WHAT IS A CLASSIC?

Cultural Memory
    in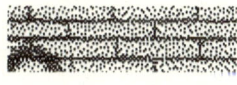
    the
  Present

Hent de Vries, Editor

WHAT IS A CLASSIC?

Postcolonial Rewriting and Invention of the Canon

Ankhi Mukherjee

STANFORD UNIVERSITY PRESS
STANFORD, CALIFORNIA

Stanford University Press
Stanford, California

© 2014 by the Board of Trustees of the Leland Stanford Junior University. All rights reserved.

This book was written with the support of the Arts and Humanities Research Council (AHRC). For further information on the AHRC, please go to: www.ahrc.ac.uk.

No part of this book may be reproduced or transmitted in any form or by any means, electronic or mechanical, including photocopying and recording, or in any information storage or retrieval system without the prior written permission of Stanford University Press.

Library of Congress Cataloging-in-Publication Data

Mukherjee, Ankhi, author.

  What is a classic? : postcolonial rewriting and invention of the canon / Ankhi Mukherjee.

    pages cm — (Cultural memory in the present)

  Includes bibliographical references and index.

  ISBN 978-0-8047-8521-1 (cloth : alk. paper)

  ISBN 978-0-8047-9525-8 (pbk. : alk. paper)

  1. English literature—20th century—History and criticism. 2. English literature—21st century—History and criticism. 3. Postcolonialism in literature. 4. Canon (Literature) 5. Criticism. I. Title. II. Series: Cultural memory in the present.

  PR478.P665M85 2014

  820.1—dc23

                          2013026231

ISBN 978-0-8047-8838-0 (electronic)

Typeset by Bruce Lundquist in 11/13.5 Adobe Garamond

For Derek Attridge

Contents

Acknowledgments   xi

Introduction   1

PART 1   THE QUESTION OF THE CLASSIC

1. "What Is a Classic?"
   International Literary Criticism and the Classic Question   27
2. What Is a Novel? Conrad, Said, Naipaul   50
3. "Best of the World's Classics":
   Derek Walcott Between Classics and the Classic   79

PART 2   REPETITION, INVENTION

4. "Pip was my story":
   Rereading, Counterreading, and Nonreading   111
5. "Yes, sir, I was the one who got away":
   Postcolonial Emergence and the Vernacular Canon   144
6. hamarashakespeare.com: Shakespeare in India   182

Postscript: The Why of the What   214

Notes   223
Bibliography   239
Index   259

Acknowledgments

What Is a Classic? is in many ways my Oxford book. I first aired the title in a job talk for a permanent post the English Faculty at Oxford, in association with Wadham College, had advertised. The topic about the Western literary canon and cultural outsiders had crystallized as I taught the undergraduate curriculum (English literature 1740–1832, 1832–1900, 1900–present) in the three preceding years as a British Academy postdoctoral fellow at Oxford, self-conscious that my diligent transmission of English literary history would always be made faintly absurd by the cultural and historical formations that I brought to bear on it. My first thanks go to the enablers and addressees of that talk at Wadham in 2006, whose successful outcome was a vote of confidence for the new book idea: Robert J. C. Young, Bernard O'Donoghue, Hermione Lee, Stephen Heyworth, Jane Garnett, Paul Giles, Valentine Cunningham, Sir Neil Chalmers (the then Warden of Wadham), and Caroline Mawson.

I am grateful to colleagues and friends at Oxford who have, in singular ways, created propitious conditions for a developing project. I continue to learn from the depth, breadth, and refinement of Elleke Boehmer's knowledge of postcolonial history and literature. I thank Patrick Hayes and Elizabeth Scott-Baumann for unselfishly sharing their research and reading early drafts. Thanks also to friends like Laura Marcus and Stefano Maria-Evangelista for stolen lunches in the thick of the teaching term during which our books in progress were generally not discussed. My graduate students in the last five years—Tomoe Kumojima, Alys Moody, Eleni Philippou, Charlotta Salmi, and Stephanie Yorke—energize my intellectual life through their bold visions and accomplishments and are gratefully acknowledged, as are the Wadham undergraduates, too numerous to name, for teaching me how to get the balance right between love and irreverence when it comes to the classics of literature I teach them course after course.

I wish to thank the following for their crucial help with specific sections and aspects of the book. The Derek Walcott chapter, which a majority of my readers at Stanford University Press liked best, would not have existed if David Damrosch did not encourage me to write it, prompting with a host of textual references. Thank you, David, for not only adding an adventure to the itinerary but also providing a road map. Ato Quayson invited me to contribute a chapter to his magisterial project, the two-volume *Cambridge History of Postcolonial Literature*, and working on an overview of postcolonial responses to the canon gave me the broader historical context for the literary examples I would develop for this book. The eminent historian (and my neighbor) Tapan Ray Chaudhuri, well aware of my idée fixe on adaptations of canonical works, recited from memory a slangy rhyme from Girish Ghosh's Bengali translation of *Macbeth*, which gave me my opening gambit for the Shakespeare chapter. Alexander Bubb, Kunal Basu, and Kalyani Ghose are also thanked for throwing out references which fired synapses and shaped ideas. My childhood friend Shantanu Bhanja sorted out an interview with the filmmaker Vishal Bhardwaj, which is, hands down, the most enjoyable hour associated with *What Is a Classic?* Martin Hägglund helped immensely with preparing my proposal for Stanford University Press. I owe thanks also to Emily Apter, Srinivas Aravamudan, Zahid Chaudhary, Pheng Cheah, Wai Chee Dimock, Debjani Ganguly, Ananya Kabir, and David Palumbo-Liu for their wise counsel and words of encouragement in different phases of the project.

I have presented fragments of the book at conferences and seminars, and in a variety of classrooms. I should like to thank the following individuals and organizations for facilitating these formative interactions with early readers and first audiences: Ron Bush (University of Oxford), Supriya Chaudhuri (Jadavpur University), Graham Huggan (University of Leeds), the Cambridge Victorian Studies Group (University of Cambridge), Brian Richardson and the Conrad Society of America (at MLA), SALA, Robert Eaglestone and the British Council, Sandra Ponzanesi (Postcolonial Studies Initiative at Utrecht University), Rebecca Beasley and the Great Writers Inspire project at Oxford University.

I am most thankful to the British Academy for a coveted postdoctoral research fellowship (2003–6), which brought recognition and resources, and the institutional space I needed to publish my first monograph and make significant inroads into this, the second. Wadham College and the English Faculty at Oxford hosted me for this fellowship, and were instrumental in making it an industrious and happy period of writing and career development. Without the funding support of the Arts and Humanities Research Council (AHRC), which helped me secure a term's research leave (and linked leave from January to July) in 2011, I would not have finished the first draft of the manuscript by autumn 2011.

I am very grateful for my editor Emily-Jane Cohen's early interest in and continued support of the project: the book wouldn't be the same without her guidance and tough love. My readers at Stanford, David Palumbo-Liu, Ato Quayson, and Sangeeta Ray, offered different combinations of affirmation and critique and saw the manuscript through a bracing revision process. Their ambition for the ideal scope and impact of *What Is a Classic?* was a reward in itself. I also thank Emma Harper for her editorial assistance, and Andrew Frisardi for his meticulous and sympathetic copyediting.

I must single out for special thanks the following friends, who have affirmed and enabled my work in words as well as actions, creating opportunities, writing tedious letters of support, and generally making me feel like the prime candidate: thank you Robert Eaglestone, Laura Marcus, Ato Quayson, and Robert J. C. Young. Purnima and Raj Mookerjee have provided tremendous emotional support in the unceremonious way profound friendships do. My parents, Chitra and Chandrachur Mukherjee, are thanked for staying telepathically linked with the highs and lows of my life despite being a continent away, and my sisters, Nayan and Dithi, for cherished moments of sisterly bonding. Finally, I mention my husband, Saumya, and daughter, Tiyash, the captive audience who lived and breathed the book with me. It would be silly to attempt to thank you though you have vitalized the book like no other: Saumya by just being yourself—calm, caring, sagacious—and teenager Tiyash with the distractions from work you create every day, which I put down to "having a life."

I dedicate *What Is a Classic?* to Derek Attridge, a key member of my dissertation committee at Rutgers University who also helped rehabilitate me in academic life after a difficult and disrupted Ph.D. process. Invaluable training and all-round guidance aside, he instilled self-belief in me when I didn't have much going for it. Derek continues to be my first phone call in times of career distress or joy, and the words of advice I trust the most. I would call this book *gurudakshina*, or the parting gift that ancient Indian custom enjoins the pupil to offer the master as a token of her respect, gratitude, and loyalty, but I am not done learning.

. . .

Earlier versions of three of the chapters were previously published. Chapter 1 is reprinted by permission of the Modern Language Association, which published my essay "What Is a Classic? International Literary Criticism and the Classic Question," PMLA (2010): 1026–42. Chapter 2 is developed from "The Death of the Novel and Two Postcolonial Writers," published in *Modern Language Quarterly* 69.4 (2008): 533–56, © 2008, University of Washington. Reprinted by permission of the present publisher, Duke University Press. An early version of Chapter 4 was published as "Postcolonial Responses to the Western Canon," in *The Cambridge History of Postcolonial Literature*, 2 vols., ed. Ato Quayson (Cambridge: Cambridge University Press, 2011), 2: 771–801.

WHAT IS A CLASSIC?

Introduction

The Western literary canon may be an abstraction elsewhere, but in the postcolony it is a key prop in an all-too-familiar scene involving a shelf of European books and a "provincial" writer who dreams of arriving at the hubs of world literature. In a 1989 UK television appearance, Derek Walcott said that the physical sensation of holding the Faber Auden and the Faber Eliot would drive him to copy out a poem in his exercise book, down to its rhyme and meter, but with the cultural content changed to correspond to a Caribbean context. "It was a complete apprenticeship, a complete surrender to modelling, because I knew that I was in a landscape that didn't have pylons and trains and autumn, or whatever."[1] V. S. Naipaul, writing about the unpromising circumstances of his English education, recalls how *Twenty Thousand Leagues Under the Sea* from the Collins Classics series was one of the first English texts read out by the headmaster, Mr. Worm, to introduce his class (fifth standard) to general reading: "He looked down at the little Collins Classic, oddly like a prayer book in his thick hands, and read Jules Verne like a man saying prayers" (*Literary Occasions*, 4). Dissatisfied with Mr Worm's idea of formative reading for impressionable boys, and increasingly influenced by his father's prolific and eccentric reading patterns, Naipaul, still under twelve, creates his own private English literary anthology: selections include speeches in *Julius Caesar*; chapters of *Oliver Twist*, *Middlemarch*, and *David Copperfield*; Conrad's Malay stories; one or two of Lamb's *Tales from Shakespeare*. Self-archiving is a recurrent pattern in the fictional and real lives of writing I describe in this book, but, while the books in this jerry-built canon fire Naipaul's ambition to become a writer, "together with the wish there had come the knowledge that the literature that had given me the wish came from another world, far away from our own" (6).

Walcott's and Naipaul's fellow Nobel winner Orhan Pamuk attributes his worldview to the influence of his father's painstakingly created library. In his Nobel lecture, "My Father's Suitcase," Pamuk describes the large library as a veritable microcosm: "Sometimes I would look at this library from a distance and imagine that one day, in a different house, I would build my own library, an even better library—build myself a world" (4). In front of his father's library, an eclectic mixture of the local, the national, and the West, the Pamuk experienced an "anguish of affiliation" (Suleri, *Rhetoric*, 148): parochial and excluded from "a life richer and more exciting than our own" ("My Father's Suitcase," 5). The center of the world, and the throbbing heart of world literature—the idea of "world" literature seemed at the time to be interchangeable with Western literature—was far enough from Istanbul and Turkey. "My father's library was evidence of this. At one end, there were Istanbul's books—our literature, our local world, in all its beloved detail—and at the other end were the books from this other, Western, world, to which our own bore no resemblance, to which our lack of resemblance gave us both pain and hope" (5). The boy's longing for this "strange and wondrous" (5) world was made acute with the realization that he lived in a country that had little interest in artists. Yet there was hope that when a writer shut himself up in a room he breached the confines of national identity to join the oceanic one of a "single humanity, a world without a centre": "All true literature rises from this childish, hopeful certainty that all people resemble each other" (7).

Pamuk's sentiments are echoed in Amitav Ghosh's Pushcart Prize–winning essay "The March of the Novel Through History: The Testimony of My Grandfather's Bookcase," in which he describes the pride of place given to the glass-fronted bookcase in middle-class Bengali households. A quarter of the novels in the bookcases in his grandfather's house, Ghosh writes, was in Bengali, the works of Bankim Chandra, Sarat Chandra, Rabindranath, Bibhuti Bhushan. The rest were in English, largely translations from European languages: Russian, French, Italian, German, and Danish. The most dust had gathered on the masterpieces of the nineteenth century, Dostoevsky, Tolstoy, Turgenev, Hugo, Flaubert, Stendhal, Maupassant. Books by Maksim Gorky, Mikhail Sholokhov, John Steinbeck and Upton Sinclair bore muted testimony to the political urgencies of a different historical era, while forgotten Nobel winners in literature—Grazia Deledda, Gorky, Hamsun, Sienkiewicz, and Andrić—brought home to the young writer the mutable criteria of taste and value. For Ghosh, the Nobel collection in this ancestral bookcase, in particular, testified to the widespread appeal of the notion of universal literature, "a form of artistic expression that embodies differences in places and culture, emotion and aspiration, but in such way as to render them communicable" (16). Like Pamuk, and echoing Italo Calvino, who declared in a 1967 Rome symposium that "a book is written so that it can be put beside other books and take its place on a hypothetical bookshelf" (*Literature Machine*, 81), Ghosh goes on to say that the sliding address to which belated novelists write is this vast and cosmopolitan "fictional bookcase," which requires them "to locate themselves in relation to it" (23).

In his well-known introduction to the Harvard Classics in March 1910, President Charles William Eliot had presented the fifty-volume "five foot shelf of books" as a mobile history of "the progress of man observing, recording, inventing, and imagining" (cited in Kirsch, "*Five-foot Shelf* Reconsidered," 1). Readers had to spend a mere quarter of an hour to improve the level of their culture, the Harvard Classics promised. The collection was intended not as "a museum display-case of the 'world's best books,' but as a portable university," observes Adam Kirsch (1). Like President Eliot's self-described archive of "recorded discoveries, experiences, and reflections which humanity in its intermittent and irregular progress from barbarism to civilisation has acquired and laid up," the canon is often represented in postcolonial fiction as portable property, a library of carefully vetted works that carries out its work of global dominance in the farthest outposts of empire. Often in postcolonial representation, the classics distil, usually for the tragically deluded protagonist, the very meaning of civilization and sanity. In Jean Rhys's *Wide Sargasso Sea*, the books in Rochester's dressing room are gradually destroyed by the West Indian climate, as Rochester himself feels poisoned and deracinated. In Tayeb Salih's *Season of Migration to the North*, the narrator stumbles upon the hidden room in Mustafa Sa'eed's house to be accosted by the replica of an English study. I quote a substantial section of this representative list,

4   *Introduction*

which tellingly includes the Koran in English (and presumably Orientalist) translation.

Books on economics, history and literature. Zoology. Geology. Mathematics. Astronomy. The Encyclopaedia Britannica. Gibbon. Macaulay. Toynbee. The complete works of Bernard Shaw. Keynes. Tawney. Smith. Robinson. *The Economics of Imperfect Competition*. Hobson *Imperialism*. Robinson *An Essay on Marxian Economics*. Sociology. Anthropology. Psychology. Thomas Hardy. Thomas Mann . . . Virginia Woolf. Wittgenstein. Einstein . . . *Gulliver's Travels*. Kipling. Housman. *The History of the French Revolution* Thomas Carlyle. . . . What play-acting is this? What does he mean? Owen. Ford Madox Ford. Stefan Zweig. E. G. Browne. Laski. Hazlitt. *Alice in Wonderland*. Richards. *The Koran* in English. (*Season of Migration*, 136–38)

The narrator of *Season of Migration to the North* likens the salon to a "graveyard," a "mausoleum," a "prison" and a "huge joke": the treasure chamber contains "not a single Arabic book" (138). Naipaul creates a similar scenario for Jimmy Ahmed, the Black Power poseur in *Guerrillas*, who lives in a house furnished with English carpets and furniture, replete with "The Hundred Best Books of the World." Jimmy is a derivative intellect whose political fantasy is carved by (mis)readings or incomplete understandings of Western political and literary masterpieces. The upshot of the historical novel is that Jimmy's revolution on the Caribbean island is tragically "dependent on metropolitan sources—both economic and literary," as Judie Newman points out (123), and is therefore unsustainable.

As I have tried to show with the literary and ficto-biographical examples above, the Eurocentric canon, routinely associated with imperial hierarchies, is usually perceived and presented as an edifying, if reformatory, force and almost always as an exclusionist corpus. In *What Is a Classic? Postcolonial Rewriting and Invention of the Canon*, I propose that the canon, and the dominant modalities in which it is received, afford a site of historical emergence through which contemporary English and Anglophone literature and literary criticism can fruitfully rethink their cultural identity and politics. The collector's love of hoarding classics is matched, in the works of Pamuk or Walcott, with a cautious expending of the literary credit, and an ethical commitment to the collection's inherent "transmissibility" (Benjamin, *Illuminations*, 66).[2] The book examines, through select events in contemporary literature and literary criticism, how the canon of literature and theory renews and transforms, achieves novel combinations, and fights obsolescence by being constantly on the move. As Naipaul states, "no literary form—the Shakespearean play, the epic poem, the Restoration comedy, the essay, the work of history—can continue for very long at the same pitch of inspiration" (*Literary Occasions*, 30). This study looks closely also at writers and critics on the move, carrying with them a transferable literary bequest that Homi Bhabha, in an essay that raises the ghosts of Walter Benjamin's "Unpacking My Library," describes as "a kind of contingent dis-ordered historical 'dwelling' bestowed upon us": "It struck me, unpacking my own library—memories of book-buying in Bombay, Oxford, London, Hyderabad, Champaign-Urbana, Jyavaskala—that it is the 'disorder' of our books that makes of us irredeemable 'vernacular' cosmopolitans committed to what Walter Benjamin describes as 'the renewal of existence'" ("Unpacking," 5). Bhabha, unpacking his crates of books upon arrival in Chicago, recalls unforgettable images ("not thoughts but images," Benjamin had emphasized) of Benjamin's wandering past that flocks the mind of the flaneur as he rifles through the cosmopolitan jumble of his old books: "Riga, Naples, Munich, Danzig, Moscow, Florence, Basel, Paris" ("Unpacking," *Illuminations*, 67). The "renewal of existence" that Bhabha cites pertains to the Benjaminian idea that, for the collector, the finding of an old book is tantamount to its rebirth and a renewal of the old world. As children, unburdened with reason and acquired frames of reference, collect things to imbue them with occult meaning and combinations, the peripatetic and "transient" collector, at home everywhere and nowhere, has an intuitive and open-ended transaction with old books. This makes for a renewal of meaning, not merely in the restive self-invention of the flaneur, but in the matter and material of the book itself as it is freed from its constrictive local and national contexts to circulate as world literature.

The "contingent dis-ordered historical 'dwelling,'" which, as Bhabha contends, is the literary legacy that attaches to vernacular cosmopolitans, is given tragicomic amplification in Salman Rushdie's memoir of his fatwa years, *Joseph Anton* (2012). Rushdie, hiding in ignominy from murderous zealots, is asked by the British police to find a pseudonym, and thinks first of a fragment of a character that he had made up, Mr. Ajeeb Mamouli, which translates literally as "Absurd Everyman." "He was Mr Odd Ordinary, Mr Strange Normal, Mr Peculiar Everyday: an oxymoron, a contradiction in terms" (*Joseph Anton*, 163). The Protection Team finds the name ethnic and unpronounceable, so Rushdie is asked to think again of a fictional name. This time he comes up with "Joseph Anton," combining the first names of Conrad and Chekhov:

Conrad, the trans-lingual creator of wanderers, lost and not lost, of voyagers into the heart of darkness, of secret agents in a world of killers and bombs, and of at least one immortal coward, hiding from his shame; and Chekhov, the master of loneliness and melancholy, of the beauty of an old world destroyed, like the trees in the cherry orchard, by the brutality of the new; Chekhov whose *Three Sisters* believed that real life was elsewhere and yearned eternally for a Moscow to which they could not return: these were his godfathers now. (165)

The pseudonym represents the consanguinity of literature and life in a catastrophic turn of events that makes life itself, Rushdie says, read like "a bad novel." But this codependency is traced to Rushdie's childhood. "Was it the fault, perhaps, of literature?" he wonders as he reviews the inexplicable decision on the part of his barely-teen self to leave behind his family in India to go to boarding school in England (*Joseph Anton*, 27). Was it a childish decision "to venture forth into an imaginary England that only existed in books?" (28). The roster of unforgettable storybook characters—Jeeves and Bertie, the Earl of Emsworth and the Empress of Blandings, Billy Bunter and his Indian classmate, Hurree Jamset Ram Singh—is seen as mobilizing the boy's outreach for an ideal community, and it is left to the mature self to realize the pitfalls of such imaginary identifications. "Elective affinities," the term coined by Goethe—which Rushdie adapts to mean conscious, not biologically predetermined, choice—applies most acutely to his extrapolations from English, American, and European literature and culture for self-definition. Fighting the lethal speech-act that is the fatwa, he seems to draw succor in his postsacral world from Hemingway's injunction of "grace under pressure" (cited in *Joseph Anton*, 395), and Conrad's "I must live until I die, mustn't I?" (*Joseph Anton*, 165). Joseph Anton is both Didi and Gogo, interposing games in a long night of despair (*Joseph Anton*, 396); he is Beckett's "mighty unnameable" (461) and Bellow's dog (422); the world he inhabits is "Gogolian," "Rabelaisian," and "Kafkaesque." "It was the breadth of human nature that allowed readers to find common ground and points of identification" (627), Joseph Anton tries to explain.

Charles Altieri sees a vital link between canonization and self-interest: canon formation, according to Altieri, works "by elaborating transpersonal principles of value that link desires in the present to forms of imaginative discourse preserved from the past" ("Idea and Ideal," 40). It is most revealing that the transhistorical canon that best serves Rushdie's personal interests includes Madame Bovary, Leopold Bloom, Raskolnikov, Miss Marple, and Salo the mechanical messenger from the planet Tralfamadore, but no one from the subcontinent. As in *Imaginary Homelands*, Rushdie argues for a model of self-generation and survival—the child as the father of man—wherein parents are not always accidental but elected, sometimes half-consciously. The belated novelist's literary output perpetuates, instead of canceling, the "polyglot family tree" of his predecessors, such as Gogol, Cervantes, Kafka, Melville, Machado de Assis: "It is perhaps one of the more pleasant freedoms of the literary migrant to be able to choose his parents" (*Imaginary Homelands*, 20–21).

Seductive as it is to trace ad infinitum the multifarious imaginary identities and identifications of historically displaced literary figures such as Rushdie, this book will strain instead to read such escapades in knowable contexts, as historically interpretable despite their dynamic resistance to national, ethnic, and cultural determinism. If literary migrants are free, and willing to choose literary antecedents, what worldly criteria determine their selection or fine-tune their calibrations of choice? In his 1991 lecture "What Is a Classic?" Coetzee narrates how he, at age fifteen, had heard a recording of Bach's *Well-Tempered Clavier*, played on the harpsichord: "For the first time I was undergoing the impact of *the classic*. . . . The revelation in the garden was a key event in my formation" ("What Is a Classic?" 10). Why does Coetzee, in the thrall of the Western classic, feign indifference to the ambient sound of vernacular African languages and culture? In renaming himself "Joseph Anton," Rushdie opts for a mediated anonymity in this memoir told in distanced, third-person narration, the subjectivity under erasure making a compensatory bid for posthumous glory in its identification with two of the most enduring names in world literature. In the context of this renaming, Rushdie's boyhood cathexis with the Western literary canon seems to not be very different from that which Coetzee self-critically interprets as "a symbolic election on my part of European culture as a way out of a social and historical dead end" ("What Is a Classic?" 18). Canons are normative, evaluative, and self-perpetuating: they also possess dialectical resources for forgings of identity that lead through the pain and shame of acculturation and deracination, as with Rushdie and Coetzee, to timeless and talismanic forms of power. The switch from "Ajeeb Mamouli" to Joseph Anton signals a defensive decision to substitute the "strange normal" Indian everyman with a name potent enough in its constellation of cultural traces to conflate Salman Rushdie with the universal and recurrent type of the artist in exile.

Is there an identifiable and agreed-upon canon of English literature in the twentieth and twenty-first centuries? How is the canon historically constituted and transmitted in our times, and how is a classic created? It seems perverse to revisit troubled ideas of canonicity for English studies in the postcolonial and global age, when the drift of English literary history has revised its temporal perspectives, with cultural identity in the era of cultural-economic globalization increasingly exhibiting symptoms of what Michel Foucault called "the epoch of space" ("Of Other Spaces," 22), a contestatory resituating of history on spatial rather than temporal axes. Are there any perennial works or masterpieces at all in the new geomorphic empire and in world literature, which is not so much a canon of texts as it is a mode of circulation, not unlike the spatial proliferation of capital itself? This study seeks to interrogate, through selected (and definitive) trends in twentieth- and twenty-first-century English and Anglophone literature, the relevance of the question of the classic for the politics of publishing, teaching, and translating core texts. It demonstrates how criticism continues to shore up the idea of literary value against mobile configurations of knowledge, technology, and expertise. If for T. S. Eliot, the classic standard was indissociable from dead languages—languages that have, ironically, been exhausted by the classics in which their energies culminated—I argue that the invention of modern classics is sustained by a dynamic and variable conversation between the past and the present of English studies, as that conversation goes from being specifically Western to being worldwide.

With the emergence of world literature, writes Wai Chee Dimock, as "a multilingual and intercontinental domain" (*Shades*, 13) with multiple geographies and chronologies, "English studies" as a category is no longer self-evident or self-contained. I ask whether, in this colloquy of different literatures in English, with no fixed canon or inviolate arbitrations, long-held literary standards of selectivity and consecration still hold. Canonicity is often seen as a normalizing agent for the anomalous, the aberrant, and the foreign, and anticanonists insist that a writer's entry into the canon represents the subjugation of the work to knowable contexts. A notorious example of the policing aspect of authoritative canonicity is Harold Bloom's *The Western Canon*, which contains a lusty defense of twenty-six authors deemed canon-worthy by the expert. Bloom goes so far as to append to the book a list of four hundred names that constitute for him the Western canon. The logic of omissions—Tagore, India's first Nobel laureate in English literature, and one of the most read, translated, and circulated of multilingual Indian writers, is left out—is too egregious for the list to be taken seriously, but it gives credence to canon debates in the Anglo-American academy that have centered on its exclusivity (and dubious inclusiveness) as well as its claims of universality. The canon has historically been a nexus of power and knowledge that reinforces hierarchies and the vested interests of select institutions, excluding the interests and accomplishments of minorities, popular and demotic culture, or non-European civilizations. As Jonathan Kramnick states, literature is long recognized to be "not the fragile troping of popular culture so much as it is the instinctive eliting of that culture" (*Making the English Canon*, 233). John Guillory lends credence to this view by pointing out that, while the rationale of Bloom's *Western Canon* is formulated at least partially in response to the perceived anti-intellectualism of the mass market, his decision to publish the book through a trade press and the appended list of canonical works gesture to "that market's perplexed desire for culture": "so the book descends, with the author's blessing, from the empyrean of the Western canon to the cloudier element of Western culture" ("Ordeal," 85). In the twentieth and twenty-first centuries, however, phenomena such as the rise of global English and world literature, American Studies, translation research, and the powerful influence of feminist, gender, and postcolonial studies in the Anglo-American academy have repeatedly challenged and sometimes altered the monolingual and Eurocentric nature of English as a discipline. This book documents and analyzes the invention of alternative canons, and the formation of what Patricia Waugh calls new "imaginary unities" (*Literary Theory and Criticism*, 71).

In the face of increasing demands for the opening of the canon to women, minorities, and postcolonial writers, Bloom argues in his 1994 work for upholding the difficulty of canonical literature and its inaccessibility to all but the smallest minority. If rarefied aesthetic value is nothing but "a mystification in the service of the ruling class," he argues, "then why should you read at all rather than go forth to serve the desperate needs of the exploited classes?" (*Western Canon*, 522). Bloom dismisses the attacks on the canon by groups he lumps under "the School of Resentment: Feminists, Marxists, Lacanians, New Historicists, Deconstructionists, Semioticians," adding that "left-wing critics cannot do the working class's reading for it" (488). Gayatri Chakravorty Spivak, whose intellectual versatility makes of her an intriguing compound ghost of the best contenders for the "School of Resentment," obviously comes to the debate from the other end of the political spectrum, but with a suspicion of minority representation that references Bloom's argument in *The Western Canon*. In *Outside in the Teaching Machine* she describes the "English major, strung tight with the excitement of learning to read the diversity of the new canon": "a bit of old masters in new perspectives, women's literature, black women's literature, a glimpse of Afro-America, the literature of gendered homosexuality, of migrant ethnicity, of the exploited in struggle" (274). Spivak's is not an upholding of unyielding principles of selectivity or Bloom's "severely artistic criteria" (*Western Canon*, 22), but dissatisfaction at the slow changing core of literature and the pitiful scale of the "reduction of the space and time spent on the old canon" (*Outside*, 271). "My argument is *against* being fully satisfied with little gains, not *for* being satisfied with nothing," she states (277).

In *Outside in the Teaching Machine*, Spivak predicts that if the study of literature in English departments remained focused on English and other metropolitan languages, without expanding into transnational literary and cultural studies, if we stopped revising the English canon altogether, English studies would stand the risk of prompting postcolonial studies to construct an anticanon of "Third World Literature (in translation)," leading to a "new Orientalism" (312). Spivak's prescient statements on reverse ethnocentrism, its rise related to an unrelenting old guard, are applicable to the alter canon suggested by the *Penguin Anthology of Twentieth-Century American Poetry*. The anthology, edited by Rita Dove, a celebrated poet, poet laureate (1993–95), and the Commonwealth Professor of English at the University of Virginia, received a scathing response titled "Are These the Poems to Remember?" in the *New York Review of Books*, leading to a controversy salaciously reported in the press as "bloodletting" (*The Huffington Post*) and "race wars" (*The Guardian*).[3] The *NYRB* reviewer was none other than Helen Vendler, A. Kingley Porter Professor of English at Harvard, and one of the most formidable American poetry critics alive, of whom Harold Bloom once said that there isn't anyone in the country who can read syntax in poems as well as she can. Vendler's review lays into the anthology on the following grounds. First, the question of selectiveness: in this new anthology of poetry of the past century, Dove has given more space to black poets than to better-known names. In fact, so keen is she on "multicultural inclusiveness" that 175 poets are represented. "No century in the evolution of poetry in English ever had 175 poets worth reading," Vendler says, "so why are we being asked to sample so many poets of little or no lasting value?" Of the twenty poets born between 1954 and 1971, fifteen are from minority communities and five are white (two men and three women), she notes. Dove has, in the name of poetry, indiscriminately included "angry outbursts" as well as "artistically ambitious meditations." What is worse, she seems to be valorizing a dumbing-down of poetry in her emphasis on accessibility, although the selections don't really support a coherent principle of organization. Finally, Vendler sees Dove's editorial persona weakened by "peculiar judgments," clichéd, imprecise, and fallacious observations, and a sloppy and showy essay style. Of Dove's description of Merrill's formal verses as "jeweled carapaces," Vendler pedantically points out that "carapaces belong, after all, to insects and tortoises": "Such cartoonish remarks are not helpful to the understanding of poetry."

Vendler is most withering on the question of her fellow critic's judgment: Dove's "brisk post hoc, propter hoc diagnosis" of the confessional poets, the paranoid projections of the "whitewashed" and implicitly racist "poetry establishment," or her enthusiastic inclusion of Amiri Baraka's rantings as a representative of the "New Black Aesthetic." She takes Dove to task for the lack of reflective distance or discernment, which prompts Dove to make heavy-handed pronouncements on literary history, heap unqualified praise on the Harlem Renaissance, and conflate biography with poetry ("Just because one describes a 'hardscrabble Appalachia' doesn't make one a hardscrabble Appalachian"). To Dove's claim that Gwendolyn Brooks's first book "confirmed that black women can express themselves in poems as richly innovative as the best male poets of any race," Vendler retorts skeptically: "As richly innovative as Shakespeare? Dante? Wordsworth?"

Dove responded angrily in the *NYRB* to what she perceived as Vendler's elitism and racism. She accused Vendler of being so selective in her own former editorial role as to be outright exclusionary: "Indeed, one of her own forays onto the anthology turf, *The Harvard Book of Contemporary American Poetry* (1985), prompted a disgruntled reader to retort on Amazon.com: 'The American Tree Becomes a Toothpick.'" Vendler, according to Dove, represents culturally entitled critics "who in their hubris believe they should be the only ones permitted to render verdicts in the public courts of literature." Bristling at Vendler's misreading of her ambivalent critical stance vis-à-vis the Black Arts movement, especially the singling out of Baraka's "knuckles in a jewlady's mouth" piece, Dove alleges that Vendler is "creepily implying that I have similar anti-Semitic tendencies." Not entirely putting to rest Vendler's snide comment about her alliterative excess, Dove writes emotionally of her desire to shield her reputation "from the slanderous slime that sticks."

The canon war between Dove and Vendler is unpleasant and disturbing, with each woman accusing the other of territorial behavior, whether it is the question of encroachment (more space devoted to black poets) or turfing out (Vendler, Dove reminds us, has her own anthology to defend), and each excoriating the other's racism, Vendler covertly and Dove overtly. Vendler's arguments upholding the literary critic's deep contextual knowledge, cultivated sensitivity to language, and carefully considered criteria of selection are justified, as is her valorization of difficult art over lazy demands for instant gratification. Isn't it uncalled-for, however, to undermine Gwendolyn Brooks through a comparison to Shakespeare or Dante, just to score a point? Vendler dismisses varieties of political poetry with her pronouncement that "a theme is not enough to make a poem" (the poetry is *not* in the pity, after all). And what exactly is Professor Vendler insinuating when she refers to Dove's canvas of "mostly short poems of rather restricted vocabulary" for her target audience "who would be put off by a complex text," especially after she has unambiguously accused Dove of pandering to black culture?

While Vendler and Bloom vehemently oppose methods of selection in which aesthetic standards are brushed aside for the political salience of a given work, John Guillory's more considered response in *Cultural Capital* expresses misgivings about the simplistic opposition between dominant and dominated cultures. Guillory cautions against the perils of identity politics in the canon debate that reduces the genius author to a representative a social group (usually a hegemonic class, while the noncanonical author stands for minorities). Clearly, the perceived disunities of culture cannot be remedied by forging cultural unities (of gender, race, sexualities, subcultures) at the level of the curriculum, for these often descend into simple allegorical structures of conflict that obscure the historical fact that gender, race, and sexuality are not interchangeable ciphers of marginality. One way out of deadlock, Guillory suggests, is to imagine the canon not as a set of books but as a "discursive instrument of 'transmission'" of institutional and pedagogic processes that canonical texts are implicated in, though not identical with (*Cultural Capital*, 56). The current study subscribes to this view of the canon as not just an archive but transmission, perpetuating a critical tradition and open to interventions that dislodge familiar reading formations. It considers questions of the canon, the formation of a valued corpus, or what Guillory describes as "an aristocracy of texts," as well as the singularity of classics ("Ideology," 339). If the canon is a conservative congealing of the "literary Art of Memory," as Bloom puts it (17), the classic is inseparable from unresolved contestations of the question "What is a classic?" and belongs to what John Guillory calls "the conflictual prehistory of canon-formation" ("Ideology," 358). This project, therefore, adopts a historical and curatorial stance vis-à-vis the historical transmission of the canon without giving up the deconstructive mode of its contestations of classic value.

Although it is impossible to dissociate literary meaning and value from the socioeconomic and institutional factors—or the history of Western hegemony over the world, for that matter—that determine them, the question of the classic signals the kind of agonistic debate that enables the literary-critical field to produce its own criteria for cultural distinction. It marks the unique time, irregular geography, and the collective life of literature; hence its continued relevance for national, diasporic, and international usages of English. A central preoccupation of this book, then, is with the role of literary criticism in articulating the time, space, and critical language for the literature of a deterritorialized world. Following Edward Said's lead, it positions the critic as an "individual consciousness" who is not a mere product of the dominant culture, "but a historical and social actor in it" (*The World*, 15). Criticism is constituted by the assumption of critical distance from the object of inquiry and the critic's calling into question his or her own emplacement and affiliations. Western critical consciousness, according to Said, has historically been predicated on the exclusion of the nonliterary and the non-European and a repression of the political dimension of all literature. There are two alternatives for the contemporary literary critic, Said states: servitude to the order of the humanities that serves the dominant culture; or, the adoption of a "secular" mode of critical scrutiny, which opposes orthodoxy and organized dogma.[4] Said's idea of secular criticism is in sharp contradistinction to national, and not necessarily religious, belief systems.[5] Aamir Mufti enjoins us to read it as Said's indictment of the exclusionary logic of nationalism, with its unscrupulous "mobilization of the filiative metaphors of kinship and regeneration": "Secular criticism seeks continually to make it perceptible that the experience of being at home can only be produced by rendering some other homeless" ("Auerbach," 107). The drift of the question "What is a classic?" is aligned to the Saidian definition of "secular criticism," both in its critique of what Said called the "mass institutions" that organize modern life and in its "exilic thrust" to seek out and speak from affiliative, marginal, and minority positions ("Auerbach," 107).

One of ways in which the minority and exilic thrust manifests itself in this book is through the destiny of the "little question mark" of its title, something Nietzsche suggested we append to our own "special slogans and favourite doctrines" (*Beyond Good and Evil*, 26). The question mark, by leaving the problem of the classic an unsolved mystery, provides an opening for a series of questions, just as T. S. Eliot's, J. M. Coetzee's, and Augustin Sainte-Beuve's inquiry of classic value precipitates its recurrence in literature and criticism. As it happens, it is also one of those frustratingly big questions that is not merely posed by the critic but that poses the critic, like Virginia Woolf's "How Should One Read a Book?" Starting its life as a talk to be given to sixty young girls in Hayes Court School in Kent, Woolf's essay wavers in its attention to the act of scrupulous reading—"do not dictate to your author, try to become him" ("How Should One Read?" 259)—as it slips into a more permeable textuality, where reading, writing, and staging are indistinguishable from each other: "The standards we raise and the judgements we pass steal into the air and become part of the atmosphere which writers breathe as they work" (269). The chief "illuminant" of this scene of reading is "the nerve of sensation," not the "gowned and furred authorities of the library" (268). Rules are made only to be perpetually overcome by the books themselves; the reader acknowledges the "considered criticism" of Coleridge, Dryden, and Johnson, but not in a spirit of sheepish conformity, and only when their ruling "comes in conflict with our own and vanquishes it" (269). "An influence is created," Woolf writes, joining text and critic in an unfixed exchange: the book morphs into a "shadow-shape," indeterminate and increasingly unauthorized, but also vital and "more varied" (269, 270). My project on literary criticism in an international frame is haunted by another big question of twentieth-century English studies: "Can the Subaltern Speak?" Spivak's revolutionary examination of gendered subalternity, is itself a strenuous exercise in non-coercive forms of knowing and representing. Read against the definitive terms of this project, it enjoins a preternatural alertness to not just voice but traces of voice consciousness, encourages critiques that take into account the enunciating subject's "geopolitical determinations," and warns against the pitfalls of precipitately recuperating and credentializing the noncanonical *as* canonical (Morris, ed., *Can the Subaltern Speak?* 238).

"It was out of the colonial small change of the great nineteenth-century achievement that—perhaps through a teacher or a friend—the desire to be a writer came to my father," writes V. S. Naipaul of the stirrings of literary ambition in his father in 1920s Trinidad (*Literary Occasions*, 31). The sense in which I use *postcolonial* in this chapter and book, as a descriptive tag for a historical category of literature, as well as a recognizable literary and critical method, derives primarily from this idea of a composite linguistic, literary, exegetical, and cultural tradition acquired as the "small change" of the global transmission of empire. Sara Suleri, in *The Rhetoric of English India*, writes: "The postcolonial condition is neither territorially bound nor more the property of one people than of the other: instead, its inevitably retroactive narrative allows for the inclusion both of its colonial past and of the function of criticism at the present time as necessary corollaries to the telling of its stories" (21–22). The key symptoms of the postcolonial literary condition, as outlined by Suleri in this rigorous and sophisticated analysis and as developed in my examination of a diverse range of English and Anglophone writing in this book are as follows: the use of English as a foreign language, even when it is, historically, the author's first language; "a spillage from history to language" (3), or the intertwining of the rhetorical and the real in cultural productions related to imperialism and its aftermath; attention to the tropological configurations of colonialism and the transference and readaptation of such tropes; knowing, recording, and imagining agonistically the psychopathology of the colonized; "a continually dislocated idiom of migrancy"

(Suleri, *Rhetoric*, 5), which reinstates vital links between colonial, national, transnational and global geographies; and a "reactive" idiom, engaged as it is in the "multiplicity of histories that are implicated in its emergence" (Suleri, *Rhetoric*, 21). The term *postcolonial* also seems relevant to demarcate an age of global imperialism that legitimates itself along the lines of Britain's nineteenth-century empire: modernization and modern communications, free trade and capital movements, war on terror, and an idea of a white civilization drawing confusedly from capitalist modernity and democracy. Nevertheless, this project on "postcolonial rewriting and invention of the canon" worries the term at every stage, in the comparatist analysis of the cultural anxieties of T. S. Eliot and Coetzee, in the polyglot possibilities of Walcott's poetry or the themes of self-transcendence in Naipaul's autobiographical fiction. It is put under particular pressure as a descriptive tag for the final chapter of the book, in which I examine three kinds of Shakespeare adaptations in India, each representing a curiously one-way cultural traffic that is uninterested in changing metropolitan paradigms of Shakespeare reception and is largely indifferent to the question of a Western audience. The first set of Shakespeare adaptations belongs to the time and the city culture of the Raj but the translation of Shakespeare for the Bengali stage, and the failed experiment of a Bengali actor playing the Moor in nineteenth-century colonial Calcutta, speak primarily to the uncanny neutrality of Shakespeare that makes the corpus so amenable to playful renomination. Similarly, the second section on Kendal's peripatetic Shakespeare troupe, and the third on Shakespeare in contemporary Indian cinema, reflect on Shakespeare as a field of knowledge that withstands creative mistranslation in a variety of local "classrooms"—be it the public school circuit of colonial India or Indian regional and English-language cinema. In these instances, postcolonial delineates not simply the vast, if ultimately undecidable, epistemic impact of the imports of empire on ethnic self-fashioning, but also unpredictable contact zones between canonical texts and readers that crystallize in out-of-context and anachronistic performances of reading.

Very few people outside academia (and perhaps the performing arts) in India today would respond to the descriptor *postcolonial* without perplexity and in good humor. Ashis Nandy points out that for many in South Asia, "colonialism was primarily an institutional arrangement and what mattered was its political economy. . . . Few saw colonialism as a way of life" (*Intimate Enemy*, 115). His *Intimate Enemy* looks particularly at the causes and symptoms of this complex disavowal "in a society so deeply concerned about the psychological" (116). Nandy also examines the pernicious after-effects of the "strange anomalies" produced by colonial rule (115). According to Nandy, "colonialism is mostly a game of categories and politics of knowledge.... As long as the game and the politics survive, colonialism, too, will survive" (117). This explains why postcolonial concerns and methods translate meaningfully from national contexts to the new empires mobilized by transnational and global forms of government, economy, and culture. Robert Young, arguing for the relevance of postcolonial studies for critical intervention in new socioeconomic phenomena such as global migration, observes that "it is no longer a question of a formal colonizer-colonized relation":

What we have instead is something almost more brutal, because there is no longer even a relation, just those countless individuals in so many societies, who are surplus to economic requirements ... forced into the desperate decision to migrate illegally across whole continents in order to survive. The postcolonial question now is how to make the dream of emancipation accessible for all those people who fall outside the needs of contemporary modernity. ("Postcolonial Remains," 27)

Finally, perhaps, the term *postcolonial* refers to the persistence of the trace that cannot, in the inexorable cultural forgetting of the indignities of foreign domination, be satisfactorily yoked to full and present historical referents, even though inequities of power and rights, uneven development, incomplete decolonization, poverty, and violence persist in countries that had experienced "colonially organised geopolitics" (Matti Bunzl et al., eds., *Postcolonial Studies and Beyond*, 8). It is easy to forget in the war of words around terminology that *postcolonial* refers to a form of critique, a historically situated method of epistemological attention, and not necessarily the interpretive resources of the works, cultures, and contexts in question. A critical attitude of unbelonging that is a difficult historic legacy for some and a matter of cultivation and (un)learning for others, the term postcolonial is a veritable "grin that hangs about without the cat."[6]

What is the relationship between postcolonial literature and world literature, and how does this determine the canon debate? "The literature around us is now unmistakeably a planetary system," states Franco Moretti ("Conjectures," 54). In a planet with more than a billion people suffering from hunger—and presumably without the use of books—this declaration seems to be asking too much of literature and the planet. Gayatri Spivak proposes the planet in *Death of a Discipline*, to override the model of differentiated globe, and as a hard-to-colonize "species of alterity." "When I invoke the planet, I think of the effort required to figure the (im)possibility of this underived intuition" (*Death*, 72). Wai Chee Dimock too advocates the planet as an "unknown quantum, barely intimated, not yet adequate to the meaning we would like it to bear" (*Shades*, 5). This study keeps in play throughout the planetary frame and the relationship between world literature and postcolonial studies, especially in relation to the structures of selectivity and prestige that have produced alternative—and relatable—canons in both fields. It undermines taxonomies that automatically align the "national" reader with the provincial, and, in extreme cases, the noble autochthon, while reserving the term *international* for the planetary expansiveness of an ideal, if virtual, Western(ized) reader, and insists that we guard against the center-periphery model of literary inequality in the world as well as the paternalistic or charitable urge to see all literary effort as equal.

This book reappraises classic work on canonicity by Harold Bloom, Frank Kermode, and John Guillory—respectively, *The Western Canon* (1994), *The Classic* (1975), and *Cultural Capital* (1993)—for a changed historical moment, marked by the emergence of a world literary system. Central to the study is the literary phenomenon of canon rewriting; the book engages rigorously with postcolonial debates on this theme. Judie Newman's *The Ballistic Bard* (1995) charts the genesis of postcolonial literature in textual violence and violations: this Manichean schema between colonial and postcolonial texts, however, reduces postcolonial literature to little more than counterreadings of master plots. Timothy Brennan's *Salman Rushdie and the Third World: Myths of the Nation* (1989) and *At Home in the World: Cosmopolitanism Now* (1997), and Graham Huggan's *The Postcolonial Exotic: Marketing the Margins* (2001), offer disenchanted critiques of the processes through which cultural fields are created and value is attributed to certain modes of postcolonial representation. The proposed work follows Brennan's and Huggan's materialist genealogy of the postcolonial canon, especially Brennan's dim view of the cosmopolitan embrace that flattens influences to reassemble Third World literature on an undifferentiated plane of value, and Huggan's critique of the mechanics of exoticist representation and consumption in a global culture industry. However, it also moves on from the antagonistic character of these works to argue for a more constructive role that the question of the canon could or should play in historical or critical reprisals of the global power relations that affect the field of postcolonial writing and cultural production.

David Damrosch's *What Is World Literature?* (2003), and Emily Apter's *Continental Drift* (1999) and *The Translation Zone* (2006), detail the ways in which literary history mirrors world history and have been influential sources for my work, which reads English literature in the framework of world literary systems and revises the traditional organization of the field of English studies around the norms of period and nation. Other key comparative literature publications in recent decades—Franco Moretti's *Modern Epic: The World System from Goethe to García Márquez* (1996), Pascale Casanova's *The World Republic of Letters* (2004), Wai Chee Dimock's *Through Other Continents* (2006), and Jonathan Culler's *The Literary in Theory* (2007)—which historicize and interrogate the rhizomatic proliferation of a global literary canon and international literary criticism, have also contributed significantly to my thinking. There is, however, no existing book-length work from the disciplinary perspective of English studies that deals with the range of topics proposed in this study: structural changes in the twenty-first-century in the once exclusively Western polity of English literary criticism, new histories of the postcolonial present, the sociology of a vernacular canon of English literature, the relationship between postcolonial and world literature (and translation studies).

The book is divided into six chapters that examine ideas of canonicity, literary tradition, counterreadings, vernaculars and translation, the "anxiety of influence," and nostalgia. The chapters are in two distinct groupings of three each. The first engages with formal considerations of the claims of a classic, read in the context of narratives, biographical and fictional, of literary ambition and metropolitan arrival. All three chapters in the first section engage with contestations of cultural capital centered on questions of literary language, genre, scope, and amplitude. The orientation of the second section is more obviously "postcolonial," and it works as an *inverse* telescope, moving from a chapter on a geopolitically diverse range of postcolonial rewritings to one on Anglophone fiction from the subcontinent, and then, finally, to a chapter on vernacular adaptations of the (Shakespearean) classic in India.

Chapter 1, "'What Is a Classic?' International Literary Criticism and the Classic Question," lays out the terms of exegesis of this study. Focusing on T. S. Eliot's and J. M. Coetzee's lectures "What Is a Classic?" I show how the question of the classic dramatizes the conflict between personality and impersonality implicit in twentieth-century conceptualizations of the critical function, giving poignant form to the latecomer's desire to be a precursor, bringing new literary value into performance, and articulating those voices dominated or occluded by what Said calls "the textuality of texts," while also affording escape to poetics, artifice, and the force field of a transnational literary space. I read T. S. Eliot's lecture "What Is a Classic?" with J. M. Coetzee's talk of the same title, later published in a collection of his essays titled *Stranger Shores*. In Coetzee's belated address, Eliot and Coetzee coalesce in the figure of the young colonial struggling to match his inherited culture to his daily experience. Eliot's assertion of a cosmopolitan destiny provides a model through which the aspiring postcolonial writer escapes the atomization of ethnicity and nationalization into modernist affirmations of impersonality and a timeless classicism. Not only is all writing doomed to be rewriting, the function of criticism too seems to be defined by its dialectical relationship with a hyperbolic literary past.

Chapter 2 examines the theme of anxiety of influence in relation to two significant postcolonial extrapolations of the Conradian narrative: V. S. Naipaul's rewriting of the intergenre novel, and Edward Said's rewriting of Conrad's autobiographical fiction and narrative theory. Through their critical and creative engagements with Conrad, Said and Naipaul reprise the history and cultural function of the novel: they revisit forms, figures, and themes of Conrad's fiction and life writing to write innovative metafictions on the novel's ability to represent.

Conrad is a formidable presence in Said's work throughout his career, from his first monograph to his groundbreaking texts of literary criticism. The influence manifests in Said's commitment to lost causes; his idea of subjectivity inseparable from history; his foundational work on the collusion of knowledge and unapparent networks of power; his enduring faith in narrative as supplement. Naipaul's rewriting of Conrad's influence manifests prominently in his portrayal of men who fight without cause or hope, and in the idea of the colonial periphery as bereft of history. Naipaul sees Conrad as reinventing the European novel of manners and social accident as a philosophical meditation on "the facts of every situation" (*Literary Occasions*, 176). The "drama and the truth" of Conrad's fiction lay not in events but "in the analysis" (179), a brooding, ratiocinative tradition that is perpetuated in the best of Naipaul's novels and narrative nonfiction.

Chapter 3, "'Best of the World's Classics': Derek Walcott Between Classics and the Classic," looks at themes that have dominated Walcott's writings: the postcolonial politics of mimesis, which tips over to comic and corrosive mimicry; unstable sets of resemblances; the relation of the postcolonial latecomer to Western poetic genealogy; disfiguration as figuration. Walcott's idea of the classic is associated in complex ways with his erudition in and love of "Latin, Greek, and the essential masterpieces" (Walcott, "Meanings," 51). For him, the classic is changeable and perfectible, and the act of relaying tradition inseparable from renewing it and creating "a fresh language" (*What the Twilight*, 79). On a related note, I examine, in the second section of the chapter, Walcott's conjugation of the past and the present in his evocation of Conrad, Eliot, and Joyce in his poetry, paying attention to his novel critical stance on ruminative, revisionary reading, which may or may not lead to writing. The familiar figure of Crusoe in Walcott's works is evoked in the third section, where I examine the different interpretive frames in which Crusoe is deployed in his poetry as well as the 1978 play *Pantomime*. The chapter concludes with an examination of Walcott's Creole modernism, which is dispersive as well as acquisitive, transcultural, and polyglot in the way it relates the satirical tradition of the Caribbean to that of the English-educated Walcott's neoclassical predecessors. Walcott, I claim, cites literary genealogy only to disavow it by posing de-composition as composition: "I decompose but I composing still," as the line goes from "The Spoiler's Return" (*Collected Poems*, 432).

Chapter 4, "'Pip was my story': Rereading, Counterreading, and Nonreading," is a historical and critical overview of the distinctive phases and categories of postcolonial rewriting. It examines the themes of influence, imitation, literary apprenticeship, and originality in relation to articulations of national literature and culture. It offers a critical analysis of postcolonial revisionism that focuses not simply on the aspect of subversive repetition but the congealing of an alternative canon of postcolonial writing to fit local needs, aspirations, and trajectories. The different sections of the chapter include an outline of the afterlives of canonical texts in the literature and cultural imaginary of the excolonies; departures from the nationalist focus of the earlier phases of postcolonial canon revision; reconstitutions of European literary genres in postcolonial literature; and their redeployment in the charged contexts of gender, class, and race. The concluding section of the chapter examines the psychological hold of the idea of the canon on the subject-in-process in postcolonial fiction, adding an unexpected new category to the range of iterative strategies that constitute belated responses to the canon: that of misreading or nonreading.

Chapter 5, "'Yes, sir, I was the one who got away': Postcolonial Emergence and the Vernacular Canon," examines the emergence of English as a global—and englobing—vernacular with reference to Anglophone literature from South Asia, focusing attention on language rather than nation as its creative principle. The term *vernacular* refers, in this instance, to both the singular idiom of South Asian literary production and the political, intellectual, and cultural parochialisms that it brings to bear on European universalities, fragmented histories that "challenge not only the idea of wholeness but the very idea of the 'fragment' itself. . . . What would fragments be fragments of?" (Chakrabarty, *Habitations*, 34–35). The geographical focus in this chapter is not meant to prioritize South Asia as a test case for postcolonial writing, and serves primarily to fully exploit my multilingual expertise in a specific area of translation and comparative work. It is also simply the case that in articulating a topic on vernacular or aberrant cosmopolitanism, I have taken on the most influential and challenging contributions in recent years toward what David Damrosch calls the "glocal" novel, where local histories are proximate with global movements, and which focus on minority existence at the edges of nations and on the peripheries of the globe.

The chapter offers two definitions of the idea of a vernacular canon: one related to the variant Englishes in Anglophone postcolonial literature, and the other involving an extensive deterritorialization of the national implications of English, which has contributed to the continental drift of English literature to "literatures in English." This chapter, which references key contemporary Indian, Sri Lankan, Pakistani, and Bangladeshi novels, as well as the unstable societies and histories from which they emanate, upholds their discrepant cosmopolitanism, which signals disaggregation and dissent in the face of engulfing global narratives.

Finally, in the last chapter, "hamarashakespeare.com: Shakespeare in India," I trace local adaptations of the Shakespearean text in Indian cinema and on the Indian stage. In a country where Shakespeare is a mandatory part of the university curriculum in English, these instances of cultural translation offer parallel instances of contestations of classic literary value in popular culture. What is the relationship of the printed text to these alien materializations? This chapter examines selected instances of Shakespeare translation in vernacular theater and cinema; details the mixed fortunes of a touring English theater company in India; examines two distinctive schools of interpretations of Shakespeare in popular Indian cinema, in English language and Hindi language, respectively.

"Of all the ways of acquiring books, writing them oneself is regarded as the most praiseworthy method," says Benjamin in "Unpacking my Library" (*Illuminations*, 60). The examples of rewriting or restaging canonical value that I have proposed in this book move from passive consumption to a dalliance with repetition and repudiation to autonomous acts of literature and criticism. As Pamuk says in his Nobel address, "I write because I want to read books like the ones I write. . . . I write because I have a childish belief in the immortality of libraries" (9–10).

PART I

THE QUESTION OF THE CLASSIC

1

"What Is a Classic?"
International Literary Criticism and the Classic Question

O lord, have patience
Pardon these derelictions—
I shall convince these romantic irritations
By my classical conventions.

T. S. Eliot

To mark the fortieth anniversary of the Man Booker Prize and the imminent announcement of the 2008 shortlist, the *Guardian* asked a judge from every year to give its readers glimpses into the "tears, tiffs and triumphs" that marked the nomination of the winning novel.[1] The resulting stories suggest that the perils of literary judgment, as borne out by rosters of glorious losers as well as by the historical fates of some of the winning tickets, could be put down largely to the fortuitous and subjective nature of the process. This short history of Booker judging, moreover, testifies to the contingent nature of synchronic critical reception. In 1970 Dame Rebecca West denounced Margaret Drabble for her novels of domestic life, remarking that "anyone can do the washing-up," in an era when "brilliant old ladies," to quote Antonia Fraser, could use the patriarchal line to seal the fate of "a brilliant young one" ("Tears, Tiffs, and Triumphs," 2). Hermione Lee recalls how Salman Rushdie's *Midnight's Children*, which has won the Booker of Bookers and the Best of all Bookers, and is "now a classic of world literature," was "by no means an easy winner" in 1981 ("Tears, Tiffs, and Triumphs," 3). Rushdie was an unknown writer who scraped through by one extra nomination and would have lost if the chair, Malcolm Bradbury, had the overruling vote. By 1983, however, the Rushdie-Coetzee battle for the Booker was likened to "a clash of continents" (Fay Weldon, in "Tears, Tiffs, and Triumphs," 4), to the detriment of candidates with lesser symbolic clout. In 2000, according to Rose Tremain, Margaret Atwood won the prize for *The Blind Assassin* not for writing her best book but "for all the times she'd nearly won it and had been pipped at the post by a lesser writer" ("Tears, Tiffs, and Triumphs," 21).

Most of us in the business of literary criticism have little to do with the ersatz and absurdity of deciding literary prizes like the Booker, and their tremendous, if dubious and short-term, impact on literary culture. "Even the most correct jury goes in for horsetrading and gamesmanship, and what emerges is a compromise," writes the novelist Hilary Mantel, a 1990 Booker panelist ("Tears, Tiffs, and Triumphs," 5)[2]. A number of judges even flag their Booker service as the definitive event that marked their turn to nonfiction and narrative journalism. But the criteria deployed in the determination of this yearly award speak to the supposedly more serious and premeditated considerations that inform academic literary criticism. No minds are changed by panel discussions, as the Booker judges note year after year, but there is the routine, familiar to literary critics, "of anatomising one's taste and judgement and then communicating it to a group," as Alex Clark, 2008 judge, puts it ("Tears, Tiffs, and Triumphs," 21). Booker judging highlights the limits of literary criticism; the triumph of creating a classic that is not unmixed with the fear of choosing the wrong book. Finally, it addresses the politics of impersonality that marks the inception and transmission of modern literary criticism. "But posterity will forget us," says English professor and Booker judge John Sutherland in the critical backlash against the 2005 choice (John Banville for *The Sea*). "Barnes, Ishiguro and—I believe—Banville they'll remember" (21).

Pierre Bourdieu's well-known work on consumption studies in *Distinction* (1986) has long exposed consumers' desires to cultivate and demonstrate a particular kind of labor informing their consumption patterns and to define their class position through it. Consumers select commodities that proclaim their sophistication in taste—hence the popularity of "educated" forms of recreation. The critical "eye" is a product of history reproduced by education: cultural consumption presupposes, Bourdieu writes, "an act of cognition, a decoding operation, which implies the implementation of a cognitive acquirement, a cultural code" (3). Bourdieu terms as cultural capital the internalization of the cultural code or the acquisition of a knowledge that equips the subject to decipher cultural relations. Prizes such as the Booker expose the vested interests behind cultural recognition, and exemplify, as James English observes, the trenchant relationship between the cultural and the economic, or "cultural and political capital." They are, to quote English, "our most effective institutional agents of *capital intraconversion*," substitutions and exchanges between different complexes of capital (*Economy of Prestige*, 10). In his insightful study of the awards industry, *The Economy of Prestige*, English argues that despite the "staggering discontinuities" between the canon at any given time and the list of past prizewinners, "it is precisely by such embarrassingly social-commercial-cultural mechanisms . . . that the canon is formed, cultural capital is allocated, 'greatness' is determined" (245).[3] I will consider the role of literary criticism in two relatable, if less commercially compromised, instantiations of literary capital and determinations of literary greatness: the twentieth-century lectures called "What Is a Classic?" that T. S. Eliot and J. M. Coetzee gave, forty-seven years apart. In each lecture the creative writer assumes the role of a critic, self-consciously taking his place in the direct succession of poet-critics—Johnson, Coleridge, Shelley, and Arnold—and his questioning is historical as well as rhetorical. Both interrogate the idea of a classic as a work of enduring value, and demonstrate, in singular ways, how literary criticism generates its classics. In his lecture, given in 1991, Coetzee even claims that "the function of criticism is defined by the classic: criticism is that which is duty-bound to interrogate the classic" ("What Is a Classic?" 19). Coetzee had reread Eliot's famous lecture in preparation for his. The two essays, read together, seem to suggest that if the classical criterion is of vital importance to literary criticism, the classic in turn is constituted by the criticism it receives down the ages. It is a peculiar codependence: the classic is that which survives critical questioning, and it in fact defines itself by that surviving. Eliot's and, later, Coetzee's investment in this question cannot be reduced to nostalgia for or valorization of the set standards and idealized attitudes of canons. The critic's quest for the classic is indeed Romantic and Oedipal, but if the classic is a fantasized point of origin it is also a new departure and signals breathless new arrivals at debates that define and contest literary modernity and the literary present.

In "Secular Criticism," an essay that sets out to define the function of criticism for our times, Edward Said describes the critic as an "individual consciousness" that is not a mere product of the dominant culture, "but a historical and social actor in it" (*World*, 15). Criticism is constituted by the "self-situating" of the critic, who assumes a distance from the collective (15). Western critical consciousness, according to Said, has historically functioned through affiliation, "a kind of compensatory order," or a cultural system, that eventually supplants the authority of the natural (or what Said calls the "filiative") order:

> Thus if a filial relationship was held together by natural bonds and natural forms of authority—involving obedience, fear, love, respect, and instinctual conflict—the new affiliative relationship changes these bonds into what seem to be transpersonal forms—such as guild consciousness, consensus, collegiality, professional respect, class, and the hegemony of a dominant culture. (20)

The affiliative order affirms and replicates filiative processes, albeit through nonbiological social and cultural structures. In the humanities, such an order is predicated on the occlusion of the nonliterary and the non-European, and arguably the political dimension of all literature. According to Said, there are two alternatives for the contemporary literary critic: unquestioning reverence for the (affiliative) order of the humanities and "the dominant culture served by those humanities" (24); or the adoption of a "secular" mode of critical scrutiny, which is oppositional toward "orthodox habits of the mind" and "organized dogma" (29). The thrust of the question "What is a classic?" is aligned to this, the second mode of doing criticism. It symbolizes a constative *and* performative epistemology, at once a long, ongoing "process of abstraction" and a timely and contingent "reaction to immediate concerns."[4] If Eliot addresses and nervously reinforces the idea of the classic as European and Eurocentric, Coetzee draws out the unspoken implications in Eliot's lecture to elaborate on the afterlife of this question in trans- or international criticism. Both versions of "What Is a Classic?" use the object of inquiry to worry the emplacement and affiliations of the literary critic. The time of the classic, both lectures testify, is the complex present of literary criticism, and its place, too, is "here."

Before launching into the Eliot and Coetzee interventions, it is necessary to mark the distinction between classics and canons. The term *classic* is closely related to the idea of canonicity but is not entirely reducible to it. The classic, like the canonical work, is a book that is read long after it was written—and that demands rereading. The classic shares with the canon the "strangeness" that Harold Bloom identifies as the greatness of canonical works: "a mode of originality that either cannot be assimilated, or that so assimilates us that we cease to see it as strange" (*Western Canon*, 3). The classic, like the canonical text, produces "startlement" rather than recognition or a "fulfilment of expectation" (3). The classic and the canonical work usher a polymorphous textuality that literary cultures value, and both involve the dimension of criticism, or interpretive traditions that contest the definition of literary value. But the classic is primarily a singular act of literature, while the canon, Guillory states, is "an aristocracy of texts" ("Ideology," 175). Canonicity implies a formation of a corpus, the congealing of the "literary art of Memory," as Harold Bloom terms it (*Western Canon*, 17), the making up of a list of books requisite for a literary education, and the formation of an exclusive club, however painstakingly contested the rules of inclusion (and exclusion) may be. The classic, however, is inseparable from the endless and unresolved contestations of the question "What is a classic?" and belongs to what Guillory calls "the conflictual prehistory of canon-formation" ("Ideology," 194). If the canon implies continuity with the past or a perpetuation of tradition, the classic is all that and something else: the survival of the classic, Kermode states, depends upon its possession "of a surplus of signifier" (*Classic*, 140).

Eliot's and Coetzee's temporal perspective—a long look back—in "What Is a Classic?" has been revised by the drift of English literary history. Cultural identity in the era of cultural-economic globalization, as Said suggests, should be conceived in terms of space rather than time: "Spatiality becomes . . . the characteristic of an aesthetic rather than of political domination, as more and more regions—from India to Africa to the Caribbean—challenge the classical empires and their cultures" (*Culture and Imperialism*, 18). Are there any perennial works or masterpieces in the new geomorphic empire and in world literature, which is not so much a canon of texts as it is a mode of circulation? How does the unitary ontology of the classic haunt the shadow constructs of postimperial selfhood? After elaborating on Eliot's and Coetzee's investment in the question, I speculate on whether the question of the classic is asked, in some form, whenever "secular canon-formation" (Kermode, *Classic*, 15) occurs in the politics of publishing, teaching, and translating core texts. Criticism in the twenty-first century continues to shore up the idea of transcendent and foundational literary value against mobile configurations of knowledge, technology, and expertise. For Eliot, the classic standard was indissociable from dead languages. In the new century, criticism invents itself and its modern classics by waking the dead, and sustaining a dynamic and variable conversation with a monolingual literary tradition as it becomes other.

"What Is a Classic?" is the title of a presidential address delivered by T. S. Eliot before the Virgil Society on October 16, 1944. The Blitz had resumed early that year, and London that summer had been introduced to "flying bombs." In June a bomb had fallen on the offices of Faber and Faber, where Eliot was editor. While business quickly resumed, Eliot was left without the use of his flat at the office and forced to commute between London and Surrey (where he lived) more frequently. He stayed in London only on Tuesday nights and fulfilled his fire-watching duties—camped on a roof, the vertiginous poet scrutinized the blacked-out city for evidence of fires after antiaircraft guns had done their job. Peter Ackroyd's biography details the benumbed existence that Eliot led in the last years of the war, negotiating days one at a time with no hope for the future (Ackroyd, *T. S. Eliot*, 268). The lectures he delivered around the time of "What Is a Classic?" do not reference the war directly, but are nevertheless chastened and enervated by its reality. The connection of "What Is a Classic?" to war work is speculative, of course: it is impossible to know if Eliot would have bothered to write this essay had the Virgil Society not held him to a presidential address, and whether this critical essay represented anything more than a tertiary thought in the master's late period. Hugh Kenner, reviewing Frank Kermode's revival of the piece in *The Classic* (1975), is convinced that "the British tradition of the ceremonial has been obligating these individual talents, and it has taken all Mr. Kermode's skill with the panel-lights and rheostats of documented learning to disguise this hollow fact" ("Footsteps of the Master").

Eliot's address, with a rhetorical question as its title, begins in a retrospective mode: "It is only by hindsight, and in historical perspective, that a classic can be known as such" (*What Is a Classic?* 10). Eliot articulates his topic by means of a desiring dialectic that pits the classic against the contingent, the racial and national against the international, the absolute against the errant. He espouses a utopian cultural homogeneity as a precondition for the emergence of the classic. A classic occurs when a civilization and a language and literature are mature and there is a community of taste and common style. A mature literature has a historical trajectory behind it, the history of "an ordered though unconscious progress of a language to realize its own potentialities within its own limitations" (11). It is the work of a "mature" mind steeped in the history of its living language and magisterial in its critical sweep of the past, present, and future. The maturity of the classic poet, according to Eliot, accrues from a consciousness of history, the poet's own as well as that of at least one other hypercivilization.

Eliot reminds us that the question "What is a classic?" is not new. I would like to look briefly at a notable historical precedent. Augustin Sainte-Beuve, an Eliot-like creator of literary value, confronted his age with the same query in the *causerie* of 24 October 1850: "Qu'est-ce qu'un classique?"[5] The word *classic*, Sainte-Beuve records, appears first in ancient Rome as *classici*, a name applied to the citizens of the first class, the only class that mattered. The classic as a mode of classification thus originates in a gesture that equates social and literary rank. Sainte-Beuve's account of the classic is at a remove from the antique ideal, but, as critics point out, it is telling that Sainte-Beuve should begin in ancient Rome, where the literary classic mirrors a privileged social class. As Christopher Prendergast comments: "The implication seems to be that, however remote Roman antiquity, it still has a lesson immensely germane to the present or to Sainte-Beuve's construction of it: namely—that the material and social conditions for the production of a 'classic' rest on the division of labour and the specialization of function" (28). In this essay, as well as the 1858 lecture that revises it, Sainte-Beuve offers several definitions of the classic that seek to broaden its spirit and scope: a true classic is an author who has enriched the human mind; the classic is an unequivocal moral truth commuted in a form that is not fixed but unfailingly large and grand, fine and meaningful, healthy and beautiful in itself. The classic has a style of its own, and is new and inimitable, an invention that is not programmable and must be recognized on its own terms. The style is new without neologism, new and ancient in equal measure, and effortlessly contemporaneous with all ages. The classic renews itself continuously to pose as a perpetual contemporary, "contemporain de tous les âges": it is a living entity, open to endless intervention in successive acts of reading and interpretation. The idea of a classic, in Sainte-Beuve's definition, is not restricted to a single work or author, but implies continuity and tradition, and the transmission of tradition. According to Kermode,

Sainte-Beuve maintains that the classic—and for him the works of Virgil are the type of all classics—is both "an index of civility" and the product of individual genius, exemplifying health, sanity, and universal values (*Classic*, 17). Ancient works are not classic because they are old, but because they are vigorous, fresh, and fit.

Sainte-Beuve's essay is an excellent case study of the difficulties attendant on asking what a classic is. Sainte-Beuve has elsewhere mounted a poignant defense of the historical situatedness and concomitant limitations of the critic. In his review of Flaubert's *Salammbô*, Sainte-Beuve wonders what the critic is to do in the face of insurmountable cultural difference, as manifested in, say, "petty local hatreds between barbarians."

How can you expect me to take an interest in this lost war, buried in the defiles or sands of Africa, in the rebellion of these more or less indigenous Libyan tribes against their master the Carthaginians, in these petty local hatreds between barbarians. What does it matter to me, this duel of Tunis and Carthage? Speak to me of the duel of Carthage and Rome, and at once I am all attention, I am involved. (Prendergast, trans., 39)

In "Qu'est-ce qu'un classique?" he nevertheless warns against the circumscribing of the canon by those who know only one language and literature, and proposes to rebuild the Temple of Taste, a canon of Indo-European classics and a veritable library of humanity. Sainte-Beuve extols Homer and, more unconventionally, European classics of the age of Louis XIV and the three unknown Homers from the East: Valmiki and Vyasa of India, and Firdousi of Persia. Despite Sainte-Beuve's cultural limitations and the racist and classist omissions from his pantheon of writers and texts, the Beuvian fantasy of the classic speaks to the dream of an international literary criticism, of a universality that is both European and transhistorical, and of the emergence of a global vernacular like English.

Like Sainte-Beuve, Eliot identifies Virgil's *Aeneid* as the originary classic of all Europe. According to Eliot, a classic mind maintains an "unconscious" balance between past tradition and the originality of its contemporary moment. As heir to the undeveloped resources of the language, the poet is driven to outdo predecessors, but that revolt serves to radicalize and recode tradition not discontinue it. Virgil is the poet of the eternal metropolis, the empire of empires, Rome. In a 1951 essay, "Virgil and the Christian World," Eliot reads Virgil as an adventist Christian and Aeneas as the prototype of a Christian hero, praising the historical imagination that synthesized pagan values with those of the Western Christian *imperium* to come. Virgil is not provincial, but Roman and European. He is a man of genius actuating the genius of his language. The classic expresses "the maximum possible of the whole range of feeling" of the people who speak that language (*What Is a Classic?* 27). After Virgil, no great development was possible in the Latin language. While the great poet—Shakespeare or Milton, say—exhausts one literary form, the classic poet exhausts, according to Eliot, the whole language of his or her time. For Eliot, Virgil is the classic criterion that rules over and outlives contesting literatures from the periphery. As Colleen Lamos argues, it probably "does not matter much to Eliot what Virgil did right that every other poet has, in one way or another, done wrong, but that Virgil stand as a marker of absolute and unquestionable literary value" (*Deviant Modernism*, 49).

"There is no classic in English," Eliot declares (*What Is a Classic?* 25). English is a living language, various, vagrant, and with possibly the greatest capacity of changing, and yet remaining itself. We may be glad, Eliot surmises, that English has never achieved perfection in the work of one classic poet, for that perfection masks the homeostasis of death. "The classic standard must come from the dead, from the tomb," remarks Lamos (49). As with Freud's *Beyond the Pleasure Principle* (1921)—another text greatly altered by the war—the death instinct seems to collude with the life instinct in propelling living languages out of historical time. A language has to fulfill its literary potential—progressively die—in order to achieve the classic immortality of Latin and Greek. According to Eliot, the "classic criterion" should be of vital importance to a language or literature, dead or alive. Without the application of the classical measure we become provincial, with distorted values, confounding the ephemeral with time-honored monuments. Without the classic, we lose our sense of the past, and the world becomes the property solely of the living, a property, to quote Eliot, "in which the dead hold no shares" (*What Is a Classic?* 30). Europe, in spite of its progressive mutilation and disfigurement, is to the war-weary, middle-aged Eliot the old organism out of which a new world harmony must develop. The bloodstream of Europe must course through all variations of language and culture that can be grouped together as European literature. The notion of the classic is inseparable from notions of empire. Eliot's universalist or imperialist classic derives from this belief that whatever happens in history, the Empire remains unchanged. As Kermode states, "the empire is the paradigm of the classic: a perpetuity, a transcendent entity, however remote its provinces, however extraordinary its temporal vicissitudes" (*Classic*, 28). Latin is the universal language, the ideal to which European vernaculars should aspire but which they can never attain. This provinciality is defensible so long as local languages and literatures do not proliferate in isolation, but maintain their position as provinces in the empire of the ideal classic—Virgil.

It is easy to read "What Is a Classic?" as a derivative essay in which Eliot places Virgil as the great pre-Christian precursor of Christianity's greatest poet, Dante, who fulfills the tradition. But the grim historical context of this dispatch makes us wonder if Eliot chose the *Aeneid*, not for its celebration of the age of Augustus, but for its prophetic testimony of the possibility of fresh civil war. Virgil's Rome is founded in blood, and Augustan pacification is laced with terror that blood could flow again. As Gareth Reeves points out, Carthage, Troy, Tyre, and Rome stand interchangeably for an exploding city that, as Eliot wrote in *The Waste Land*, "cracks and reforms and bursts in the violet air" (*T. S. Eliot*, 31). "What is a classic? It is not a new question," said Eliot in his Virgil Society address (*What Is a Classic?* 7). The real question is why Eliot revisits this tired and curatorial attitude to reclaim the classic as a work of foundational value. Was the effort war work, as Ackroyd claims (*T. S. Eliot*, 268)?[6] Did his difficult present make the melancholic poet turn to a philosophical meditation on history?

In *T. S. Eliot: An Imperfect Life*, Lyndall Gordon sees "What Is a Classic?" as revealing "Eliot's own concern with destiny" (383). Eliot speaks to two peoples, English and American, not only allies in war but heirs to a common culture, embodied in his own person. A few years before the address, Eliot had edited a selection of Kipling's verse. Kipling, Eliot said in his introduction, had "a universal foreignness" and yet could see more clearly because he was "alien." He had "a sense of the antiquity of England, of the number of generations and peoples who have laboured the soil and been buried beneath it, and of the contemporaneity of the past" (Gordon, *T. S. Eliot*, 383–84). Like Kipling and Conrad, Eliot positioned himself in relation to England as a powerful insider who was also an outsider. As Rushdie once claimed, "The only people who see the whole picture . . . are the ones who step out of the frame" (*Ground Beneath Her Feet*, 43).

In a tribute to T. S. Eliot, on 26 September 1986, at the unveiling of the blue plaque at 3 Kensington Court Gardens,[7] Ted Hughes made a distinction between "great" and "truly great" poetry. "Great poetry is poetry of a distinctive national character," while truly great poetry, Eliot's poetry, is, "of this new, unprecedented psychic simultaneity of all cultures, this sudden, inner confederation of all peoples, subjected as they are, under the tyranny of modern history, to a single spiritual calamity" (*Dancer to God*, 10). Coetzee, however, is less forgiving of the "psychic simultaneity of all cultures" in Eliot's *Geist*. In a lecture titled "What Is a Classic?" given in Graz, Austria, in 1991, Coetzee says that what struck him when he reread Eliot's famous lecture in preparation for his present one was that "nowhere does Eliot reflect on the fact of his own Americanness, or at least his American origins, and therefore on the somewhat odd angle at which he comes, honouring a European poet to a European audience" ("What Is a Classic?" 2). As Coetzee points out, Eliot's project involves not only inventing a fully European identity for Virgil but also claiming for England a problematic European identity. Coetzee wonders "how and why Eliot himself became English enough for the issue to matter to him. . . . "Why did Eliot 'become' English at all?" (3). The motives, according to Coetzee, were confused and complex: Anglophilia, a strong identification with the English middle class, a certain American self-loathing. Arguably, the world wars were instrumental in turning Eliot's *avant guerre* cosmopolitanism to a paranoid and displaced nationalism. Marjorie Perloff speaks of Eliot's increasing alienation from the public sphere and politics of Europe: "Indeed, after *The Waste Land*, what we know as modernism was to lose its Utopian edge and become much darker, its face no longer turned to the 'new' in the same way" (*21st-Century Modernism*, 41). His alienation also had something to do with what Helen Vendler terms "the dilemma of idiom" (*Coming of Age*, 64): Eliot and other American poets of his generation encountered a lack of a serviceable style as they came of age. "England is a 'Latin' country," Eliot had proclaimed in 1923 (Kermode, *Classic*, 20). By 1944, Eliot was an Englishman or a "Roman Englishman" (Coetzee, "What Is a Classic?" 3).

According to Coetzee, Eliot uses the story of Aeneas as a fable of exile followed by "home-founding" to evoke the topography of his own life history, appropriating the cultural weight of the epic to back himself. If Aeneas is recast as an Eliotic hero, a fugitive from a ruined city, Virgil is characterized as a rather Eliot-like "'learned author'" (5).[8] Eliot is remaking and resituating his national identity by inserting it in a Western European and what Coetzee identifies as a Catholic cosmopolitanism, the internationalism of the learned elites represented by Dante. Coetzee marvels at the way Eliot fashions a new identity not on the basis of "immigration, settlement, residence, domestication, acculturation," as mere mortals do, but by co-opting a convenient nationality and then resituating it within a larger narrative of cosmopolitanism (7). He is, as Coetzee says, claiming "a line of descent less from the Eliots of New England and/or Somerset than from Virgil and Dante" (7). In this fabrication of genealogy Eliot is not alone among the Modernists. In his 1929 essay "Dante . . . Bruno.Vico . . . Joyce," Beckett compares James Joyce's "desophisticated" idiom and his writing, which is "not *about* something," but "*is that something itself*" (*Samuel Beckett*, 4: 504, 503), to Dante's "vulgar." "They both saw how worn out and threadbare was the conventional language of cunning literary artificers, both rejected an approximation to a universal language" (506). Eliot is akin to Joyce and Beckett in making exile a precondition of new and supranational art, and in relishing the freedom it afforded to choose one's predecessors. "Where Eliot went wrong," notes Coetzee, "was in failing to foresee that the new order would be directed from Washington, not London and certainly not Rome" (6). Coetzee does not, however, outmode Eliot's notion of provincialism, which implies an eternal metropolis.

"What is a classic? It is not a new question," Eliot had said by way of introducing his topic. So what is Coetzee's investment in this old question, and how does he answer it? It is impossible not to see a vexed affiliation between the Eliot and Coetzee, particularly the fictionalized Coetzee of *Boyhood* and *Youth*. Coetzee's autobiographical protagonists match the description of Eliot and Ezra Pound that he provides in "What Is a Classic?": "young colonials struggling to match their inherited culture to their daily experience" ("What Is a Classic?" 7). *Boyhood* details a hilarious incident—the young John pretending to be Roman Catholic because he thought it had something to do with Rome—that plays on Eliot's insistence on the nobility of Latinity. In a send-up to Eliot's early poetry of deracination, rootlessness, and self-invention, the narrator of Coetzee's autobiographical fiction, *Youth*, says "each man is an island . . . [and] you don't need parents" (*Youth*, 3). "There is no dishonour in electing to follow Eliot," John speculates (the "electing to follow" is telling, after the disavowal of genealogy and national affiliation in both novels), and the antihero's mobility narrative negotiates Eliotic critical issues: Englishness, civilization versus barbarism (and philistinism), metropolitan urbanity, Latinity, the grip of Europe on the colonial imaginary. Halfway through his lecture, Coetzee tellingly embarks on "an autobiographical path" (he says it is methodologically reckless but will successfully dramatize the issue ["What Is a Classic?" 9]). Eliot the provincial, we learn, is indeed a pattern and figure of the author. Just as Virgil spoke across the ages to Eliot, Coetzee, age fifteen, had undergone the impact of the classic: an afternoon in the back garden in the suburbs of Cape Town, the music of Bach from the house next door, "after which everything changed" ("What Is a Classic?" 10). Does the classic choose and enthrall us, or do we choose to be thus elected and reconfigured by a transcendent ideal? Was that experience in the garden mystic or material, Coetzee wonders?

[Was] I symbolically electing high European culture, and command of the codes of that culture, as a route that would take me out of my class position in white South African society and ultimately out of what I must have felt, in terms however obscure or mystified, as an historical dead end—a road that would culminate (again symbolically) with me on a platform in Europe addressing a cosmopolitan audience on Bach, T. S. Eliot and the question of the classic? ("What Is a Classic?" 10–11).

"Every writer who desires to be read . . . has to seek admittance to the canon—or, more precisely, *a* canon," says Derek Attridge of the processes of canonization operative on Coetzee's novels: "unless we are read, we are nothing" (*J. M. Coetzee*, 74). Coetzee's fashioning of his literary and cultural genealogy in the classic mold is inseparable from the writerly desire to be recognized and judged favorably by the classic's exacting standards. And his ambivalent attitude toward the legacy of the classic reflects his misgivings about the transmission of knowledge in the humanities: the acquisition of disinterest and autonomy by subscribing to transcendent values that comes with an inescapable sense that to be educated is to be incorporated in the knowledge economy.

According to Coetzee, the classic is historically constituted by the criticism it receives down the ages. "What is a classic?" is thus an unanswerable question. The classic is that which survives ideological determination as well as skeptical questioning—in fact it defines itself by surviving. Coetzee evokes the "great poet of the classic of our times, the Pole Zbigniew Herbert," to set in motion the antagonism between the classic and the barbarian: "not so much an opposition as a confrontation" ("What Is a Classic?" 19).

It is not the possession of some essential quality that makes it possible for the classic to survive barbarism. Rather, "what survives the worst of barbarism, surviving because generations of people cannot afford to let go of it and therefore hold on to it at all costs—that is the classic," Coetzee asserts, echoing Herbert (19). The classic is also radically new: impossible to predict and difficult to welcome. Coetzee shows a strong affinity with Eliot in the way he brings his topic to a close. According to Eliot, the classical criterion is of vital importance to literary criticism. Coetzee takes this idea to its logical limit: "The function of criticism is defined by the classic: criticism is that which is duty-bound to interrogate the classic. Thus the fear that the classic will not survive the de-centring acts of criticism may be turned on its head: rather than being the foe of the classic, criticism, and indeed criticism of the most sceptical kind, may be what the classic uses to define itself and ensure its survival" (19). As with Sainte-Beuve's "Qu'est-ce qu'un classique?" the classic as well as the critical appraisal of the classic have a "function," an ostensible aspect of which is to attest to the viability of and embolden the very tradition of close critical "testing": "The criterion of testing and survival is not just a minimal, pragmatic, Horatian standard (Horace says, in effect, that if a work is still around a hundred years after it was written, it must be a classic). It is a criterion that expresses a certain confidence in the tradition of testing, and a confidence that professionals will not devote labour and attention, generation after generation, to sustaining pieces of music whose life-functions have terminated" (18). According to Sainte-Beuve the function of the classic as well as of critical investment in the question of the classic is to act as a dyke ("une digue") in the face of rising barbarism and anarchy.[9] The term *function*, when applied to the work of literary criticism, has the Arnoldian resonance of "preserving and defending something seen as under threat" (Prendergast, *Classic*, 46), and is applicable equally to Sainte-Beuve's, Eliot's, and Coetzee's task of interpreting and evaluating the classic. This discussion of the function of criticism is a telltale moment in the Coetzee essay. The author-critic is justifying the high seriousness of his present endeavor; he is also activating the idea of the classic for the contemporary writer. "What is a classic?" is another way of asking, "What is borne across?" or "Who reads me?" or, in a more Beuvian mode of address to the higher mortals, "What would they say of us?" The subsistence of the classical criterion, combined with the absence of a definitive classic in English, must also fuel the modern writer's hope, to quote Coetzee's predecessor, "that I . . . may be able to write something which will be worth preserving" (Eliot, *What Is a Classic?* 25).

As Coetzee points out in his lecture, Eliot does not mention his wartime circumstances except in passing, to let his auditors know that "accidents of the present time" ("What Is a Classic?" 8) had made it difficult for him to access scholarly materials for the lecture. It could be argued that Eliot parenthesizes the raging war so as not to let the timely critical consideration of the European classic be overwhelmed by one of the greatest crises in European history and possibly because the reality of the event would defy any act of aesthetic containment. It could also be argued that Coetzee's engagement with this question, too, takes the distant impress of his own conflictual social reality. The apartheid regime fell apart in 1990, a year before Coetzee's lecture. Coetzee's back garden, like Eliot's war-ravaged London, is represented as timeless, spaceless, and universal. Coetzee's reexamination of metropolitan versus provincial or classic versus barbarian in this lecture could be said to refer obliquely to the relationship between South African cultural production and international aesthetic paradigms and to the 1990s South African cultural debates to find a new settlement between domestic and international discourses. Coetzee's evocation of the function of criticism brings up the ghosts of Eliot and Arnold and a duty to eschew the antinomian "inner voice" that urges "doing as one likes" and attune oneself instead to the higher authority embodied in the literary canon. This turn away from the "new" to what Eliot valorized as the "present moment of the past" (*Selected Essays*, 22) could be read as Coetzee's increasing alienation from the South African public sphere, its institutional and academic politics, notably the debates and disputations on the shaping of a national culture. Finally, the quest for the classic and the need to be accommodated in the classical category are symptoms of "a kind of upward race-mobility" (Spivak, "Burden," 276) that is Coetzee's burden as much as it is Eliot's.

"What is a classic?" is easily mistaken for a snobbish and conservative question that signals entrenched cultural privilege and overreach. In the context of increasingly globalized structures of labor, trade, environment, warfare, and knowledge, however, the question of the classic is no longer bound to class imperatives, "cognitive acquirement," or the power-knowledge nexus of a colonial canon. The literary canon itself has become a site of unresolved struggles, no longer perceived as a mainstay of transhistorical values but as an "abstraction from history," an institutional means of exposing people to "ideological overdeterminations" (Altieri, *Canons*, 24). In the twenty-first century, the idea of the classic also has to measure up against floating populations; transnational politics within national borders; mobile configurations and diffusions of knowledge, technology, and expertise; and global English. We are, as Arjun Appadurai states, functioning in a world "characterised by objects in motion": "These objects include ideas and ideologies, people and goods, images and messages, technologies and techniques. This is a world of flows. . . . It is also, of course, a world of structures, organizations, and other stable social forms. But the apparent stabilities that we see are, under close examination, usually our devices for handling objects characterised by motion" ("Grassroots Globalization," 5). Does the classic criterion speak to the planetary system of literature rising out of the movement of capital, commodities, services, and discourses, or does it pose a veritable constraint on such flows? And if the classic ideal could be renovated for a postcolonial, global world, would it inevitably replicate global capital and what Ian Baucom calls the "globalizing imaginary" (*Out of Place*, 168) by synchronizing and homogenizing historical difference or differentiation, and creating a centralized (not constellated) literary studies? In *What Is World Literature?* David Damrosch presents "world literature" not as a canon of texts but as a dynamic field, a mode of circulation and reading whereby books exist in literary systems beyond their culture of origin.[10] The literary corpus that constitutes world literature at any given time is not fixed, but variable. The ways in which the works of world literature are read are also (ideally) variable. A given work may enter into world literature and fall out again, depending on the "complex dynamics of cultural change and contestation" (*What Is World Literature?* 6). "The history of the world is the slaughterhouse of the world, reads a famous Hegelian aphorism; and of literature," says Franco Moretti. "The majority of books disappear forever," Moretti adds, citing the example of the canon of nineteenth-century British novels, whose two hundred titles account for about half of one percent of all novels published in Britain during the century ("Slaughterhouse," 207). Similarly, very few secure a quick and permanent place in what Damrosch terms the "limited company of perennial World Masterpieces" (*What Is World Literature?* 6). Damrosch's definition of a masterpiece makes it nothing other than a modern classic. There is a superficial difference between the two, in that while the classic is a work of lasting value, identified primarily with Greek and Roman art, and often closely associated with imperial hierarchies, the masterpiece can be an ancient or modern work and need not have any foundational cultural force. The greatness of the masterpiece, however, seems to lie in its perpetuation and redefinition of a cultural standard of excellence, in its high difficulty level, and in its participation in classic ideal, as it were: "In this literary analog of a liberal democracy the (often middle-class) masterworks could engage in 'a great conversation' with their aristocratic forebears, a conversation in which their culture and class of origin mattered less than the great ideas they expressed anew" (*What Is World Literature?* 15). Damrosch discredits the culture of "presentism" that entails opportunistic, erratic, and often unhistorical appropriations of the past for a perpetual present (17). The canons of the earlier periods, suggests Damrosch, should be reexamined and opened up rather than abandoned, and a masterpiece is a work in which the past is thus reconfigured and put to use.

Damrosch's views on literary masterworks are relatable to Frank Kermode's suggestion in the concluding pages of *The Classic* that the "imperial classic" has given way to "a modern version of the classic," which is plural, secular, and "a permanent locus of change" (139–40). Kermode seems to present the modern version of the classic as both plenitude and lack. The classic ideal is a "surplus of signifier" (140), exceeding the claims of an interpreter or a generation of interpreters: the plenitude of the modern classic allows it to be adapted to the specific demands of different cultures. And the classic is a teeming lack, which invites readers to make and remake meaning. Kermode briefly pauses to consider "classic characteristics"—"'a fine awareness of human relations,' and a certain maturity" (133)—but his analysis glosses over the constitutive depth and magnitude of a classic work that invites and organizes successive readings. It is as if the classic can only be determined retroactively and across a hermeneutic gap, the survival of the classic being the greatest proof its ontic status. Kermode is content to shore the classic as a complex indeterminacy, which has allowed us "our necessary pluralities" (121), and that in turn reduces the classic to a temporary and replaceable touchstone for modern literature and criticism. In this schema, the values of the "originary culture" are routinely outmaneuvered by those of the "receiving culture" (Damrosch, *What Is World Literature?* 126). Surely classics are important for "the quality of the questions they ask and the concerns they exhibit, rather than for the thematic answers they propose," as Charles Altieri argues in his critique of Kermode ("Hermeneutics of Literary Indeterminacy," 89)? Damrosch's concept of the "masterpiece" reinvents the classic more effectively for a post-teleological age. It augments Kermode's sequential narrative (the classic as "an essence available to us under our dispositions, in the aspect of time"; Kermode, *The Classic*, 141) with dynamic networks of dialogue and exchange with the past that reflect human diversity, new forms and maps of belonging, and what Coetzee, in *Diary of a Bad Year*, calls "the continuity of the human story" (189). Coetzee's shorthand for the classic in this experimental novel, a set of "strong" (and "soft") opinions strongly evocative of Vladimir Nabokov, is "the perduring" (190).

"What is a classic?" is a question of outliving and "postness" or of living in an age that seems to come after the end of history. As my readings of Eliot and Coetzee show, the relation to classic is in a sense equally "post" or postcolonial for both Eliot (American, and also English in relation to Virgil and Dante) and Coetzee. In their roles as literary critic, both seem to subscribe (in varying degrees) to the fantasy that literary culture is instrumental and produces beliefs and ideas that unify or order culture. And it is the outsider, like Coetzee, reading at university in the 1950s the modern classics Eliot and Pound, who is more interested in constructing tradition, since his own relation to it has to be constructed, not assumed. As Pascale Casanova observes: "The irremediable and violent discontinuity between the metropolitan literary world and its suburban outskirts is perceptible only to writers on the periphery, who, having to struggle in very tangible ways in order simply to find 'the gateway to the present' (as Octavio Paz puts it), and then to gain admission to its central precincts, are more clearsighted than others about the nature and the form of the literary balance of power" (*World Republic*, 43). The question of the classic is closely related to the "worlding" of an international literary criticism for the twenty-first century. For writers and critics emerging from the "suburban outskirts" of the "metropolitan literary world" (as repeated attacks on the elitism of Edward Said, Homi Bhabha, and Gayatri Spivak show, however, it is impossible to fix the location and provenance of "the most deserving marginal"), it is not simply a case of accessing the culture of imperialism, but, to quote Spivak, the "persistent critique of what one must inhabit . . . an incessant recoding of diversified fields of value" (*Outside*, 61). "What is a classic?" is a question that has no single or unified answer.

It is self-confirmatory and effective to some extent, of course, but is also posed as an incomplete and unfulfilled quest and "a yearning for conceptuality" (Said, *World*, 52). As the Eliot and Coetzee lectures demonstrate, the question of the classic dramatizes the conflict between personality and impersonality implicit in twentieth-century conceptualizations of the critical function: it gives poignant form to the latecomer's desire to be a precursor, to bring new literary value into performance, to articulate "those voices dominated, displaced, or silenced by the textuality of texts" (Said, *World*, 53), while also affording escape to poetics and artifice, impersonality, and the force field of a transnational literary space.

"For every major poet a cloud of minor poets, like gnats buzzing around a lion," notes the poetaster of Coetzee's autobiographical *Youth* (20). The classic question is inevitably tied with anxieties around major and minor statuses in a disciplinary context, since they are also contestations between the majority and minorities. Though the deconstructive impulse is to "decenter the desire for the canon," Gayatri Spivak is right to sound a cautionary note: "a full undoing of the canon-apocrypha opposition, like the undoing of any opposition, is impossible. . . . When we feminist Marxists are ourselves moved by a desire for alternative canon formations, we work with varieties of and variations upon the old standards. Here the critic's obligation seems to be a scrupulous declaration of 'interest'" (*Spivak Reader*, 110). If the question "What is a Classic?" is historically implicated in what Spivak often calls the "epistemic violence" of colonial canonical norm, its deconstructive logic of evaluation provides the terms for counterquestioning—"What subject-effects were systematically effaced and trained to efface themselves so that a canonic norm might emerge?" (110)[11]—and reterritorializing the idea of the canon. It is my argument in this chapter that the question of the classic, especially when posed with "a scrupulous declaration of 'interest,'" provides metropolitan twenty-first-century critical humanities with a viable, sustainable, and ethical means of judging literary works and demarcating the literary field. "Either there were aesthetic values, or there are only the overdeterminations of race, class, and gender," says Bloom unequivocally of secular canon-formation (*Western Canon*, 487). Needless to say the overdeterminations of race, class, and gender are too real, and they persist but indeed they should not lead to dubious negotiations between aesthetic standards and social engineering. Neither should texts be read and canonized for the politics of blame they embody. It is equally absurd, however, to deny the cultural embeddedness of aesthetic standards, as Bloom tends to do. While it is impossible to dissociate literary meaning from immediate historical contexts and alignments as well as wider networks of publication and redistribution, I have argued that the question of the classic generates value criteria that enable the literary-critical field to subvert global relations of force with a different kind of international conversation. The event of the classic, neither fully situated in history nor entirely transcendental, marks what Dimock calls the "nonstandard space and time," a unique and irregular geography and chronology of what can be the disaggregated but shared life of literature (*Other Continents*, 4). International literary criticism should not ideally have any traffic with reconstructed territorial borders. Yet, the two lectures by Eliot and Coetzee testify to the unstable relationship between the classic as preeminently European-national and the classic as the locus of the transnational. As Antoine Compagnon points out—and his observations are based on the qualitative differences between Sainte-Beuve's 1850 essay and its reprisal in his opening lecture at the École normale supérieure in 1858—Sainte-Beuve himself is "divided between an open, global and generous vision of universal literature, and a national view, and it takes him two steps to come down, or back, from the universe to the West, and from the West to his own village" ("Sainte-Beuve and the Canon," 1195).[12] The traditional discourse on the classic follows the logic traced by Derrida in his essay "Onto-Theology of National-Humanism," the experience of the European modern claiming to be universal against the backdrop of imperialism and the rise of nationalisms. To borrow from Derrida's description of Fichte's *Discourse to the German Nation*, the discourse of the classic in the Sainte-Beuve or Eliot mode tends to essentialize nationalism "to the point of making it an entity bearing the universal and the philosophical as such" ("Onto-Theology," 11). A nation's fantasy of self-identification always assumes philosophical form, Derrida observes: "This philosophy, as structure of nationality . . . can show up as spontaneous philosophy, an implicit philosophy but one that is very constitutive of a non-empirical relationship with the world and a sort of potentially universal discourse 'embodied', 'represented', 'localised' (all problematic words) by a particular nation" (10). Derrida has spoken elsewhere about the way Europe claims to stand for the universal.[13] Coetzee, in pointing out Eliot's Americanness and his co-opting of a "convenient nationality," is challenging this hegemonic logic, and to some degree making it harder for his readers to conflate his status to that of the "traditional" apologist of the classic. Yet Eliot's lecture on the classic shows that the national (or national-as-universal) protocols of the classic are by no means stable, thriving as they do on iterability and cultural performance. The desultory binary evoked in Eliot's and Coetzee's essays—the global and the local or national—might even turn out to be a productive one in the way twenty-first century literary criticism interprets acts of literature. The classics of South Asian English, to cite an example, work neither in a universalist way nor as reified particularity, as the enduring appeal of Salman Rushdie's *Midnight's Children* has recently shown.[14] Postcolonial literature in English has undergone cultural globalization in its inexorable move toward Western markets and readerships, but it is also a heterotopic site, a mash-up of continuities, discontinuities, repetitions, and displacement. The self-determination and future of that literature cannot any longer be meaningfully be related to a hyperreal cultural Europe that stands as "an entelechy of universal reason," (Chakrabarty, "Postcoloniality," 3), as Casanova ends up doing by way of delineating global literary space. Hierarchy, inequality, and the uneven distribution of goods and values have not only determined the staggered ascendancy of postcolonial global literature, they seem to retain a tenacious grasp over its strategies of reversal and reinvention. In the widely acclaimed *The World Republic of Letters*, Casanova groups the specificities of emergent literatures under headings such as "Small Literatures," "The Assimilated," "The Rebels," "The Tragedy of Translated Men," or "The Revolutionaries." V. S. Naipaul's complex extrapolations of English ethnicity and his melancholic Englishness are grossly misinterpreted in Casanova's literal-minded reading: "V. S. Naipaul, born on the outer edges of the British Empire, is an outstanding example of a writer who wholly embraced the dominant literary values of his linguistic region; who, in the absence of any literary tradition in his native country, had no other choice but to try to become English" (*World Republic*, 209). Naipaul is consequently relegated to the category of "Assimilation," "the lowest level of literary revolt, the obligatory itinerary of every apprentice writer from an impoverished region having no literary resources of its own" (207). Casanova falls back on the certitudes of the center-periphery model of literary critical history, failing new epistemologies of comparison and connection: "To speak of the centre's literary forms and genres simply as a colonial inheritance imposed on writers within subordinated regions is to overlook the fact that literature itself, as a common value of the entire space, is also an instrument, which, if re-appropriated, can enable writers—and especially those with the fewest resources—to attain a type of freedom, recognition and existence within it" (Casanova, "Literature," 9). The literary world system, in this appraisal, is the final asylum for nonwinning and nonhegemonic writers if they are to win freedom, recognition, and consecration. Literature from "subordinated regions"—nations with diverse populations and polyglot cultures, multilingual literary traditions, and the tangled cultural legacies of different forms of domination—are doomed therefore to be negatively determined as literature written against a putative Western center in the disaffected registers of assimilation, translation, rebellion, and revolution. The metropolitan literary establishment, Casanova seems to suggest, is the singular object cause of any activity in peripheral literary cultures, as also the final address in their eager movement from nationality to universality. And that establishment seems to have banished critics from the republic, and is consequently not self-reflexive or self-divided in any way, just as national literatures seem devoid of literary-critical agon. As Joe Cleary observes in his review of Casanova's book, "*The World Republic of Letters* attaches no importance to the discipline as a serious arbitrating variable in its own right." While Casanova mentions individual critics, her world system is powered by writers and publishing (and award) industries and one of the book's key oversights is that of "the relative strengths or the different dispositions of nationalized literary critical establishments or university systems" (Cleary, "World Literary System," 213).

International criticism is not simply locatable in areas of underdevelopment or uneven development surrounding what Casanova identifies as "central precincts." As Eagleton points out, English literature in the twentieth century has been largely written by Americans, the Irish, Poles, and Indians (*Exiles and Émigrés*, 9), and a similar case for foreignness could be made for literary criticism and theory emanating from the Western academy. The postcolonial and global world has witnessed the return of what Spivak calls "demographic, rather than territorial, frontiers that predate and are larger than capitalism," and "parastate collectivities," which make unsustainable national anchoring and the traditional differentiations and bindings of political space (*Death*, 14). I urge a way of thinking about the relation of Eliot and Coetzee, two very different "outsider" writers, to mainstream British literature—not how we think of them (American and South African, or metropolitan cultural arbiter and postcolonial critic), but how *they* position and imagine themselves, which is often as out of place, emergent, or coming after and as needing to rewrite perduring pasts, real and invented. In the end, the question and concept of the classic is perhaps always that of the outsider.

2

What Is a Novel?
Conrad, Said, Naipaul

"I've no more judgment of what is fitting in the way of literature than a cow," Conrad wrote in a letter to Edward Garnett on August 24, 1897 (*Collected Letters*, Vol. 1, 375). Conrad's direct or indirect expositions on the form and function of the novel have, however, proved highly influential in anticipating the futures of the colonial novel.[1] This chapter examines two significant postcolonial extrapolations of the Conradian narrative and theories of the novel: V. S. Naipaul's rewriting of the heart-of-darkness tradition and the intergenre novel, especially its sense of "unrest," pervasive uncertainties about a dying world order as well as an emergent modernity; and Edward Said's affiliation, as writer and critic, to the interpretative strategies discursively posited by Conrad's fiction, autobiographical writing, and metacritiques. Both reprisals of Conrad's work reinforce the enmeshing of politics and aesthetics in the question of the novel. They demonstrate a preternatural attentiveness to the empirical and psychic conditions that precipitate narrative, but are equally influenced by the conviction that art is autonomous and "the essential story itself seems opposite to the conditions of its telling" (Said, *World*, 92). These rewritings of influence are valuable also in the way they position as literary predecessor and pioneer a writer whose pervasive sense of foreignness and secondariness in relation to the English establishment makes him an unlikely candidate for whisking latecomers to the canon, his grand induction as canonical English writer in F. R. Leavis's 1948 *The Great Tradition* notwithstanding.

In *Conrad and Imperialism*, Benita Parry presents the ideological contradictions that make Conrad the artist of "the divided mind" (3), and although it has been convincingly argued by Said that one of the "two visions" of empire—the Western and imperialist one—usually prevails, unresolved moments of ambivalence are key to the appeal of Conrad for a certain generation of postcolonial writers, caught between worlds.[2] "Conrad in his 'colonial fictions' did not presume to speak for the colonial peoples nor did he address them," goes the first line of Parry's well-known argument (1). Nevertheless, Conrad transformed the genres of colonial fiction by making them reflexive and vigilant of their own precepts and underlying assumptions. According to Parry: "These innovations from within the forms of the given mode produce a contrapuntal discourse where the authentic rendering of imperialism's dominant ideological categories is undercut by illuminations of the misrecognitions and limitations in a form of cognition which saw the world in black and white and admitted only a restricted area of reality to its purview" (2). Yet—and Parry's argument is punctuated with conjunctions that emphasize the unexpected nature of the qualifying information, and that give her utterances a curiously unfinished quality—Conrad's fictions do eventually "invite the closing of ethnic ranks, and confirm western codes as human norms and the ultimate measure of moral standards" (2). According to Parry, Conrad's double vision makes it inevitable that his fictions, despite their dispassionate mediations of the "misrecognitions and limitations" of the western imagination, will have "affinities with writing he despised" (2). While he breaks with the colonial tradition of representing the other hemisphere as either "a metaphysical landscape" or a primitive one, and questions in multifarious ways the moral justification of European domination, the contestations in the novels, material or spiritual, "invariably issue as victories for the West" (3). The fictions are "radically subversive" in the way they expose the "heterodox values within western traditions" (empiricism counterposed to skepticism, "the fascination of material advantage" to "the restraint of abstract ideas") and bring these into dialogue with what Parry calls "foreign alternatives" (4). However, when there is an impasse between Western traditions and alternative structures of experience, the fictions "effectively intercede to decide the contest between two cultures as if they represented two unequal moral universes" (4).

On Conrad's attitudes to imperialism, Parry's critical appraisal is not alone in giving with one hand what it takes away with the other.[3] Conrad's scrutiny of empire is especially valuable in the way it reveals the disjunctions "between high-sounding rhetoric and sordid ambitions." "But," Parry adds in her characteristic style, "to read these works as univocal denunciations of imperialist mores, motives and dreams is to overlook those textual processes which not only leave imperialist assumptions intact but originate perceptions of a latent idealism indwelling in what was manifestly a soulless project" (10–11). If the very terms of imperialism's operation are questioned by the texts, Parry is claiming here that they also manage to imbue it with greater intelligibility and a redeeming moral ambivalence: "With the intercession of this discourse, the texts themselves become accomplices in the life-lie necessary to the existence of a world that can neither be defended nor disavowed" (11). Such texts are unmistakable accomplices in the life-lie of an imperialist culture; they articulate a veritable colonial theology—and they are texts that, nevertheless, are generative of what Parry calls "estranging devices" (21), which galvanize speculation and argument on the material practices and cultural frameworks that sustained imperialism. Conrad revises the realist novel's febrile responsiveness to its historical process by presenting a discourse that has equivocation, misrecognition, irony, and despair staggering its seeming collusiveness with the changing ideologies of imperialism and an emergent globalization. Conrad's ambiguous style serves well to convey his contradictory values and authorial tendency "to judge without judging" (Brantlinger, *Rule of Darkness*, 273); "Impressionism is the fragile skein of discourse which expresses—or disguises—this schizophrenic contradiction as an apparently harmonious whole," as Brantlinger puts it (257). Similarly, at the level of characterization, Conrad simultaneously "presumes and undermines" an identity between person and place, relying on "the fixities of nineteenth-century nationalism to define his characters even as he charts a world in which they are all out of joint" (Gorra, *After Empire*, 555). Conrad's is a unique kind of historical fiction in which characters like Marlow and Almayer do not live where they belong or belong where they live: it exemplifies, through its out-of-place characters, the "capacity of the intuitive self to breach the historical ego," to quote from the Guyanese writer Wilson Harris's tribute to his predecessor ("Tradition," 86).

In a spirited defense of *Heart of Darkness* against the charge of racism brought to it by Chinua Achebe, Harris sees the novel as irreducible to the historical context out of which it emerges: "The capacity of the intuitive self to breach the historical ego is the life-giving and terrifying objectivity of imaginative art that makes a painting or a poem or a piece of sculpture or a fiction endure long beyond the artist's short lifetime and gives it the strangest beauty or coherence in depth" ("Tradition," 86). The echoes of Conrad's ideas on literature and history, or the continued relevance of true art beyond its immediate sphere of influence, are unmistakable here. "Art is long and life is short," Conrad says in Hippocratic cadences in the preface to *The Nigger of the "Narcissus"* (1). Art, however, is ineffable, "inspiring," "difficult," and "obscured by mists" (1), what Harris describes as possessing "the strangest beauty." The aim of art, "difficult and evanescent," is the momentary instantiation of "the truth of life": "a moment of vision, a sigh, a smile—and the return to an eternal rest" (*Nigger of the "Narcissus,"* 3). Art, Conrad muses, speaks "to the sense of mystery surrounding our lives," and as such it evinces a "subtle but invincible conviction of solidarity that knits together the loneliness of innumerable hearts" (xlviii).[4] It binds together "the dead to the living and the living to the unborn" (xlviii). Art is long, despite the fleeting durations of the effect of art and the reader's enrapt attention, because its immanence is fully realized in the relays of meaning between the dead, the living, and the unborn. Harris reinforces this tentatively articulated notion of solidarity, calling *Heart of Darkness* a "frontier novel," one that can and will culminate in the future: "By that I mean that it stands upon a threshold of capacity to which Conrad pointed though he never attained that capacity himself" ("Tradition," 87).

Harris's own *Palace of the Peacock* (1960), set in the Guyana interior, and charting a surreal journey up river by Donne, a white Creole rancher, and his motley, multiracial crew in search of the Amerindian settlement or mission, has often been compared to *Heart of Darkness*, as has *The Secret Ladder*, which reprises the themes of the *Palace of the Peacock*, and is the last novel of the "Guiana Quartet." The journey in *Palace* does not lead to the unspeakable abominations of the colonizer's mind, but is "a psychological and alchemical quest" for self-integration, as Michael Gilkes observes, and of the integration of the multiracial Guyanese society (*Wilson Harris*, 39). Not conquest, but a dream of reclaiming the interior, sending down roots, and developing the rich hinterland and its cultural heritage. The seven-day journey brings death and devastation, as in the Conrad novella, and the deepening cycles of exploration are beset with epistemic uncertainty and terror, but also the possibility of multiple interpretive options: "Everything turning different, changing into everything else Ah tell you" (Harris, *Palace*, 111). In the end, the bafflement of the worldly quest hardly matters: "Each of us now held at last in his arms what he had been for ever seeking and what he had eternally possessed" (152).

In his well-known essay "Henry James: An Appreciation," Conrad vests dramatic energy and urgency in the praxis of the novel, "carried out in the darkness against cross gusts of wind swaying the action of a great multitude. . . . It is rescue-work, this snatching of vanishing phases of turbulence, disguised in fair words, out of the native obscurity into a light where the struggling forms may be seen, seized upon, endowed with the only possible form of permanence in this world of relative values—the permanence of memory" ("Henry James," 103). Life does not narrate, so art (re)writes history. The task of the novel is to capture "vanishing phases of turbulence," and articulate them from the "native obscurity" of undifferentiated sensation in the service of literary language and cultural memory. This notion of art as conferring coherent and enduring value to random life recurs with added poignancy in the Conradian traces of Naipaul's fiction, especially where it speaks of a colonial pre-text that has ruined "raw" experience, jeopardizing the rescue work of aesthetic recall. Ralph Singh, the protagonist of Naipaul's *Mimic Men*, discovers the always already edited nature of his memory as he attempts to write the history of Isabella. "My first memory of school is of taking an apple to the teacher. This puzzles me. We had no apples on Isabella. It must have been an orange; yet my memory insists on an apple. The edition is clearly at fault, but the edited version is all I have" (109–10). Like the quality of his memory, Ralph Singh's world is "mixed and secondhand," as Naipaul said of his own society (*Literary Occasions*, 168), and symptomatic of colonial schizophrenia, shame, and fantasy. "There in Liège . . . was the true, pure world. We, here in our island, handling books printed in this world, and using its goods, had been abandoned and forgotten" (*Mimic Men*, 175). *The Mimic Men*, however, "is not about mimics," Naipaul states in his Nobel lecture: the condition of colonial mimicry, dire though it is, does not debilitate narrative. Despite the enervated narrator and the deep-seated malaise of the societies that he attempts to speak for, the novel *tells*, carries on the rescue work, and consigns to literary memory "how the powerless lie about themselves, and lie to themselves, since it is their only resource" (*Literary Occasions*, 193).

Conrad's appeal to the postcolonial writer is also inseparable from the question of language. In the "Author's Note" to *A Personal Record*, Conrad says emphatically that "if I had not known English I would not have written at all" (*Mirror of the Sea and Personal Record*, vi).[5] His use of English is neither a matter of deliberate choice nor one of "adoption," Conrad protests. He qualifies the disclaimer by saying that there may have been adoption, only *he* did not adopt but was adopted. "And as to adoption—well, yes, there was adoption; but it was I who was adopted by the genius of the language, which directly I came out of the stammering stage made me its own so completely that its very idioms I truly believe had a direct action on my temperament and fashioned my still plastic character" (v). This is uncannily similar to the idea of election proposed by Coetzee and Eliot in relation to the classic, as elaborated in the first chapter of this study. "His first identification was not with Britain or the British, but with the language, on learning which he discovered that his 'faculty to write in English' . . . was natural to him," observes Geoffrey Galt Harpham (*One of Us*, 155). When Conrad learned English in his twenties, he had already abandoned Polish for French, so it was not simply a substitute for the mother tongue. Neither did he try to convey a Polish intellectual and emotional character through English. The turn from filiation to affiliation, which Said associates with modernism, or the privileging of imagined and recombinant identifications over cultural and national identity, is particularly applicable to the complexity of Conrad's modes of belonging. His English was not a translation from Polish, just as the English use of multilingual postcolonial writers like Said or Naipaul does not accord privileged status to a Palestinian or Caribbean-Indian consciousness. Conrad used English as the most expedient medium for conveying the denaturalization and excursiveness of his own international identity: "To express himself in English was all at once to become a man, a seaman, a Brit, and a cosmopolitan citizen of the world" (Harpham, *One of Us*, 158). Clearly, then, what Conrad presents as the choiceless choice of writing in English is at least partly related to the status of English as a lingua franca and an emergent world language. "Conrad felt himself to be adopted by a language that had long specialized in adoption," comments Harpham wryly (157). The "adoption," however, was by no means an easy cultural assimilation into the Anglo-Saxon or European canon, and Conrad's works are often best read in a globalist, not nationalist or even transnationalist framework.

A novel like *Nostromo* bears little resemblance to novels written in French, English, or Russian, as Said points out in *Beginnings*. In fact, it is "most profitable to compare the novel with novels written in the more insecure, individualistic, and nervous American tradition" (110).

Conrad, the outsider writer negotiating conflicting modes of existence, is not merely a symbol of the discontents or unclassifiable remainders of literary modernism. He draws attention to the fact that twentieth-century literary production in Britain is inconceivable without the socially marginalized or the foreigner, "the exile and the alien" (Eagleton, *Exiles and Émigrés*, 10), and also that without the heterogeneity or broader frameworks that the exile and the émigré brings into play, "the erosion of contemporary order" cannot be situated or understood (15). While he joins the ranks of Joyce, Lawrence, Pound, and Eliot (and the later generation of Hemingway, Beckett, and Auden), who evoke the Lukácsian transcendental homelessness constitutive of Anglo-American modernism, Conrad's is also a special case, Ian Watt argues: "For one thing, Conrad did not choose his exile—the fate of his family and his country forced it on him; and for another, Conrad's exile was much more absolute—with very minor exceptions he did not write about his own country, and he wrote nothing for publication in his native tongue" (*Conrad*, 32). Conrad's appeal to transitive intellectuals like Said and Naipaul surely lies in this unresolved tension between itinerancy and belonging, between the three lives of Conrad (in Ukraine, on the sea, and as naturalized British citizen) and their reflections, distortions, and elisions in art. The fragmentary vision of the novels, with discontinuities that generate "a bewildering variety of competing and incommensurable interpretive options" (Jameson, *Political Unconscious*, 208), foreshadow the works of Said and Conrad in being unmistakably autobiographical. To quote a relevant observation made by Timothy Brennan on Edward Said, the writing "relies on the creation of a persona . . . a peculiar combination of invention and circumstance" ("Edward Said and Comparative Literature," 24).

This chapter looks closely at questions of the relationship of the novel to the displacement and dissonance of life that, according to Lukács, gives it its definitive form. Conrad ushers, for Said and Naipaul, the Foucauldian "epoch of space," a contestatory resituating of history on spatial, rather than temporal axes, and as simultaneity.[6] My analysis of Said's and Naipaul's investment in the Conradian narrative engages with their well-known dealings with Conrad's metropolitan imperialism to focus additionally on another area of connection and juxtaposition: "a vision of literature and a lesson of history," to quote Bhabha's well-known formulation (*Location of Culture*, 148), as transmitted through the prolepsis and the radical aesthetics of the (Conrad) novels. Finally, it examines the formative influence on postcolonial writers of Conrad's representation of the exile's loss of home and language in the new metropolitan setting as "irredeemable, relentlessly anguished, raw, untreatable, always acute" (Said, *Reflections on Exile*, 555).

Conrad and Narrative

> Deep within the tarnished ormolu frame, in the hot half-light sifted through the awning, I saw my own face propped between my hands. And I stared back at myself with the perfect detachment of distance, rather with curiosity than with any other feeling, except of some sympathy for this latest representative of what for all intents and purposes was a dynasty; continuous not in blood, but in its experience, in its training, in its conception of duty, and in the blessed simplicity of its traditional point of view on life.
>
> It struck me that this quietly staring man whom I was watching, both as if he were myself and somebody else, was not exactly a lonely figure. He had his place in a line of men whom he did not know, of whom he had never heard; but who were fashioned by the same influences, whose souls in relation to their humble life's work had no secrets for him.
>
> CONRAD, *The Shadow-line*

The long quotation from Conrad's *The Shadow-line* describes a remarkable scene of identification-in-alienation, or reviewing oneself as other, albeit an interpretable other. The nameless narrator of the tale has been appointed commander of the ship and is entering his cabin for the first time. Here, the intimate enclosure of the room becomes a symbol of the tradition he is accidentally elected to, a dynasty "continuous not in blood, but in its experience."[7] This is a rare instance of self-affirmation in a novel exploring the problem of human isolation, made all the more fleeting by the irony of the professed "sympathy." The sense of entitlement the foreign interloper feels in relation to "a line of men whom he did not know . . . but who were fashioned by the same influences" becomes the basis of his possession of space. The narrator speaks, with the collective agency of what Homi Bhabha calls the "pronominal and postnominalist" "I," just as the narrator of *The Nigger of the "Narcissus"* speaks as an "I" at times and as "we" at others. "I" is an arbitrary signifier which, however, through the performance of repetition of the "symbolic agency of history," becomes the "sign of the interstitial difference through which the identity of meaning is made" (*Location of Culture*, 233–34).[8] I would like to juxtapose this scene with one from Conrad's *A Personal Record*, where a similar dialectic of avowal and disavowal marks Conrad's description of his unlikely turn to fiction. Imagining a domestic episode where he is seen to be making a scene about the housekeeper (the landlady's "anaemic daughter," in this case) misplacing his pen, he writes: "If anybody had told me . . . that a devoted household, having a generally exaggerated idea of my talents and importance, would be put into a state of tremor and flurry by the fuss I would make because of a suspicion that somebody had touched my sacrosanct pen of authorship, I would have never deigned as much as the contemptuous smile of unbelief" (*Mirror of the Sea and Personal Record*, 91). Earlier in the book Conrad aligns himself with the "most unliterary of writers, in the sense that literary ambition had never entered the world of his imagination" (90), but his self-criticism, he qualifies, is not a smoke screen for the megalomaniac's self-regard. As in the mirror scene in *Shadow-line*, *A Personal Record* valorizes the "detached, impersonal glance" upon oneself that unsparingly records the fallible, changeable self at a temporal and cultural distance (92). As in life, so in art. "Never the wholly incorporated and fully acculturated Englishman, Conrad therefore preserved an ironic distance in each of his works," Said says of the historical Conrad (*Culture and Imperialism*, 25). And as with the episode in *Personal Record*, the uncertainty and hesitation of this moment eventually gives away to a quiet justification of the "prose artist of fiction," albeit one who shares with other artists

> the conception of a purely spectacular universe. . . . Even the writer of prose, who in his less noble and more toilsome task should be a man with the steeled heart, is worthy of a place, providing he looks on with undimmed eyes and keeps laughter out of his voice, let who will laugh or cry . . . even he has his place amongst kings, demagogues, priests, charlatans, dukes, giraffes, Cabinet Ministers, Fabians, bricklayers, apostles, ants, scientists, Kaffirs, soldiers, sailors, elephants, lawyers, dandies, microbes and constellations of a universe whose amazing spectacle is a moral end in itself. (*Mirror of the Sea and Personal Record*, 93)

Not deserving entry into the captain's cabin or the House of Art, as the interloper knows too well, "there is no retainer so devoted as he who is allowed to sit on the doorstep" (*Mirror of the Sea and Personal Record*, 94).

These textual instances in *Shadow-line* and *Personal Record* shed light on crucial aspects of Conrad's relation to narrative: the concept of a mysterious vocation; niggling self-doubt and scrutiny ameliorated by a devotion to the efficacy of shared genealogies and codes, whether in the tradition of seafaring or that of art; the suspension of personality ("undimmed eyes" and "laughter out of his voice"), which in turn helps maintain optimal distance from the object of inquiry, "not so near as to be strangled but not so far away that discourse becomes garrulous and untroubled," as Harpham puts it (*One of Us*, 100).⁹ They also provide vital links between Conrad and two postcolonial writers, both given to presenting themselves as coming after Conrad, and, as Naipaul states, from the "mixed and secondhand world[s]" into which they were born. In both textual instances, recognition—face-to-face with the specular double in the propitious setting of a new office or with the belated discovery of one's true vocation—is haunted by lives left behind and darkened by survivor's guilt. The "Familiar Preface" to *A Personal Record* ends defensively, stating that even if the author has put down his memories "without any regard for established conventions," they are not entirely without system or purpose:

They have their hope and their aim. The hope that from the reading of these pages there may emerge at last the vision of a personality; the man behind the books so fundamentally dissimilar as, for instance, "Almayer's Folly" and "The Secret Agent," and yet a coherent, justifiable personality both in its origin and in its action.... The immediate aim, closely associated with the hope, is to give the record of personal memories by presenting faithfully the feelings and sensations connected with the writing of my first book and with my first contact with the sea. (xxi)

The hope that there may emerge at last, with the author's hard-fought right to utterance, "the vision of a personality," is clouded with doubt, and "good reasons for not writing at all" (xx). "And yet in truth I was by no means anxious to justify my existence," insists the narrator later in the *Personal Record* (94).

The other aspect of Conrad's presentation of narrative that has far-reaching implications for the critical practice of Said and Naipaul—and a host of writers discussed in this book—is a belief in the interimplication of biography and autobiography, literature, literary criticism, and craft (not least the work of prose). Conrad approvingly quotes the French novelist and essayist Anatole France as saying, "The good critic is he who relates the adventures of his soul amongst masterpieces" (*Mirror of the Sea and Personal Record*, 96). Without the animation of personal experience—the glimpses of "strange beasts" the "hair's-breadth escapes," the "sufferings"—criticism risks looking like "a mere feat of agility on the part of a trained pen running in a desert" (97). "To snatch in a moment of courage, from the remorseless rush of time, a passing phase of life is only the beginning of the task," Conrad writes in Paterian (and Schopenhauerian) cadences in the preface to *The Nigger of the "Narcissus,"* read often as his *ars poetica*. "The task approached in tenderness and faith is to hold up unquestioningly, without choice and without fear, the rescued fragment before all eyes and in the light of a sincere mood" (xlix). Without choice and without fear—the reference is again to the obscure urge to write, the impossible and necessary task of giving narrative form to the formless and "remorseless rush of time," and to *create*, without fear, the meaning of passing events. It is impossible to definitively assess whether this urge to represent the ineffable serves as a manifesto for literature or criticism. Conrad's writing involved sensation and interpretation, "acts of both remembering and analysis," as Collits observes (*Postcolonial Conrad*, 65). As the oft-cited passage from *Heart of Darkness* goes, the meaning of an episode lies "not inside like a kernel but outside, enveloping the tale which brought it out only as a glow brings out a haze" (*Heart of Darkness*, 20). The inside of the tale is not an essence; the relationship of the outside and inside is not reducible to that of surface and corresponding depth. Meaning cloys to the tale as a haze, waiting for the search light of the critic to unravel its dark life. Referring to the "Author's Note" in *The Heart of Darkness*, Collits enjoins the readers of Conrad to make a categorical distinction between "sincere colouring" and "another art altogether," that of interpretation and analysis, and the antimimetic impetus that gives the novel's theme "a sinister resonance, a tonality of its own, a continued vibration" (*Postcolonial Conrad*, 65). Ian Watt has famously called this critical method "delayed decoding," the interpretive gap between impression and understanding whereby an outcome is depicted before the cause of that outcome is satisfactorily presented. As he further explains: "It served mainly to put the reader in the position of being an immediate witness to each step in the process whereby the semantic gap between the sensation aroused in the individual by an object or event, and their actual cause or meaning, was slowly closed in his consciousness" (*Conrad*, 270). Michael Gorra supports Watt's influential formulation with his own observation that every one of the major novels "began as a story, a story forced into length by Conrad's need to explain, to circle back through time, excavating motive and pursuing its consequences" ("Joseph Conrad," 548). It is perhaps the embeddedness of the works—and their writer—in a colonial context of market capitalism that made it imperative for Conrad to pose the problems of novelistic form against questions of world history. "By choosing colonial settings for his work, he made it impossible to maintain a comfortable distance between aesthetics and politics," Collits remarks (*Postcolonial Conrad*, 40).

In *Joseph Conrad and the Fiction of Autobiography*, billed as "a phenomenological exploration of Conrad's consciousness" (7), Said compares Conrad's assumption of a literary self-disguise with that of Henry James. Quoting Leon Edel on James, Said says that Conrad too found it necessary to lead an "open ritualistic life that masked the private life" (60). In *The Mirror of the Sea*, the first autobiographical work he wrote, Conrad seems to find it easier to reflect himself in the sea, using it as a mirror to throw a mess of self-images to the public. His *Personal Record* too expressed the secret of his life as a parallel between the writing and his sea experience, and Conrad urged his correspondents to look in that correspondence for the "heart and essence" of his life. However, Conrad was not a person for an "orderly" biography, "auto or otherwise," he said, and life could never be rendered as "a sort of Cook's Personally Conducted Tour—from the cradle to the grave," as he wrote to Edward Garnett (*Joseph Conrad*, 63). Writing and life were, for him, "like journeys without maps, struggles to win over and then claim unknown ground," Said states (63).

Said looks at Conrad's letters for themes and patterns, "certain dynamic movements or structures of experience (mechanisms)," that correspond to structures in fiction (*Joseph Conrad*, 12). *Joseph Conrad and the Fiction of Autobiography* records the difficulty of reconciling both—writing and life—and as such it validates the crucial function of the critic-as-phenomenologist (Said). First of all, as Conrad acknowledged in a letter to Graham, "life is long—and art is so short" (*Joseph Conrad*, 47), its economy eclipsed by the atomistic singularity of life. The past, especially—its obscurity, difficulty, and loneliness—cannot be commuted to a present-tense narrative. Next there is the "fluid . . . evading shape" of the story (*Joseph Conrad*, 49), as Conrad writes in a letter to Garnett during work on "The Rescuer" and the persistence of style, order, and grammar. The work of art hurtles to an expedient end: life goes on. There was also the difficulty of a starting point. Other writers, he said (in a letter to Garnett on June 19, 1896), "know something to begin with"—anecdote, dialect, tradition, history, "some tie or some conviction of their time, or upon the absence of these things, which they can praise or blame" (54). His own sensations and impressions tended to weaken, Conrad said dramatically: "my very being seems faded and thin like the ghost of a blonde and sentimental woman, haunting romantic ruins pervaded by rats" (54). In the absence of a starting point, Conrad's work of writing, to quote his own words, was like "quarrying [my] English out of a black night, working like a coal miner in his pit" (55). Conrad's achievement, according to Said, is that he nevertheless ordered the chaotic onrush of his experiences into "a highly patterned art" that reflected and controlled the realities with which it deals with fidelity (*Joseph Conrad*, 196).

Conrad is "a *cantus firmus*, a steady groundbass to much that I have experience" (*Reflections on Exile*, 555). Besides being the subject of Said's doctoral dissertation and first book, Conrad is a formidable presence in *Culture and Imperialism*, where Said examines the relations between narrative and cultural groupings, and narrative and geography. This text is also source of the much-cited chapter in which Said talks about the "two visions" of the colonial novel (*Heart of Darkness*), one historically circumscribed and the other an open-ended critical inquiry into (to quote Said from an interview) "the mechanisms, and presuppositions and situatedness and abuses of imperialism" (Kaplan et al., eds., *Conrad*, 288). The widely used coinage "exilic marginality," which owes its origin to the essay in *Culture and Imperialism*, has served not only to describe Marlow, standing "at the very juncture of this world with another, unspecified but different" (24), but also Conrad and Said himself. In Said's meditation on Freud and the non-European, *The Heart of Darkness* features prominently in an impassioned defense of the historical and ideological determination of an otherwise extraordinary writer:

Rather than leaving Conrad's compelling portrait of Leopold's Congo in an archive labelled as the dead-end rubbish bin of racist thinking, it seems to me far more interesting to read Conrad's late-nineteenth-century work as—in all sorts of unforeseen proleptic ways—suggesting and provoking not only the tragic distortions in the Congo's subsequent history but also the echoing answers in African writing that reuse Conrad's journey motif as a topos to present the discoveries and recognitions of postcolonial dynamics, a great part of them the deliberate antitheses of Conrad's work. (*Freud*, 24)

Clearly, Said is referring to Chinua Achebe's denunciation of Conrad as "a bloody racist," and urging instead a more discriminating and subtle reading of *Heart of Darkness*. According to Said, Conrad's novella not only shows an uncanny prescience of "Congo's subsequent history," but also anticipates and makes possible the "echoing answers in African writing," Achebe's included, that are, ironically, posed as "deliberate antitheses" of Conrad's work. Achebe himself, judgmental though he is of Conrad's ideology, "relents to the ambivalence of the novel as an aesthetic form, rewriting Conrad in some of his novels painstakingly and with originality" (*Culture and Imperialism*, 76). It is true that Tayib Salih's *Season of Migration to the North* and V. S. Naipaul's *A Bend in the River* would be unimaginable without the ideological insinuations of Conrad's novel. Echoing Eliot's formulation of the symbiotic relationship between past tradition and new (individual) talent, Said states that Conrad's writing, in turn, is "actualized and animated by emphases and inflections that he was obviously unaware of, but that his writing permits" (*Freud*, 25).

Said returns to Conrad also in the way he conceptualizes, in his 1985 book, *Beginnings*, the idea of the novel as "beginning intention" (79). Incidentally, he cites the trope of journeying back to the beginnings of time in *Heart of Darkness* as the inspiration for the exploration of beginnings in the book of the same name. "I mean, one can't repeat Conrad," Said says in the interview with Peter Mallios, "but one can go back to the very idea of beginning in some way that had been unexcavated before" ("Interview with Edward W. Said," 296). In the 1983 book *The World, the Text, and the Critic*, the themes of writing and its negation, writing and the reconstitution of negation, so crucial to the formulation of his first book on Conrad, return with a vengeance. "Conrad tried to use prose negatively for the transcendence of writing and the embodiment of both direct utterance and vision" (109): it is an aesthetic whereby authorship is refracted in a variety of negative narrative and quasi-narrative contingencies, where affect struggles to achieve true expression in the way that inert substances like silver or ivory are transmuted into value, and where the delayed decoding of narration presents life as tragically diminished and defeated through representation.

Writing a comparative analysis of Conrad's novels and Nietzsche's philosophy, Said remarks that they differed in the way they shaped their modes of critical reception for what they perceived alike as the self-destroying nature of history. But, if Nietzsche cautioned against "aesthetic anthropomorphisms" and let the debilitating recurrence of the past blast an opening into the future, Conrad embraced the difficulty of aesthetic ordering and saw the recurrence of the past as primarily a hauntology of the present that needs to be worked through in writing.[10] Said speculates that the dissimilarity between Nietzsche's and Conrad's relationship to history could be attributed to the latter's "deepest commitment as a writer . . . to the narrative form, which of itself finds the recurrence of past and present normal and congenial" (*Reflections on Exile*, 81–82). In Said's other writings on Conrad's narrative, however, the Nietzschean echoes of Conrad's theory of language and the novel ring louder. "To have chosen to write . . . is to have chosen in a particular way neither to say directly nor to mean exactly in the way he had hoped to say or to mean," Said says of the acutely felt incommensurability of words and meaning in Conrad's art of fiction (*The World, the Text*, 90). Conrad saw the sinewy strength of narrative as capable of sustaining the antitheses of "the motivated, the occasional, the methodical and the rational," on the one hand, and "the aleatory, the unpredictable, the inexplicable," on the other (92). The narrative, consequently, becomes an "alternation in language of presence and absence" (95), in the way the writer's express intention is exceeded by the phenomenal world that the reader is privy to see, or in the way the reflective narrator negotiates the contesting claims of contradictory versions of the same story. This essay, "Conrad: The Presentation of Narrative," first published in *Novel* in 1974, has proved extremely influential in shaping the history of postcolonial reception of Conrad. I would like to claim further that it has, through its phenomenological framing of Conrad's intellectual formation and narrative experiments, shaped Said's subsequent critical approaches to the aesthetic histories of (post)colonial cultural production, including his own. Conrad makes "highly imaginative distinctions within English," Said observes, giving the example of the numerous "languages" within *Heart of Darkness* (*The World, the Text*, 99). By repossessing and reconstituting received language into voices, the outsider writer stages his originality. Again, there is in Conrad the curious sense of being chosen by his vocation that has come to define the irrational ambivalence of desire for and disavowal of metropolitan arrival in non-English writers of English.

It was I who was adopted by the genius of the language, which directly I came out of the stammering stage made me its own so completely that its very idioms I truly believe had a direct action on my temperament and fashioned my still plastic character. . . .

All I can claim after all those years of devoted practice, with the accumulated anguish of its doubts, imperfections and falterings in my heart, is the right to be believed when I say that if I had not written in English I would not have written at all. (*The World, the Text*, 98–99)

These lines from the 1919 preface to *A Personal Record*, cited in *The World, the Text, and the Critic*, do not signify for Said a cultural outsider's shrewd glossing of hard-won social gains as accidentally acquired. In "Conrad: The Presentation of Narrative," Said conveys instead a moving account of the novelist grappling with the difficulty of writing in English, his years of "devoted practice," combative attempts at perfecting perception, pitch, idiom, and dissemination, and his extraordinary care in delivering his narratives. "Conrad's writing was a way of repeatedly confirming his authorship by refracting it in a variety of often contradictory and negative narrative and quasi-narrative contingencies," Said concludes (*The World, the Text*, 109). Years later, writing about the negative determinations of and avoidance of direct representations in his own authorial life, Said says, "better to wander out of place, not to own a house, and not ever to feel too much at home anywhere" (*Out of Place*, 294).

Conrad also surfaces in the discussion of lost causes in *Reflections on Exile*. At the level of style and theme, Conrad gives Said the notion of "elaboration." Fantasy is elaborated and worked over and translated to practical, worldly realities, resulting in the echoic, reverberative quality of richly intertextual writing. Subjectivity, even subjectivity in the diegetic universe, is inseparable from its elaboration in historical context. As Said explains later in an interview, "What's really interesting about the world we live in—and this is obviously what the great artist develops obsessively—is the fact that there is a kind of labor in all human activity which is similar to the labor you can see in a tapestry or a piece of music. This is a labor that is elaborated, worked over, what the French call *travaillé*" ("Interview with Edward W. Said," 294). Orientalism, Said writes, is a working over, an attempt to "inventory the traces upon me, an Oriental subject, of the culture whose domination has been so powerful a factor in the life of all Orientals" (*Orientalism*, 24). Said's term for this Gramscian task, which threatens to collapse the (Oriental) subject into its object of inquiry (Orientalism), this awakening from knowledge to self-knowledge, is "critical elaboration" (25).

Public and private history and self come together again in the elaboration of Said's own "fiction of autobiography," a genre that he describes plainly as the imposition of narrative on a disorganized, scattered, and decentered life, under the indictment of "an ugly medical diagnosis" (*Reflections on Exile*, 555) of cancer in the fall of 1991. It is now that he realizes with some finality that "Conrad had been there before me," although, he adds with sly humour, "Conrad was a European who left his native Poland and became an Englishman, so the move for him was more or less within the same world" (*Reflections on Exile*, 556). If in his critical appraisals of Conrad, Said had noted, and not without ambivalent identification, the preponderance of exilic auto-ethnography in Conrad, he now imbibes from his predecessor the former's desire, as expressed in *Nostromo*, to "write down once and for all a true account of what happened" (*Reflections on Exile*, 568). The writing of a memoir is made all the more urgent by the historical reversals through which the three locales of Said's pre-political life have been radically altered: Palestine is now Israel; Lebanon, after decades of of civil war, is no longer "the stiflingly boring place" he spent his summers in; and colonial, monarchical Egypt has been written out of existence since 1952. The imaginative constructions of autobiographical fiction—for both Conrad and Said—promise to create life for keeps because life itself is (and I quote George Levine here) "so determinedly attenuated, so mechanically inhuman, and because life refuses to be true" (*Realistic Imagination*, 290).

The Death of the Novel: Conrad and Naipaul

"The novelist, like the painter, no longer recognizes his interpretive function; he seeks to go beyond it; and his audience diminishes," Naipaul writes wistfully, drawing his essay on Conrad to a close (*Literary Occasions*, 180). And so the world, which is always turning new, goes by unperceived, caught by the camera for easy circulation and consumption, its difficult, atomistic meanings unmeditated upon—"there is no one to awaken the sense of true wonder" (180). The great societies that produced the great novels of the past have died: the novel as a form is no longer authentic, efficacious, and inspired. The art of fiction, Naipaul said in a 1973 interview, is a "curious, shattered thing," and the imaginative writer must turn to nonfiction—journalism—to articulate a deliberate and "fair response" to their world ("Novelist V. S. Naipaul Talks," 368, 367). I begin this section on Conrad and Naipaul with the discussion of a novel that seems heavily influenced by and fixated on Western forms of the realist novel, but which, nevertheless, enacts a death of the romance of the novel. At first glance, the literary act in question seems to perform what Geoffrey Hartman, in his review of Bloom's *Anxiety of Influence*, described as a *"danse macabre* or 'dramatic mimesis' which alienates person into persona, self into role, and every intended revolution into a degraded repetition of the past" (27). Can the literary psyche of the once-colonized, haunted by the preemptive nature of language, epistemology, and representation itself, negotiate the anxiety of influence without commemoration, repetition, or revisionism? Could the postcolonial novel ever claim "innocence of influence" (28)? I address these questions in my examination of Naipaul's translations of the English canon in his novels of marginalization, disenfranchisement, and also, equally, individuation.

In his 1905 essay on Henry James, mentioned above, Conrad writes of his own obdurate belief in man's triumph over entropy: "When the last aqueduct shall have crumbled to pieces, the last air-ship fallen to the ground, the last blade of grass shall have died upon a dying earth, man, indomitable by his training in his resistance to misery and pain, shall set this undiminished light of his eyes against the feeble glow of the sun" ("Henry James," 104). Men without a cause fighting lonely battles in the dark places of the earth; mimic men of the new world—Naipaul's great novels draw on these two Conradian commonplaces. Just as D. H. Lawrence once said of Conrad, Naipaul is one of the "Writers among the Ruins" (*Collected Letters*, 1: 152). In *The Mimic Men* (1967), Eden, a West Indian "Negro," is maddened by fantasies of absolute power, like Kurtz and Lord Jim: "Eden had fixed on Asia as the continent he wished to travel in; he had been stirred by *Lord Jim*. His deepest wish was for the Negro race to be abolished; his intermediate dream was of a remote land where he, the solitary Negro among an alien pretty people, ruled as a sort of sexual king. Lord Jim, Lord Eden" (162–63). In *An Area of Darkness* Naipaul says controversially that the novel genre is of the West, and Indian approximations of the genre are symptomatic of the postcolony's unscrupulous cultural syncretism; they are a form of Indian self-violation. His meditations on colonial mimicry in *The Mimic Men* and other novels ironically enact this tragic codependency. Ralph Singh's first stabs at writing in *The Mimic Men* evoke in painstaking detail Conrad's first attempts at writing (as recorded in *A Personal Record*), at thirty-two, in a London boarding house. Naipaul, indeed, "found that Conrad—sixty years before, in the time of a great peace—had been everywhere before [him]" (*Literary Occasions*, 170). Naipaul's *Bend in the River* draws its title from *Lord Jim* and shadows Conrad's symbolic journey through Africa in *The Heart of Darkness*. Salim cuts a last-of-the-race figure in Central Africa: "no family, no flag, no fetish" (*Bend*, 63). For Salim, the difficult Africa of bush and villages always overruns modern Africa—everyone around him seems immobilized in the face of certain death. The African bush has crept back on the ruins of a departed machine civilization, and black men have assumed the lies of white men. Similarly, Naipaul's *A Congo Diary*, like Conrad's *Congo Diary*, is a journey without maps and a phobic figuration of Africa. Zaire is a country where "history has vanished" (Naipaul, *Congo*, 9), its post-teleological existence made more trenchant and tragic when contrasted with the excursiveness of the Westernized journalist's movement upriver. Naipaul takes in the aftermath of empire with increasing unease and anger: "The Empire of things. Exporters of what civilization? The perishable" (*Congo*, 42). When his steamer passes through settlements and cultivated land, instead of the primeval jungle that Marlow's journey upstream promised, Naipaul seems petulant about the precursor text's felt breach of faith.

The starting point of any comparison of Naipaul and Conrad is usually Naipaul's essay, "Conrad's Darkness," first published in *The New York Review of Books* in 1974 and revised and reprinted as "Conrad's Darkness and Mine" in *Literary Occasions*. This remarkable essay ushers a new phase in Naipaul's own understanding of himself as a writer and marks his turn from the novel toward nonfiction. Naipaul shares with the Polish émigré the predicament of being raised in one world and willing himself into becoming an artist in another, England. "It came to me that the great novelists wrote about highly organized societies," he writes. "I had no such society; I couldn't share the assumptions of the writers; I didn't see my world reflected in theirs. My colonial world was more mixed and secondhand, and more restricted. The time came when I began to ponder the mystery—Conradian word—of my own background" (*Literary Occasions*, 168).[11] The essay maps journeys, psychic and other, in which Naipaul keeps coming up against Conrad's legacy: "I found that Conrad—sixty years before, in the time of a great peace—had been everywhere before me. Not as a man with a cause, but a man offering . . . a vision of the world's half-made societies as places which continuously made and unmade themselves, where there was no goal, and where always 'something inherent in the necessities of successful action . . . carried with it the moral degradation of the idea.' Dismal, but deeply felt: a kind of truth and half a consolation" (*Literary Occasions*, 170–71). In a conversation with Rachel Donadio after the publication of *Bend in the River*, however, Naipaul insists that Conrad had had "no influence on me": "Actually, I think *A Bend in the River* is much, much better than Conrad" ("Irascible Prophet"). The best part of Conrad's *Heart of Darkness*, Naipaul goes on to say, is the reportage part. "The fictional part is excessive and feeble. And there is no reportage in my thing. I was looking and creating that world. I actually think the work I've done in that way is better than Conrad" ("Irascible Prophet"). Naipaul also dismisses the idea there might be a direct link between his Conrad essay and subsequent works in which he expatiated on some of the same places and themes. "These things might appear like that. But that's only for a person on the outside," he says ("Irascible Prophet"). Unsurprisingly, "a different picture emerges from Naipaul's bibliography," writes Donadio ("Irascible Prophet"). After the Conrad essay, Naipaul had in fact followed Conrad's itinerary to the Congo—the subject of his nonfiction essay on Mobutu, "A New King for the Congo" (1975), and of *A Bend in the River* (1979); and to Aceh, Indonesia, for *Among the Believers* and *Beyond Belief*.

"Conrad's Darkness and Mine" details Naipaul's complex Oedipal filiation with Conrad as his colonial predecessor, as well as his identification with and alienation from the cultural work of the colonial novel. "To understand Conrad," Naipaul writes, "it was necessary to begin to match his experience" (*Literary Occasions*, 171). Following in step with Conrad's narrative strategies meant that it was necessary "to lose one's preconceptions of what the novel should do and, above all, to rid oneself of the subtle corruptions of the novel or comedy of manners" (171). Rob Nixon notes that Naipaul's automatic finding of a literary predecessor in Conrad presents the latter "as neither an invented nor a chosen starting point but a natural one" ("Preparations," 179). The perceived embeddedness of Conrad's writing in the colonial context in turn perpetuates the heart-of-darkness tradition in Naipaul's own work. The crimping of time between "sixty years before" and "now" underscores Conrad's and Naipaul's fatalist imaginings of the colonial periphery as always already trapped in the mythic past and devoid of creativity and enterprise: static and stultifying, it is "impervious to change, bereft of history" ("Preparations," 179). Conrad's art substantiates the Said commonplace that "without empire, there is no European novel as we know it" (*Culture and Imperialism*, 58–59) and Naipaul finds in Conrad a post-dated prescience about the world's "half-made societies" (*Literary Occasions*, 170). "Conrad's value to me is that he is someone who sixty to seventy years ago meditated on my world, a world I recognize today. . . . His achievement derives from the honesty which is part of his difficulty, that 'scrupulous fidelity to the truth of my own sensation'" (*Literary Occasions*, 173). Naipaul's *Enigma of Arrival* is reminiscent of Conrad's cautious historical contextualization of his novelist self in the *Personal Record*, and shows the writer imagining himself "not as extraneous to England but as a part of it, and of England in the narrowest and most provincial sense," as Gorra puts it (*After Empire*, 91). England in *Enigma* stands for Englishness, the canon and the Jamesian house of fiction, and if Naipaul stakes his claim on the great tradition, he also shows how little is at stake. For the landscape of *Enigma* is a veritable heart of darkness, a no man's land of remnants and relics of other efforts and lives: "Grass to hay to earth" (*Enigma*, 82). The world that the narrator had hoped to enter was in fact turning to dust and ruination: Jack dies, as do his father-in-law, Brenda, Mr. Phillips, Alan, Shiva (Naipaul), and Sati, the Naipaul sister. The ruined country house and the lives destroyed in its wake are linked to the ruination of British imperialism, although ruin so complete that it cannot be set right or remade is also perfection. The narrator's yearning for perfection takes the form of a pleasurable dalliance with death.

Naipaul's *Bend in the River* (1979) is another belated arrival, this time at a Conradian dark place. The novel rewrites and reworks Conrad's *Heart of Darkness* and *Congo Diary* as it commemorates Conrad's notorious fictional journey. Naipaul finds much that is mind-expanding in global travel, Conrad-style: "It showed me a changing world and took me out of my colonial shell; it became the substitute for the mature social experience—the deepening knowledge of a society—which my background and the nature of my life denied me" (*Finding the Centre*, x). However, as Rob Nixon correctly points out, Naipaul's historical predilection to Conrad's internationalism converges with a retrogressive literary affiliation: "the Western tradition of 'doing' Africa via *Heart of Darkness* . . . the net effect is the image of a continent still debilitated by a measure of figurative arrest" (*London Calling*, 91). It is hard to conclude whether the travelogue novel that is *A Bend in the River* charts a narrative of decolonization, a coming out of the "colonial shell" as it were, or reinforces stereotypes about backwardness and atavism in its racist representations of Africa.

As in Conrad's novel, Salim's Africa experience is a misadventure predicated on a series of misrecognitions. The protagonist Salim journeys from the East African coast to a town at the "bend in the river" of a central African country, but it is not destination-bound travel. "I . . . thought of myself as a man just passing through. But where was the good place?" he speculates early in the novel (*Bend*, 110). Salim keeps shop and rides a short-lived economic boom in the river town before a tide of history washes him away. Salim's imagined community in the heart of Africa is a predictable assortment of colonial miscreants: Indar, the mimic man who will modernize Africa; Father Huismans—the neocolonialist with the heart and covetousness of a museum curator's—whose beheading is treated nonchalantly, as if it were an acceptable professional hazard for missionaries; Raymond, the black man's white man; Yvette, his child-woman bride; and "Big Man," the hyperbolic presence that is the country's totalitarian president. Salim himself is negatively characterized: insecure, pessimistic, nervous, melancholy about the world. His people came long before the Europeans did, but the community "was antiquated and almost at an end" (17).

"Nobody's going anywhere. . . . Everyone wants to . . . run away. But where? That is what is driving people mad," says Ferdinand to Salim as he hands the latter back his life and liberty (319). Ferdinand is the aspirational new African of Mobutu's Zaire, who has imbibed the mind of Europe through his Domain education; the son of a sorceress who has now risen to the post of regional commissioner. Salim, however, sees him as a victim of the savage history of the land, not as its agent. There is no way out for Ferdinand in *A Bend in the River*—like many others in the novel he seems to stagnate—though all around him it is a world in motion. Ferdinand is one of the many who have gone back to the old ways of Africa with modern tools like the machine gun. Without rule of law or civic liberties, the country was now "too small for its tribal hatreds" (235). In Naipaul's Africa, dawn was always receding into darkness, and time was running backward.

"Imagination, not invention, is the supreme master of art as of life," writes Conrad in *A Personal Record*: "An imaginative and exact rendering of authentic memories may serve worthily that spirit of piety towards all things human which sanctions the conceptions of a writer of tales, and the emotions of the man reviewing his own experience" (*Mirror of the Sea and*

Personal Record, 25). The melancholia of Naipaul's fiction and nonfiction can be related to the failure of this kind of imagination in a nonmourning of the past and a refusal of loss. In *A Bend in the River*, Indar sees in Salim the signs of prolonged grieving for lost totalities, and urges him to break free from the past, which has been their prison. "It isn't easy to turn your back on the past. It isn't something you can decide to do just like that. It is something you have to arm yourself for, or grief will ambush and destroy you" (*Bend*, 164). "The past was simply the past," says Salim by way of explaining his family's and his own rejection of history (12). The family continues to live as it has always lived, because of a lack of distance or diachronic perspective with which to assess its own cultural location. But the other polarity of postcolonial subjectivity, as embodied by Nazruddin and Indar—hybrid, exogamous, centrifugal—does not prove efficacious either. In Naipaul's work, the nightmarish European metropolis is as inimical to romantic self-fashioning as the nightmarish bush. Riding an airplane (for the first time) out of Africa is no cause for jubilation in Salim—for him, the flight, and later, the London hotel room, trap the dead air of benumbed, suspended lives. London itself has atrophied to the dimensions of an Indian-run corner shop. Europe is nothing like its mythologized older self, and has not achieved the promise of modernity: it is something "shrunken and mean and forbidding" (*Bend*, 269). London was central as long as it had the colonial peripheries, a sacrosanct ideal unreachable for address (or immigration). But now the postcards have arrived from the empire's dark destinations, as have millions of fugitives from dreadful places. Salim, like Indar, indoctrinated in the Manichean ideology of a colonial time, is distracted by this chaotic plurality and cultural in-mixing, and cannot make a sum of London's parts. "I traveled everywhere by underground train, popping down into the earth at one place, popping up at another, not able to relate one place to the other, and sometimes making complicated interchanges to travel short distances" (272). Salim has merely exchanged one airless chamber for another. The idea of "the other place," "comforted only to weaken and destroy" (285). Salim makes it his business to return home to Africa despite the grim realization that there is no going back and nothing to go back to. *A Bend in the River* gives us the parting image of men lost in the back of beyond, but staying dreadfully busy.

Despite his protestations, Naipaul shares with Conrad a mode of telling a story that is part reportage and part fiction: this narrative style successfully addresses questions that are both cosmic and of large international political consequence. Naipaul, however, faults Conrad for regarding fiction "not as something of itself, but as a varnish on fact" (*Literary Occasions*, 176). If, as Naipaul writes of "The Lagoon," a typical Conrad tale gives poignant form to "passion and the abyss, solitude and futility and the world of illusions" (*Literary Occasions*, 163), the impasses caused by the mutually opposed force fields of "passion" and "abyss" are summarily resolved through the inexorable novelization of Conrad's vision. The meaning of the novels is not elaborated in performance—what the Conrad novel *is* happens to be more significant than what the Conrad novel *does*—and the story always remains fixed: "It is something given, like the prose 'argument' started at the beginning of a section of an old poem. Conrad knows exactly what he has to say" (176).

The justification that Naipaul provides for the bounded nature of Conrad's vision implies a strong autobiographical affiliation: "It is the complaint of a writer who is missing a society, and is beginning to understand that fantasy or imagination can move more freely within a closed and ordered world. Conrad's experience was too scattered; he knew many societies by their externals, but he knew none in depth" (*Literary Occasions*, 179). According to Homi Bhabha, "The 'unhomely' is a paradigmatic postcolonial experience" (*Location of Culture*, 142). Naipaul's homelessness describes and repeats the trauma of diasporic movement endured by Conrad and is haunted by an old fear of being reduced to nothing, of feeling crushed—the old colonial anxiety of having one's individuality destroyed. The scene from *Heart of Darkness* that most haunts Naipaul presents Marlow, traveling upriver toward Kurtz, as he finds at a deserted outpost a book titled *An Inquiry into Some Points of Seamanship*. Marlow, like Naipaul, imaginatively identifies with the reader, for whom the book sheds valuable light on the surrounding darkness and the imperial traffic that it conceals. This scene, Naipaul writes in "Conrad's Darkness and Mine," addressed a "political panic" in his youthful self: "To be a colonial was to know a kind of security; it was to inhabit a fixed world. And I suppose that in my fantasy I had seen myself coming to England as to some purely literary region, where, untrammelled by the accidents of history or background, I could make a romantic career for myself as a writer" (*Literary Occasions*, 170). The old seamanship manual, with its "honest concern for the right way of going to work" (170) in the midst of entropy, is the cultural correlate of the "purely literary region," the metropolis that promises the young colonial a deracinated, desacralized, and aesthetic existence in a time after history. Reading this passage, Sara Suleri asks why Naipaul, resolutely refusing to remember the crucial plot twist in *Heart of Darkness* when Marlow actually meets the previous owner of *An Inquiry*, focuses instead on "Marlow's grim appreciation of the guilty single-mindedness that attends on reading" (*Rhetoric*, 152). The individual is none other than the Harlequin at Kurtz's inner post, a border-crossing and shape-shifting creature who accidentally completes the circuit of transmission between oppressor and oppressed, Eurasia and Africa, Kurtz and Marlow. "The spirit of adventure," Marlow observes, "seemed to have consumed all thought of self so completely, that, even while he was talking to you, you forgot that it was he—the man before your eyes—who had gone through those things" (*Heart of Darkness*, 93). Suleri contends that "Naipaul invites his readers to conceive of him as the Harlequin. He chooses to become that comic figure of incessant arrival, and in so doing inscribes himself as strongly on *Heart of Darkness* as in that tale the Harlequin makes *An Inquiry* serve as the occasion for his own ciphered marginalia" (*Rhetoric*, 152). Just as the Harlequin represents an emergent national narrative of professionalism, Naipaul the arriviste postcolonial writer is to be seen transversally through the symbolic determination of the canonical empire novel. Thus canonicity is the trope through which Naipaul despairs of historical chance while also consecrating colonial history and heritage and conceptualizing an evolving postcolonial modernity to come. To quote Suleri again, "The writer invokes the authority of a prior text, be it Conrad or colonial history; in the posture of a respectful reader, however, he manages to recast himself as a character in the former tale in such a way that it becomes a frame, a preparation for his continuing plot" (152).

Naipaul's novel *Guerrillas* is often compared to Conrad's *The Secret Agent: A Simple Tale*, the book that Conrad did not create but "found" and subsequently "edited": "The subject of *The Secret Agent*—I mean the tale—came to me in the shape of a few words uttered by a friend in a casual conversation about anarchists or rather anarchist activities; how brought about I don't remember now," writes Conrad in the "Author's Note" to *Secret Agent* (xxxv). The friend in question was Ford Madox Heufer (later Ford), who had told Conrad that the man blown to bits in the attempt on the Royal Greenwich Observatory was an imbecile and that his bereaved sister had committed suicide afterward. The other factual source for *The*

Secret Agent was an assistant police commissioner's book of recollections, which detailed the dynamite attacks in London. The absurd cruelty of the Greenwich Park explosion cried out for an intervention from the author who, on completing *Nostromo* and *The Mirror of the Sea*, had given himself up "to a not unhappy pause" (xxxv): "It was at first for me a mental change . . . in which strange forms, sharp in outline but imperfectly apprehended, appeared and claimed attention as crystals will do by their bizarre and unexpected shapes" (*Secret Agent*, xxxvii). While Conrad makes of the process of crystallizing this story—the story of Winnie Verloc—a matter of dutiful attending to "bizarre and unexpected shapes" that coerced his narrative intervention, he emphasizes also the pathological and compulsive dimension of his authorship of this tale: "There had been moments during the writing of the book when I was an extreme revolutionist, I won't say more convinced than they [the real-life extreme revolutionists] but certainly cherishing a more concentrated purpose than any of them had ever done in the whole course of his life" (xxxix). The text's anarchic element manifests in dehiscence, kinship between unlikely doubles, "madness and despair" (xxxix). The narrator says that in their own ways the most ardent revolutionists, like everyone else, seek "the peace of soothed vanity, of satisfied appetites, or perhaps of appeased conscience" (*Secret Agent*, 102). Inspector Heat feels an affinity for the burglar, because they are guided by the same instincts and conventions. The assistant police commissioner lingers in Brett Street as if he were a member of the criminal classes. Verloc senses subtle moral affinities between himself and Vladimir. The professor notes that "the terrorist and policeman both come from the same basket. Revolution, legality—counter moves in the same game; forms of idleness at bottom identical" (74). The unsophisticated and obtuse Winnie, convinced that things don't bear too much looking into, is an unlikely double of the author, who in the novel's preface identifies with the human impulse to shrink from explanations. Again, like the author, Winnie defies human nature to go beyond the world's love of surfaces in her perverse quest of depth (motives and meaning): like the artist, she necessarily restages the violence she confronts, transforming it from brute accident to the radical simplicity of an abstraction ("the fact of a man blown to bits for nothing even most remotely resembling an idea" [xxxv]). Conrad's world muddles the distinction between civilization and ape, progress and atavism, human and mechanical functions, conservative ends and anarchic means, and good and evil in such a manner that rapacious opposites come to constitute a "simple," if incredible, tale of the simple truths of life.

Like *The Secret Agent*, Naipaul's *Guerillas* fictionalizes current events. It is based on the violent life and hanging of the Trinidadian Michael de Freitas, also known as Abdul Malik or Michael X, a leader of the Black Power movement in the 1960s. He was "the Black Power man who was neither powerful not black," as Naipaul wrote in a journalistic account, "Michael X and the Black Power Killings in Trinidad" (*Return of Eva Peron*, 22–23).[12] Malik was "made by words, his and other people's" (51).[13] He remade his past and posited a future with stories. It was in London that he had picked up the rhetoric of the Black Power movement and had become, Naipaul writes, a "Negro." Malik was also a writer who left behind an unfinished novel, in which an Englishwoman visits Malik's "well-appointed" and "English-looking" house (*Return of Eva Peron*, 60), develops a fatal fascination for him, and then disappears from the story. "This was a literary murder, if ever there was one," Naipaul adds in the postscript to "Michael X and the Power Killings in Trinidad" (94). Art foreshadows and precipitates cataclysmic life: Malik murders in the paroxysms of a fantasized rape and violation. He is a hollow man made of hollow words, not real but "a hollow succession of roles" (25).

Naipaul goes over the same ground in *Guerrillas*, which is "not so much a copy of an 'original' in Malik, as a copy of a copy," states Judie Newman. "Malik himself is portrayed as profoundly imitative, the ultimate mimic man" (*Ballistic Bard*, 125). Neil ten Kortenaar reads *Guerillas* as "a novel about a failed novelist" ("Writers and Readers," 322). While "Michael X and the Black Power Killings in Trinidad" offers a cultural commentary on a historical event, *Guerillas* becomes increasingly inscrutable as it proceeds. The key characters, Jimmy and Jane, are described as "unreadable." Roche cannot read Jane's moods, and chides her in turn on misreading phenomena: "You have the world in front of your eyes, and yet it's funny how your mind prints out comic strips all day long" (*Guerrillas*, 29). Jane is initially attracted to Roche, because "he seemed to make accessible that remote world, of real events and real action, whose existence she had half divined" (49), but Roche is no more of a mover or a doer than she. His logical and controlled public performances belie panic, paranoia, and cowardice. In his writing, as in his political and social role playing, there seems to be no conviction or an overriding framework of belief, and this in turn makes him fail to capture the personal costs of political torture. As Meredith Herbert, a local radio presenter and politician, says of Roche's book on the experience of torture in South Africa, "You write as though certain things merely happened to you, were forced upon you" (209). Roche admits in the throes of the uprising that he "cannot read these people" (179). He and Jane are compelled to inhabit a hallucinatory reality that they have not authored and are too paralyzed to break free of: "You mean we just have to sit here and watch this happen?" muses Jane (195). There is also no meaningful communication between the novel's diagrammatic characters. Jane, who, Roche decides, was "without memory" and nothing more than "what she did or said at any given moment" (100), dramatizes the historical weightlessness of other characters in the novel like de Tunja, Meredith, or Roche himself, who continue to live as unreflectively as ever. It is as if, as John Mellors states, the fictional characters were denied growth and mutability by the foregone conclusion of the real story ("Mimics," 117). Insofar as the novel is generically and historically determined as the chief source for a certain tradition of representing subjectivity, this conclusion signals nothing less than the death of the genre. In putting down the old form, Naipaul reaffirms the necessity and impossibility of making the European novel live anew.

Yet the repressed returns in *Guerillas* via a narrative that is laden with allusions to canonical works of literature. The name of Jimmy Ahmed's commune is Thrushcross Grange, and his house is fortified with imported English furniture and "The Hundred Best Books of the World." In Jimmy's novel, Clarissa picks up a copy of *Wuthering Heights* and imagines the crowd hailing Jimmy as a leader: "This man was born in the back room of a Chinese grocery, but as Catherine said to Heathcliff 'Your mother was an Indian princess and your father was the Emperor of China'" (62). Jane and Roche recall the turbulent Jane and Rochester of *Jane Eyre* as also the humbler and emasculated Rochester of Jean Rhys's *Wide Sargasso Sea*. Richardson's Clarissa is invoked in a powerful rape fantasy where Jimmy is both Lovelace and Clarissa. Jane reads *The Woodlanders*, Thomas Hardy's novel about a threatened agrarian community, in the context of a failed pastoral experiment.

Significantly, *Guerrillas* also writes back to *The Secret Agent*, evoking an alienated reality, a surplus existence over sense, a certain dislocation and disease in the order of the historical being. Conrad's *The Secret Agent*, like *Guerrillas*, had alluded to a historical event, to which it disclaimed any relation. Conrad had stated simultaneously that the story was based on the inside knowledge of a certain event in the history of active anarchism *and* that it was purely a work of the imagination. Conrad's ambivalence prefigures Naipaul's colonial schizophrenia: both authors are secret agents, torn between protecting and destroying the authority vested in the canon. Ralph Singh's aesthetic credo in *The Mimic Men* serves Naipaul and Conrad equally: "I write, I know, from both sides. I cannot do otherwise"(*Mimic Men*, 191).

Bhabha suggests that Naipaul draws from Conrad "a vision of literature and a lesson of history" (*Location of Culture*, 104). In Naipaul's reappraisal, Conrad stands for a singleness of literary intention that survives the corruption of causes, of authenticity besmirched and innocence lost. His work speaks to the postcolonial latecomer of a sense of right conduct and honor achievable only through the acceptance of "customary" norms that are the signs of culturally cohesive "civil" communities. These aims of the civilizing mission speak, in Bhabha's view, with a peculiarly English authority derived from the customary practice on which both English common law and the English national language rely for their authenticity and appeal. As Naipaul reflects, "All the novels I had read were about settled and organized societies, and I was aware of a slight fraudulence in applying a form created by that type of society to the squalor, disorder, and shallowness of my own" ("Writing is Magic," 117). He nevertheless "translates" Conrad from Africa to the Caribbean "in order to transform the despair of postcolonial history into an appeal for the autonomy of art" (Bhabha, *Location of Culture*, 107). This practice is intimately related to Naipaul's invention of himself as an English writer, nowhere more poignantly documented than in the autobiographical *Enigma of Arrival*. Naipaul's "homecoming" to the Wiltshire estate of Waldenshaw in this novel has two historical implications: it signals the irreversibility of his departure from his Caribbean island in 1950, and the stirrings of a new life "in the ancient heart of England." This England, "a garden country suffused by an ambience of Constable, Ruskin, Goldsmith, Gray's *Elegy*, and Hardy; of chalk downs, brookside strolls, footbridges, bridle paths, Stonehenge, and delicate beds of peonies," was, of course, a literary idea (*Enigma*, 111).

3

"Best of the World's Classics"
Derek Walcott Between Classics and the Classic

"First and foremost, like Eliot's 'major poet,' he steals," states Rei Terada, explaining why Walcott is a "magpie poet" (*Derek Walcott's Poetry*, 209).[1] Also, like the magpie, Walcott "throws nothing away" (209). Terada's influential work on Homeric mimicry in Walcott's *Omeros* intricates several themes that have dominated Walcott scholarship: the postcolonial politics of mimesis, which tips over to comic and corrosive mimicry; unstable sets of resemblances that defer presence through metonymic proliferation; the relation of the latecomer to Western poetic genealogy; disfigurement and/as figuration. Homer is not the only predecessor figure for the poet-narrator, Terada points out. There is Joyce, or more specifically, Joyce's Bloom; Shakespeare; characters drawn from non-Homerical classics; the figure of Christ. If *Omeros* is structured on a series of parallels, however, Terada enjoins the reader to move beyond the fun-house mirror correspondences between "Walcott's Helen to Homer's, Achille to Achilles, Philoctete to Philoctetes, and so on," and question, instead, "our impulse to perceive, and hence to create, likenesses—especially when such questioning becomes an overt theme of the poem itself" (183–84).

Taking its cue from Terada, the present chapter goes beyond anatomizing the dense allusiveness of Walcott's work to examine his renovation and invention of classics in the present tense of a postcolonial and postnational world. In "Reflections," Walcott says of the African-American artist Romare Bearden's cutouts that "they may be like Greek vases, but they are *simultaneous* concepts, not *chronological* concepts" (240). Walcott's rewriting of the (Homeric) classic, in *Omeros* and related works, I argue, should be seen as a comparable art of simultaneity, or of succession posing as simultaneity, which makes short work of the spatio-temporal translation between the Aegean and the Caribbean. "Joyce is a contemporary of Homer (which Joyce knew)," as Walcott states ("Reflections," 241). This chapter explores the many aspects of Walcott's engagement with and creative reprisals of the "Best of the World's Classics": his affinity with the Greco-Roman classic in the shadow of Homer; his rewriting of Conradesque travel; his bemused examination of the classical status of modernist writers like Joyce, Eliot, and Rhys; his shifting strategies of using Creole in a mode that is reactive in relation to the classic; his own multinational self-representation.

Walcott says matter-of-factly that "great poets sound both like themselves alone and like all the great poetry written" ("Young," 5). In his case, the upward mobility narrative of the hero as artist involved "the interior life of poetry," as well as "the outward life of action and dialect": "The writers of our generation were natural assimilators. We knew the literatures of empires, Greek, Roman, British, through their essential classics; and both the patois of the street and the language of the classroom hid the elation of discovery" (*What the Twilight*, 4). Walcott talks about assimilation as if it were a starting point, the onset of a fierce apprenticeship that is a creative, and not a self-consciously critical mode. He dismisses the colonial paradigm of an Old World original and New World mimicry: "There was no line in the sea which said, this is new, this is the frontier, the boundary of endeavour, and henceforth everything can only be mimicry" ("Caribbean," 8). The poet becomes himself by acquiring the demons that are the artists of the past, he had argued in "Young Trinidadian Poets" (5). "One's own voice is an anthology of all the sounds one has heard," Walcott states in an interview with Leif Sjöberg (*Conversations with Derek Walcott*, ed. Baer, 83).[2] The febrile intertextuality of Walcott's work, however, is liable also to be interpreted as symptomatic of a cultural belatedness that leaves poets overwhelmed by the influence of strong precursors: Homer, Virgil, Dante; the metaphysical poets; Shakespeare; the theater of Synge, Strindberg, and Brecht; the poetry of Yeats and Hart Crane, Dylan Thomas, Pound, Eliot, and Auden. "Has Derek Walcott developed a voice altogether his own, the mark of a major poet, or does one hear in him the composite voice of post-

Yeatsian poetry in English?" asks Harold Bloom dubiously (*Derek Walcott*, 1). According to Bloom, if he doesn't rate Walcott as highly as John Ashbery or Seamus Heaney, Geoffrey Hill or James Merrill, Jay Wright or Anne Carson, it is possibly because he sets too high a value upon "the agonistic element in poetry" (1). Bloom has famously stated elsewhere that a strong poem is "achieved anxiety" (*Anxiety*, xxiii). Influence-anxiety, in the Bloomian sense, has little to do with temperamental anxiety: he uses the term *anxiety of influence* to demarcate a "matrix of relationships—imagistic, temporal, spiritual, psychological—all of them ultimately defensive in their nature" (xxiii), which defines the relationship between poets and their powerful forerunners. However, instead of agonistic misprision, through which the latecomer talent simultaneously acknowledges and disavows tradition, he finds in Walcott's *Tiepolo's Hound* an untroubled adaptation of the nuanced cadences of Wallace Stevens (*Derek Walcott*, 3). In an essay in the same collection edited by Bloom, Helen Vendler labels Walcott "derivative," relating it to the "unhappy disjunction between his explosive subject, as yet relatively new in English poetry, and his harmonious pentameters, his lyrical allusions, his stately rhymes, his Yeatsian meditations" (27). Reading Walcott's "Ruins of a Great House," Vendler is reminded of Yeats's "Meditations in Time of Civil War," "On a House Shaken by the Land Agitation," and *Supernatural Songs*. She sees this tension between content and style reach breaking point in sentences such as "How choose / Between this Africa and the English tongue I love?" Vendler seems oblivious to the self-mocking irony of a poetic utterance which is presenting itself as the catachresis of poetic utterance, a Yeatsian adaptation that is avowedly *not quite* Yeatsian because of its confused allegiances and clashing imperatives (Africa and the English tongue). The patois ends in "an unlikely 'literary' note," she states (27).

Walcott is perhaps the "mulatto of style" he himself describes in "What the Twilight Says," Vendler helpfully offers.[3] "He was in all things 'a divided child,' loyal to both 'the stuffed dark nightingale world of Keats' and the 'virginal unpainted world' of the islands," states Vendler (27). A divided child, trying to reconcile poetry with theater, the act of writing plays with a vocation in theater direction, poetic truth with literal truth, the use of patois with aspiration for high diction. Mixed diction, however, Vendler argues, is yet to legitimize itself as a literary or aesthetic resource: a "macaronic aesthetic," that uses two or more languages at once, has never been sustained in poetry at any length (31). "It seemed that his learnedness might be the death of him," Vendler comments, "especially since he so prized it" (27): "He will remain for this century one of its most candid narrators of the complicated and even desperate destiny of the man of great sensibility and talent born in a small colonial outpost, educated far beyond the standard of his countrymen, and pitched—by sensibility, talent, and education—into an isolation which deepens with every word he writes" (32). There is, however, little sign of the damning isolation Vendler diagnoses for the overeducated and overreaching Walcott in the way he critically appraises his "*simple* schizophrenic boyhood" (my emphasis, *What the Twilight*, 4), and the "heretical reconciliation" that his poetry seeks to make between the outer world and the world of poetry, esoteric, ordered, and often nonreferential (or aberrantly referential) to its own geopolitical provenance ("The Figure of Crusoe," 35). In *Another Life*, Walcott wishes that his identity and heritage—"wrenched" by two competing styles as well as what he, in *Tiepolo's Hound*, calls "the horizon's hyphen" (97)—is soldered by "one body of immortal metaphor" (*Tiepolo's Hound*, 236). Walcott neither downplays the "malarial enervation" (*What the Twilight*, 4) of the colonial condition nor the messianic role thrust upon the "man of great sensibility and talent" that Vendler mentions. "The self-inflicted role of martyr came naturally, the melodramatic belief that one was the message bearer for the millennium, that the inflamed ego was enacting their will. . . . If there was nothing, there was everything to be made. With this prodigious ambition one began" (*What the Twilight*, 4). The Antillean poet is a "stripped man" like Crusoe, "driven back to that self-astonishing, elemental force, his mind" (*What the Twilight*, 70). The basis of the Antillean experience is a "shipwreck of fragments, these echoes, these shards of a huge tribal vocabulary, these partially remembered customs, and they are not decayed but strong" (*What the Twilight*, 70). On these scattered fragments of Antillean memory, and on the collective amnesia over lost Aruac signs and hieroglyphs, Walcott grafts the mimetic learning of an accidental colonial education, with its mistranslations and fortuitous errors, "typographical mistakes" that, however, function as poetic "revelation" ("Caligula's Horse," 138). In "The Caribbean: Culture or Mimicry?" he states: "What has mattered is the loss of history, the amnesia of the races, what has become necessary is imagination, imagination as necessity, as invention" (6). In *Omeros* Walcott speaks affirmatively of a "reversible world," where remembering and forgetting are interchangeable activities. Paul Breslin reads this idea of reversibility as "a property of space, such as microcosms suddenly grow larger and macrocosms smaller." "Places that a European might think of as peripheral, like the Jacmel Church in St. Lucia, become centers, and places that loom large in European history, like Versailles, become secondary, less important than the palm trees of a Caribbean island," Breslin explains ("Derek Walcott's 'Reversible World,'" 18). This is probably what Wilson Harris means when he writes, in "Tradition and the West Indian Writer," that to "create a *native* tradition of depth," the Caribbean writer must pay attention to "the smallest area one envisages, island or village, prominent ridge or buried valley, flatland or heartland," until each thing "is charged immediately with the openness of imagination" (31). The burden of history is not so much put aside as it attritions through what Walcott calls the "widening amnesia" (*Collected Poems*, 60) of a tropical land, where the rain forest, the swamp, or the beach have had all traces of visible history wiped out by a fierce tropical climate.

For the poet who famously said, in his poem "The Schooner *Flight*," "I had no nation now but the imagination" (*Collected Poems*, 8), history is lack, a void created by physical and psychic violence. It is also a nonevent, a history of the people "which they did not commit," fabricated to support doctrines of sin, guilt, and expiation through which collusive imperial religion justified colonial servitude ("The Star-Apple Kingdom," *Collected Poems*, 387). There is no history "but flux, and the only sustenance, myth," Walcott writes in "The Muse of History" (*What the Twilight*, 12). In this essay, Walcott admires the great poets of the New World who have looked beyond the trauma of history to articulate instead a vision "capable of enormous wonder" of "the greatest width of elemental praise of winds, seas, rain" (*What the Twilight*, 38). Disavowing the "literature of recrimination and despair" (*What the Twilight*, 37) and the history of "ennui, defence, disease" (*Another Life*, 70), and defying the loneliness that ensues from routine objectification as historical victims ("time that makes us objects, multiplies / our natural loneliness" ["Crusoe's Journal," *Collected Poems*, 93]), Walcott seeks healing, waking, and absolution from history in new beginnings to be found in new words, and in the retrieval of "something rooted" that is yet "unwritten" ("Hic Jacet," *Gulf and Other Poems*, 70).

"What's new about a classic is that it stays new"

Discussing Charles Augustin Sainte-Beuve's formulation of the "modern classic" in relation to the writings of Du Bellay, Christopher Prendergast emphasizes Sainte-Beuve's linking of the classic to the doctrine of *renovatio*. Sainte-Beuve's "classique dans toute la force du terme [classic in every sense of the word]" involves "a practice of 'grafts' and 'transplants' from old to new, whereby . . . one imitates in a spirit of freedom, warmth, emulation, one does not translate" (Prendergast, *Classic*, 262).[4] Walcott's relationship to the subject of the classic, similarly, is hardly describable as an article of blind faith. For him, the classic is changeable and perfectible, and the act of preserving and relaying tradition is inseparable from renewing it. The modern classic, Sainte-Beuve had stated, is not an imitation of the past. As such, it is not immediately perceivable as classic: it disturbs and shocks in its newness and has to be claimed in successive acts of interpretation and reinterpretation (Prendergast, *Classic*, 262). In an interview with Nancy Schoenberger, Walcott speaks in Beauvian cadences on the possibility of the modern classic: "What's new about a classic is that it stays new. You have your debts to your predecessors; your acknowledgement is a votive acknowledgement. Seamus Heaney recognized in a review that 'The Schooner *Flight*' opens like *Piers Plowman*. You put that there deliberately: 'as this reminded me of that, so let it remind you also.'" ("Interview," 17). The fusion of classical myth with island characters is, of course, not just a literary conceit but a reflection of the history of decoding and recoding the West Indies, where such names are remainders of what Ramazani calls a "violent colonial imposition" (*Hybrid Muse*, 55). Odysseus, Helen, and Hector are household names and "very ordinary symbols" in the Caribbean, Walcott explains:

> I was just talking to somebody in St. Lucia the other day, and he said: "I see you have somebody called Hector." And a lady said to me: "There's a Hector who has a shop in St. Lucia"—in Gros Ilet, the same village. And of course Achille . . . is another name that is common. Now these names have been given to these people—are given, *because* . . . Well, first of all, the slavemaster gives a name because he thinks that the slave has the attributes of Achilles, or of Caesar, or Pompey. ("On *Omeros*," 38–39)

Parallelisms caused by "chance / or an echo" (*Omeros*, 100): Walcott attributes the correspondences to historical contingency and also the time-honored literary custom of mediating the world through the mythopoeic. As seen in *Another Life*, the answer to the question, "Boy! Who was Ajax?" is simply that Ajax is a

> lion-coloured stallion from Sealey's stable,
> by day a cart-horse, a thoroughbred
> on race days. (*Another Life*, 16–17)

In another instance in the same text, a "tattooed ex-merchant sailor" is likened to Odysseus, and Janie, "the town's one clear-complexioned whore / with two tow-headed children in her tow," is Helen (*Another Life*, 18). "History" is changed to "metaphor," Walcott says in *Omeros* (193). Names "are not oars / that have to be laid side by side, nor are legends" (*Omeros*, 312–13): the ebony Helen in *Omeros*, wearing a yellow cotton dress and carrying cheap sandals, is herself unperturbed by the history of her classic marble counterpart. And yet the images coalesce compulsively, mixing up the histories of Troy's Helen and the unimportant island Helen:

> These Helens are different creatures,
> . . .
>
> but each draws an elbow slowly over her face
> and offers the gift of her sculptured nakedness,
> parting her mouth. (*Omeros*, 313)

In Major Plunkett's political unconscious a third Helen, the Caribbean island that is often referred to as "the Helen of the West Indies," commingles with the two Helens of the *Omeros* poet. As Robert Hamner puts it: "He sees her village as another Troy, the island's Pitons as her breasts, the Battle of the Saints as her Homeric conflict. These people have no Parthenon, and Latin is replaced by native dialect, but he [Plunkett] can envision their athletic contests as Olympiads. Thus Hector and Achille run marathons and wrestle not for victory's laurels or shields but to win Helen" (*Epic*, 46). The historian shares with the poet a laughable infirmity, this inability to see Helen

> as the sun saw her, with no Homeric shadow,
> swinging her plastic sandals on that beach alone,
> as fresh as the sea-wind. (*Omeros*, 271)

Yet, doubling, echoing, troping, and analogizing seem inevitable for postcolonial self-representation and automobility. This is particularly true of the character of Philoctete in *Omeros*, drawn from Philoctetes of Greek legend, "the man with the wound, alone on the beach," but also signifying, through his excruciating physical suffering, the indelible memory of New World African slavery.[5]

He believed the swelling came from the chained ankles
of his grandfathers. Or else why was there no cure?
That the cross he carried was not only the anchor's

but that of his race. (*Omeros*, 19)

Jahan Ramazani correctly points out that Philoctete, who has little credibility as a Caribbean fisherman, "seems to have wandered out of Greek literature and stumbled into a textual universe where he suddenly embodies the colonial horrors perpetrated by the West." As Ramazani elaborates, "To highlight his reliance on a culture of slavery to indict the practice of slavery, Walcott pointedly refers to the institution as 'Greek' ([*Omeros*,] 177) and ironically adduces 'the Attic ideal of the first slave-settlement' (63), even as he turns a Greek hero into his synecdoche for all the damage wrought by slavery and colonialism" (*Hybrid Muse*, 55). Ramazani calls Walcott neither "Eurocentric" nor "Afrocentric" but "an ever more multicentric poet of the contemporary world" (64). Taking the idea of multiple centers, which diffuses the ontic clout of a putative imperial center, I would claim further that Walcott's complex relationality to local and international frameworks of reference marks the emergence of a nonidentificatory politics. When he proclaims in "The Schooner *Flight*": "I have English, Dutch, and nigger in me, / And either I'm nobody, or I'm a nation" (*Collected Poems*, 346), "one thinks," Brodsky remarks, "not so much about blood as about language. . . . And it is from this height of 'having English' . . . that the poet unleashes his oratorial power" ("Sound," 165–66).

A fine example of the politics of nonidentification *as* multiple identification is Walcott's poem "Hotel Normandie Pool," where the poolside of a Port of Spain hotel is reimagined as the setting for the Black Sea exile of Ovid. In this poem, the Odyssean drifter, a staple of the Walcott narrative poem, is Ovid, the shape shifter of *Metamorphoses* and *Tristia*, derided by "slaves" and "Romans" alike for displaying "the fickle dyes of the chameleon" (*Collected Poems*, 444). "Ovid" appears in the poem as a white male tourist "with a robe of foam-frayed terry cloth" (441). He materializes, as if on cue, in response to the Aquarian poet's prayer for transformation to his sign, water: "Change me, my sign, to someone I can bear" (440). As Terada observes, it is difficult to distinguish "Ovid" from the poet who conjures him up. Both speak the dead language of Latin and share the consanguinity of stone statues: "'Quis te misit, Magister?' And its whisper went / through my cold body, veining it in stone" (442). The condition of homelessness is common to both, which, in the case of the Walcott persona, additionally hints at a social or domestic breakdown that necessitates his spending a New Year's morning around "the cold pool in the metal light" (439).

The specular economy of the poem, with its myriad reflective surfaces, spatial metaphors, and what Terada calls "visual rhymes" (where objects resemble, reflect, image, and insinuate each other), makes the graphic artist Ovid a most fitting muse (*Derek Walcott's Poetry*, 138).[6] Exile, perhaps, is preferable to domicile, the poet wonders, and Ovid reassures that though he was overcome with feelings of alienation at first—"I missed my language as your tongue needs salt"—his exilic consciousness eventually generated "reflections that, in many ways, / were even stronger than their origin" (443). Local politics, "corruption, censorship, and arrogance," according to Ovid, "make exile seem a happier thought than home" (442). Ovid turns out to be one of Walcott's "mythical hallucinations" (*Omeros*, 31), from whom the living poet seeks an "approving nod." As Walcott had stated in an interview: "What keeps me awake is tribute—to the dead, who to me are not dead, but are at my elbow. All I ask is an approving nod from them, as Verrochio may have nodded at Leonardo, his assistant, or was it vice versa?" (*Conversations with Derek Walcott*, ed. Baer, 83). The achieved mutuality between the figures, however, does not quite justify the overwrought classical analogies in this lyric. Why drag the ghost of Ovid to make sense of "the disfiguring exile of divorce," especially since it is beyond the consolation of words (441)?

> Why here, of all places,
> a small, suburban tropical hotel,
> its pool pitched to a Mediterranean blue,
> its palms rusting in their concrete oasis? (*Collected Poems*, 445)

"Because," the poet has Ovid cattily retort, "to make my image flatters you." (445).[7]

In implying that a figment of the poet's imagination is likely to be Ovid-shaped, Walcott is perhaps harking back to a schoolboy aspiration, when he was, as he writes in "Homecoming: Anse La Raye," one of the "solemn Afro-Greeks eager for grades" (*Selected Poems*, 47).[8] In *Afro-Greeks: Dialogues Between Anglophone Caribbean Literature and Classics*, Emily Greenwood highlights the intellectual formation that led to classical extrapolations in the works of a generation of Caribbean writers: "That it is possible to write this book at all is due to the fact that several of the writers who dominated Caribbean literature in the twentieth century were schooled in Latin and ancient history, and sometimes Greek under a colonial school curriculum in the period roughly 1910–60" (8–9).[9] Walcott says himself that the foundation of his education was "rigid": "Latin, Greek, and the essential masterpieces" ("Meanings," in *Critical Perspectives*, ed. Hamner, 50). In "What the Twilight Says," he mentions the Walcott brothers' daily negotiation of European cultural diktat with the elemental "native beat" (*What the Twilight*, 19): "On the verandah, with his back to the street, he began marathon poems on Greek heroes which ran out of breath, lute songs, heroic tragedies, but these rhythms, the Salvation Army parodies, the Devil's Christmas songs, the rhythms of the street itself were entering the pulse beat of the wrist" (20). By making Ovid, the classic poet and prophet of mutability, interchangeable with the Caribbean "successor," Walcott is also highlighting the culture of references, free-form choice, and what Marlow, in *Heart of Darkness*, calls the "choice of nightmares" that is the prerogative of the cosmopolitan twentieth-century writer (Conrad, *Heart of Darkness*, 62). The joys of cross-cultural adaptations, however, are made irrelevant by the tendency of the evening sky to defy or exceed representation. This is a richly ambiguous end to "Hotel Normandie Pool," the effect heightened by indeterminate syntax and irregular rhymes, where it is uncertain if we are looking at nature or an artist's rendering of nature even as the poet debunks the power of art to mediate or represent:

At dusk, the sky is loaded like watercolour paper
with an orange wash in which every edge frays—
a painting with no memory of the painter. (*Collected Poems*, 445)

Ovid has disappeared, or remains unsummoned as muse. Clearly, as Walcott writes in "Gros Islet," the "Classics can console. But not enough" (*Arkansas Testament*, 34). With dusk comes the suspension of human figuration and voice, or at least the kind practiced by the "invisible, exiled laureate" (*Collected Poems*, 445). Hints of death abound: death of the author, the "death of consciousness," as Terada puts it (*Derek Walcott's Poetry*, 142), the self-defeating nature of autotelic art. The fruit bat swings ominously on its branch like a funeral bell, but its message, if there is any to be intercepted, is necessarily "tongueless" (*Collected Poems*, 445).

In Walcott's work, the love of classic literacy militates endlessly and interestingly with his avowed aim of abandoning the metanarratives and grand themes of history. From time to time, he makes resolute gestures of discarding the great book, as in an early poem, "Greece."

The body that I had thrown down at my foot
was not really a body but a great book
still fluttering like chitons on a frieze,
till wind worked through the binding of its pages
scattering Hector's and Achilles' rages
to white, diminishing scraps, like gulls that ease
past the gray sphinxes of the crouching islands.
I held air without language in my hands. (*The Fortunate Traveler*, 35–36)

The great book is a thing of critical mass and quickening life, livid with passion and staining the world with language. In "Greece," the poet can breathe freely and write inventively only after he has consigned the great book and its indictments to the elements. "Now, crouched before the blank stone, / I wrote the sound for 'sea,' the sign for 'sun'" (*The Fortunate Traveler*, 36). This too, however, is a rewriting of the Adamic inaugural gesture, not to mention the history of previous attempts by writers to find the original story. A similar stance informs *Omeros*, where the poet confesses, upon meeting the spirit of his ancient Greek predecessor, that he has not read the Homeric epics "all the way through" (*Omeros*, 283). He has, instead, "heard / your voice in that sea, master" (283). Again, when asked about the epic proportions of "The Schooner *Flight*" in an interview, Walcott mischievously retorts: "The only epical thing in "The Schooner *Flight*" is the width of the sea, for which I'm not responsible. It's not my intention to have a hero who takes on battles, who becomes an emblematic figure. The fact is, critics are looking for a repetition of the past; one wants a sort of *Iliad* in blackface. Writers won't do that" ("Interview," 17). In *Omeros*, a trip down memory lane in chapter 12 leads the poet to his childhood home, now a printery, and the specter of his father. The poet is the long-lost Telemachus to Odysseus, Aeneas to the guiding light of Anchises. Warwick Walcott is also the slain father of Hamlet—he has died of an ear infection and is now materialized to ghost write the course of his son's life. The hauntology of Shakespeare is unreservedly evoked, with the dead father wittily punning on the "Will" to write poetry that the son has inherited from his father.

I was raised in this obscure Caribbean port,
where my bastard father christened me for his shire:
Warwick. The Bard's country. But never felt part

of the foreign machinery known as Literature. (*Omeros*, 68)

Warwick Walcott leads the poet down Grass Street toward the harbor of Castries. They come across Warwick's local barbershop, whose presiding deity is the town anarchist. In this remembered scene, the "foreign machinery known as Literature" is momentarily domesticated and contained in the barber's collection of *The World's Great Classics*, proudly displayed on a varnished rack.[10] Warwick's—and, by extension, Walcott's—initiation into canonical literature (and their shared calling) thus takes place in a room surrounded by rusted mirrors, where the classic toga is replaced by a pinned sheet, and where curled hairs falling to the floor foreshadow the writerly commas of the future. When the father returns again in book IV, he urges Walcott to live out the amplitude promised by *The World's Great Classics*, casting his shadow on the "flagstones, histories . . . rivers, great abbeys . . . those streets that History had made great" (187). *The World's Great Classics* make two more appearances in book VI, first amid the flotsam of imperial paraphernalia that overcrowd Plunkett's mind on the morning of Maud's death:

gold-braid laburnums, lilac whiff of lavender,
columned poplars marching to Mafeking's relief.
Naughty seaside cards, the sepia surrender

of Gordon on the mantel, the steps of Khartoum,
The World's Classics condensed . . . (262)

In Plunkett's state of shock, private memory becomes indistinguishable from the collective memories of nation, empire, Englishness and Imperial service. *The World's Great Classics* reappear on the next page, this time as a ground bass that conjoins the lives of the Plunketts with that of the poet. The classics belonging to his father's barber are like the morning glories and bougainvilleas that grow attached to Caribbean homes, a box set of transcendent values shared by disparate groupings of perishable lives.

"Works that attain a lasting status as classics of world literature are ones that can weather a variety of tectonic shifts in the literary landscape," says David Damrosch (*What Is World Literature?* 186). This insight is validated in the way the portable property that is *The World's Great Classics* is positioned or repositioned in Walcott's novel-in-verse of St. Lucian life. Despite their incongruous location, the classics in the barber shop are instantly recognizable for the ambition, aspiration, and cultural perfectibility they synecdochally signify. They are portals to the great cities of the world that Walcott must visit before returning to St. Lucia, failing which he is bound to feel parochial and diminished, as did his father. The force of classics in the barbershop is not just in their universal appeal, but countercultural, as the association with the anarchic barber suggests, and errant—the classics invite acts of reclaiming and reversibility and sustainable relays and switches of cultural authority. The last section of the first book of *Omeros* ends with Warwick enjoining his son in Shakespearean cadences ("O Thou, my Zero") to write into historical existence the lives of the women colliers from his childhood, to take ancestral rhymes from the rhythm of the feet walking up that coal ladder, and to give, in return, "those feet a voice" (*Omeros*, 76).

"The greatest reader in the world": After Conrad, Eliot, and Joyce

A key aspect of Walcott's revisionism with regard to the Western literary canon is his rewriting of Conrad, as he does in the African section of *Omeros*. In book III of *Omeros* the sea-swift inveigles Achille into the thickets of his African past. It was, "like the African movies / he had yelped at in childhood," Achille says (*Omeros*, 133). The "unreeled" river is a mess of familiar images: naked mangroves, knotted logs, yawning hippopotami, screeching monkeys swinging from trees. Like Marlow's journey to the "earliest beginnings of the world" (*Heart of Darkness*, 92), Achille's return is a backward flow of time through "primeval mud," "primeval forest," and "prehistoric earth" (*Heart of Darkness*, 81, 95). In *Omeros*, however, Africa is mythopoeic space, not the blank canvas of Africanist discourse, devoid of history and culture, or minatory, with what Conrad called "the unseen presence of victorious corruption" (*Heart of Darkness*, 138). It provides the backdrop for Achille's self-discovery and self-recovery, which begins with a specular encounter with Afolabe, his father: "he knew by that walk it / was himself in his father, the white teeth, the widening hands" (*Omeros*, 136). In this father-son encounter, Afolabe and Achille become sympathetic extensions of an impinging ancestral world:

> The only interpreter
> of their lips' joined babble, the river with the foam,
> and the chuckles of water under the sticks of the pier,
> where the tribe stood like sticks themselves, reversed
> by reflection. (136)

Afolabe wants to know the provenance of Achille's name, which the latter can hardly provide. The genealogy of Achille's name is not relatable to African trees, rivers, or persons, and, confronted with this revenant from the future, the tribe begins to grieve the rootlessness and cultural amnesia that will plague its unborn generations. Bit by bit, through ritual, litany, and everyday acts of communal bonding, the long memory is reconstructed for Achille, but, unexpectedly, this restoration brings about alienation and homesickness. As with countless imperial travel narratives, Achille's sense of ethnicity and identity congeals away from home, at a remove from his everyday reality. In his dream he leaves Africa for a willful return to the New World across three centuries and an undersea world of coral meadows, sunken galleons, skeletal remains, and remainders of lost treasures.

This chapter on lost genealogy is neither a journey in the heart of darkness tradition, nor a reversion to a primordial past. Achille's ambivalence toward a restored homeland and identity is foreshadowed by the ambivalence of the narrator: "Half of me was with him [Achille]. One half with the midshipman [Plunkett] / by a Dutch canal" (*Omeros*, 135). The journey that began with Helen's abandonment of Achille circles back lovesick to where she, stripping sheets along a wire in Hector's yard, hears the moaning of a dove. The sound seems to emerge from abyssal pain in her heart.

> It was not the song
> that twittered from the veined mesh of Agamemnon,
> but the low-fingered O of an Aruac flute. (*Omeros*, 152)

The narrator extricates the local goddess from one classical reference to embed her representation in yet another. She is not Clytemnestra, reveling in the misery of the fallen Agamemnon, but a Penelope, "in whom a single noon was as long as ten years" (153). The African section of *Omeros*, galvanized by ideas of a return to and retrieval of native belief and structures of feeling, and written in conscious opposition to the futility and despair of the heart-of-darkness tradition of European travel writing, seems oddly uninterested in the possibility of an Afro-Caribbean literature in English that is immune to the insinuating referential networks of the Western literary canon. Literature, Walcott speculates later in the poem, is perhaps as much a victim of ideological determination as history:

When would my head shake off its echoes like a horse

shaking off a wreath of flies? When would it stop,
the echo in the throat, insisting, "Omeros";
when would I enter that light beyond metaphor? (271)

"The Fortunate Traveler," the title poem of the first volume written after Walcott's move to the United States, powerfully evokes Conrad and the specter of the Dark Continent only to baffle recognition through its antinomian charge. The poem writes itself through sinuous modifications, substitutions, and reversals. The heart of darkness is not Africa, we are told, but "the core of fire / in the white center of the holocaust" (*Collected Poems*, 461). In fact, the very binarism of light/dark or civilization/barbarism that structures phobic configurations of the non-West is debunked through a shoring of criminal evidence against the sinister north, the list of whose atrocities prompts the poet to substitute "Anno Domini" with the desacralized temporal marker "After Dachau." The South is, by contrast, radiant with "man-lit, sulphurous, sanctuary lamps" and faith (462). In this modern-day excursion, the business of empire is done through air travel, not sea voyage. The spatial diffusion and extensiveness of this empire are insidious, perceived only in the inequalities and uneven development they visit on the world, and in the hunger of millions of stateless ("shoreless"; 457) creatures:

      fires
drench them like vermin, quotas
prevent them, and they remain
compassionate fodder for the travel book. (462)

There is a crucial change in this revision in that the Marlow figure in the poem, the fortunate traveler, is probably a migrant in Europe, not a native.

"One flies first-class, one is so fortunate" (457), the narrator says sarcastically, though this seems to be lost on Helen Vendler, who doubts that Walcott titled the new book "entirely ironically" (*Derek Walcott*, ed. Bloom, 28). The self-critical tone of the poem suggests, not merely European unease over its history of empire, but the colonial's guilt of deracination and his implication in ongoing narratives of neocolonial capitalism. The insistence of an Afro-Caribbean genealogy is felt in the way the historical trajectory of the slave ship's journey is reversed as the protagonist travels from Bristol to St. Lucia. The glamor of globetrotting, for the narrator, is forever marred by the unforgettable association of global travel with human traffic and slavery: "Indeed, indeed, sirs, I have seen the world. / Spray splashes the portholes and vision blurs" (460).

The title, "The Fortunate Traveler," is adapted from Thomas Nashe's *The Unfortunate Traveller* (1594), detailing the misadventures of Jack Wilton. The choice of precursor text is interesting in the way its genesis seems to validate the latecomer poet's appropriative gesture. Nashe too was a borrower, it turns out. He had adapted the matter and genre of the Spanish picaresque novel to write an English counterpart, which was singular nevertheless in its use of tragicomedy, the humanization of its picaro, and in that Nashe's protagonist, traipsing over western Europe, was more cosmopolitan than Spanish rogue-heroes. Walcott borrows his title from a consummate mimic to write a richly intertextual poem that cites not merely Conrad and Eliot, but the immediate contexts and biographical aspects of the works, as well as the histories of their critical and cultural reception. The allusive title, as well as the profession of the narrator ("A Sussex don, / I taught the Jacobean anxieties"; 458) humorously allude to Eliot's facility with Elizabethan and Jacobean material. The opening of the poem not only evokes the anomie of the "Unreal City" articulated unforgettably by Eliot, but also the influence on it of Baudelaire's "fourmillante cité":

> I sat on a cold bench
> under some skeletal lindens.
> Two other gentlemen, black skins gone grey
> As their identical, belted overcoats,
> crossed the white river. (456)

In Baudelaire's "Les sept vieillards," which Eliot cites as a source in the notes to *The Waste Land*, the speaker sees a decrepit old man through the yellow fog on the banks of the Seine. Eliot evokes this scene in his description of a winter noon mired in brown fog, when the speaker in *The Waste Land* is approached by the Smyrna merchant. In Walcott's poem, "Rotting snow" flakes from "Europe's ceiling" and the poetic persona, an executive with a "square coffin manacled to my wrist," is part of the spectral swarm of city workers purged of individuality and racial difference ("identical, belted overcoats," "black skins gone grey") in the oblivion of common suffering (456). Unsurprisingly, though innovatively, Walcott uses *The Waste Land*, which Robert Lehman aptly calls "a poetic anamnesis of literary history" ("Eliot's Last Laugh," 74), to do the police in different voices.[11]

Similarly with Conrad, not only is *Heart of Darkness* the inspiration for Walcott's critique of "imperial fiction" (*Fortunate Traveler*, 460), he is influenced also by its reverberations in culture over time, its ubiquitous presence as intertext in successive narrations of the colonial condition. The protagonist of "Koenig of the River," aimlessly poling his canoe up river, feels "bodiless," hollowed out by the force of a foregone conclusion:

Koenig felt that he himself was being read
like the newspaper or a hundred-year-old novel. (*Collected Poems*, 381)

The Kurtz-like Koenig is (poetic) fiction imitating fiction, or fiction imitating the obscure lives in the declining empire that are no more substantial than the ghosts of empire fiction,

      like a man stumbling from
the pages of a novel, not a forest,
written a hundred years ago. (*Collected Poems*, 380)

In "The Fortunate Traveler," Walcott, Paula Burnett observes, seems to draw more heavily from a Conrad mediated by Chinua Achebe's "An Image of Africa" than the author-function of the novels, and is influenced also by the visual register of *Apocalypse Now*, Francis Ford Coppola's Hollywood adaptation of the *Heart of Darkness* (Burnett, *Derek Walcott*, 186). "The distinct references in Achebe's discussion to Albert Schweitzer, Nazism, Arthur Rimbaud, and Haiti, all of which Walcott incorporates in his poem, warrant a firm assertion of intertextual genealogy," states Burnett (186). Burnett misses the echo of Haiti, the city where the speaker of the "Fortunate Traveler" images a starving, hydrocephalic child in "a gecko pressed against the hotel glass" (*Collected Poems*, 457), from Achebe's essay. Haiti was where Joseph Conrad had had his first encounter with a black man, Achebe notes, a meeting which "fixed my conception of blind, furious, unreasoning rage" ("An Image of Africa," 9). The swarm of locusts in Achebe's *Things Fall Apart*, seen in the novel as a sign of divine retribution, returns in this poem with a biblical charge, but the poet presents the threat of vengeance with a vision of hope in the obtuse survival of insects:

still, through thin stalks,
the smoking stubble, stalks
grasshopper; third horseman,
the leather-helmed locust. (*Collected Poems*, 463)

Achebe observes in "An Image of Africa" that while the Western imperialist desire—and design—to set Africa up as a foil to Europe's spiritual grace has had many cultural manifestations, the brutalizing racism of these representations have been widely condemned since. What seems to escape censure, however, is the literary classic, such as Conrad's *Heart of Darkness*: "His contribution . . . falls into a different class—permanent literature—read and taught and constantly evaluated by serious academics" (Achebe, "Image of Africa," 2). Walcott's use of Achebe in an active rewriting of the heart-of-darkness tradition in "The Fortunate Traveler," which restores what Achebe calls the "human factor" occluded by Conrad's representations of the South ("Image of Africa," 9), is perhaps testimony to the fact that "permanent literature" remains so through critical vigilance, evaluation, and fresh contestations of its implications and ends.

The ghost of Conrad returns, with that of Joyce, in "Volcano," in *Sea Grapes* (1976), a unique example of Walcott's lifelong interest in the anxiety of influence, in that it emphasizes the definitive role of "rereading" in the filial impulse that prompts rewriting. From the start, it is made clear that the speaker does not distinguish life clearly from literary representation. As he meditates on the virtuous dead, Joyce and Conrad, sea derricks seem to glow like the ends of cigar, and, Walcott suggests, the volcano at the end of *Victory*.

If there is a colonial context in the way the poet decks the island scene with borrowed feathers, however, it remains understated. It is brought out instead in the authorial predicament the interloper (postcolonial) poet shares with the Irish writer of English and the Polish émigré.

Walcott has talked elsewhere about the expectations surrounding an emergent Caribbean voice, and the inevitable comparisons: "Reading Joyce, you have, of course. Even Stephen, Son of a pastiche. Some article I read by whatshisnamenow, in a Life and Letters yes, predicting that someday a new Ulysses will come forth out of these emerald, ethnic isles, and sure that he had put his finger on me. Imitation, imitation, when will I be me?" (*Another Life*, 164). There are many evocations of Joyce and Joycean effects in Walcott's work. In "Leaving School," Walcott reminisces about St. Mary's College in Castries and his teachers, the Irish Brothers of the Presentation, the atmosphere summoning that of his "current hero, the blasphemous, arrogant Stephen Daedalus" ("Leaving School," *Critical Perspectives*, ed. Hamner, 31). In *Omeros*, he "reverses and honours" Joyce, rewriting Stephen's theories of *Hamlet* in *Ulysses* to make the artist not a self-propagating father—the Wordsworthian idea of child as self-begotten, and the father of man—but a bereft orphan son (*Omeros*, 68). In the Dublin section of *Omeros* he pays tribute to the artist manqué figures in *Ulysses* and *Finnegans Wake*. Joyce is "our age's Omeros, undimmed Master" (*Omeros*, 200). In a brilliant dovetailing of the Joycean and Walcottesque narrative, the poet of *Omeros* enters a pub in Dublin where even a dog's bark is replete with Wakean echoes ("Howth"! "Howth"!) to find "Mr Joyce" leading the assembled singers, "Dead . . . in fringed shawls," as Maud Plunkett plies the piano (201). In "Volcano," however, the poet finds a different way of shadowing the afterlife of Joyce and Conrad, what the thunder said in Eliot, and Melville's leviathans:

One could abandon writing
for the slow-burning signals
of the great, to be, instead,
their ideal reader, to be, ruminative,
voracious, making the love of masterpieces
superior to attempting
to repeat or outdo them,
and be the greatest reader in the world. (*Selected Poems*, 104)

Ruminative, voracious reading, that is not an abdication of writing, but a necessary counterforce for acts of reading that have lost the sense of awe: "so many people can predict, / so many refuse to enter the silence" (*Selected Poems*, 104). True to the nature of other poems from *Sea Grapes*, "Volcano" marks the mixture of the acid and the sweet that, according to Walcott, characterizes the great poetry of the New World ("Muse of History"; *What the Twilight*, 41). There is a new equation reached between "obsession and responsibility" ("Sea Grapes"; *Selected Poems*, 87), and Baugh is correct to note that the poems in *Sea Grapes* show the gnarled poet "ripen towards awe, humility and gratitude" (*Derek Walcott*, 106).

Crusoe, "craftsman and castaway"

If questions of cultural and political decolonization are indistinguishable in Walcott's imagining of a postcolonial Caribbean, a crucial figure in this agonistic struggle against European cultural domination and toward cultural autonomy is Daniel Defoe's archetypal castaway, Robinson Crusoe. "One might . . . expect a Caribbean reworking of Defoe's archetypal imperialist to adopt an adversarial response, but predictably perhaps Walcott's Crusoe proves to be far more complex," observes John Thieme (*Derek Walcott*, 78). Crusoe, for Walcott, is the "stripped man" driven back to his mind and that "shipwreck of fragments, these echoes, these shards of a huge tribal vocabulary, these partially remembered customs" (*What the Twilight*, 70). He is, as Terada points out, the Caribbean postcolonial intellectual, between worlds, stranded on an island and in his intellectual solitude, arduously reconfiguring the fragments of a tribal past in novel gestures of ordering a Caribbean first book (*Derek Walcott's Poetry*, 155).[12] He is "Craftsman and castaway" (*What the Twilight*, 69), wracked by loneliness and defeated by a "racking sun" (71), and impotently looking on his slave Friday's progeny, "Black little girls in pink / Organdy, crinolines" walking "in their air of glory / Beside a breaking wave" ("Crusoe's Journal"; *Collected Poems*, 72). In the "Figure of Crusoe," Walcott likens him to Adam, Proteus, Columbus, God, Ben Gunn the pirate, Prospero, a missionary who educates Friday, a sea traveller from Conrad, Stevenson, and Marryat ("Figure of Crusoe," 35–36). Crusoe is a naturalist and a beachcomber, head full of fantasies of innocence, and trying heroically to capture through figurative language "a green world . . . without metaphors" ("Crusoe's Journal"; *Collected Poems*, 93). Crusoe is also his author, Daniel Defoe: "He is also Daniel Defoe, because the journal of Crusoe, which is Defoe's journal, is written in prose, not in poetry, and our literature, the pioneers of our public literature have expressed themselves in prose in this new world" ("The Figure of Crusoe," 36). Crusoe and Daniel Defoe coalesce in the figure of the West Indian writer, shaping, with the bare necessities of language and in a profane style, a saga of shipwreck and salvaging. This Crusoe-Defoe is not Prospero, "lord of magic," for he "does not possess the island that he inhabits" ("The Figure of Crusoe," 37). He acts out of conscience, not the ruler's sense of entitlement, and pragmatic good sense:

> like Christofer he bears
> in speech mnemonic as a missionary's
>   the Word to savages,
> its shape an earthen, water-bearing vessel's
>   whose sprinkling alters us
> into good Fridays who recite His praise,
>   parroting our master's
> style and voice, we make his language ours,
>   converted cannibals
> we learn with him to eat the flesh of Christ. ("Crusoe's Journal," *Collected Poems*, 93)

The subject of the poem slides effortlessly from Crusoe to Friday. The Columbus-like Crusoe delivers the Word to his colonial charges. The cannibal Fridays imbibe the power of sublimation from much used and abused missionary texts to learn with him "to eat the flesh of Christ." Parroting the master's style, the slave accidentally makes New World language.

Pantomime, Walcott's 1978 play, which he describes in an interview with Edward Hirsch as "a farce that might instruct" (*Critical Perspectives*, ed. Hamner, 74), also builds on the themes of misrule and role reversal in relation to the master-slave dialectic. The plot develops from the hotel owner and Englishman Harry Trewe's idea of staging a Robinson Crusoe pantomime with his waiter Jackson Phillip to entertain guests during the tourist season. Jackson is a retired Calypsonian, and Harry, a failed music hall player himself, tries to enlist his services for a staging of the Defoe novel where he will play the autochthon, Friday, and Jackson a "black" Crusoe, in a "picong" or mash-up of two disparate cultural traditions. The ensuing drama, however, is intense, unpredictable, more tragicomic than farce, and menacing in the way it entertains real and imagined threats of violence. Despite his initial reservations, Jackson is drawn into the act, and is soon playacting and acting out with gusto the contradictions and conflicting ideologies of his real-life and pantomime parts. He rewrites the Defoe classic by introducing the problematic of class between the Crusoes of the world and their Man Fridays.

Jackson: For three hundred years I served you. Three hundred years I served you breakfast in . . . in my white jacket on a white veranda, boss, bwana, effendi, bacra, sahib . . . that was my pantomime. Every movement you made, your shadow copied . . .
(*Stops giggling*)
. . . and you smiled at me as a child does smile at his shadow's helpless obedience, boss, bwana, effendi, bacra, sahib, Mr. Crusoe. (*Remembrance and Pantomime*, 112)

Harry, increasingly uneasy at the historical echoes and political implications of what he devised as a light entertainment, tries to stop Jackson:

We're trying to so something light, just a little pantomime, a little satire, a little Picong. But if you take this thing seriously, we might commit Art, which is a kind of crime in this society. . . . I mean there'd be a lot of things there that people . . . well, it would make them think too much, and well, we don't want that . . . we just want a little . . . entertainment. (*Remembrance and Pantomime*, 124).

But Jackson, true to his allegiance to Calypso, an art form that emerged largely due to the sanctions on African expressionism, finds his voice and comes into being in the face of this ban.

While Harry's reasons for putting on the jape—boredom, insomnia, "the terror of emptiness" in an empty boarding house on a still tropical afternoon (135), or his anticipation of "the humor and impact" (110) of an unusual black and white collaboration—are less than convincing, Jackson's anxiousness about performing with his white employer (and the unmanageable nature of performativity) are given sensitive and nuanced representation. In the beginning of the play we find Jackson peevishly complaining about the racist implications of the hotel parrot's "Heinegger, Heinegger."

I know your explanation: that a old German called Herr Heinegger used to own this place, and that when that maquereau of a macaw keep cracking: "Heinegger, Heinegger," he remembering the Nazi and not heckling me, but it playing a little havoc with me nerves. . . . Language is ideas, Mr. Trewe. And I think that this precolonial parrot have the wrong idea. (99)

Harry Trewe's imperviousness to this perceived injury is one of many ways in which Jackson is made to feel invisible, insignificant, a cipher in a colonial exchange: when Jackson objects to Harry's cavalier state of undress in his presence, for instance, Harry unthinkingly says, "There's nobody here" (103). Inexorably drawn into the Harry's plot for the pantomime, Jackson injects a mischievous, deconstructive mimicry, more menace than resemblance, which replicates authoritative discourse, especially its representation of the savage races, and imitates also the native's futile gesturing toward cultural origins and self-invention. He exasperates Harry with muddled English words ("You mispronounce words on purpose, don't you, Jackson?"; 138) and by inventing a nonsensical 'African' language ("Kamalongo kaba!"; 114) designed to destabilize European terminology. He also petulantly renames Defoe's Friday "Thursday." Jackson revels in activating stereotypes about the black man's derivative symbolic and cultural apparatus and his propensity to violence and cannibalism. Throwing the dead "racist" parrot across the room, he teases Harry with "One parrot, to go! Or you eating it here?" (155). Noting the sinister resonance of this scene with those in *The Seagull* and *Miss Julie*, Harry says, predictably, "You people create nothing. You imitate everything" (156).

If the two men's radical incommunicability and mutual distrust come to a head in the course of the Robinson Crusoe "game" (106, 118), it is because neither can suspend his Manichean worldview even in the make-believe scenario. When Jackson suggests a revisionist reading of Crusoe's shipwreck involving a big white bird and the black explorer, played by him, Harry comically insists on keeping intact the color correspondence of the code switchings:

Harry: Okay, if you're a black explorer . . . Wait a minute . . . wait a minute. If you're really a white explorer but you're black, shouldn't I play a black sea bird because I'm white?
Jackson: Are you . . . going to extend . . . the limits of prejudice to include . . . the flora and fauna of this island? (122)

As Baugh points out, much of the fun of *Pantomime* "derives from the parody of classics of the 'great tradition of English literature—not only Robinson Crusoe, but also Coleridge's 'Rime of the Ancient Mariner'" (*Derek Walcott*, 134). If Harry is irritated by Jackson's pronunciation of "mariner" as "marina," his own absurd attempts at depicting a "racially other" sea-bird offend Jackson by undermining the latter's alternative interpretation of Crusoe's landing.

Harry: Kekkk, kekkk, kekkk, kekkk!
(*Stops*)
What's wrong?
Jackson: What's wrong? Mr. Trewe, that is not a sea gull . . . that is some kind of . . . well, I don't know what it is . . . some kind of *jumbie* bird or something.

The collaboration reaches an impasse, and Harry "fires" the resentful Jackson from the act-in-progress, a move that decisively changes the power balance of the play from "one of them 'playing man-to-man talks'" (139) to both characters angrily accosting each other. Jackson refuses to let Harry dismiss the theatrical:

You see, it's your people who introduced us to this culture: Shakespeare, *Robinson Crusoe*, the classics and so on, and when we start getting as good as them, you can't leave halfway. (124)

This, perhaps, is yet another variation on Caliban's "You taught me language" (*The Tempest*, 1.2.363–64), only Jackson is not simply acknowledging a debt of vocabulary but citing the colonial legacy of a predominantly European cultural education that the Caribbean artist has opportunistically used and subverted in order to survive.

It is perhaps this idea of subversive imitation that makes Harry set up an imaginary opposition between classical and Creole acting. What passes for Harry's "classic acting" is an inflated style and turgid, melodramatic prose: "O silent sea, O wondrous sunset that I have gazed on ten thousand times, who will rescue me from this complete desolation" (142). Creole acting, on the other hand, is marked by pragmatic, down-to-earth observations and a plain style. "He is not sitting on his shipwrecked arse bawling out . . . 'O silent sea, O wondrous sunset,' and all that shit," Jackson exclaims. "No. He shipwrecked. He hungry" (148). Where "classical" acting subsumes local detail in universalized abstractions, the Creole perspective throws into doubt the existential posturing of the European castaway by pointing out: "*There are goats* all around him" (146). Walcott sends up Harry's comic attempts to arrogate the cultural authority of the classic to his music hall antics, emphasizing the persistence of the old colonial habit of evoking a classic standard that serves as the arbiter and measure of relative art forms. The play also makes ironic comment on the affinity between "Creole acting" and the representational strategies of the classic in question. *Robinson Crusoe*, despite its allegorical aim of commuting the physical world into a typology, adopts realism, a method that captures in elaborate and well-realized detail both the receptivity of its protagonist to the natural phenomena that surround him, goats included, and the adaptational efforts that follow. *Pantomime* ends with an uneasy reconciliation between the men, along the lines of what Henry Louis Gates, following the work of William Labov, identifies as "separate development" (*Signifying Monkey*, xix). Discrediting the ludic role reversal between Crusoe and his Friday, as playfully suggested by Harry Trewe, as a viable solution for the inequalities of power between master and slave, and discrediting also the role of *Robinson Crusoe* as a formal antecedent for economic and artistic self-sufficiency in the colony, the Trinidadian opts for more transparent business relations ("Starting from Friday, Robinson, we could talk 'bout a raise?"; 170), even when the business in question is entertainment. He turns also to the black tradition of Caiso, a folk art that refuses to attune itself to culturally hegemonic forms.

Creole, Insect, Animal

Jackson's return to Calypso at the end of *Pantomime* provides a great starting point for a discussion of Walcott's shifting strategies of using Creole. In "What the Twilight Says," Walcott had argued that "what is needed is not new names for old things, or old names for old things, but the faith of using old names anew" (*What the Twilight*, 9). Accordingly, in "The Spoiler's Return," the old names of Juvenal and Rabelais, Rochester, Quevedo, Juvenal, Maestro, Martial, Pope, Dryden, Swift, and Lord Byron, classics of literature Walcott had studied at university, are written in (reconstituted) heroic couplets and enunciated in Calypso rhythm and Creole accent. The transfigured names, the poet says, "salted my songs, and gave me their high sign" (*Collected Poems*, 438). Spoiler is a literary parasite who calls on the "Old Brigade of Satire" to endorse his gift of mockery (*Collected Poems*, 433): Dryden, Swift, and Lord Byron, but also the "Old Brigade" of calypsonians, and Old Masters such as Attila, Executor, Lion, and Tiger (Baugh, *Derek Walcott*, 163). The "Spoiler 'chorus' brings together the European and Caribbean, the scribal and the oral, and what Brathwaite called "the 'great' and 'little' traditions" that Creole societies try to mediate (*Development*, 309). It is as if Walcott is creating an impossible and audacious "creole continuum" between Standard English and Caribbean vernaculars, and also between the European literary canon and an emergent Caribbean one.[13] The poem is polyvocal and choric, polymorphous in its enjoyment, and draws on the richly intertextual tradition of libertine satire, as exemplified in Rochester's "Satyr," with its echoes of Boileau, Hobbes, Montaigne, and Horace. As Terada observes, "Walcott's impulse to allude coincides happily in Spoiler's polyglossia with satire's *need* to allude." Terada draws attention to Walcott's use of "a language of mimicry for a mode of mimicry": "the constant awareness in creole that one is in effect alluding to other languages and ringing changes upon them suits creole to satire" (*Derek Walcott's Poetry*, 109).

Wai Chee Dimock makes a larger claim in *Through Other Continents*, where she equates creolization to an inherent centrifugal force in literature itself, which makes it multiply its "lines of filiation," overcoming time and distance. Literature, Dimock claims, "is a creole tongue not only in the commingling of languages, but equally in the commingling of expressive media" (159). While this argument seems particularly relevant for a multicultural literature such as English, it does not explain whether the recombining and absorptive powers of a lingua franca result in a secondary process of creolization that leaves in the peripheries its autochthonous other. Walcott's metropolitan creolizing validates and legitimates Creole as medium appropriate for high (English and comparative) literature. What is less clear in poems such as "The Spoiler's Return" is whether he sees Creole as having grammatical possibilities beyond serving as nonstandard English in the contact zone.

But who is the title character of "The Spoiler's Return"? Theophilus Phillip, a renowned Calypsonian of Trinidad and Tobago, who flourished in the 1940s and 1950s, and was known as the "Mighty Spoiler." In the poem he has returned to Laventille from hell and sends up Port of Spain in coruscating satire. The Spoiler's "voice" channels John Wilmot, Earl of Rochester, through the Calypso of "The Bedbug."

Were I, who to my cost already am
One of those strange, prodigious creatures, Man,
A spirit free, to choose for my own share,
What case of flesh and blood I wished to wear,
I hope when I die, after burial,
To come back as an insect or animal. (*Collected Poems*, 433)

The first four lines are Rochester's, taken from "A Satyr Against Reason and Mankind," while the last two lines of this quote are from Spoiler's "Bedbug," winner of the National Calypso Crown of 1953. The first stanza in Rochester's satire runs as follows:

Were I (who to my cost already am
One of those strange, prodigious creatures, man)
A spirit free to choose, for my own share
What case of flesh and blood I pleased to wear,
I'd be a dog, a monkey, or a bear
Or anything but that vain animal,
Who is so proud of being rational.

To the first four lines Walcott grafts the original words of the calypso sung by Theophilus Philip, his claim that he has heard "when you die, after burial / you have to come back as some insect or animal" (Baugh, *Derek Walcott*, 163). Following the Calypso Spoiler, Walcott's persona chooses to come back as a bed bug to bite "big fat women" (*Collected Poems*, 433), the corpulent flesh of the morally corrupt. The "Spoiler chorus" involves not only Rochester and the Mighty Spoiler but Donne (who is seemingly confused with Rochester as having praised "the nimble flea"), and also Dryden and Pope, whose mock-heroic coronations in *MacFlecknow* and the *Dunciad*, John Thieme notes, are evoked in the crowning of "King Bed Bug the First" or "Lord" Rochester (21). Mock coronations of carnival queens and kings, however, are also indigenous Trinidadian practices, so the relation between classical or neoclassical satirical tropes and their Caribbean counterparts is not easily reduced to questions of colonial mimicry. The conceptual similarity between the two kinds of satire is posed instead as a historical coincidence that speaks to epistemological continuities in nonadjacent literatures. It is evident that the political unconscious of satire is characterized by the "commingling of expressive media," which, according to Dimock, makes literature itself a "creole tongue." Take for example the familiar engraving on the cover of Pope's *Dunciad*, of the ass bearing the work of the dunces, the lumber that bestows on it not learning but unmistakable dullness. The image is thick with learned allusion, from Aristophanes' *Frogs* to the smarting wisdom of Latin proverbs. The thistle-chewing ass occurs in Swift's *A Tale of a Tub* as well as Dryden's *The Medall*. "The Spoiler's Return" does not reference the self-important ass as such, but its venal imagery of crabs, sharks, goats, vermin, lice, not to mention the evocation of the arses of "big fat women" or the metaphorical "Fame behind," taps into not just the iconography but the sensorium of Augustan satire, making comic and gothic its unforgiving rendition of modernity, rationality, and their vicissitudes. It is, however, made evident that the likeness accretes meaning and cross-references in the "European" mind of the poet, trained to reduce the world to its synthetic imagination: there is no suggestion in the poem that the Mighty Spoiler had any truck with his neoclassical proponents of satire. A similar kind of accidental affiliation can be seen at the level of prosody, where the Calypso meter seems to approximate the condition of the heroic couplet. Walcott's Spoiler writes in iambic pentameter or the Caribbean four-stress line, which can be heard as iambic pentameter—again, it is only in the economy of the poem that Calypso's similarity with the mock-heroic tradition is fleetingly entertained.

Walcott's Creole poetry is a vital part of his own multinational identity politics. It uses definitive local situations to revisit the experimental temporal forms of modernism: the uncanny simultaneity of tradition, the subversion of the chronotope of what Bakhtin calls national historical time, and the valorization of non-standard sequence over that of official history. Besides claiming a transnational and transhistorical vantage point, it shapes his authorial self-presentation as metaphysically marginal, and the idea of the world or world literature as "one / island in the archipelagoes of stars" (*Collected Poems*, 360–61). Emily Apter, describing Maryse Condé's relationship to the British novel vis-à-vis a Caribbean gothic, states that her engagement with classics is not simply a ruse to gain literary pedigree; nor is it unduly influenced by postmodernist code switching, reversal of high and low characters, and a studied undermining of the authorial subject.

Condé's fiction downplays the ethics of reversal in favour of a preoccupation with the transmission of literary voice. . . . It is as if Cathy's famous line in *Wuthering Heights*, "I *am* Heathcliff," typically read as testimony to the breakdown of the autonomy of the sovereign subject, or as an instance of pathological overidentification, could be translated as Condé saying "I *am* Brontë." ("Global *Translatio*," 183)

This interpretation is particularly apt for Walcott's comic portrayal of a writing hell at the end of "The Spoiler's Return," where he rubs shoulders with "cadaverous Dante" and "big-guts Rabelais," literary reputations "wide as oceans when compared with mine" (*Collected Poems*, 438). Mollifying the coarse patois with technical versification and lofty themes, Walcott seems to insist that return though he might to a local context, he is no "bland as a green coconut" local writer (435).

I conclude this chapter with a reading of Walcott's poem on Jean Rhys, a fellow Caribbean grappling with the burden of a bifurcated history and opposing modes of figuration. In "Jean Rhys," the portrait of the Caribbean artist as a child is imagined in "faint photographs / mottled with chemicals" (*Collected Poems*, 427). The act of literature proves to be an event that forces the question of the disparity of figure (Rhys) and ground (Dominica): Rhys's poetics of white Creole anomie is like a "white hush between two sentences," crystallizing, processual, refusing to cross over to a zone of cultural equivalency, refusing full translation into either metropolitan or regional language.

And the sigh of that child
is white as an orchid
on a crusted log
in the bush of Dominica,
a V of Chinese white
meant for the beat of a seagull
over a sepia souvenir of Cornwall,
as the white hush between two sentences. (428)

Walcott describes a Caribbean scene of fierce beauty that can also be a "furnace of boredom" for the restless, excursive mind of a world traveler: the poem captures the lost moment of movement when random details of lived experience give rise to, and are monumentalized in, narrative.

the cement grindstone of the afternoon
turns slowly, sharpening her senses,
the bay below is green as calalu, stewing Sargasso. (428)

At the poem's end, "Jean Rhys" appears with

her right hand married to *Jane Eyre*,
foreseeing that her own white wedding dress
will be white paper. (429)

This surrender to the vocation of writing is staged in the context of the unlived-out life of petit-point representations of unseen London scenes, embroidered on hammock cushions by aunts doomed "to fall / into the brown oblivion of an album" (429), visual representations eventually destroyed by the relentless Caribbean sun. Dreams of metropolitan arrival, too, are eventually defeated by its reality, as recorded in Rhys's stories of misrecognition and betrayal, and the shattering isolation, alienation, and cultural disenfranchisement of the Creole migrant in London. Perhaps the young artist selects a more memorable form of death in choosing affiliation to the Western canon. This is comparable to a moment in "What the Twilight Says," when the Caribbean artist feels "a fear of that darkness which had swallowed up all fathers" in the "dialect-loud dusk" of voluble, ambient, and demotic poetry (*What the Twilight*, 28); "madly in love with English," he chooses at that moment to prolong "the mighty line of Marlowe and Milton" (*What the Twilight*, 10).[14] As described in "Ruins of a Great House," the icons of the Great House of English literature, decaying in the Caribbean climate like other relics of a brutal plantocracy, are "perplexed / In memory," as both "Ancestral murderers and poets": "My eyes burned from the ashen prose of Donne" (*Selected Poems*, 7).

PART 2

REPETITION, INVENTION

4

"Pip was my story"
Rereading, Counterreading, and Nonreading

"It was as if a Briton, of the time of Severus, had suddenly written a poem in good Latin," read the 1829 *Oriental Herald Review* appraisal of the 1827 and 1829 volumes of Henry Derozio's poetry (*Derozio*, ed. Chaudhuri, 415). This was high praise indeed by a reviewer (possibly J. S. Buckingham, the editor of the *Oriental Herald*) who had earlier puzzled over the viability of Indian writing in English: The very language ... can hardly be called English" (415). The poet in question was Henry Louis Vivian Derozio, a Calcutta "Eurasian" of Portuguese and Indian ancestry, and a pioneer Indian English writer. Derozio's poems imagined and apostrophized a unified India from the limited scope of the plains of "Bhaugulpore" or the rock of "Jungheera" and gave tremulous form to its nascent nationalist imagination. These elegiac poems of India situate Derozio as a belated arrival to the once glorious but now subjugated country. In "Harp of India" (March 1827), for instance, he writes:

Thy music once was sweet—who hears it now?
Why doth the breeze sigh over thee in vain?
Silence hath bound thee with her fatal chain;
Neglected, mute, and desolate art thou,
Like ruined monument on desert plain! (439)

Derozio's "postcoloniality" inheres not in dates but in the postimperial tone of the unmistakably nationalist poetry. And his enthusiastic appropriation of the English literary canon to write of the emancipation of India foreshadows the predicament of the postcolonial writer, whose conscious or unconscious affiliation and allusiveness to the Western literary tradition is an inheritance that is often as unwanted as it is labored for. "The brilliant hues of the Byronic sunset flung their glow over Derozio's sky," said E. W. Madge in his famous 1904 lecture on Derozio at the YMCA Hall in Chowringhee, Calcutta. "His style has been termed the echo of Byron, Moore and L. E. Landon" (Madge, *Henry Derozio*, 23). Lines from *The Fakir of Jungheera* attest that Scott heavily influenced Derozio, as did the radicalism of Shelley. Commentators recommended reading of a more severe nature, Elizabethan and Augustan texts instead of Byron's poetic romances, Moore's "Lallah Rookh" and Saunders's "Troubadour," or Letitia Landon's "extatic damsels, whose only occupation is to kiss—and die."[1] "How much better for him, had his attention been directed to the volumes of Shakespeare and Milton," the *Oriental Magazine* speculated. "Their delineation of human character and the passion of the one, and the sober and classic Muse of the other would have constrained him to reflect [before he] sat down to write his thoughts."[2] The critique was specifically targeted at Derozio's luxuriating in the works of his immediate predecessors in England, which precluded a humbler, more studied imitation of classics. The figure who has since been reclaimed in twentieth-century postcolonial criticism as an iconoclast, revolutionary, and possibly the first Indian nationalist poet, was widely perceived in his time as a creative reader but a derivative colonial writer, whose borrowings, according to the *Oriental Magazine* were "like diamonds that sparkle on the person of an Indian king, which instead of lighting up the beauty of the countenance by their lustre, dazzle the eyes and destroy the effect of the natural appearance" (*Derozio*, ed. Chaudhuri, 39).[3]

Harold Bloom defines canonicity as a "strangeness, a mode of originality that either cannot be assimilated, or that so assimilates us that we cease to see it as strange" (*Western Canon*, 3). Both definitions are relevant for Derozio's youthful imbibing of the canon without registering its strangeness, as it were, and for the strangeness and recalcitrance of the canon that made for failed interpellations. The young poet did not see his relationship to English classics as one of unqualified adoration or imitation. He was no apologist of the empire, and had, in fact, worried in print about the practicability of colonization. As the *India Gazette* of October 30,

1828, proclaimed, he had "some title to be considered as a national poet"—Derozio was, after all, "a son of the soil, born, bred, and entirely educated in India," unlike other expatriates and "Eurasians" who wrote "in a state of modified exile, yearning after other climes and modes of life" (*Derozio*, ed. Chaudhuri, 399). Derozio's canonical extrapolations were primarily in the service of an emergent corpus of Indian writing in English and constitute an important milestone in the history of the usage of English as a global vernacular for social and political mobilization and contestations of modernity in the colony. Derozio's "The Harp of India," written in the style of Moore's "The Harp of Erin," is not simply clever imitation but marks the canny deployment of a serviceable form and style to give expression to a subjugated collective imagination attempting national self-definition in Derozio's time:

—but if thy notes divine
May be by mortal wakened once again,
Harp of my country, let me strike the strain! (*Derozio*, ed. Chaudhuri, 439)

The Cuban writer Roberto Fernández Retamar calls Caliban the symbol of "our *mestizo* [hybrid] America," adding, "I am aware that it is not entirely ours, that it is also an alien elaboration, although in our case based on our concrete realities" ("Caliban," 27). Do postcolonial rewritings help revive and sustain the Western canon of literature in alien elaborations? Does postcolonial studies' emphasis on the literary consequently run the risk of settling into what Vilashini Cooppan calls "a catalogue of thematics and a canon of fiction and poetry, in which characteristic concepts of hybridity, creolization, and diaspora are not contextualized within related discourses of colonial and imperial knowledge . . . subaltern opposition, and subject formation?" ("Interconnections," 279). The present chapter examines various kinds of canon revision in postcolonial literature: reading for contrapuntal meanings of colonial texts; cultural translations and transmissions of classic works; creative and critical acts of rewriting that lead to the formation of an alternative canon for a postcolonial, global age. Canonicity itself is a changeable attribute, selective yet inclusive, the reading practices of the canon (and the politics of curriculum formation and publication that congeal around the same) kept vital through reinventions and hybridizations of the "literary." The canon can be related to what Antonio Benítez-Rojo describes as "dynamic states or regularities that repeat themselves

114 *"Pip was my story"*

globally" (*Repeating Island*, 2–3), and this chapter studies manifestations of canonicity in postcolonial literature as repetitions of dynamic states.

The afterlives of Shakespeare in the colony testify to the efficacious use of a canonical literary figure to inaugurate dissident textual systems, narrative traditions, and subcultures. I have devoted Chapter 6 to popular adaptations of Shakespeare in India, but would like to briefly reference the genealogies of Shakespeare teaching, criticism, and adaptations in erstwhile colonies, which have been instrumental in determining what Ashis Nandy identifies as the paradigms of "sanity, rationality, adulthood, and health" (Nandy, *Intimate Enemy*, 118) imposed on the colonized. Harish Trivedi notes that "the complex fate of loving Shakespeare while living in India is a classic instance of the colonial double-bind." "Can eminent English or American academics in this day and age proclaim the love for Shakespeare obtaining in their respective countries with such straight faces, or is such a strong sentiment on our part in some ways overcompensatory?" asks Trivedi bemusedly. Given the inequitable distribution of power in academic scholarship and criticism, he wonders also about the relevance of voices in the postcolony to mainstream Shakespeare studies. "Can such a difference of critical sensibility, if permitted free play, generate any new Shakespearean meanings universally worth having, or is the disjunction too great to allow of any bicultural dialogic engagement?" (*Colonial Transactions*, 39).

Trivedi documents the mixed fortunes of Shakespeare reception in colonial India: the unflagging appeal of Shakespeare translations from around 1870 to the first decades of the twentieth century, the nationalist boycotting of the likes of Smarajit Dutt ("Slavery enforced by brute force is degrading enough. . . . But slavery of the mind is truly a hundred times more deplorable") in the 1920s, and the subsequent camp warfare between translators (*Colonial Transactions*, 31). One group saw in Shakespearean heroes an emancipatory force for "the idlers of India" (31), while the other asserted the supremacy of Sanskrit literature. Following the Indian Independence in 1947, Shakespeare studies entered an apolitical phase, its popularity unabated. By 1979 Raghuvir Sahay would say of his translation of *Macbeth* that he had "sought to universalise the story without deliberately Indianizing it in any way" (33). During the 1980s and 1990s colonialism, race, and gender became key interpretive tools for studying Renaissance literature and culture in the Anglo-American academy, and Shakespeare was political again: as Francis Barker and Peter Hulme argue, if English colonialism had previously been little more than the historical backdrop for Shakespeare's *Tempest*, colonial discourse was now seen to be central to the play's thematic as well as formal concerns, constituting one of its "dominant discursive con-texts" ("Nymphs and Rapers," 198).

The rise of "postcolonial Shakespeare," ironically, coincided with the declining relevance of plays like *The Tempest* for African and Caribbean intellectuals, who had used it for articulating anticolonial resistance till the 1970s, a decline Rob Nixon jestingly attributes to the play's lack of "a sixth act which might have been enlisted for representing relations among Caliban, Ariel, and Prospero once they entered a postcolonial era" ("Caribbean," 576). In his close examination of the role of Shakespeare in South African English Studies, from its inception in the nineteenth century through the cultural and political regime changes in twentieth, David Johnson makes us aware of two realities, or two versions of Shakespeare: one relates to the colonial audience's perception of Shakespeare in the classroom as "the greatest living writer" (*Shakespeare*, 3), while the other refers to metropolitan assessments of an oppositional Shakespeare in the colonies, whereby African intellectuals are seen to reaffirm the importance of Shakespeare, "not passively or obsequiously, but through what may be described as a series of insurrectional endorsements" (Nixon, cited in Johnson, *Shakespeare*, 4). What these two Shakespeares—the conservative Shakespeare in the Athlone Teachers Training College in Paarl, and the radical Shakespeare of the Rob Nixon article—add up to, Johnson says, is a third figure, "Shakespeare." "'Shakespeare' is a body of texts produced, disseminated, contested, institutionalized, performed, and criticized over a long period of time by a wide variety of social agents" (5). In the value contestations of Shakespeare for the postcolonial present, the question that is often overlooked is the speculation with which Johnson ends his study: could we have ever chosen a different set of texts?

The phenomenon of canon revision is often subjected to the limited interpretive protocols of Ashcroft, Griffiths, and Tiffin's *The Empire Writes Back* (1989), which draws on Rushdie's "The Empire Writes Back to the Centre," itself a play on the *Star Wars* movie *The Empire Strikes Back*, to argue that the development of independent literatures in the postcolony depended upon the "abrogation" of the constraining power of colonial epistemes, and the "appropriation of language and writing for new and distinctive usages" (*Empire Writes Back*, 6). As Ashcroft, Griffiths, and Tiffin state, "Writers such as J. M. Coetzee, Wilson Harris, V. S. Naipaul, George Lamming, Patrick White, Chinua Achebe, Margaret Atwood, and Jean Rhys have all rewritten particular works from the English 'canon' with a view to restructuring European 'realities' in post-colonial terms, not simply by reversing the hierarchical order, but by interrogating the philosophical assumptions on which the order was based" (*Empire Writes Back*, 32). Provocative though the idea is of all "dominated literatures" having "an inevitable tendency towards subversion" (32), the "empire writes back" formulation is fundamentally flawed in the way it relates all contestations of modernity in the non-Western world to what is perceived as the primal trauma of colonization. Ashcroft, Griffiths, and Tiffin treat such contestations as interlinked strategies that "reveal both the configurations of domination and the imaginative and creative responses to this condition" (32). Who writes back to the center validating the postcolonial nation, and for whom? What are the exclusions and occlusions on which such a unifying narrative voice is articulated, which are often also the structural exclusions of unified and bounded nations? Is it retribution or transcendence (or both)? In an essay on Benedict Anderson's theses on the novel and the nation, Jonathan Culler wonders if a distinction can be made between the old-fashioned novel, "whose narrative voice easily encompassed characters unknown to each other and created 'in the mind of the omniscient reader' the community to which they could belong," and works such as Vargos Llosa's *El hablador*, which refutes "the possibility of inventing a voice that can include all those who might be claimed by the nation" (32). Postcolonial rewritings of canonical novels function to some extent as protest literature but their deeper cultural significance lies, not in an oppositional framing of selfhood-nationness, but in their imagining of a "community without unity," as Culler describes it, drawing on Jean-Luc Nancy's idea of "communauté désoeuvrée," *community as difference*, rather than "fusion, sublation, or transcendence" ("Anderson and the Novel," 32). This imagining of a "community without unity" applies equally to the problem of the nation (and the impossible task of forging national identity as self-same) and a diverse, international literary community that such interventions into canonicity address and actively mobilize.

In the obsolescence of a definitive imperial "center" from the second half of the twentieth century to the present, the stranglehold of "writing back" reduces postcolonial writing to dead letters, and must make way for alternative ways of reading postcolonial literary production. Postcolonial rewriting does not simply pertain to the cultural anxiety of the belated text, but is a detangling and undoing of the accreted values and what Sara Suleri calls the "unramified time" of the Western canon (*Rhetoric*, 151). In a well-known example, Edward Said initiates an inventive rewriting of Charles Dickens's *Great Expectations*, urging acts of reading that connect the 1861 *Bildungsroman* to a "much older and wider experience between England and its overseas territories" than that represented by the metropolitan history of British fiction (*Culture and Imperialism*, xv). He enjoins the reader not to treat the book "as a novel about self-delusion, about Pip's vain attempts to become a gentleman" (xiv), but examine the significance of its wider geopolitical scope—Magwitch's Australia and Pip's Orient—for a less static and more politically aware reading of the novel. And such critical intervention, Said assures us, derives less from "a kind of retrospective vindictiveness than from a fortified need for links and connections" (xxi). Only thus can the "insidious and fundamentally unjust" separation of Europeans and natives under imperialism be supplanted with a humanist renegotiation of the common history: "The task then is to describe it as pertaining to Indians *and* Britishers, Algerians *and* French, Westerners *and* Africans, Asians, Latin Americans, and Australians despite the horrors, the bloodshed, and the vengeful bitterness" (xxii).

"The postcolonial," according to Gyan Prakash, "exists as an aftermath, as an after—after being worked over by colonialism" ("Postcolonial," 8). "We are always *after*," says Gayatri Spivak—"after the empire of reason, our claims to it always short of adequate" ("Poststructuralism," 228). Bloom's theory of influence is also predicated on the idea of a time lag—a great work has symbolic preeminence because it came before—and this stealthy connection between historical precedence and novelty has haunted literary production in the erstwhile colonies. It is as if "history were like a series of children being born one after the other from past to present *ad infinitum*" (Said, *World*, 155). Said warns against the easy application of the concept of belatedness on all forms of repeating discourse: "An irreducibly serial, filiative conception of sociohistorical time such as this totally obscures the interesting problems of emergence, in which cultural phenomena are not simply ascribed priority of a miraculous birth, but are treated as a family of ideas emerging 'permanently in discourse'" (155). He advocates instead affiliative models of repetition, such as the one described by Marx in *The Eighteenth Brumaire*, where repetition is not symptomatic and immediate, but an analytic technique of belated regrouping and redisposition. Gyan Prakash, too, moves away from the idea of mimicry, however subversive, stating that postcolonial literature and literary criticism in the twentieth and twenty-first centuries occupy a space that is neither inside nor outside the history of Western domination but in a tangential relation to it. This is what Homi Bhabha calls an in-between, hybrid position of practice and negotiation, or what for Spivak constitutes the catachrestic action of "reversing, displacing, and seizing the apparatus of value-coding" ("Poststructuralism," 228).

More often than not, the Western canon is a subject of fantasy against which the postcolonial *Bildungsideal* pits its narrative mechanism. While the European metropolis often stands for the disappointment of history for hopeful arrivistes—for Jean Rhys, for example, the convoluted trajectory from the West Indies to London was a veritable "voyage in the dark"—the canon is represented time and again as a derealized body, untouched by the depredations of history, which directly or indirectly mobilizes postcolonial self-invention and renewal in the English language. Postcolonial responses to the canon often signify a historical becoming, the third person of dialogue becoming first and second person: canonicity, to quote Sara Suleri, becomes a trope through which the belated writer delineates and occasionally rewrites "the strange interaction of power and debasement that constitutes colonial history" (*Rhetoric*, 152). In a world of transnational exchanges and traffic, where national literatures have been galvanized by literary globalization, canon revision often takes the form of a rhizomatic reading and writing, which invent the canon as "extraterritorial," with "random radii linking a text to an ever more dispersed readership" (Dimock, "Literature," 178). Discrediting both territorial sovereignty and numerical chronology, and conceptualizing literature as a medium that makes non-synchronous entities collide, these rewritings are constitutive of "a global process of extension, elaboration, and randomisation . . . [that] turns literature into the collective life of the planet. Coextensive neither with the territorial regime of the nation nor with the biological regime of a single human being, this *life* derives its morphology instead from the motion of words: motion effected when borders are crossed, when a new frame of reference is mixed with an old, when foreign languages turn a native tongue into a hybrid" ("Literature," 178).

The twentieth- and twenty-first centuries offer a wide variety of writing in the reactive mode—Creole, Caribbean, African, Australian, South Asian, North American, Scottish, and Irish—that have been inspired, influenced, or negatively determined by questions of canonicity and cultural transmission. Rewritings of the canon occupy a wide spectrum, ranging from literary works with strong or muted echoes of European texts to radical reappraisals of European literary genres or movements. European cultural forms such as the travelogue, the *Bildungsroman*, the detective story, the Gothic and the Romantic, the epistolary novel, tragedy and melodrama, the Shakespearean sonnet or the Cubist poem, have undergone postcolonial translations in the works of Rhys, Achebe, Salih, Naipaul, Seth, Suleri, Ghosh, Rushdie, Walcott, Atwood, and Coetzee, and this chapter will look at selected examples of a wide variety of counterhegemonic appropriations of the canon. The chapter takes into consideration another key feature of postcolonial revisionism: the postcolonial critic's "worldly self-situating" and responses to the canon which take the form of setting literary texts "in the world" (Said, *World*, 8). The task of recuperating and reinstalling Austen in our world—or Joyce and Conrad, for that matter—Rajeswari Sunder Rajan argues, "is not one critical 'approach' among others, propagated by postcolonial critics, but an inescapable historical imperative of our times" (*Postcolonial Jane Austen*, ed. Park and Rajan, 3). It is an engagement that is attentive to all forms of relations of domination and that identifies their complicities with the present. Moreover, postcolonial literary criticism has increasingly undermined the model of mimicry that any act of rewriting evokes, and which locates the other as a fixed phenomenological point, opposed to the self. Homi Bhabha's articulation of "the Third Space of enunciation" (*Location*, 37) makes the structure of meaning and reference in colonial and postcolonial discourse an ambivalent and self-contradictory process. Bhabha finds in the disruptive temporalities of enunciation the unstable site where the borders between subjects and objects or practices are continually rearranged: "The meaning and symbols of culture have no primordial unity or fixity . . . the same signs can be appropriated, translated, rehistoricized, and read anew" (*Location*, 37). In the foreword to Franz Fanon's *Black Skin, White Masks*, he turns Fanon's idea of the hysterical ambivalence—black skin, white masks—of colonial pathology into an altogether philosophical meditation on the idea of self as its alienated image, not self and other, but the alienated and othered self psychically integrated to constitute colonial identity. One of the key recuperative tasks of the postcolonial critic is that of interpreting the ambivalent space and disjunctive present of cultural statements, and this critical ethic frames and supplements the literary examples I have discussed in this chapter.[4]

Comparativism and Contrapuntality

In her essay "In the Neocolony: Destiny, Destination, and the Traffic in Meaning," Mary Louise Pratt writes of a young Colombian *guerrillera*, who in April 1999 had escaped to the jungle with one of the captured soldiers she had been assigned to guard. For five days the fugitives traveled through the forest to an army post where she laid down her arms. She justified her betrayal thus: "*Me gusto su piel Blanca* [I liked his white skin]" (459). She had not, she claimed, joined the guerrillas voluntarily—her mother had sold her to the cause when she was ten years old. The story, Pratt reports, appeared in a Mexican newspaper with the headline "New Romeo and Juliet." The Shakespearean image, Pratt writes, is noteworthy, because "the much more obvious parallel lay in Mexico's own mythology, in the story of La Malinche. Shakespeare, and his current Hollywood revival, however, trumped the hemispheric imaginary" ("In the Neocolony," 459). The last colonies have become independent and globalization is widely seen as supplanting the vestiges of European imperialism, but, as Pratt points out, "white skins continue to seduce, brown-skinned daughters continue to be sold, and imperial myths continue to generate meanings, desires, and actions" (460). The incomplete decolonization of the mind would seem to justify the persistence of the postcolonial as a historical marker of our times. "Is 'postcoloniality' a state which has been achieved, or one to which we aspire?" speculates Pratt. Her argument is that the term *postcolonial* is perhaps most useful as a way of historically situating and interrogating one's coloniality. The prefix *post-*implies change and discontinuity, the assumption of a critical distance, which facilitates a belated understanding of the workings of empire. Pratt suggests that the pre-positional *post-* be used to call forth "not a subject paralyzed between nostalgia and cynicism in a Fukuyaman 'end of history,' but a subject newly capacitated to read the present in light of a broadened, more discerning, reading of the past. This subject is oriented not toward a future frozen in a post-progress eternity but toward a renewed anti-imperial, decolonizing practice" (460). The postcolonial critic faces the complex intellectual challenge of apprehending imperial dynamics in their continuing transformations. As Mary Pratt cautions, if one seeks simply to establish the continuity across time of a "colonial legacy" one will fail to explain the processes by which this legacy has been and continues to be invigorated and reintegrated into a changing world through continuing permutations of its signs, practices, and traditions. The phenomenon of postcolonial rewriting reflects the decolonization of postcolonial literature itself, the move from the phase of "nauseating mimicry," as Fanon termed it, to one in which former colonies defined their own literatures and cultures aggressively from within (*Wretched*, 48). Peter Childs's edited volume *Post-Colonial Theory and English Literature* brings together the best-known examples of such revisionism. These include reworkings of *Tempest* by Lamming, Césaire, and Mannoni in the late 1950s to the early 1970s for black political and cultural ends; fictional and critical reappraisals of the history, geography, and mythology of *Robinson Crusoe*; and postcolonial assessments of class, gender, and race in *Jane Eyre*. The collection examines reworkings of the "darkness" of Conrad's *Heart of Darkness*, the phobic and racist figuration of the dark and mute heart of the colonized, in fiction and critical exegeses, and also the role of the Conrad text in shaping anticolonial responses. It also discusses belated responses to a mode of colonization embodied in Kipling's *Kim* that works not through ethnocide, deportation, and slavery but, to quote Thomas Richards, through "the mediated instrumentality of information" (*Imperial*, 23).

According to Rob Nixon, Caribbean intellectuals used Shakespearean texts to get out of what Lamming describes as "the mausoleum of [Western] historic achievement" ("Caribbean," 58). George Lamming's nonfictional *Pleasures of Exile* rewrites the history of Shakespeare's Caliban for the future, offering poignant testimony to the experience of West Indian immigrants arriving in Britain in the 1950s, their faces turned in expectation toward the anglophone Caribbean that had yet to achieve decolonization and self-determination. Lamming usurps Caliban's unforgettable cry, "You taught me language; and my profit on't / Is, I know how to curse" (1.2.363–64), to articulate the British-Caribbean writer's fear that colonized as he is by language, he is condemned to live out the slave's destiny forever. Rob Nixon sees in Lamming's extrapolation of Shakespeare, not simply an aggressive gesture of manipulating the meanings of a European text to bear on Caribbean history, but "the desire to mount an indigenous countertradition, with a reinterpreted Caliban from 1611 and the contemporary, about-to-be-liberated Antillean of 1959 flanking that tradition" ("Caribbean," 66). These rewritings also forge links between the "indigenous countertradition" and the internationalism that the writers aspire to. Rhys's *Wide Sargasso Sea*, the celebrated retelling of *Jane Eyre* from the point of view of Bertha Mason Rochester, the white Creole wife of Brontë's Rochester, foregrounds, through historic displacement, the increased visibility and audibility of the Creole returning to the metropolis in the 1950s. Similarly, the reworkings of *Heart of Darkness* in fiction by Naipaul, Harris, Emecheta, and Salih, not only reemphasize the role of racist representations of Africa in shaping Euro-Atlantic modernity's knowledge projects, but also appropriate what Brantlinger calls the "imperialist adventure romance" (*Rule*, 264) to chart thwarted metropolitan arrivals and bitter homecomings.

In Naipaul's *A Bend in the River*, which reworks Conrad's fictional journeys in *Heart of Darkness* and *Congo Diary*, the travelogue novel leads nowhere, even as African bush gives way to the metropolis of London. Salim thinks of himself as a man passing through: "But where was the good place?"(*Bend*, 110). If, in Naipaul's Africa, dawn was always receding into darkness, the London that the protagonist escapes to is also something "shrunken and mean and forbidding" (269). Salim returns to Africa simply because the idea of the "other place," "comforted only to weaken and destroy" (272).

In Tayeb Salih's *Season of Migration to the North*, Mustafa Sa'eed is the troubled figure of Kurtz, who reverses the fictional heart-of-darkness trajectory by leaving Sudan for London. In London, his sexual conquests seem to reenact the ancient Arab victory over Europeans—his violence toward a series of English women, who are seduced and driven to suicide by him, could also be interpreted as a correction of the modern European supremacy over the dark continent ("I'll liberate Africa with my—"; 122). Women become veritable Desdemonas in their "Christian sympathy" toward him, an attitude that often succumbs to the desiring production of a "primitive naked creature holding a spear in one hand and an arrow in the other hand, hunting elephants and lions in the jungle" (35–36). He fabricates and populates their Orientalist fantasy, "a den of lethal lies," eventually to act out its venal stereotyping of the Arab and African as inherently brutal and bestial. Mustafa Sa'eed is himself a lie, a revenant, and a mess of contradictory selves: Richard, Hassan, Charles, Amin, and Mustafa. After serving a prison term for murdering his English wife, Sa'eed returns to the Sudan to a sleepy village along the banks of the Nile. No one knows of his past except the narrator, a native of the village who, too, has returned to Africa with an English education, and Sa'eed finishes decanting his life story little by little only to disappear in the floodwaters of the Nile. It is as if there is "no escape, no place of safety, no safeguard" for the translated man (*Season*, 135). After his death, the narrator discovers in Sa'eed's mud house a secret room, an exact replica of the salon in his London apartment: the bookshelf, heaving with masterworks of the Western humanistic tradition, and which the narrator likens to "A graveyard. A mausoleum. An insane idea. A prison. A huge joke. A treasure chamber," contains "not a single Arabic book" (138).

It is important not to reduce the phenomenon of postcolonial rewriting of canonical texts to the "first in the West, and then elsewhere" formula of global time, as Dipesh Chakrabarty puts it (*Provincializing*, 6). Aamir Mufti suggests that such hierarchical modalities of knowledge be supplanted by a "global comparativism" that stems from the realization that "societies on either side of the imperial divide now live deeply imbricated lives that cannot be understood without reference to each other" ("Global Comparativism," 478). Mufti's avowed model is Said's notion of "contrapuntality," elaborated in his 1984 essay "Reflections on Exile" and more fully in *Culture and Imperialism* in 1993. Contrapuntality speaks to Said's vision of the robust combination of discrete traditions in the modern era, and of a "transnational, even trans-human perspective on literary performance" (*Culture and Imperialism*, 45). It is, as Mufti says, about "opening up" and "crossing over" ("Global," 477), and elicits a radical rethinking of our modes of critical and cultural reception. Tayeb Salih's masterpiece lends itself to such a reading. As critics like Saree Makdisi and Barbara Harlow have pointed out, the novel writes back not only to Conrad's *Heart of Darkness* but to Shakespeare's *Othello* and *King Lear*. It is presented in the old *hakawati* style of Arabic oral tradition, and also contains elements of the Arabic literary technique of *mu'arada*, a dialectical process involving at least two writers, the first of whom writes a poem that the other will deconstruct by writing along the same lines, but reversing the meaning.

It reenacts the Oedipal scenes and hallucinatory psychological realism of Freudian case studies. Finally, through the revived political and cultural awareness of the narrator in the final pages of the novel, Salih traces what Said calls "the voyage in" (*Orientalism*, 24), shoring up progressive, libertarian alternatives to the Orientalist way of seeing. In his interpretation of *Season of Migration to the North*, Mufti states that the migration should be read as "the emergence of an oppositional consciousness that is neither fully inside nor entirely outside metropolitan, Western culture, a critical consciousness that will undertake a radical critique of Western culture" ("Global," 482). For Mustafa Sa'eed, the "Black Englishman," this trajectory is bookended by the aphasic self-loathing of "I am no Othello: I am a lie" (*Season*, 37), and the political awakening of "I am no Othello: Othello was a lie" (*Season*, 98).

The narrator of *Season of Migration to the North* is presented explicitly as a foil to Sa'eed. Mustafa Sa'eed, born in 1898, the year that saw the collapse of the Sudanese resistance to Kitchener's army, is educated in Britain while Sudan is still under British control. The narrator's years in Britain, spent acquiring an English degree, on the other hand, takes place in the years following the independence of Sudan. Sa'eed returns to his motherland "not a local man," while the narrator strenuously asserts his allegiance to the here and now: "But I am from here, like the palm tree standing in the court of our house. It grew in our house, not in another house" (53). Despite this ideological and generational gap, the narrator finds himself as marginalized and ineffective in the cultural community as Mustafa Sa'eed seemed voluntarily to have been. He fails to claim Hosna Bint Mahmoud for himself or save her from a catastrophic marriage, leading to the murder of Wad Rayyes and Hosna's suicide. "Schooling and education have made you soft. You're crying like a woman," scoffs Mahjub at him (109). Shocked and disoriented at the turn of events, and his own failure to foresee or thwart the murderous course of action, the narrator reaches the riverbank and starts swimming to the north of the Nile. At a halfway point between the north and the south, he is fatally immobilized, but we are told that at least the ideological impasses of his previous life have given way to a newfound lucidity: "All my life I never chose of made decisions. Now I choose" (171). This choice or avowal, whatever it is, is contingent and of the instant: Salih stops short of promising that the narrator's epiphany will have a salutary or enduring effect on the double consciousness of the Westernized Arab.

Saree Makdisi sees in *Season of Migration to the North* "the counter-narrative of the same bitter history" of modern British imperialism as that narrated in *The Heart of Darkness*: "Salih's [novel] participates (in an oppositional way) in the afterlife of the same project today, by 'writing back' to the colonial power that once ruled the Sudan" ("Empire," 805). While this is undeniably true of the reactionary energies of Salih's novel, it is also obvious that its closing lines, which evoke the darkness that engulfs the narrator at the very instance of his individuation, seem to suggest that such a counter-narrative has little meaning or function in the possibility of a decolonized future for Sudan. In my reading, the most burning issue of Salih's novel is not that it reverses the heart-of-darkness trajectory by supplanting Africa with Europe, but that it marks a cultural reconciliation with and a departure from colonial history that paves the way for the European novel to reinvent itself in Africa. Sa'eed, the mimic man, had left behind the record of a "life story" that was empty barring a one-line dedication: "To those who see with one eye, talk with one tongue, and see things as either black or white, either Eastern or Western" (*Season*, 152). The vision of the novel, in other words, could not be realized for the lack of a predisposed readership. The very fact that the narrator, unlike Sa'eed, can indeed convey a life story seems to imply that there is, finally, a reader in place to complete the transmission circuit of a story neither black nor white, Eastern nor Western.

Nation, Narration, and the Repeating Novel

In *The Moor's Last Sigh*, Salman Rushdie pokes fun at Homi Bhabha's "DissemiNation," with its elaboration on "the 'double and split' time of national representation" (Nation and Narration, 295), by making the critic Zeeny Vakil labor on a study of Aurora Zogoiby's works that is verbosely titled "Imperso-Nation and Dis/Semi/Nation" (329). Elsewhere, Rushdie comments scathingly on the twinning of the narratives of the novel and nation-state:

> The progress of a story through its pages towards its goal is likened to the self-image of a nation, moving through history towards its manifest destiny. Appealing as such a parallel is, I take it, these days, with a pinch of salt. Eleven years ago, at the famous PEN congress in New York City, the world's writers discussed "The Imagination of the Writer and the Imagination of the State." . . . Striking how many ways there were to read that little "and." For many of us, it meant "versus." (*Step Across*, 65)

Postcolonial canon revision, whether it is in the form of rewritings and adaptations of great books, or critical reappraisals of European masters, tends also to be read along the axiomatic of "nation and/is narration," although the nation itself is seen in twentieth-century evaluations as a revenant, an entity that is "imagined" through overlapping synchronic and diachronic frames (Benedict Anderson), one that is performatively posited and split in enunciation (Homi Bhabha), or a ghostly remainder of the organismic theories of nation, neither fully living nor fully dead (Pheng Cheah). The "nation and narration" theme has been crucial in formulating postcolonial interpretations of texts, and has even been successfully applied to writers who are markedly "nonnational." We can consider the example of *Semicolonial Joyce*, a collection of essays edited by Derek Attridge and Marjorie Howes, which aims to situate Ireland's colonial history in Joyce's work, despite the "limited compatibility" between postcolonial studies and Joyce's writing (3). According to Attridge and Howes, Joyce's writings, in their dealings with questions of imperialism and nationalism, "evince a complex and ambivalent set of attitudes, not reducible to a simple anticolonialism but very far from expressing approval of the colonial organization and methods" (3): "Joyce's achievement," the critics argue, "cannot be understood without relating it to the Irish struggle for independence—regarded not merely as a storehouse of images, characters, and narrative possibilities, but as a bitter, complex and protracted conflict, with a history still alive in Irish political memory, a constantly changing course during Joyce's lifetime, and an unforeseeable future" (16). *Semicolonial Joyce* follows the lead of scholarship by Vincent Cheng, Enda Duffy, Emer Nolan, David Lloyd, and Colin MacCabe to revise and rewrite a history of critical reception that has neutralized Joyce's politics and relegated his works to the homogenous empty time of the classic. Enda Duffy calls *Ulysses* Joyce's definitive "guerrilla text" (*Subaltern*, 5), which has had a secret life as a postcolonial novel. While Joyce's postcoloniality remains arguable, Joyce scholars are clearly less ambivalent about his antagonism to cultural nationalism and speculate whether his "revolution of the Word" (Lloyd, *Anomalous*, 5) and deconstruction of conventional literary norms and grammar are comparable to political acts of disavowing colonial and nationalist ideologies. The "postcolonializing" of Joyce aims to counteract his mainstreaming or canonization, a process that Lloyd condemns as "a process of appropriation, abstracting works from their dialogical relation to traditions which the canon cannot accommodate" (Anomalous, 8). Postcolonial revisions of Joyce bring into play the vexed question of the nation in Joyce as they follow the trace of a writerly desire that is anticolonial yet not strictly nationalist, and that speaks to what Terry Eagleton calls the "free state" of Joyce's fiction (*Heathcliff*, 257), free from the limitations of both art and nationalism.

In the case of the postcolonial novel that is a rewriting of a preexistent, canonical novel—"literature about literature," to quote Charles Altieri ("Organic and Humanist Models," 220)—the complex dialectical process that is revisionism is often reduced to the act of wresting from European cultural matrices the legitimation for national histories or cultural migrancy. Even Rob Nixon's sophisticated reading of V. S. Naipaul perpetuates the ubiquitous "nation/narration" theme in the way he sees Naipaul co-opting opposing styles of authorship from Victorian literature—the "semiethnographic, distanced, analytic mode" and the "autobiographical, subjective, emotionally entangled mode" (*London Calling*, 15)—to produce an ethnographic account of colonial and neocolonial societies which doubles as coruscating auto-ethnography. Naipaul's rewritings of Conrad in *Guerillas* (1975) and *A Bend in the River* (1979), Rob Nixon observes, are narrations of the world's half-made societies in the "*Heart of Darkness* tradition" (*London Calling*, 124), the fractured form of each novel mirroring and sometimes elaborating the irremediable imperfections and fragmentedness of its sociocultural milieu. J. M. Coetzee's *Foe*, a rewriting of *Robinson Crusoe*, similarly, is often read as an allegorical narrative of the South African nation, albeit a "complex and multivalent" one that leads to a "nonallegorizable interpretation" (Cooppan, *Worlds Within*, 205, 206).[5] As I have argued elsewhere, Coetzee's literary reworkings "never claim to capture the social in a full and present analysis": it is a narrative mode in which the political material is sublated in the aesthetic mode and the tricky dissemination of language and the literary becomes "an isomorphism for a postcolonial condition that is processual and that never stops realising itself" ("Death of the Novel," 552). Can Coetzee's rewriting of *Robinson Crusoe*, which ends with a spectacular undoing of the historical preexistence of *Robinson Crusoe* as well as the possibility of *Foe*, be confidently claimed as a "reconfigure[d] South African national novel," on the conviction that "the island is South Africa," Susan Barton the "well-intentioned but ineffectual white liberal," and Friday its "oppressed majority" (Cooppan, *Worlds*

Within, 204)? Writing of the hauntology of Dostoevsky in Coetzee's novels, especially *The Master of Petersburg* (1994) and *Diary of a Bad Year* (2007), David Attwell finds no easily translatable or interchangeable relationship between Dostoevsky's Russia and Coetzee's own historical situation. What the Coetzee text inherits instead is a Dostoevskian "ingestion and sublimation of the madness that infects the culture" ("Coetzee's Estrangements," 240). Attwell qualifies this reading by adding that the literary-historical framing and multilayered allusiveness of the novels so defamiliarize the nation space referred to that perhaps a reexamination of social relationships can be explored *de novo*.

I bring this section to a close with a discussion of Keri Hulme's *The Bone People* (1984), a novel which flirts with the "nation and narration" theme to expose its tautological meaninglessness and reveal the sedimented idealization that obfuscates the limits of its intelligibility or applicability. When the novel won the Mobil Corporation Pegasus Award for Maori Literature (it went on to win the Booker in 1985), the New Zealand author C. K. Stead famously said that it was "a novel by a Pakeha which has won an award for a Maori" ("Keri Hulme's *The Bone People*," 104). Stead pointed out that Hulme was not brought up speaking Maori (though she is of part Maori descent), and alleged that her use of Maori culture in the novel was "willed, self-conscious, not inevitable, not entirely authentic" (104). According to Stead, Kerewin seemed more Irish than Maori, "word-obsessed, imaginative, musical, unstable, something of a mystic, full of blunder and swagger, charm and self-assertion" (106). As Margery Fee's response to Stead has demonstrated, this kind of pernicious cultural essentialism fosters a constricted sense of minority group membership. Can majority group members never speak as minority members? Is there no difference between imperialist distortions of Polynesian culture by Melville, Ballantyne, Stephenson, and Maugham, to name the prominent eighteenth-, nineteenth-, and twentieth-century cultural travelers, and the transformative visions through which Fourth World writers imagine, project, or safeguard "a living, changing culture?" (Fee, "Who Can Write?" 243).

The distinction between Maori and Pakeha (white New Zealander) cannot, of course, be fully grasped along the binaries of "European" and "native": Pakeha writers usually have faint cultural contact with Britain (or Scandinavia, for that matter), while the terms Maori and Maoritanga (or Maoridom) are themselves the products of a postcolonial consciousness, for, as Murray Martin points out, "the Maori were in fact prenational and tribal rather than national" ("Who Is the Colonist?" 490). Questions of authenticity are further unsettled by in-mixing and racial hybridization. Kerewin in *The Bone People* is first perceived as Pakeha, though she is one-eighth Maori. She feels spiritually and culturally Maori rather than European, despite her long estrangement from live Maori culture: "Now it feels like the best part of me has got lost in the way I live" (62). Again, Hulme makes a distinction between English-Pakeha and Irish-Pakeha through the plot detail of Simon's Irish provenance, and his mystic traffic with ghosts, auras, and lights on people, which evokes the nativist, primitivist turn of the Irish revivalist movement. The fourth (and final) section of the novel further muddles the distinction by showing how the Maoris are emigrants too, who, like the European arrivals, came to the island on boats; only the old Maori lived in concordance with the spirit of the islands ("Mauri"). "Maori" is more a state of mind than an ethnicity: as Tiaki tells Joe, the new Maori changed, forgot to nurture land, and fought among themselves—ceased to be Maori, in other words.

Kerewin Holmes is a painter in the grip of a powerful artist's block. A lottery windfall has helped her secure for herself a life of isolation in a Tower, a vaunted "pinnacle" that gradually closes on her as a "prison" (*Bone People*, 8). She meets Simon, a mute, blond, blue-eyed boy who has washed up on the island in a boat wreck, and his foster father, factory worker Joe. The three characters are revealed to be deeply troubled and dysfunctional in singular ways: Kerewin, intensely self-regarding (though not self-loving) and solipsistic, is estranged from her family, a lack she feels keenly if not chronically; Joe, deeply traumatized by the untimely deaths of his wife and son, struggles to care for the foundling Simon, whom he smothers and batters alternatively, his drunken rage in part the acting out of repressed pedophiliac tendencies, which he aligns with his hidden and abhorred homosexuality; and Simon, one of the world's "maimed" (17), a sexually and physically abused child wracked with terrors and given to pathologically self-destructive behavior, yet capable of redemptive gestures of unconditional love. The three come together despite themselves, and start an unconventional relationship that makes their inward-looking lives more social and companionate, but which eventually amplifies their psychic maladies to breaking point. Joe attempts suicide and Kerewin nearly dies, but both are magically healed and reconciled to their mythic pasts after a phantasmagoric journey through—or a symbolic homecoming to—the precolonial realms of Maori myth and legend. The band of three leaves the Tower to start life as in a shell-shaped house in Taiaroa, a model of apartness that is nonetheless connected and nonisolable. The boy, despite the ravages of Joe's last recorded beating, is "mainly calm and good as bread." There is even a reassurance from Joe that with the new communal structure of care for the child and mutual vigilance between his immediate guardians, there will be no more violence: "It's all over now" (538).

Is the book a reconciliation between the postcolonizing discourses of a settler colony and its post-colonialized voices, as Simon During describes it ("Postmodernism?" 373)? The novel, which evokes unease and ambivalence, not least in its matter-of-fact depiction of homophobia and pitiless child abuse, and ends with a polysemic, if also frustratingly indeterminate and vatic, symbol of the double spiral, does not seem to have any such clear-cut political message. Simon Gillayley, the little boy who inadvertently orchestrates the "commensalism" or communal living with which the novel ends, is rendered mute as well as deaf, too broken—"the quick light is dimmed, the dancer's grace is gone" (*Bone People*, 538)—to be the guarantor for a sustainable future of intergenerational or cross-cultural harmony. The novel is curiously unreflecting about its own interventionist agency, and seems ambivalent at best about the generative power of the literary as it struggles to find terms that adequately describe its hard-won imaginative unities: "maybe there aren't words for us yet?" (*Bone People*, 478). The figure of the artist—Kerewin—is portrayed as sharing the autistic spectrum of Simon, acquisitive of influence, Judeo-Christian, American, British, and Maori, but unable or unwilling to commute the esoteric vision to realist or abstract representation. "Gimme something escapist, Narnia or Gormenghast or Middle Earth, or . . . " Kerewin jokingly says to herself and perhaps of her aesthetic (*Bone People*, 16). The interior monologues of each of the three characters do not develop into dialogic patterns or circulate freely in the text: despite the emotional encounters, there is no mutual recognition between Joe, Kerewin, and Simon, and the social reconciliation of the novel's ending is achieved largely through supernatural means. The narrative drive of the novel is blocked, especially toward the end, by opaque symbols, talismans, giant teeth, and putrescent genitalia.

The Bone People is not a postcolonial rewriting of a canonical text, but an intriguingly echolalic novel that evokes Tolkien, C. S. Lewis, Melville, Woolf, Shakespeare, Joyce, and Yeats. "There is just about everything in her [Kerewin's] library," the novel tells us (32). Michiko Kakutani described it as having "the overall form of a Shakespeare comedy," with characters moving from "a state of unhappy isolation, through a period of turmoil, into a new world that holds the promise—or at least the possibility—of harmony and redemption" ("No Headline"). The remote and relatively uninhabited South Island evokes the occult magic of *The Tempest*, as also its philosophical inquiry into the meaning of civilization and barbarism, the relationship between knowledge and power, or intelligence and magic, and questions of original ownership (Caliban's "This island's mine by Sycorax my mother"; 1.2.333). Simon reminds readers of the "little changeling boy" in *Midsummer Night's Dream*, who arrives from elsewhere, and over whom a custody battle rages between Oberon and Titania. Puck says of Titania that "She, perforce, withholds the loved boy" (2.1.26), the compulsive pattern replicated in Joe's love for Simon. The novel draws also from *Robinson Crusoe*, playfully so in the scene where the fabric of Kerewin's solitude is rent by the apparition of a little scuffed sandal and footprints in the beach leading to her garden. Simon is the "European arrivant" in the New World, only this is no Robinsonade, and he "does not bring language, technology, rational discourse, or new social hierarchies as his portmanteau," as Elizabeth DeLoughrey points out ("Island Writing," 811). It is tempting to see a crude avenging impulse in the way the white boy is scapegoated for the autochthonous and colonized subject's historical despair and rage, but such a reading would travesty a visionary text that discredits cultural isolationism and unfailingly promotes imagined identifications over filial or historically predetermined ones. As even C. K. Stead says, *The Bone People* "creates a sexual union where no sex occurs, creates parental love where there are no physical parents, creates the stress and fusion of a family where there is no actual family" (104). It makes a man not 100 percent Maori the custodian of the dormant spirit of the land, and a blond, Irish child the tremulous soul of the Maori family and "marae."

Rewriting Genre

According to Leela Gandhi, postcolonial literature treats the colonial encounter as a "textual contest" and a "bibliographic battle," but as I have tried to show in this chapter, this agonistic relationship defines merely one aspect of postcolonial appropriations of European literary genres (*Postcolonial*, 141). As Spivak wittily remarks, "The invention of the telephone by a European upperclass male in no way preempts its being put to the use of an anti-imperialist revolution" (cited in Alcoff, "Problem of Speaking," 115).[6] Postcolonial efforts to rewrite European genres are not limited to the mobilizing of anticolonial resistance, and have often been deployed to formally articulate individual and collective awareness and identifications, imagined communities, and the social contract in the postcolonial state. Notes, novels, diaries, letters, and autobiographies have proliferated in Indian literature since the mid-nineteenth century, but, as Dipesh Chakrabarty observes, they are unique in the way they fail to deliver bourgeois subject formation or the buried life as readily as their European counterparts. "Our autobiographies are remarkably 'public' . . . when written by men, and they tell the story of the extended family when written by women," Chakrabarty claims of life writing published in India between 1850 and 1910 ("Postcoloniality," 25). These are not poor copies of Western models. Instead, the particularities of regional literary and cultural traditions make evident the limitations of the model (Western) autobiography, such as the blind spots of self-observation and the limits of self-knowledge; the impossibility of self-transparency or neutrality; the false opposition of private and public; the counterfeit nature of memory, psychic recall, and regroupings of self.

Imaginative literature has long been one of the most irrepressible and effective modes of decolonization and postcolonial revisionism in Africa. The historian Ade Ajayi famously privileged Kole Omotoso's historical narrative, *Just Before Dawn*, over the twelve volumes of Nigerian history commissioned by the Nigerian government. The modern African history play came to being in a cultural desert, "arrested by a cultural policy which represented European drama as the ideal," to quote Oyeniyi Okunoye ("Dramatizing," 228). This is particularly true of the settler colonialism in East Africa, where the systematic oppression of indigenous cultural production led to the rise of a radical theater, committed to "unearthing the buried history of the struggle and resistance," as Ngũgĩ described it (*Moving the Centre*, 98). In *The Trial of Dedan Kimathi*, Ngũgĩ and Mugo synthesize the Christian belief in the messiah with African songs, myths, and old notions of heroism to present the portrait of a traditional hero. A belated consciousness also shines through in the collaborator's shared mistrust of capitalism, which provides continuity between the history of slavery and the plight of the dispossessed in the postcolonial era. In Ngũgĩ and Mugo's intervention, the struggle for independence in Kenya, which culminated in the Mau Mau war, is theatricalized, and I quote Michael Etherton here, "not only as a war against colonialism and imperialism but also a class war which is by no means over" (*Development*, 167).

The *Bildungsroman* and *Künstlerroman*, showcasing, as they do, upward mobility and ambition in bourgeois society, have been widely used in postcolonial delineations of the colonial upstart or the emergent artist, the social climber, the parvenu, and mimic man. Bruce Robbins points out that "the young person's 'coming-of-age' story and the immigrant's 'coming-to-America' story . . . are also concerned, if only inadvertently, with attaining greater access to economic goods and services" ("Portrait," 411). Tsitsi Dangarembga's *Nervous Conditions*, Tayeb Salih's *Season of Migration to the North*, Jamaica Kincaid's *Lucy*, V. S. Naipaul's *The Mystic Masseur*, Doris Lessing's *In Pursuit of English*, Caryl Phillip's *The Final Passage*, Hanif Kureishi's *The Buddha of Suburbia*, Amitav Ghosh's *The Shadow Lines*, and Zadie Smith's *White Teeth*—to mention a few notable examples—are self-conscious and sometimes ironical adaptations of the Western novel of intellectual formation and socialization. An interesting variant of the *Bildungsroman* in 1980s India is the "Nationsroman," which Priya Joshi defines as "novels of the nation, including I" (*Another Country*, 260). Allan Sealy's *The Trotter-Nama*, Salman Rushdie's *Midnight's Children*, and Shashi Tharoor's *The Great Indian Novel* answer to this category, emphasizing the importance of the novel form in foregrounding questions of identity in markedly national and postnational space.

Naipaul's use of the *Künstlerroman* for *The Mimic Men* is startling in the way it insists on the nonrelation between the individual's rise and the well-being of the social whole. Disenchanted with his stint as a political leader on the island of Isabella, Ralph Singh discovers that he has no affinity with the culture and politics of the Caribbean states where his ancestors arrived as immigrant laborers. He repairs to London and the Home Counties to document the broad history of the impact of European imperialism, but writes a personal memoir instead. Like the charlatan heroes of *The Mystic Masseur* and *A House for Mr Biswas*, Ralph Singh ends up a stateless actor: "I could never feel myself as anything but spectral, disintegrating, pointless, fluid" (*Mimic Men*, 61). Naipaul's autobiographical work *The*

Enigma of Arrival confounds most of the conventions associated with mobility narrative or the portrait of an artist as young man in *Künstlerroman* mode. The book identifies itself as a novel, but asks to be read as literary autobiography. The novel's form reminds Patrick Parrinder of a predecessor text, a "fictional literary memoir, George Gissing's *The Private Papers of Henry Ryecroft*," though, as Parrinder himself points out, Gissing did not live in the settings he describes, as Naipaul does (*Nation*, 402). At times Waldenshaw has the atemporal quality of a pastoral, with Naipaul celebrating "the gift of the second life in Wiltshire, the second, happier childhood as it were" (*Enigma*, 83). At others, the grand, ruined house stands for the insurmountable legacy of empire that "explained my birth in the New World, the language I used, the vocation and ambition I had" and also, in the end, "explained my presence there in the valley, in the cottage, in the grounds of the manor" (*Enigma*, 191). *The Enigma of Arrival* is not about the colonial's bittersweet reconciliation with the England of Constable, Ruskin, Goldsmith, Gray, and Hardy. Nor does it document the "creation, maintenance, decay, and cross-fertilization of the national identity," as Parrinder seems to suggest. The benighted traveler does find himself at the quayside of arrival, as in Giorgio de Chirico's painting *The Enigma of Arrival*, but with the sinking realization that the "antique ship has gone" (*Enigma*, 99).

Accidental to the postcolonial rewriting of the canon is the invention of voice. In a paper given to the English Institute in 1979, Edward Kamau Brathwaite describes the use of unconventional English in Caribbean poetry. "You may know of the Caribbean at least from television, at least now with hurricane David coming right into it," he says teasingly, before providing a potted history of the archipelago to account for the prevalence of conquistador languages over Amerindian, African, and Asian languages ("English," 17). English is one of the imposed official languages in the Caribbean—there is also Creole English, a mixture of English and other imported languages on the islands, and "nation language," the language of slaves and laborers and servants of imperial masters. Nation language, Brathwaite states, is English in terms of its lexicon, but not in terms of its syntax, "its rhythm and timbre, its own sound explosion" (21). Nation language is different from dialect, which Brathwaite treats as a perversion or inferior version of an official language, and should be treated as a special area of development in Caribbean English that represents the African aspect of the New World heritage. It "is like a howl, or a shout, or a machine-gun, or the wind, or a wave" (21). Interestingly, Brathwaite evokes the imperial classic standard twice to describe the genesis of the anti-imperial nation language. The forerunner of nation language is Dante Alighieri, he says, who argued in *De vulgari eloquentia* (On Eloquence in the Vernacular; ca. 1304) that his own Tuscan vernacular should replace Latin as the most natural means of verbal expression. More recently, Braithwaite writes, T. S. Eliot had unwittingly inspired many a mainstream poet to move from Standard English to nation language by introducing "the notion of the speaking voice, the conversational tone" (33). It was Eliot's recorded voice, property of the British Council (Barbados), which turned the nation poets on. The "dry deadpan delivery, the 'riddims' of St. Louis," resonated with Caribbean poets listening to the dislocations of Bird, Dizzy, and Klook. This unlikely allegiance, besides shedding light on the vast and diversified range of motivations mobilizing creative adaptations of European models, complicates Eliot's status as a mainstream "English" poet. While Eliot was to become the undisputed literary arbiter in the cultural capital, it is also sadly true, Brathwaite reminds us, that "the establishment could not stand Eliot's voice" (54).

The problem of finding expedient form for new content, so crucial to the postcolonial rewriting of genre, is brought up by Coetzee in his 1980 acceptance speech for South Africa's most prestigious literary prize, the CNA award. Coetzee makes a clear distinction between provincial, national, and metropolitan literature. Can the "bodies of writing in English coming out of Africa" be deemed as "national literatures," Coetzee asks (cited in McDonald, *Literature Police*, 304).[7] With "passion, imagination, fluency, enough sense of what the world is like and what it could be like, and one or two other qualities," the writer does not lack for things to say, Coetzee observes. The problem is that "what you can say, what you can think, what you can feel" are defined and delimited by formal considerations and structures that were "not easily changed, much less invented" (cited in McDonald, 304). Literary history shows that forms do not move as easily from the periphery to the center, or from periphery to periphery, as they do from center to periphery: important modifications of literary form tend not to take place on the periphery but "where the overlay of old forms is densest and where the resistance of old form to new expression is felt most oppressively, that is to say in the cultural centres of the civilization, which I will gather under the name of the metropolis" (304). The relationship of the South African writer to the metropolis, Coetzee concludes disquietingly, "is not all that different from what it was seventy years ago" (304). What the CNA award seeks to recognize and nurture, then, is not an emergent national literature, but an accreted provincial literature that continues to draw on a cosmopolitan literary heritage. Coetzee does not imply that provincial literature is derivative minor literature, but his pitting of the provincial as a counterforce within the national, which aspires to the very material and symbolic hegemony that it proposes to dismantle, remains unconvincing. This is a most curious disavowal of the national definition and, perhaps, delimitation of the artist by one of South Africa's most international writers: by defending the idea of the "provincial writer," Coetzee seems to be "attempting to position himself on an alternative, necessarily inexact, and specifically literary map and to create space for his own metropolitan 'affiliations,'" observes Peter McDonald (306).

The colonial legacy of the tension between metropolitan form and nonmetropolitan cultural expression, or the relationship between the "new" to the "present moment of the past," is reworked in a very different way in Derek Walcott's aesthetic. "We think of tradition as history," claims Walcott in the "Muse of History" (*What the Twilight*, 54). Instead of a tradition that is deadening and deterministic, and privileges sequential time, however, Walcott proposes a tradition that is invented by imagination and synthesizes past and present. "Poetry conjugates both tenses simultaneously: the past and the present" (*What the Twilight*, 69–70). In this 1974 essay, Walcott speaks of the way the Caribbean is looked at: rootless, mongrelized, ruined, no real people but fragments and echoes. The victims' history is both the deep amnesiac blow—the loss of genealogy and cultural memory in the sea-crossings—and a remembered past of slavery and brutalization. And the history of heroes is a sordid affair, which proves equally debilitating. As Walcott states, "In the New World servitude to the Muse of History has produced a literature of recrimination and despair, a literature of revenge written by the descendants of slaves or a literature of remorse written by the descendants of masters" (37). Walcott interprets the anxiety of history that haunts the West Indian as a "shame and awe of history," which makes the rage for identity degenerate into "incoherence and nostalgia." He valorizes the effort of those "patrician writers" who hold in awe the very tradition that they break: "These writers reject the idea of history as time for its original concept as myth, the partial recall of a race. For them history is fiction, subject to the fitful muse, memory. Their philosophy, based on a contempt for historic time, is revolutionary, for what they repeat to the New World is its simultaneity with the Old" (37). For the mature writer, however, the anxiety of influence is not a matter of being enslaved to the past, but a creative condition of being "inhabited by presences" (37). Walcott's own influences, Breslin notes, are postmodern, premodern and antimodern ("Cultural Address," 324). His poetry brings into play the works and words of classic modernists such as Conrad, Crane, Eliot, Joyce, Pound, Dylan Thomas, and Yeats ("I blest myself in his voice," the speaker of *Omeros* [200] says of the spectral presence of Joyce while traveling in Ireland), alongside less canonical moderns like Césaire, Chamoiseau, Harris, Glissant, and Rhys. His work bears complex testimony to what Christopher Ricks calls the "predicaments and responsibilities of 'the poet as heir'"(*Allusion*, 9), but the legacy is carefully imagined and the past history marked as nonsynchronous or out of sync with the "here" and "now" of global modernity.[8]

Nonreading as Rereading

In a compelling analysis of Tsitsi Dangarembga's *Nervous Conditions* (1988), Joseph Slaughter argues that the novel studiously addresses the generic attributes of the *Bildungsroman*—"self-sponsorship" and "human personality development" leading to the promise of egalitarian "citizen-subjectivation"—only to show up the limitations of the classic literary form in conveying the coming-of-age story of a Shona girl in colonial Rhodesia. Dangarembga's celebrated novel begins with the shocking yet all-too-familiar disavowal of filiation characteristic of the genre: "I was not sorry when my brother died" (vii). Tambudzai is an accidental mobility hero, whose schooling is made possible only because her brother Nhamo's death creates the vacancy for a new ward for her uncle. Babamukuru, a colonial mimic man and headmaster of the Mission School, had sponsored the boy's education as a gesture of "emancipation" toward his improvident and hapless extended family, and Tambu, the next child in line, feels elated at the animistic self-fulfillment of her wildest dreams: "I, I was triumphant. Babamukuru had approved of my direction. I was vindicated!"

(57). She leaves her old life of grinding poverty and unpaid labor behind to acquire a Western education in Umtali, a trajectory that sees her finally win one of the two places in the prestigious convent school of the Sacred Heart: "Another step away from the flies, the smells, the fields and the rags; from stomachs which were seldom full, from dirt and disease, from my father's abject obeisance to Babamukuru and my mother's chronic lethargy" (186). Her story, which is tangled in the life stories of four other women, her cousin Nyasha and mother Mainini, and aunts Lucia and Maiguru, is largely one of the elaboration of Tambudzai's "finely tuned survival system" (64) that extrapolates cannily from theoretical and practical sources of information to carve out a secure and viable socioeconomic future for herself. The novel, however, ends not with triumphalism, but with the faltering articulations of an ill-repressed discontent, whose full realization cannot be diegetically contained in the present narrative and will eventually "fill another volume" (208). Tambu's story remains "unassimilable to the conventions of the idealist *Bildungsroman*," Slaughter argues, "whose democratic norms of citizenship do not match the forms of social and civil participation available either to the marginalised black majority generally or to native women specifically" (*Human Rights*, 230).

The engine room of Dangarembga's novel, which draws its title from Sartre's description of the psychic debasement of the subjugated colonial,[9] is the question of how newness enters a ravaged and enervated society, and how regime change is engineered, suffered, and occasionally baffled by the protagonists of the *Bildungsroman*. In this instance, it is an overlapping series of febrile transitions that Dangarembga describes through the growth narrative of Tambu's life: colonial and neocolonial rule to national consciousness and democracy, traditional patriarchy and colonial paternalism to the first stirrings of women's liberation, the "old ways" of a preindustrial culture giving way to what Tambu nervously calls "progress" (*Nervous Conditions*, 150).[10] Babamukuru, the scholarship boy who went to South Africa and England to return with degrees that would mitigate "the meagreness of his family's existence," is the instigator of the family's reversal of fortune, but Dangarembga slyly insinuates his mother—Tambu's grandmother—as the original agent of change for negotiating a pact with the white missionaries, who would educate her bright and hardworking son in exchange for the slave's vow to "endure and obey" (19). Tambu's dreams of advancement are inseparable from the lessons of economic self-sufficiency she has imbibed from working in her grandmother's plot of land. She readily transfers her admiration of her grandmother to Babamukuru, whom she imagines the missionaries sizing up as "a good boy, cultivatable, in the way that land is, to yield harvests that sustain the cultivator" (19), and on whose career development she models her own fantasies of authority and authorship.

There is another ubiquitous, if not always perceptible, factor affecting social change in *Nervous Conditions*: "It's the Englishness," Tambu's mother states unequivocally (207). "Englishness" provides the content and form of postcolonial disfiguration and reconfiguration in the novel. Babamukuru's formidability is related to his "having devoured English letters with a ferocious appetite" (36). Ironically, his daughter Nyasha's failed incorporation of food later in the novel is connected to the vicissitudes of that very "Englishness" that her father had eaten and digested well. Nyasha's notions of the desirability of the svelte womanly frame and subsequent rejection of food seem at first to be related to her exposure to Western cultural trends in England: it could also be interpreted as the deracinated African's disavowal of the fecund female form, primed for the marriage market back home, and used as collateral in its transactions. Reading (English) and eating are passionately conjoined once again with Nyasha, whose experiments with hunger, which turn pathological eventually, follow an incident whereby her devouring of that great English novel of "social and sexual redemption," as Kate Millett described it in *Sexual Politics* (242)—*Lady Chatterley's Lover*—is rudely interrupted, the book confiscated by her father. Nhamo's and Tambu's English education brings about a forgetting of Shona that Dangarembga describes as a cultural aphasia: to be educated, it would seem, was to render oneself particularly vulnerable to a violent erasure of will. It results in a parody of feminine passivity in Tambu, and in Nhamo's case, is superstitiously related by his mother to his spiritual and material undoing

The most insidious source of "Englishness" to mobilize the story of Tambu's *Bildung* comes from Nyasha's "various and extensive library": "I read everything from Enid Blyton to the Brontë sisters, and responded to them all. Plunging into these books I knew I was being educated and I was filled with gratitude to the authors for introducing me to places where reason and inclination were not at odds" (94). Joseph Slaughter's interpretation of *Nervous Conditions* as a "dissensual *Bildungsroman*" that challenges the emancipatory fictions of the idealist *Bildungsroman*, especially its promise of reconciling the particularities of inclination with universal Reason, is predicated on this key plot detail of Tambu and the "fairy tales." Slaughter groups under the generic term "British *bildungsromane*" (*Human Rights*, 232) the American Louisa May Alcott's *Little Women*, alongside the novels by Enid Blyton and the Brontës, the "Dilthean misreading" of which supposedly fosters in Tambu a deluded exceptionalism and faith in the colonial discourse of development, corrected eventually by a crushing historical awareness (*Human Rights*, 239). The novel, however, is largely silent on the specificities of the textual interactions between Tambu and the *Bildungsromane*: does she grow to distinguish between the cultural contexts and formations of Alcott, Blyton, and the Brontës? In her reception of these novels as motivational literature, is she the governess in *Jane Eyre* and *Vilette*, the culturally invisible and paralogical figure for whom the regulative logic of the narrative finally relents, or the mad woman in the attic, for whom it doesn't? We are not told whether in Tambu's interpretive schemas questions of race elide with the occlusions of class in the novels. How can a Shona peasant girl possibly relate the experience of the Mission School to the jollities of the English boarding school experience promised by Malory Towers or St. Clare's? How does her conflicted adolescent sexuality and self-image relate to that of the clever, confident, growing girls in largely bourgeois contexts? Dangarembga's disregard for the singularity of these classic texts points to yet another function of the canon for postcolonial reinvention, which the instrumental modality of Slaughter's study of the historical conjunctions between literary form and international human rights law entirely misses: Tambu can author her story precisely because she hasn't quite read the ones that colonial history had put in place for the natives' discursive formation. The canon of English literature functions as horizon, a limit case, luring the parvenu and the picaro, yet becoming irrelevant as the Manichean logic of self and other, or center and periphery, fitfully gives way to a more deconstructive modality of "expansion."

Lloyd Jones's *Mister Pip* (2007), which starts out with an episodic reading of Charles Dickens's *Great Expectations*, but which evolves into the "Pacific version" of the great novel (*Mister Pip*, 149), is as much about reading Dickens as it is about creative misreading, anachronistic interpretation, and the valorization of a viral textuality that not merely collapses author and reader functions but also the critical distance between living and reading. *Mister Pip* takes place in a small village in Bougainville, an island "no bigger than a cow pat" (7) in the South Pacific. Set in the 1990s, when this Papua New Guinea island was in the throes of civil war, it is told from the perspective of a precocious and restless thirteen-year-old girl. Eighty-six days have passed since Matilda's last day of school, when Mr. Watts, the only white man on the island, reopens the school and tells the children he will introduce them to Mr Dickens. "I will be honest with you. I have no wisdom, none at all . . . whatever we have between us is all we've got. Oh, and of course Mr. Dickens"(16).

"It was a new sound in the world," Mathilda says of the time when the first lines of *Great Expectations* are read out to the class (18). The reverence with which Mr. Watts treats the text, holding it up in one hand "like a church minister" and pronouncing it "the greatest novel by the greatest English writer of the nineteenth century" (18), is easily transferred to his pupils as they realize for the first time that Mr. Dickens was a book, not a visiting white man who could be prevailed upon for antimalaria tablets, aspirin, generator fuel, beer, kerosene, wax candles, and household repairs. In a belief system where white was "the colour of all the important things, like ice-cream, aspirin, ribbon, the moon, the stars" (4), it is believable to the reader that a novel endorsed by the last white man on the island as the greatest ever written comes to occupy the symbolic centrality that it does, both in the classroom and in the wider culture's contestations of meaning. Mathilda describes the readings as affording the kids "another world to spend the night in" as the rebels and the army "redskins" slaughtered each other (20). The history, geography, and culture of Dickens's novel are largely lost on its auditors, though its themes, particularly the imbrications between love and loss, death and individuation, and the breathtaking violence of Pip's coming-of-age story, translate effortlessly. The children do not always comprehend the characters' motivations and compulsions, but "Mr Watts didn't really know either" (80).

In an interesting twist, the New Zealander Jones gives us a scene of canon revision which involves the protocols and vagaries of oral transmission, not (re)writing. For two months (December 10, 1991, to February 10, 1992), the children have an audio of the novel, and just when Mr. Watts is about to delegate the task of reading the text aloud to his pupils, the copy of *Great Expectations* goes missing. In a period of escalating political tension on the island, the class is given the assignment of reconstructing the book from memory, not mere plot detail, but voices, conversations, actual words. "However," Mr. Watts concedes, "if we can get the gist of what is meant, that will be something, at least" (113). The task of shoring the fragments becomes an object lesson in the unpredictable and unprogrammable way in which great texts are received and retained, by common and ideal readers alike: a chance, everyday remark from her mother ("Do you not have a shadow of your own to play with?" [114]) reminds Mathilda of the unmistakable tone of Estella's exchanges with Pip. The task of fabricating "Mr Dickens' greatest book" (111) sheds light also on the ways in which the belated writer cathects to the precursor on his or her own terms, in the light of the political and cultural exigencies of their historical moment. The canon, Jones seems to be suggesting, is always the "successor's creation," made by the living "for the needs of the living," as Bloom says, paraphrasing T. S. Eliot's famous thesis on tradition and individual talent (*Anxiety*, 19). Mr. Watts offers an exemplary instance of creative recounting when he recites *Great Expectations* to the rambos, enthralling them with story each night to avert the night's inevitable business of death. The improvised Dickens retelling extrapolates freely from his life and the lives of the islanders, the book coming alive in the slippage between Dickens's *Great Expectations* and Watts's great expectations. The rebels, who listen on "with their mouths and ears open to catch every word, their weapons resting on the ground in front of their bare feet like useless relics" (142), fall for Mr. Watts's lie that he is Pip, and it is his story.

 Matilda closely identifies with the orphan protagonist, Pip, and even builds him a beachfront shrine. She seems to survive the most horrific personal and historical trauma with little more than the power of story, a classic novel of formation (*Great Expectations*) that builds character and gives her hope. Reality seems to cancel out fiction when "redskin" soldiers mistake Pip for a rebel fighter, but in the end Mr. Watts's and Matilda's faith in literature's transfiguring power holds. Matilda emerges a postcolonial subject "newly capacitated to read the present in light of a broadened, more discerning, reading of the past" (Pratt, "In the Neocolony," 460). As with Dickens's *David Copperfield*, the body of the novel provides the backstory for the inaugural act of authorship with which it ends as Mathilda sets aside her thesis on Dickens's orphans to write about the Mr. Dickens she had known, who "used to go about barefoot and in a buttonless shirt" (*Mister Pip*, 218). As a child, Mathilda had felt peevish about the way her interaction with *Great Expectations* could only be "a one-way conversation," for there was no "talking back" (*Mister Pip*, 39), no scope whatsoever to intervene in the characters' self-destructive trajectories. The adult Mathilda has a difficult realization in the Dickensian heart of England—in Mr. Dickens's study in Eastgate House—that in being forced by Mr. Watts to intervene in Pip's story, ineffectual though it had seemed at that time, she had found her recalcitrant voice: "Pip was my story, even if I was a girl, and my face black as the shining night" (219). It was another thing altogether that what she now had to say would be impossible to assimilate in the scholarly register of Dickens studies and would perhaps not be readily counted as the aesthetic, sociocultural work buttressing international "citizen-subjectivation" either.

5

"Yes, sir, I was the one who got away"
Postcolonial Emergence and the Vernacular Canon

"English in culture, like the dollar in economics, serves as the medium through which knowledge may be translated from the local to the global," observes Jonathan Arac in "Anglo-Globalism?" (40). The literatures in English emerging from the subcontinent in recent years testify to Arac's statement in complex ways. They lend some credence to the center-periphery model of "writing back," where a source literature is rewritten and radicalized by the borrower, and where the (one-sided) transaction demonstrates both the inequality of the historical affiliation and what Franco Moretti calls the persistent "asymmetry in international power" ("Conjectures," 56). They also, however, disturb this dated model of interconnection: by commanding a new spatial politics of the periphery and new morphologies, these literary interventions put in place new structures of difference that demand commensurate modes of critical reception. With about one and a half billion nonnative speakers, "English has become the world's own language," as Harry Bingham remarks ("You say potato," 3). Bingham, the author of *This Little Britain*, a study of the evolving history and definition of Britishness and its far-reaching implications for the increasingly anglophone world, observes that "there will shortly be as many English-language speakers in China as there are in the entire English-speaking world put together" (3), and offers further evidence for the global supremacy of English. The official dictionary-based word count of English is five hundred thousand (to German's two hundred thousand, and the one hundred thousand word count of French), but the actual number, if American English, slang, and dialect are taken into consideration, runs to a million. English clearly dominates in fields such as the Nobel Prize in Literature, if we count by language and not country (twenty-six laureates to thirteen for France), and the index of the most-translated authors of all time is dominated by four Brits in the top five places (Agatha Christie in first place, Enid Blyton in third, Shakespeare and Barbara Cartland in fourth and fifth respectively). Bingham, however, draws a self-congratulatory conclusion when he gives the commodious English language, which all evidence would relate to a changeable and planet-wide collectivity of language users, strictly national coordinates: "In the end, it's hard to survey all these facts and not draw the obvious conclusion: that we Brits have some natural affinity to words and literature, the way Germans 'do' music, and the French 'do' visual art" (3). In this chapter, I discredit cultural interpretations that relate English usage to Britishness—naturalized, acquired, or pined for—and challenge readings such as Bingham's that insinuate a link between global sales figures of English-language texts and structures of class and race mobility predicated on not just using English but "becoming English." I argue instead that English is a veritable cosmopolitan vernacular, its transregional and transethnic scope enhanced by regional adaptations in contact zones, and chart the rise of what John Guillory calls, albeit in a different literary historical context, an "English vernacular canon" (*Cultural Capital*, x).

Kipling's "Letters of Travel" in *From Sea to Sea* begins with the author at loose ends, pondering his course of action for successive years. A possible direction is inadvertently suggested by a creature he most hates, the "Globe-trotter": "He, sitting by my chair, discussed India with the unbridled arrogance of five weeks on a Cook's ticket. He was from England and had dropped his manners in the Suez Canal. 'I assure you,' said he, 'that you who live so close to the actual facts of things cannot form dispassionate judgments of their merits. You are too near. Now I—' he waved his hand modestly and left me to fill the gap" (*From Sea to Sea*, 208). Kipling wryly notes the accoutrements of the globe-trotter, from his new helmet to his deck shoes. His thoughts turn to the object of his visitor's touristic attention, India, "maligned and silent India, given up to the ill-considered wanderings of such as he—of the land whose people are too busy to reply to the libels upon their life and manners" (*From Sea to Sea*, 208), and resolves with alacrity to stage a countermovement:

> It was my destiny to avenge India upon nothing less than three-quarters of the world. The idea necessitated sacrifices,—painful sacrifices,—for I had to become a Globe-trotter, with a helmet and deck-shoes. In the interests of our little world I would endure these things and more. I would deliver "brawling judgments all day long; on all things unashamed." I would go toward the rising sun till I reached the heart of the world and once more smelt London asphalt. (208)

The globe-trotter, Kipling says, "is extreme cosmopolitan," refusing "to be steadied" (312).[1] This damning observation is made in the context of a rocky sea voyage aboard the P & O S.S. *Ancona*, crammed with "Globe-trotters" who, Kipling adds, "will be sick anywhere" (312). The cosmopolitanism of the vernacular canon of English literature could similarly be read as derogation and dissemination, acquisitive of syntax and phoneme but not steadying itself or slowing down enough to become an accountable category. Our poststructuralist suspicion of totalizing systems, however, allows for a less damning view of the dynamism and adaptability of English as a cosmopolitan medium than Kipling's; I even argue that we could see in its linguistic and conceptual borrowings and syncretism not a greedy epistemology, but a longing for unbelonging, or belonging to what Said called a "noncoercive human community" (*World*, 247).

In *Cultural Capital: The Problem of Literary Canon Formation*, John Guillory examines the formation of a vernacular curriculum in eighteenth-century England. "Vernacular canon," in this historical context, refers to a curriculum whose language, grammaticality, and epistemic orientation no longer engage with standards derived from Greek and Roman classics. *Vernacular* thus becomes a byword for "unofficial," "non-Latin," nationalist (as defined against what Guillory calls "the multilingual cultural internationalism of the Renaissance humanists" [76]), minor, and common. If the vernacular canon emerges as an alternative to a body of high canonical literature that, by definition, claims the seriousness and cultural capital of the scriptural canon, it does so through its democratic promise of mediation between varying levels of literacy and in its commitment to the standardization of vernacular languages. However, as Guillory observes: "While the standard or 'common' language seems to efface social stratification by making language itself the vehicle of a common national identity, the 'literary' language reinstates at another level a linguistic difference by which the upper classes can continue to mark their cultural distinction" (78). The vernacular canon in the eighteenth and nineteenth centuries operates as a standardizing influence on the language of the masses, and is, in its turn, regulated by "literary" texts at the higher levels of the school system (79).

Guillory's discussion of the eighteenth-century vernacular canon is useful for reading the late-twentieth and twenty-first century phenomenon of "literatures in English" and investigating questions of audience, reception, and recognition mobilizing the same. It is, of course, absurd to read English and anglophone literature judgmentally along the binaries of "high" and "low" or "literary" and "vernacular." Gayatri Spivak describes the complexity of the relationship between British literature and what was once called "Commonwealth literature" as "collaborative/parasitical/contrary/resistant" ("Burden," 285). "Proper English" in the twenty-first century tends to be negatively determined concept, its ontic essence most concretely grasped in terms of what it is not. Exocentric models such as General American or Received Pronunciation are no longer adopted in teaching policy, and Standard English, Guillory states, "has dwindled to an impoverished scribal formulaic that takes refuge in the fortress of composition, where it defends itself against the continual invasion of barbaric tongues" (*Cultural Capital*, 81). The invocation of the "vernacular canon," therefore, merely provides an informative paradigm for exploring the gap between written and oral languages, between idiolects and the global babble of sociolects, between institutional programs of assimilation and standardization and inexorable processes of nonstandardized literization (and social reproduction) that result in new currencies of exchange, "different but complicit," to quote Spivak ("Burden," 285).

I also use *vernacular* in the sense of variant and localized usages of English, not "parochial" or "regional." English in the subcontinent signals social access and class privilege and is the language of "literary sophistication and bourgeois civility," as Aijaz Ahmad points out: "All else is regional, hence minor and forgettable" (*In Theory*, 75). The selection of anglophone novels that I relate to the constitution of a vernacular canon cherishes its dialectical difference while rebuffing a provincial definition. The Indian or Pakistani English novel is equally opposed to the nationalist and antihybridist tendencies of the postcolonial state. Spivak's formulation of the paradox of translation could be applied to the recombinatory language politics of the narratives in question: "The verbal text is jealous of its linguistic signature but impatient of national identity" ("Translation," 21).

In "The Cosmopolitan Vernacular," an excellent article on the Sanskrit cosmopolis and the rise of the Indian vernacular at the beginning of the second millennium, Sheldon Pollock argues that not only does the vernacular reconfigure the cosmopolitan, but the two "produce each other in the course of their interaction" (7). Moreover, "Although not all cosmopolitan languages may initially be vernaculars . . . many vernaculars themselves do become cosmopolitan for their regional worlds" (7). If the superior attraction of a language like Sanskrit, in its prevalent medieval usage as *kāvya* (poetics) and *praśasti* (political encomiums), was its uniformity and a certain transethnic character that made it impossible to date or localize a work of Sanskrit literature, local languages like Kannada, Pollock argues, aspired for regionalism as well as "supraregionality" (28). The vernacular turn in precolonial India was in fact brought about by the cosmopolitan elite, such as Pampa, the tenth-century court poet of a Cālukya overlord in western Andhra, who, despite the formidable rank and status his Sanskrit erudition bestowed upon him, sought in the regional language a composite medium for the literary and political self-definition of a "vernacular polity."[2] In premodern globalization, the global and local, Pollock states, should not be analyzed as "pregiven, sharply defined cultural formations, the former as the exogenous, great tradition, the latter as the indigenous, little tradition," as area-studies courses are wont to do, but regarded instead as a "congeries of constantly changing repertoires of practices" (32–33).

Homi Bhabha's argument in "Unsatisfied: Notes on Vernacular Cosmopolitanism," speaks to Pollock's historical analysis of the twin narratives of emergent regional polities and the rise of cosmopolitan vernaculars. Defining the vernacular against the excursive spatial imagination of Martha Nussbaum's definition of cosmopolitanism in "Patriotism and Cosmopolitanism," where the self is at the center of a series of concentric circles that move through cycles of familial, ethnic, and communal affiliation to the telos of humanity as a whole, Bhabha locates it in a space "that somehow stops short (not falls short) of the transcendent human universal" (42). Drawing on Anthony Appiah's insight that "humans live best on a smaller scale" and his valorization of circles "narrower than the human horizon"— the country, the town, the street, the business, the craft, the profession—as "the appropriate spheres of moral concern," Homi Bhabha sees the cosmopolitanism envisaged in a marginality or metonymy as providing "an ethical entitlement to, and enactment of, the sense of community" ("Unsatisfied," 42).[3] Vernacular cosmopolitanism, Bhabha states, is that experience of modern living that Julia Kristeva, in *Strangers to Ourselves*, has called "the cosmopolitanism of those who have been flayed," the experience of indeterminate communities living in interstitial zones between the private and the public, between greedy nationalism and an even greedier commodification of the world.[4] The new cosmopolitanism, Bhabha states, needs to be defined by an *unsatisfaction*, an unachievable domestication of the universal: "Unsatisfied, not because it is mimetically in/non-adequate, but because 'unsatisfaction' is the sign of the movement or relocation of revision of the 'universal' or the general" ("Unsatisfied," 48). In what follows, then, I explore the "unsatisfied" and discrepant cosmopolitanism of the vernacular canon of South Asian English, starting with its linguistic aberrations and experimentations, and moving on to thematic concerns that could be said to vernacularize English by opening it up to demographical diversity, making it mediate new disasters, emergences, and new ways of being modern.

The Language Riot

If, in Chapter 1, where I discuss T. S. Eliot and J. M. Coetzee, the question of the classic seemed inseparable from the logic of "provincials" arriving at the metropolitan center, this chapter references a reverse movement in the colonial history of excursive imperial travel from the center to the peripheries. It is possible to say that English literature came to India with the passing of the Charter Act of 1813, as a potted history of this inaugural moment of British cultural domination will reveal.[5] The Charter Act, which renewed the East India Company's charter for commercial undertakings in India, marked a new interest in and responsibility toward native education. It also relaxed controls over missionary work in India, an action that would contribute to the growing influence of English education in the country. England's involvement with colonial education was a consequence of the English Parliament's conflict with the East India Company, and its increasing unease over reports of the profligacy of the company's merchants. While the eighteenth century had seen a flowering of Orientalism, which Gauri Viswanathan describes as "a tacit polity of reverse acculturation, whose goal was to train British administrators and civil servants to fit into the culture of the ruled" ("Currying" 88), the first three decades of the nineteenth witnessed the countermovement of Anglicism, which drew on English principles of government and jurisprudence to restructure the codes of public conduct for British administrators. The Charter Act promised that "a sum of not less than one lac of rupees shall be annually applied to the revival and improvement of literature, and the encouragement of the learned natives of India."[6] Despite its lack of specificity the Charter Act was widely interpreted by administrators like Thomas Macaulay to mean Western, not Oriental, literature, and led eventually to the passing of the English Education Act of 1835, which would oblige Indian natives to acquire not just a rudimentary knowledge of the English language but a liberal education in English literature. Orientalist learning began to wane as the rulers discovered more efficacious ways of inducing Indians in the hierarchical structures to create a bureaucratic mediatory class between the British officers and the masses.

As the scholarship of Gauri Viswanathan has shown, educational development in British India differed from England in that it was freed from the domination of Church-controlled education, which mandated a classical curriculum for the aristocracy and religious studies for the lower classes, with the eclecticism that we now associate with the literary curriculum in place only in the last quarter of the nineteenth century. The strict controls on what Viswanathan calls "Christianizing activities" ("Currying," 95), stemming from the fear of native rebellion, made British rulers turn to English literature to discipline and manage natives. The noninterference in religious matters—and this turn to a desacralized education to instill in their subordinates the Christian values of piety, morality, and benevolence—led to a curious decriminalization, dehistoricization even, of the colonial ruler, with the corpus of English literature functioning as an ideal Englishman: "Making the Englishman known to the natives through the products of his mental labor removed him from the plane of ongoing colonialist activity—of commercial operations, military expansion, administration of territories—and de-actualized and diffused his material presence in the process" ("Currying Favor," 103). The cultural work of English in the "moral and intellectual suasion" of natives (85), however, eventually had the opposite effect, though it was not by any means the chief instigator of nationalist and anticolonialist ardor. As Modhumita Roy observes,

"If Milton and Shakespeare were included in the curriculum as a 'disguised form of authority' . . . it is important to bear in mind that knowledge of English also introduced the Indians to the ideas of Voltaire, Thomas Paine . . . the scientific writings of Newton and Davy, all of which were translated and circulated among the literate classes" (Roy, "'Englishing' India," 103). Interestingly enough, in post-independence India, the chief objectives of introducing English language and literature in the colonial educational curriculum turned out to be the very factors that guaranteed their survival in the erstwhile colonies: the need for the unification of a linguistically diverse country through a common currency; the facilitation of new forms of mobility generated by industrial modernity; the creation and expansion of an indigenous bourgeoisie; the safeguarding of secular values from the regressive and conservative energies of the religious extreme. In the conflict of interest between "national unity" and "powerful regional aspirations symbolically represented by the vernacular languages" (Ganguly, "Language Question," 673), English emerged in the postcolony as the link language, or a neutral and pan-Asian language. Similarly, in the newly created state of Pakistan, English was the official language (and Urdu the national language). While in Bangladesh, Bengali has been the medium of instruction—and English the second language—since 1974, the cultural hegemony of English is perpetuated in the way the elite are educated in English medium schools that borrow wholesale from the British curriculum, and, also, in recent years, from the American and Australian systems.

> The language I speak,
> Becomes mine, its distortions, its queernesses
> All mine, mine alone. ("An Introduction," 727)

These lines from Kamala Das's "An Introduction" capture the dialectical relationship between a language and its vernacular uses. Das insinuates that a queer performativity is intrinsic to the adopted language as well as being the defining feature of its transmission. The multilingual Das's English language poem is particularly apt for this discussion as it sees English as not just "a surrogate Englishman in his highest and most perfect state," a beguilingly universalist literature that proved instrumental in the cultural indoctrination of colonized peoples, but a language that is vagrant, perfectible, and in the throes of change.[7] The English vernacular canon subscribes to both Pollock's and Bhabha's formulation of an unachievable cosmopolitanism that is written into the very grounds of the flowering of the local, and its use of a global language reveals the possible differentiations and dispersals of the idea of the global ("All mine, mine alone"). The foreignizing of English, of course, is not merely a symptom of the crisscrossing flows of economic globalization. As Robert Young points out, "English has always been voracious, insatiable, languishing in a constant state of desire for other languages to partner with" ("English," 204). It could be argued that the susceptibility of English to linguistic interference and its genius of remaining identifiably "English" despite hybridizations singularly resonate with the anglophone writer's firsthand experience of the translatability and adaptability of English in a colonial education system. Often, it speaks to the fantasy of "free intelligence" and a "frontierless nation" shared by the rootless and what Rushdie calls "the deliberately uprooted" intellectual (*Step Across*, 67).

The promise of freedom that writing in a hegemonic language holds out to the indigenous writer has various aspects. First, it signals a break from compromised nationalist interests that seek a literal restitution of the precolonial past. As Rushdie states in *Imaginary Homelands*, "We will not be capable of reclaiming precisely the thing that was lost; . . . we will, in short, create fictions" (10). The fictions, these invisible cities and imaginary homelands, could well be created with artistic license, "in CinemaScope and glorious Technicolor" (10). Reading English literature in an Indian classroom affords the student "an entry, however remote, into a geopolitical rather than merely national 'Indian'-ness," observes Gayatri Spivak: "It is from this base that R. K. Narayan can speak of 'English in India' as if it were a jolly safari arranged by some better-bred version of the India Tourist Board; and, conversely, it is also on this base that a critical study of colonial discourse can be built" ("Burden of English," 276–77). Second, as Robert Young shows with the example of Vikram Seth's *A Suitable Boy*, the 1998 Hindi translation of which was forced to excise an episode for fear of offending a caste-conscious readership, writing in English allows the Indian writer to bypass the moral police dogging literary production in *bhasha*, or regional languages. Third, the English vernacular canon provides continuities between double lives and parallel lives, just as the multeity of the English literary critical tradition was instrumental in linking Edward Said's exilic poetics and his involvement in Middle East politics with his ivory-tower concerns as literary critic and English professor: "There are links between the two worlds which I for one am beginning to exploit in my own work" ("Beginnings," 14). The terms of such engagement, for Said, were not always "harmony and resolution" but "intransigence, difficulty, and unresolved contradiction."[8] And finally, reading the European canon out of cultural context, as V. S. Naipaul did in Trinidad, is perhaps inseparable from the desire for a canon of one's own, or of creating legitimizing fictions that will usher in and sustain new and revolutionary linguistic and narrative forms. Naipaul's Nobel lecture, "Two Worlds," evokes the cultural void from which a young Vidia forged materials for his autobiographical fiction: "I could find in no book anything that came near my background. The young French or English person who wished to write would have found any number of models to set him on his way. I had none" (*Literary Occasions*, 192). What, then, are the terms of this alternative canon formation? Who makes it to the list and who monitors it? "This is a simple game: sales and prizes," says William Dalrymple, author, cultural commentator, and curator of the Jaipur Literary Festival (Dalrymple, cited in Shah, "Pakistan's Literary Boys' Club"). The logic of this statement may be implacable, but what is harder to anatomize in the sales- and prize-driven business of international recognition is the quality—or set of qualities—that enables vernacular newness to enter English language and literature. The most obvious novelty value of anglophone fiction is its breathtaking linguistic diversity or the "Hazaar fucked" English, as Upamanyu Chatterjee calls it.[9] Here are some well-known examples from writers of Indian origin. G. V. Desani said of his 1948 novel, *All About H. Hatterr*, that "this book isn't English as she is wrote and spoke" (*All About H. Hatterr*, 16). A mess of Babu English, Queen's English, bazaar-talk, *Hatterr* is crammed with puns, riddles, jokes, malapropisms, ephemera from regional languages (English, Hindi, Sanskrit, Tamil), classical allusions, and Anglo-Indian argot. In his introduction to the novel, Anthony Burgess compared the language of the book to "the English of Shakespeare, Joyce and Kipling, gloriously impure" (*All About H. Hatterr*, 10). Desani's "rigmarole English" stains the "goodly, godly tongue" (17), his parodying of the *Bildungsroman* enacts an unlearning of dominant modes, and his gaze on the ways of the Occidental people achieves a comic reversal of the ethnographical intent of Orientalism. In the novel, Hatterr's cosmopolitan aspirations are exposed to be bourgeois, Western, out-of-joint with emergent Indian modernity, and we could argue that this pattern is repeated in the history of the modern English novel in India, with the old kind of cosmopolitanism—normative, universalistic—steadily supplanted by discrepant and vernacular cosmopolitanisms. Perhaps the best example of this can be found in R. K. Narayan's stories of small-town South India. As Naipaul puts it simply, "Narayan wrote in English about Indian life." He wrote in a foreign language from within his culture and within a Hindu cosmology, fluently and unaffectedly. His English, Naipaul says, "was so personal and easy, so without English social associations, that there was no feeling of oddity" (*Literary Occasions*, 25).

Narayan's untroubled use of English for stories of Indian life is contrasted by the intense self-alienation of Raja Rao, about which Meenakshi Mukherjee writes in her essay "The Anxiety of Indianness." In his 1938 foreword to *Kanthapura*, Raja Rao states: "The telling has not been easy. One has to convey in a language that is not one's own the spirit that is one's own. . . . I use the word 'alien,' yet English is not really an alien language to us. It is the language of our intellectual make-up, like Sanskrit or Persian was before—but not of our emotional make-up" (cited in Mukherjee, "Anxiety," 2607).[10] Mukherjee details the ways in which Raja Rao sets up his acquired language against the contesting claims of memory and myth, oral tales, fabulation, gossip, and the sensory overload of everyday life in a village on the slopes of the Sahyadri Mountains. Mulk Raj Anand and Ahmed Ali also used English for indigenous narrative material in the 1930s: in each case, the use of English represents a curious compromise formation between estrangement from the legacy of imperialism and a process of mutation, translation, and a new cross-cultural relation. If R. K. Narayan's use of English enabled him to create what Meenakshi Mukherjee identifies as "Hindu upper-caste pan-India, resistant to change, eternal and immutable" ("Anxiety," 2608).[11] Anand wrote in English to claim a wider circulation for his tales of the socially downtrodden. "The English-writing intelligentsia in India," he stated, "was thus a kind of bridge trying to span, symbolically, the two worlds of the Ganga and the Thames through the novel" (quoted in *Another Country*, 211). Similarly, Ahmed Ali used English to retrieve the lost stories and the unofficial history of pre-British Delhi because he did not want his readership to be confined to "a narrow belt rimmed by Northwest India," as Joshi comments (*Another Country*, 212). While he borrowed the language and novel form from English literature, his cultural influences were Arabic, Persian, and Hindustani. Joshi describes Ali's *Twilight in Delhi* as engaging in "a complex transaction with both anglicist and Oriental priorities combined in a project to reinscribe a new history of India on terms different from and even irrelevant to the versions presented by the colonial state" (*Another Country*, 212).

Later writers like Suniti Namjoshi downplay the easy equivalence of English and Indian languages evident in the realist mode of the 1930s, highlighting instead the enabling gap, in metropolitan India, between a lived-in culture and "the cultural load of the learnt language," English: "If two realities are possible, then the next thought, that perhaps multiple realities are possible, isn't far away" (Namjoshi, in Hanscombe and Namjoshi, "Writing," 391). Namjoshi, like Vikram Seth in *Beastly Tales*, uses English to evoke fabulist traditions from Aesop, La Fontaine, the Panchatantra, and the Hitopadesa, mixing genres like the novel, fairy tale, fable, and fantasy to project her utopian vision of a society of sexual dissidents and/as animals. Pidgin English, or what Mulk Raj Anand called "pigeon Indian" (cited in Srivastava, "Pidgin English," 62), Rushdie's irrepressible chutneyfied "Angrezi," Amitav Ghosh's use of the acrolects of Indian intelligentsia (and, in a more colonial context, the "floating lexicon" of Hobson Jobson he showcases in *Sea of Poppies*), V. S. Naipaul's "Oxford" English, "Guru English," a term Srinivas Aravamudan coined to describe the idiom of religious cosmopolitanism, gentrified 'Babu English,' the urban metropolitan English of the "St. Stephen's School of Literature," Gautam Malkani's "Londonstani" or British-Asian gangsta-speak, all testify to the differing and deferring relays of English.[12]

If Salman Rushdie's role in putting South Asian anglophone fiction on the global marketplace is central, "so dominating that he has gobbled up his predecessors, who now seem like clouds to his sun," as James Wood aptly put it in the *New Republic* ("Noisy Pluralism," 32), it is also undeniable that his insouciant language use was instrumental in the breakthrough as well as in shaping the terms of its critical reception. Rushdie made of English "a placeless, free-floating noumenon," to borrow Jahan Ramazani's phrase describing the phenomenon of a modernist and transnational poetics, entrenched in the local yet far-reaching in its translocations, performative in essence and always on the move ("Modernist Bricolage," 446). Michael Gorra says of Rushdie's prose that it is "the omnium-gatherum of whatever seems to work, sprinkled with bits of Urdu, eclectic enough even to accommodate cliché, unbound by any grammatical straightjacket"

(*After Empire*, 133). Phrases from Rushdie's *Midnight's Children* (1981), such as "handcuffed to history" (9), "no escape from recurrence" (284), "national longing for form" (291), "the chutnification of history" (458), "the bomb in Bombay" (462), not to mention "midnight's children" itself, have become critical touchstones for the *soma* of metropolitan postcolonial literature and culture. Rushdie's fiction is "current-events collage, articles clipped from a newspaper" (Brennan, "Cultural Politics," 114), and the pyrotechnics of his maximalist English bespeak "consumed multitudes" (*Midnight's Children*, 9): epics, scriptures, classics, the philosophy and politics of history, histories and theories of the novel, high and low cinema, the excitable signage and graphemes of colonial and diasporic cities, all presented in the dream logic of a cosmopolitan Indian's cultural memory, shoring fragments deeply ingrained in the national psyche, and others that are barely assimilated or repressed. Bishnupriya Ghosh calls this idiom "a new kind of Indian *vernacular*," which "can be decoded only with recourse to *situated* or contextual knowledges" ("Invitation," 126). Giving the example of *The Moor's Last Sigh*'s Jamibhoy Cashondeliveri, whose name evokes country-and-western star Johnny Cash, Ghosh notes the process of recoding whereby the "at-home-in-the-world" image of the country singer is displaced on the "uprooted and fallen Parsi boy's angst" (142). With an overload of similar cross-cultural references, misprisions, and incomplete translations, the trilogy of *Midnight's Children*, *Shame*, and *The Moor's Last Sigh* valorizes untraceable genealogies and barely-contained and unfinished aesthetic histories of nations.[13]

Language in Rushdie novels is often powerful enough to reduce characterization to the vicissitudes of naming, writing, acts of enunciation, and the diegetic narrator's voice. Tragicomic incarnations of the Joycean insight that modernity confers an epidermis rather than a soul, characters wear words like soul-skin, veil, flag. Omar Khayyam in *Shame* is the namesake of a Persian poet who achieved lasting fame not in his native country, but through Fitzgerald's translation and reworking of his verses: the fictional Omar Khayyam Shakil consequently lives out the destiny of the name as an off-centered, out-of-place, "translated" man (*Shame*, 29). Aadam Aziz in *Midnight's Children* is the Adamic figure of Indian modernity, while Shiva, named after the lord of destruction, automatically takes to messianic violence. In *Haroun and the Sea of Stories*, Rushdie's catastrophic revisionism of the Koran in the *Satanic Verses* is repeated covertly in the literal, scribal act of "Pagination and Collation" (or putting papers in chronological order and chapter groupings) involving the Guppee army, which comprises of pages, "thin persons in rectangular uniforms" (*Haroun*, 116).[14] In the *Satanic Verses*, the clash between obdurate nativism and untroubled metropolitan assimilation, the opposing if also complicit poles of migrant experience, is staged in the form of a musical shouting contest between Saladin Chamcha and Gibreel Farishta as the two men plummet from the hijacked Air India flight 420. Gibreel croons (albeit in translation) Indian movie star Raj Kapoor's famous song from the film *Shri 420*, "Merā jūta hai Jāpānī [Oh, my shoes are Japanese. These trousers English, if you please. On my head, red Russian hat; my heart's Indian for all that]" (*Satanic*, 5). Chamcha (in the shortened form of the less pronounceable Chamchawala), whose name now has the slangy connotation of "toady" and an "ass-kisser," as Spivak puts it (*Outside in the Teaching Machine*, 247), hits back with an exaggerated rendition of "Rule Britannia": "Chamcha carolled through lips turned jingoistically redwhiteblue by the cold, 'arooooose from out the aaaazure main.' Farishta, horrified, sang louder and louder of Japanese shoes, Russian hats, inviolately subcontinental hearts, but could not still Saladin's wild recital" (*Satanic*, 6). This prolepsis of identity in language is not allowed psychological depth, complexity, or growth as the narrative unfolds: if anything, the characters accrete more literary and cultural signifiers to become mythic ossifications of otherwise perishable and forgettable selves. Gibreel develops a schizophrenic messiah complex, wishing to redeem 1980s London "all the way from A to Z" (*Satanic*, 322), while Saladin the mimic man is deranged by the projections of his own voice as he becomes an anonymous phone call.

Arundhati Roy describes language as "the skin of my thought" (Abraham, "Interview," 91), and Roy's *God of Small Things*, which Pankaj Mishra has described as "the most important Indian English novel since Salman Rushdie's *Midnight's Children*" (cited anecdotally by Tickell, introduction to *God of Small Things*, 17), brings to Rushdie's febrile language experimentations the quality of automatic and symptomatic thinking. Aijaz Ahmad says of Roy's debut novel that it is "actually *felt* in English" ("Reading," 118). Ahmad describes Roy as "the first Indian writer in English where a marvellous stylistic resource becomes available for provincial, vernacular culture without any effect of exoticism or estrangement, and without the book reading as a translation" (118). Roy achieves this by breaking the decorum of grammar and style, by diverting, reversing, and arresting linear narrative, preferring small over big, and connecting the smallest things to the biggest. The twins, Estha and Rahel, grow up in a world transitioning from their grandfather Pappachi's unreflective Anglophilia to their uncle Chacko's disaffection as a Westernized Indian ("We belong nowhere"; *God of Small Things*, ed. Tickell, 53), and transitioning also from a traditional sense of community, with its legitimated domestic rape, violence, and perversions, to a society of the excommunicated, as made inevitable by the love affair between their mother and the "untouchable" Velutha. The twins use the English language not to regulate experience but to mimic its absurd excess of signifier and skip around the abyss of nonmeaning that is the flip side of the excess. Their mother's lack of legal status or *locus standi* becomes the incomprehensible but ominous-sounding "Locusts Stand I"; the decoupling of words from the tyranny of signification makes for a contemplation of brute sound, "boot" or "sturdy"; words broken down into semantic units are randomly combined to form new sound and meaning constellations (barn owl / Bar Nowl). The twins also read backward, a tendency which makes the Australian missionary Miss Mitten describe them as having "Satan in their eyes" (transcribed instantly as "nataS in their seye"; 60). "A yellow hoarding said BE INDIAN, BUY INDIAN in red. 'NAIDNI YUB, NAIDNI EB,' Estha said" (58). The nonmimetic repetition implicit in reversing words, sequence, and time is to be read against the fabric of law-abiding Ayemenem life, held together by acts of systematic learning, cautious remembering, and reminding: Baby Kochamma's insistence on the twins' memorizing of canonical texts and prayers, the children's (Estha, Rahel, Comrade Pillai's son and niece) attempted or achieved feats of recitation, Kochamma's own pitiless record of "Things She'd done for People, and Things People Hadn't Done for Her" (98), not to mention the specter of intractable "Love laws," or "laws that lay down who should be loved, and how" (33). The twins read things back to front as if to ferret out meaning from the obscure and the spasmodic, and through random, unmotivated acts of transgression (such as reading back to front). These child narrators present without irony or embitterment the hopeless non-correspondence between name ("Orangedrink Lemondrink man") and referent (fearsome predator of children), or sensation and even its most forensic literary or historical figuration, a failure encapsulated best in the idea of "History's smell." "They smelled its smell and they never forgot it" (55).

Roy's vernacularization of English also involves the use of Malayalam words and phrases, some translated, others inviting the reader's inference and conjecture. Christine Vogt-William reads in the latter strategy "a form of resistance to demands that literature conform to either accepted varieties of American or British English or the diverse regional languages of India" ("'Language is the skin,'" 402). This is also Roy's way of naturalizing English as it is unspectacularly mixed up in everyday bilingual or multilingual use, no questions asked. The issue, with Roy and other anglophone novelists, of course, is not "Why Malayalam?"—or Hindi or Bengali, for that matter—for these are regional languages with hypertrophic histories and viable futures, but: "Why English?" or why the admixture of English and its other? Tahmima Anam's *A Golden Age* (2007), which commemorates the year of the Muktijuddho, or the Bangladesh Liberation War, from the perspective of a woman and mother, is written in English, though the battle of tongues in the crucible of 1971 was waged between Urdu and Bengali. Anam, who is of Bangladeshi origin, was born five years after the civil war, grew up in Paris, New York, and Bangkok, and was educated at Mount Holyoke College and Harvard. She attributes her desire to write to "stories about the war" relayed by her parents (*Golden Age*, 276).[15] Interestingly, despite the plethora of vernacular literature—films and documentaries, nationalist songs, novels—on the events and aftermaths of 1971, Anam said in a 2007 interview, "There have been so many novels to come out of India, and there are noted writers from Pakistan, but no one has told my story" ("PW Talks"). English, in the shadow of this second partition of Bengal (the novel, of course, is written thirty-six years after the event), thus loses its colonial ramifications to become the sole transparency through which Anam's "postmemory" of this inaugural moment in the national narrative of deltaic Bengal is conveyed to the world. The use of English to convey Bangla cultural self-definition, nevertheless, raises uneasy questions: Who is this novel written for? Why should an English-language novel about the 1971 civil war in what was then East Pakistan be allowed to supersede Bengali literary and cultural representations of the same? Is the line of descent for the thematics and plotting of Anam's realist novel Western? Anam lists as her literary models the novelists of the American South: Faulkner, O'Connor, Cather. "There's something about the South that really reminds me of Bangladesh—the climate, the delta, the way the environment takes over the imagination" ("First Look"). How privileged and exceptional is this "excess of belonging," to use Aijaz Ahmad's term for late-capitalist forms of transnational or multinational affiliations?[16]

The weakest sections of Monica Ali's 2003 *Brick Lane* are perhaps the letters in broken English dispatched by the protagonist's sister Hasina from Dhaka. Ali's first novel charts the *Bildung* of young Nazneen, who arrives in the East End of London after an arranged marriage with a much older man. The story unfolds in the claustrophobic space of a council flat, a loveless marriage, and a pinched and penniless existence in Tower Hamlets, London. A parallel narrative of gender oppression and feminine self-loathing in a regressive and patriarchal society is proffered through the letters written to Nazneen by her sister Hasina, who has remained in Bangladesh and is hurtling from a financial crisis to another, moral one in the course of the novel. Why would a pair of literate, Bangla-speaking sisters with no formal English education recourse to English at all? Admittedly, the letters are part of an English-language novel on the Bangladeshi diaspora, but could Ali have not presented these in the neutral English of translation, instead of attempting a bizarre interlingual translation that reads like a mockery of vernacular English? "*Sometime I feel to run and jump like goat. This is how we do on way to school. But not much room for running here and I sixteen year old and married woman*" (*Brick Lane*, 19).

Hasina's snapshots of a present-day Bangladesh reference a disastrous change from rural to industrial economy, hellish cities, rampant corruption, a disgruntled and woefully underperforming workforce that thrives on trade unionism and crippling strikes. "*University is also close down. All students hold protest. They rallying for right to cheat*" (122). They alternately correct and corroborate Nazneen's daughters' misgivings around Bangladesh as a backward country where daughters are married off to tyrannical men, and where they don't have toothbrushes or toilet paper (329, 331). The "translation" of Hasina's narrative, however, fails dismally to capture the rhetoric or affect of her subaltern voice.

"The ploy of creating a stylised Indian English remains suspect and actually replicates the staged English of colonial literatures," says Tabish Khair (*Babu Fiction*, 125). Peculiar language, however, is hardly the signal characteristic of vernacular English as this chapter seeks to define it. South Asian literary production in English is reformed, not just through an "idiom and imagery" that reflects "the consciousness of Indian speakers," as Khair enjoins it to do, but in the political, intellectual, and cultural parochialisms that it brings to bear on European universalities, fragmented histories that, to quote Chakrabarty, "challenge not only the idea of wholeness but the very idea of the 'fragment' itself" ("Radical Histories," 757). The fragments testify, in varying degrees of engagement, to the legacy of colonialism, especially in its epistemic stranglehold on questions of modernity, law, and civilization; the rise of transnational capitalism, denationalization, and global economic and cultural flows; "delocalised transnation[s]," as Appadurai calls diasporic communities, a formulation that is perhaps equally applicable to cultural collectives and terror cells (*Modernity at Large*, 172); globalization as neocolonialism and the uneven development of classes in erstwhile colonies. The Pakistani novelist Kamila Shamsie's *Burnt Shadows* (2009) begins in a cell in Guantánamo, where the subject is undressing under military supervision in readiness for his orange jumpsuit: "The cold gleam of the steel bench makes his body shrivel. As long as it's possible, he'll stand. *How did it come to this*, he wonders" (1). To construct the genealogy of the naked prisoner of war, the novel journeys through five countries and sixty years, through the last days of the Second World War in Japan to the eve of Partition in India; through Pakistan in the 1980s, a backdrop for American dealings in Afghanistan, to a calamitous development of the America-Afghanistan nexus in the 9/11 World Trade Center attacks and the subsequent "war on terror." This powerful and almost inescapable imbrication of personal stories with complex, overlapping transnational structures and global forms of power marks the anglophone novels I wish to discuss in the next section, all published to wide acclaim.

Invisible, Accidental, and Reluctant (Vernacular) Cosmopolitans

The Booker Committee that judged the 2008 competition lauded its winning entry, Aravind Adiga's *The White Tiger*, for the way in which it deals with "pressing social issues and significant global developments."[17] In this section I will discuss *The White Tiger*, Mohammed Hanif's *A Case of Exploding Mangoes*, and Mohsin Hamid's *The Reluctant Fundamentalist*, moving on to include Nayantara Sahgal's *Rich Like Us* and Indra Sinha's *Animal's People*.

Besides providing exemplary instances of the transculturation of the twentieth- and twenty-first-century Indian and Pakistani novel in English, these texts introduce yet another category in what Emily Apter describes as the "marketing of Third World difference" (*Translation Zone*, 100): the reluctant or accidental cosmopolitan. Before elaborating on this, I would like to briefly consider a less marketable, if less legible, variety of vernacular cosmopolitanism, associated with the figure of the *invisible* vernacular cosmopolitan, who does not overtly prefer one term over the other, nor does he or she serve as a mediating mechanism between the two. In Amitav Ghosh's *The Shadow Lines*, the narrator's uncle Tridib is a classic armchair cosmopolitan, longing for "everything that was not in oneself" (29). With his "vast reservoirs of abstruse information" (*Shadow Lines*, 8), Tridib is an unmistakable social type, however rare and cherished the actual specimen—the hypereducated and work-shy Bengali "traveller/imaginist[s]," to quote Meenakshi Mukherjee (*Perishable Empire*, 138). "Mesopotamian stellae, East European jazz, the habits of arboreal apes, the plays of Garcia Lorca, there seemed to be no end to the things he could talk about," the narrator fondly recollects (9). Tridib's invisible vernacular identity (a type of Bengali intelligentsia, in this case) lies in the cosmopolitanism that he wears so lightly, in his frontierless intellectual affinities, and the covert acquisitiveness driving his multiple enthusiasms.

In the opening scene of Michael Ondaatje's 2000 novel *Anil's Ghost*, the protagonist Anil emerges from the terminal of Katunayake airport at sunrise and is reminded of Kipling's "By the Old Moulmein Pagoda Looking Eastward to the Sea," in which the Burmese dawn is described as coming up abruptly "like thunder out of China 'crost the bay." She is in fact reminded of the visceral sensation of reading the poem as a schoolgirl in the United States—"she knew she was the only one in the classroom to recognize the phrase physically"—and also of her qualified agreement with the poem's description, for "it was never abrupt thunder to her" (9). Anil Tissera is a forensic anthropologist on contract with a Geneva-based NGO, who has returned to Sri Lanka after fifteen years to gather evidence of government-sponsored atrocities in the ongoing civil war. The detail of the Kipling poem is cunningly inserted to warn from the start that this is a native informant who will deploy unconventional conjunctions and "structures of equivalency" (Apter, *Translation Zone*, 102). The expatriate Sinhalese Anil, who mainly speaks English, like the cetologist Piya in Amitav Ghosh's *Hungry Tide*, is a creature of compound allegiances, her national and cultural identity subsumed in the dictates of a vocation or profession. "For me, home is where the Orcaella are," says Piya, with reference to the objects of her scientific inquiry, the Gangetic dolphins of the Sunderbans. "She was a foreigner; it was stamped in her posture, in the way she stood, balancing on her heels like a flyweight boxer, with her feet planted apart. Among a crowd of girls on Kolkata's Park Street she might not have looked entirely out of place, but here, against the sooty back-drop of the commuter station at Dhakuria, the neatly composed androgyny of her appearance seemed out of place, almost exotic" (*Hungry Tide*, 3). This is the Delhi businessman Kanai Dutt's description of his first sighting of the American Indian Piya, but could just as easily be a description of Anil, whose counterperspective is valuable precisely because she returns to the country of her origin as neither an outsider nor a prodigal insider. As such, she—and Piya—prove to be eminently suitable to form what Joseph Slaughter terms "surrogate micropublics," alternatives to the national public sphere, which transgress "national, political, linguistic, ethnic, class and gender boundaries" (*Human Rights*, 193).

It would be absurd to suggest that either Ondaatje or Ghosh valorizes privileged figures of deracinated intelligentsia in novels that strain to memorialize history's forgotten victims. Anil's interaction with the local archeologist, Sarath Diyasena, proves transformative in the way she learns to understand the vagaries of "truth" and what the latter calls "the archaeological surround of a fact" (*Anil's Ghost*, 44). Similarly, Piya's experience in the Sunderbans leads to a recalibration of her own environmental beliefs and interventionist ethics. The novel ends with her return to the Sunderbans on an international conservation project, for which she seeks the guidance of Nilima, Kanai's aunt and a social worker, whose tireless work with the Badabon Trust bespeaks a lifetime's dedication to sustainable development in the tide country, and who will ensure that local fishermen are involved. In *Anil's Ghost*, Sarath sacrifices his life for the contraband intelligence that will let the international expert complete her report before getting out of the country alive. Anil is, in the end, "the American or the Englishman [who] gets on a plane and leaves," as Sarath's brother Gamini had once remarked caustically (*Anil's Ghost*, 285). However, despite the finite scope of their involvement, figures like Anil and Piya are portrayed in the novels as conduits of redemptive power-knowledge and stand for a reattachment, or what Bruce Robbins terms "attachment at a distance," between metrocosmopolitan provenance and identity and parastatal contexts of belonging ("Introduction," 3).

Returning to the topic of accidental or reluctant participants of cosmopolitanism, Aravind Adiga's Man Booker Prize–winning novel *The White Tiger* is strongly evocative of Benjamin Disraeli's *Sybil; or, The Two Nations*, which is plotted around the existence of two nations, the rich and the poor. Disraeli contrasts the oligarchy's acquisitiveness and conspicuous consumption, a result of the dangerous liaison between "Venetian politics, Dutch finance, and French wars," with scenes of abject suffering of the working-class poor (book 1, chapter 3, 46). Disraeli, however, had little political sympathy with the "Two Nations" theory held by his Chartist characters, and in his novel the marriage between the working-class girl and the aristocratic hero quickly loses its subversive charge when it is revealed that Sybil is highborn. The novel eventually discredits the Two Nations theory by showing the poor as not a united front but quarreling factions. Disraeli's interest in the "condition of the people" ultimately serves a pernicious Tory paternalism, which mandates that the aristocracy and Church look after the physical and moral condition of the degraded multitudes in exchange for trust and obedience. Adiga's book is a disenchanted narrative of the Indian growth story that plays on the Two Nations theory: the novel, however, also charts viable pathways of insurgent individualism, which disturb codified social categories in contemporary India and draw attention to the changing size and definition of the middle class. Unlike Disraeli, Adiga explicitly attacks the benighted ruling class, but his representation of the subaltern is not free from cautionary projections about the brutality of the poor and the inevitability of violent proletariat uprisings. Adiga fails to make knowable or identifiable the character of an underdog like Balram, whose name and date of birth are not even his own, but arbitrarily imposed by the state, and who remains excluded from the constitutive transactions of civil society till the end.

White Tiger is structured as a series of letters written over a period of seven nights. The author-narrator is Balram Halwai, formerly of the village of Laxmangarh in Bihar, who subsequently arrives at the prosperous suburb of Gurgaon, near Delhi, to work as chauffeur for the younger son and daughter-in-law of a feudal family, and who now lives incognito in cybercity Bangalore. The missives are addressed to Wen Jiabao, the prime minister of the People's Republic of China, who is scheduled to visit India soon. The mobility narrative that ensues in staggered installments is a grisly tale of deception, ambition, and blackmail, which reaches its logical limit with the murder of his master for a bag of money (with which Balram would reinvent himself as a New Indian entrepreneur).

The ostensible reason for writing to the premier of the People's Republic of China—and, as Sanjay Subrahmanyam points out, the framing device is reminiscent of John Barth's "Petition" from *Lost in the Funhouse*, addressed to the King of Siam ("Diary," 42)—is Mr. Jiabao's purported wish to meet Indian entrepreneurs "and hear the story of their success from their own lips" (43). India may lack "drinking water, electricity, sewage system, public transportation, sense of hygiene, discipline, courtesy, or punctuality," but it does have an embarrassment of entrepreneurial riches, Balram asserts (4). He sees himself as one of Bangalore's most successful (though unknown) entrepreneurs, and offers his life story, which would also serve as contrapuntal narrative vis-à-vis the airbrushed official story presented by the Indian government. Balram relentlessly presents two Indias: the shining new malls, with their squalid counterparts for service staff; luxurious apartment complexes named Windsor Manor A and Buckingham Towers B, with derelict living quarters for servants in the basement; the architectural sublime of industrializing India juxtaposed with slums (where the construction workers live); Johnnie Walker whisky and whisky third class ("English" liquor men and "Indian" liquor men); "Men with big bellies, and Men with Small Bellies" (64); real blonde prostitutes for rich punters and counterfeit blondes for the less privileged—"What do you expect, for seven thousand? The real thing costs forty, fifty" (235). The narrative conjures a grinding existence for have-nots in country and city alike in a sparse style reminiscent of Munshi Premchand's Hindi chronicles. Adiga provides a comprehensive etiology of the postcolonial state's nervous condition: incurable communal prejudices, the inexorable march of free-market capital, migration of labor from village to cramped industrial centers, extreme inequality between the classes, the chicanery of the so-called leaders of the people, the corruption of the Indian left.

Balram's misadventures take him from the world of "Darkness," the stagnation and ruination of the Indian village and small town, to the world of "Light," the metropolitan destinations of hordes of immigrant workers. His master, Mr. Ashok, is an American-educated feudal heir who has recently returned to India, and whose father and brother have willed him away from a provincial life in Dhanbad to the bigger game that is cosmopolitan Delhi. At first Ashok seems different from the "old-school master"

(112) that is his brother Mukesh or his father, the Stork: Westernized and superficially liberal, he is initially made uneasy by the inequitable distribution of wealth and goods between the classes and the widespread corruption of Indian society. He is married to the Christian and Indian-American Pinky, who feels equally thwarted and estranged in the Hindu family carceral and the country. Balram puts up with the indignities of his servile existence with customary deference tempered with customary mischief: "A time-honoured servants' tradition. Slapping the master when he's asleep. Like jumping on pillows when masters are not around. Or urinating into their plants. Or beating or kicking their pet dogs. Innocent servants' pleasures" (185). He largely conforms to his class role, and is dutiful even, till the "story gets much darker" (113). In a fit of drunkenness, the desperately unhappy Pinky Madam takes the wheel and runs over a street urchin, and Balram is forced to sign a statement of culpability. The hit-and-run accident is quickly hushed, but a horrified Pinky walks out of the marriage. Ashok comes unstuck in the face of this development and his behavior toward Balram reverts to atavistic master-slave exchanges. "The landlord inside him wasn't dead, after all," notes Balram wryly as Ashok violently accosts him for aiding his wife's escape to the airport (182). Balram's responses lurch confusedly from contempt to pity to rage as Ashok succumbs to a life of drunken debauchery: "Do we loathe our masters behind a façade of love—or do we love them behind a façade of loathing?" (187). As his employers shamelessly pander to politicians to cover up a massive tax fraud, Balram finds himself deranged with fury. In *Sybil*, Disraeli had highlighted the correlation between the felonious origins of the Venetian oligarchy and the moral disorientation of their subjects. Balram makes a similar point: "once the master of the Honda City becomes corrupted, how can the driver stay innocent?" (197).

Adiga deftly demonstrates how the increasingly psychotic Balram cathects with abject, occluded others and an objectal world—the large dark fruits in a cellophane bag, the buffalo in the butcher's quarter in Old Delhi, the line of defecators in the slum where construction workers lived—in the absence of meaningful human communication between the stratified classes. The relationship between master and slave is one of physical intimacy and cultivated distance. "I swear, I was ready to make a full confession right there . . . had he said the right word . . . had he touched my shoulder the right way," Balram claims (257). Ashok's growing nonregard for Balram precipitates an inevitable violent correction, as prefigured in the cautionary tales in the *Murder Weekly*. Balram hatches a lethal plot to get his hands on the minister's ransom, justifying it as an act of revenge, not avarice, and as the cleansing violence of an insurrectionary world:

> *And even if you were to steal it, Balram, it wouldn't be stealing.*
> *How so?* I looked at the creature in the mirror.
> *See—Mr Ashok is giving money to all these politicians in Delhi so that they will excuse him from the tax he has to pay. And who owns that tax, in the end? Who but the ordinary people of this country—you!* (244)

He kills Mr. Ashok on a rainy night with an empty bottle of Johnnie Walker Black Label, crushing his skull and slitting his throat, and disappears to Bangalore with seven hundred thousand rupees cash.

Adiga's use of the epistolary form is strategic for the transmission of the autobiographical tale of "a Half-Baked Indian" (10), whose access to education is fortuitous, discontinuous, and tragically incomplete: "Sentences of history or mathematics remembered from school textbooks (no boy remembers his schooling like one who was taken out of school, let me assure you), sentences about politics read in a newspaper while waiting for someone to come to an office, triangles and pyramids seen on the torn pages of the old geometry textbooks which every tea shop in this country uses to wrap its snacks in, bits of All India Radio news bulletins" (10–11). The epistolary novel unsettles the notion of unitary authorship with its constitutive doubleness—doubleness of author (the writer of the letters and the writer of the novel), as well as the doubleness of the reader (the addressee of the letter and the reader of the novel). It induces a related ontological uncertainty around the question of temporality. Are we reading the letters as they are written, or in the form in which the intended addressee receives them? Does the fact of the letters' publication and dissemination in the public sphere imply that the missives were intercepted? Who owns the letter, the sender, receiver, or interceptor? The abstract ideality of the letter in *White Tiger*, instead of offering a contrast with the materiality of bodies that it circulates between, heightens the reader's sense of the immateriality of Balram Halwai's body.

"Neither you nor I can speak English, but there are some things that can be said only in English," goes the first line of Balram's first letter to Wen Jiabao (3). In Vikram Seth's *A Suitable Boy*, a farmer says, "If you talk in English, you are king," to the anglicized Mann Kapoor (501). Balram keenly imbibes the English spoken in the backseat of his car along on that hunch, but not enough to speak the language—as he assumes would also be the case of the Chinese premier. Sanjay Subrahmanyam points out, "We are meant to believe—even within the conventions of the realist novel—that a person who must really function in Maithili or Bhojpuri can express his thoughts seamlessly in a language that he doesn't speak" ("Diary," 43). This logical inconsistency, however, testifies to the larger point that Adiga is making about the unslakable global aspirations of local capital (and the insinuation of the global in the local in a hypermediated information economy). As Dipesh Chakrabarty said of Marx's philosophical category of capital, it is always "planetary (or global) in its historical aspiration and universal in its constitution" ("Universalism," 654). Balram Halwai's narrative medium does not mix Indian languages or appropriate the accreted Indian English that more virtuoso auditors like Vikram Seth or Upamanyu Chatterjee effortlessly use. Adiga purportedly *translates* to English the thoughts of a man devoid of an English education, but while the cognitive and affective structures of Balram Halwai's musings may resonate as Indian, the language and idioms are not drawn from North Indian vernaculars. Shoddy colloquialisms like "kissing some god's arse," "wasted himself through buggery," "Time to dip my beak in her," "half-baked," and "mutt" sound like a mixture of the urban dictionary the Indian student picks up in his years abroad and an estranged, almost Orientalist, take on Indian slang and patois. "What does Balram sound like," Sanjay Subrahmanyam wants to know: "Whose vocabulary and whose expressions are these? On page after page, one is brought up short by the jangling dissonance of the language and the falsity of the expressions. This is a posh English-educated voice trying to talk dirty, without being able to pull it off" ("Diary," 9). More positively, perhaps, the inauthentic translation that is *The White Tiger* marks the evolution of a global and nonsynchronic language as it negotiates the conflicting speeds of diverse histories. It is the botched success story of an Indian underdog told in the language of the most mobile strata of international capitalism and a world literary system. And while Adiga's novel marks the emergence of a universal language, the stability of universals is simultaneously undermined through the historical difference that his "translation" struggles to neutralize.

The White Tiger has the ingredients of a thriller, except that the revelation of the murderer—"I slit Mr Ashok's throat" (42)—comes in the very first chapter of the book, and the narrative does not consequently move inexorably and seductively toward exposure followed by expedient resolution. Mohsin Hamid's *The Reluctant Fundamentalist*, shortlisted for the 2007 Man Booker Prize, works better in this respect. The novel begins with what looks eerily like a hostage situation, as Changez, a bearded Pakistani man, detains an American in a restaurant in the Old Anarkali district of Lahore with his life story: "I noticed that you were looking for something; more than looking, in fact you seemed to be on a *mission*, and since I am both native of this city and a speaker of your language, I thought I might offer you my services" (*Reluctant*, 1). The narrative that follows is a dramatic monologue in prose. Changez plies his listener with food and drink while teasing out his life story, the tale of a young Muslim boy from a shabby-genteel background who was educated at Princeton on a scholarship and went on to work at Underwood Samson & Company, a New York firm specializing in ruthless appraisals of ailing companies on the verge of takeovers. Ace student Changez knows by his senior year that he is "a perfect breast, if you will—tan, succulent, seemingly defiant of gravity" (5), and is momentarily euphoric over landing the job at the valuation firm. The other Princeton privilege he holds dear is his growing friendship with Erica, the American princess with a troubled past, and the cultural access this alliance provides.

The development plot and the romance plot in Changez's life trundle onward despite occasional digressions, detours, and misrecognitions, and Changez predictably loves New York ("I was in four and a half years, never an American; I was *immediately* a New Yorker"; 37), until 9/11 erupts on his TV screen and the world political scene, changing lives forever. His girlfriend, Erica, who has a melancholic attachment to her dead lover, cannot withstand the powerful nostalgia that 9/11 invokes. Changez is surprised to feel elation at the thought that "someone has so visibly brought America to her knees" (83). He gradually allows himself to feel the bewilderments, cultural estrangements, and rage of a reacculturated Muslim in post-9/11 New York and an out-of-joint nation. In his role as purveyor of American expansionism he identifies with Christian boys, captured by the Ottoman empire and brainwashed to fight ferociously against their own people: "I was a modern-day janissary, a servant of the American empire at a time when it was invading a country with a kinship to mine and was perhaps even colluding to ensure that my own country faced the threat of war" (173). His willing and untroubled assimilation thus far is rudely interrupted by intractable cultural difference. Erica disappears, a possible suicide; Changez chucks the American dream to return to Pakistan a secular nationalist.

The East-West clash of cultures that leads to Changez's reinvention in America is prefigured early in the novel. During a summer trip to Greece with fellow Princetonians, the island of Rhodes, fortified by ancient ramparts against the Turks, "much like the army and navy and air force of modern Greece," gives Changez pause for thought. "How strange it was for me to think I grew up on the other side!" (26). Despite the distributive and redistributive flows of capital, labor, texts, and commodities brought about by globalization, Hamid suggests that the West and the East still strain to find nationalist identity in reactive or contestatory modes. This colonial interpretative framework, however, dulls the edge of Hamid's political critique. Hamid neglects to look more strenuously at the depredations, corruptions, and failures of modernity in the postcolonial state. In his discussion of Pakistan after 9/11, Hamid focuses on the terrifying brinkmanship between the nuclear neighbors India and Pakistan following the December 2001 terrorist attack on the Indian parliament, and especially the role played by America in pressurizing Pakistan (through India). He does not, however, mention two key indigenous developments that rocked Pakistan in 2002: terrorist outrages *within* the country that threatened to destabilize the transition to democracy following the October parliamentary elections, and growing anxieties concerning the future of civil-military relations following the transition. Changez may have returned home, but American cultural imperialism still remains his main frame of reference. He pays his class dues to continue to receive the *Princeton Alumni Weekly*. He writes a single letter each year—which is always returned unopened—to Erica on the anniversary of her disappearance.

An intriguing feature of the narrative voice in *The Reluctant Fundamentalist* is the absence of what Isobel Armstrong, in her review of Browning's poetry, calls "the nervous energy of thinking itself, the halts and blocks of the effort" (93). The story of Changez's radicalization in the event of a neocolonial war is punctuated with lovingly detailed accounts of quotidian bourgeois life in peacetime Pakistan: the Punjab Club memberships of the fading aristocrats, the carefully maintained Toyota Corolla, the Christian bootlegger who delivers booze in a Suzuki pickup, the rolling blackouts and gaudy lights of Lahore by night, the *brothers* and *sons* that appear in the signage of filial businesses. The point that Hamid is making—with subtle irony, of course—is that Changez is possibly not a fundamentalist at all, and his posturing as such is an indictment of the unequivocal message that America's war on terror sent to the global south: if you are not with us you are against us. It is, however, not made perfectly clear what Hamid means by fundamentalism—Changez's activities, if his words to the American are to be believed, seem to be confined to advocating, on campus, "a disengagement from your country by mine," training students to see the parallels between war and international finance, and pressing on them "the merits of participating in demonstrations for greater independence in Pakistan's domestic and international affairs" (203). Can fundamentalism be redeemed as a mode of "focus[ing] on the fundamentals," as the Underwood motto goes?

M. H. Abrams identifies an important feature of the dramatic monologue when he points out that the speakers in monologues are generally unconscious of their deepest truths. Changez—one of literature's endless talkers, like Balram Halwai—is interchangeably a self-conscious casuist and an unconscious self-deceiver. The dialectic setup in the first paragraph of the novel—"native of this city" and "speaker of your language"—translates, in Changez's dealings with the stranger, to a menacing game of identification and difference with a symbolic America. The American is clearly in the wrong place at the wrong time: a time of what Bhabha calls "the living perplexity of history" (*Nation*, 306), and a fluctuating space, that "zone of occult instability" that marks the emergence of a violent national consciousness (Fanon, *Wretched*, 227). The resolution of the novel is brilliantly ambiguous: is Changez, the political gadfly, the anti-American rabble-rouser, the quarry, a Kurtz waiting for his Marlow, or is he choreographing with manic calm the decapitation of yet another agent of American interests? Changez's sly reference to the story of the Headless Horseman from *The Legend of Sleepy Hollow* keeps in play both possibilities: "I must admit, I am sometimes reminded of the sound of those spectral clip-clops when I go for nocturnal walks by myself. How they make my heart pound! But clearly you do not share my pleasure at this thought; indeed you appear decidedly anxious" (194–95). Again, is Changez's painstaking annulment of the idea of America the inevitable consequence of his late patriotism, or was his decision to quit "just the superior opportunism of a well-trained appraiser of ailing companies, who knows which way the wind is blowing," as James Lasdun puts it ("Empire Strikes Back," 2). The one-sided conversation remains intelligent until the end, in plain queen's English, without a trace of waywardness, vernacular eccentricity, or slang, stiffening in rare instances to signal defensiveness or a deliberate withholding. It ends as the best dramatic monologues do, to quote James Kincaid, with a "careful balance of the humorous and awful, the detached and immediate" ("Rhetorical Irony," 236).

The White Tiger and *The Reluctant Fundamentalist* are "glocal" novels, to use a term used by David Damrosch with reference to nongovernmental groups in the 1990s that sought to "think globally, act locally." To quote Damrosch: "In literature, glocalism takes two primary forms: writers can treat local matters for a global audience—working outward from their particular location—or they can emphasize a movement from the outside world in, presenting their locality as a microcosm of global exchange" (*How to Read*, 109). Adiga pitches for a global audience—just as Balram Halwai writes to a pan-Asian development narrative—playing native informant, albeit a fallacious one, through the misadventures of a character who is both an insider and an outsider. Adiga seems to rethink globalization in the postcolony by making a minority figure negotiate its power and pitfalls. With Hamid, the trajectory is reversed: the excursiveness of Changez's journey to America and his professional identification with the transnational New Yorker are both undone by the final return to Pakistan and filial, national structures. Both Balram and Changez are "self-translator[s]," to borrow a term used by Emily Apter to describe Edward Said (*Translation Zone*, 60). Both fleetingly bring about an enfolding of the opposing values and cultures of postcolonial nation and world for self-divided, "glocal" readers.

The most insouciant of the three major works I will discuss in this chapter is Mohammed Hanif's *A Case of Exploding Mangoes*. Unlike *The White Tiger* or *The Reluctant Fundamentalist*, Hanif's novel is not set in twenty-first-century India or Pakistan. The ostensible subject matter is the mysterious death of General Muhammad Zia ul-Haq, president of Pakistan between 1978 and 1988, aboard the plane *Pak One*, which crashed, killing General Zia, a host of senior army generals, and the American ambassador to Pakistan, Arnold Raphel. *A Case* plays on the polysemous signification of a "case": the crates of mangoes that were loaded on the plane (and that may have contained a can of nerve gas, which debilitated the pilots); a case for investigation that counts, among its suspects, a blind woman, a snake, a mango-loving crow, a canister of nerve gas, an army of tapeworms; and the shell of the imposing C-130 Hercules that is, however, rigged, and a powerful symbol of the ponderous body politic in Pakistan eviscerated from within. The narrative obsessively circles the case (and the cases) in the months preceding the crash, dissociating it from the larger politics of the U.S. standoff with the Soviet Union in Afghanistan. This is, after all, the 1980s, when America colluded with General Zia to train and equip the Afghan mujahideen as they fought their Soviet foe.

The novel's protagonist is Ali Shigri, a junior trainee officer in the Pakistani air force. Like Balram Halwai and Changez, he is a survivor, "the one who got away" (3), the hero of the *Bildungsroman* or what Priya Joshi calls the "nationsroman" (*Another Country*, 260), who acutely suffers the depredations of history yet lives to tell the tale. Ali is increasingly convinced that his father, Colonel Quli Shigri, was murdered on the orders of General Zia and hatches a complex plot to avenge the death, implicating in the process comico-pathological military types and the squadron laundryman's snake. The thickening of the plot in the countdown to the assassination has a parallel narrative that shows General Zia's paranoid descent into a comic state of psychic dereliction in the last months of his life. Through his case study of the increasingly befuddled Zia, Hanif satirizes, with implosive comic effect, the pernicious liaison between religious mania and militarism that haunts Pakistani politics. In a telling moment, the president's head is lodged between Pakistan's national flag, and the flag of the Pakistan army, as he is probed by the gloved and lubricated finger of a Saudi doctor. He looks at the army flag, and at the famous slogan underneath the crossed swords that the Founder of the Nation had given the country as its birthday present and motto: "Faith. Unity. Discipline."

Suddenly, the slogan seemed not only banal and meaningless to him but too secular, non-committal, almost heretical. . . . He felt the doctor's breath on his arse. . . . It also dawned on him that when the Founder came up with this slogan, he had civilians in mind, not the armed forces. This slogan, he told himself, had to go. His mind raced, searching words that would reflect the true nature of his soldiers' mission. Allah had to be there. Jihad, very important. (82–83)

The novel is densely populated with what Salman Rushdie, in *Satanic Verses*, called "temporary human beings, with little hope of being declared permanent" (*Satanic*, 264). The homosexual Baby "O," Ali's friend and lover in the air force academy, with his penchant for the perfume "Poison"; Bannon, the American drill inspector, who regales cadets with dubious stories of his homicidal activities in Operation Bloody Rice in Vietnam; Brigadier TM, who didn't miss his parachute landing target even in death (he was murdered, actually, and landed on the bull's eye regardless). Then there is General Zia, ruthless, violent, and emotionally incontinent, behaving "like a twelve-year-old having a bad birthday" on his frequent visits to Mecca: "He threw tantrums, he cried, he smashed his head against the black marble wall of the Khana Kaaba, he sprinted around it as if he was in some kind of competitive run, not on a pilgrimage" (*A Case*, 155). And finally, at the Fourth of July party hosted by Arnold Raphel, there appears a bearded Saudi known as "OBL" who works for "Laden and Co. constructions," and is a valuable guest of the local CIA chief.

Hamid and Hanif extrapolate freely from the experiences of Westernized, upper-middle-class Pakistanis, who grew up in the 1980s. An article in the *Guardian* has quoted Hamid as saying that for Pakistan's minority English-speaking elite, who had lived an insulated lifestyle up to the 1980s, the oppressive dictatorship of General Zia was a "dramatic wrenching change": "Great fiction comes from the tension that produces those dramatic political developments" (Shah, "As Their Country"). The effrontery of Mohammed Hanif's English-language novel is breathtaking, reminiscent of Heller and DeLillo, and sometimes its verbal energy obscures its clear-eyed prescience about the deep dysfunction and corruption of postcolonial states, and the way history repeats to claim its symbolic due. The novel makes optimal use of the fictional possibilities of such a breakdown: its technique entails a working over of the realist novel with tricks of consciousness, dreams and nightmares, and local and European fables that give tentative and provisional form to the phantasmagoria of history. With its allusion to García Márquez's *Chronicle of a Death Foretold*, a novel where the death of the main character is announced on the very first page, *Case* asks readers to question its own originality and truth claims as narrative fiction, given that the plot shadows a well-documented historical life with a foretold outcome. Hanif's novel starts too with the announcement of imminent death. "You are a pervert, comrade," says Ali Shigri to Obaid, who reads García Márquez as they fly out together on a mission for the last time. While Hanif dabbles in the marvelous and the surreal, the profoundest absurdity of the novel derives from the history it narrativizes: medieval torture carried out with modern Philips irons, a gang-rape victim sentenced to be stoned to death (for she has unwittingly committed adultery with her attackers), Obaid's fascination for the soaring hero of *Jonathan Livingstone Seagull* in a novel full of plummeting men, the military dictator with an eye on the Nobel Peace Prize. The novel draws on a transnational, global English, the collective language that is carried around and traded with, and that Said, in his memoir, *Out of Place*, sees "dominated by a small handful of perceptibly banal systems deriving from comics, film serial fiction, advertising, and popular lore that was essentially at street level" (200). Hanif uses English (and also the conventions of the *Bildungsroman*) as if they were his own to commute the acrolects, sociolects, and idiolects of a failed state.

The last couple of novels I discuss in this chapter deal with class disparity and extreme poverty in the postcolonial, neoliberal state. Speaking of the depersonalizaton of colonized peoples, Albert Memmi states that the subjugated race always bears "the mark of the plural" (*Colonizer*, 129)—the colonized subject is never allowed individuation and stands for a faceless multitude. This colonial paradigm applies also to the representation of poverty, which seems to be limit case of cultural representations of class conflict in India, or a category that operates beyond class (as in underclass or lumpenproletariat). Poverty remains an unquantifiable term and indeterminate concept, related to complex social forces that cause hunger and human abjection. Nayantara Sahgal's, Indra Sinha's, and Aravind Adiga's portrayals of the evils of the neocolonial state seem to involve representations of the poor as animal, and also the poor as the collective unconscious of (or at best a temporal condition of transition for) the upwardly mobile Western or expatriated observer. How, then, does literature reconcile the discourse of class with the phenomenon of poverty? How does minority consciousness emerge and how is it sustained? Is the poverty theme the gothic monster that is entertained in South Asian cultural production only to be forcefully expelled?

In his short book *The Open: Man and Animal*, Giorgio Agamben accepts Heidegger's perplexed but ultimately privative account of the human as the discloser of being. It may indeed be, as Agamben argues, that the name and being of man is always in question, that *Homo sapiens* does not designate a species, but rather an "anthropological machine" for the production of the human, but this indeterminacy is lifted into the very condition of man's exceptionality and privilege. Agamben follows Heidegger in defining man as the being that must heroically—and, it seems, uniquely—ask itself the question of its own being. Agamben offers an account of the machinelike process whereby the species "man" is produced. He shows how identificatory characteristics emerge once the "animal" is posited as something negative in order for the human to be determined by way of a negation of the negation: "The equating of the negation of the negation with positivity is the quintessence of identification" (27). Agamben revises Heidegger when he defines human freedom as a function of its proximity to, rather than distance from, animal life.

Agamben looks forward to the demise of the anthropological machine, the "device for producing the recognition of the human" (26): to render inoperative this machine that governs our conception of man would not mean to search for new—more effective or more authentic—articulations of this conception, but rather to display "the central void, the hiatus which—within the human—separates man and animal" (92). Agamben's positive biopolitics is thus a call for the human being to appropriate "his own concealedness, his own animality, which neither remains hidden nor is made an object of mastery, but is thought as such" (92). The novels that I will now discuss bear testimony to this condition of bare life, where the machine is stopped in the "reciprocal suspension of the two terms, something for which we perhaps have no name and wherein that which is neither animal nor man settles in between nature and humanity" (92).

In Nayantara Sahgal's *Rich Like Us*, set in the murky world of post-Emergency Delhi, the red-haired Cockney memsahib Rose forges an unlikely psychic alliance with a beggar, first described as "altogether a great bone arch, more insect than animal, inching diagonally across the road on its knees" (10). Mr. Neuman, the representative of a foreign multinational, who has just been the beneficiary of Rose's stepson Dev's obsequious attention—Dev wants to start a cola ("Happyola") factory—is made to ponder the absurdity of his briefing, "If they'd do like we do, they'd be rich like us," in the context of the extreme disability a worker without working parts represents (10). The figure of the beggar in a gloomy, decrepit tomb, "part of the moss-covered wall" (290), becomes a logical copula that brings together different narratives of dispossession in the novel, including that of Rose, an unhappy hybrid of wife and mistress, local and foreign, subject and object of her own anthropological gaze. Acutely vulnerable to the injustices of a totalitarian state, the beggar brings home, for Rose, Gandhi's doctrine that service of India means wiping the tears from every eye. Rose had forgotten the phrase "until the handless beggar who couldn't wipe his own tears brought it back to her" (143). When Sonali, the idealistic civil servant, goes back to the scene of Rose's disappearance—not far from the beggar's habitat—to carry out her friend Rose's wish to give the man artificial limbs, she retrieves the story of Rose's murder that seems of a piece with the beggar's story of his violent disenfranchisement from his land. In the totalitarian biopolitics of the Emergency era, entire human ways of life are excluded from the political and the civil (or included in these registers as bestial): life not worthy of being lived, which is eventually exterminated or left to die.

This commingling of human and animal can also be seen in Adiga's Booker-winning novel about the Indian parvenu, Balram Halwai, which I have discussed earlier. Indra Sinha's Booker-shortlisted *Animal's People* (2007) describes the body of the socially abjected as it has morphed into a four-footed beast. The protagonist, Animal, is posthuman, the residue of a human catastrophe, the gas leak at Union Carbide's Bhopal factory in December 1984 (the book is a fictional reworking, of course, and the Bleak House of Bhopal is renamed "Khaufpur").[18] Animal is a picaro, only this "beastly boy," this human animal, is a trenchant reminder of what Rob Nixon, quoting Giancarlo Maiorino, identifies as "the antihumanist core of the picaresque" ("Neoliberalism," 453).[19] As Nixon observes, Sinha deploys Animal's physical form "as not just consequence, but a condensation of occluded transnational economic relations. His picaro is literally outlandish, his twisted body the physical manifestation of extraterritorial, offshore capitalist practices" (453). Animal is an extreme example of the physical and environmental fallout, visited on the bodies of the poor, of actions carried out long-distance by global overlords. He is "unique, but not exceptional," Nixon points out: "In his singularity he serves as a synecdoche for the spectrum of mutations to which Khaufpuris have been subjected over time, ranging from the celebrated singer with now-ravaged lungs to the chatty Kha-in-a-jar, a double-headed, bottled fetus that envies Animal his external, unbottled freedoms" (453).

Joseph Slaughter's work on the parallel histories of the *Bildungsroman* and international human rights law is applicable to the ways in which

Adiga and Sinha capacitate and chart the subjectivation of their antiheroes. In the tradition of the *Bildungsroman*, these novels explore the limits of democratic citizenship, the meaning of being human, and the question of equal and inalienable rights: "From the perspective of human rights, we might recognize *Bildungsroman* . . . as the name of a function, the generic label that good reformists repeatedly give to texts that perform a certain kind of incorporative literary social work" ("Enabling Fictions," 1411). Animal is living testimony that there is no biological, existential, ethical, and economical common ground between the rich and the poor. As the old woman, disfigured by toxicity, tells the Kampani lawyer: "You were making poisons to kill insects, but you killed us instead . . . was there ever much difference, to you?" (*Animal's People*, 306). He lives in a twilight world of superstition and hearsay and conflicting discourses that articulate the broken logic of his "unnatural" body (78). His self-awareness is described by a primal moment of social abandonment, when children at the orphanage call him "animal," and emancipatory narratives such as the activist Zafar's, which redefine him as "especially abled" (23). His cosmology is divided between a half-hearted subscription to Chunaram's karmic Hinduism, with commensurate rewards in successive lives ("a better deal next time round") lined up in exchange for the suffering endured in the present, and the skeptical realization that this might, by the same logic, tie his abnormal body to the "evil things I did in my past lives" (240). Animal's debased, animal-like survival is ringed around by the detritus of industrial capitalism, forcibly proving that globalization is multispeed and uneven: Kampani, the multinational corporation responsible for making Khaufpur the "world capital of fucked lungs" (230); "Amrika," a hyperbolic America that is both poison and cure for this small town; the "tape mashin" that was left by a foreign reporter, and that enables the transmission of the unlettered Animal's tale; the ubiquitous and mistranslated Hollywood (Animal calls the act of spying "jamesponding," or James Bonding). Animal's existence prompts philosophical insights on the fungible borders of human, inhuman, and machine, and offers an excoriating critique on the plight of the subpoor under the aegis of neoliberalism. More importantly, his obtuseness to narratives of progress and self-improvement—he refuses corrective surgery for his crippled body—sounds a hopeful note that not all bodies can be superseded in the inexorable drift of history into World-history.[20] In a climactic scene, Animal is wracked by hallucinations caused by thirteen poisonous Datura pills. He is in an animated forest, and, for the first time in the novel, finds himself the predator, not quarry, not merely a freak show objectified by the "Eyes," his unseen readers-tormentors, spying on him from a distance, but one who is free to visualize his subjectivity in the scene. Sinha does not implausibly add psychological depth to the character, but lets it proliferate in pictorial surfaces. Animal's center of (un)consciousness registers the inexorable drift of sustainable creaturely life: "a tree gobbles the monkey's bones, tree grows tall, shining fruits appear among its leaves, a monkey sits on a branch eating the moon" (345). His thoughts of survival are not sustained by an illusory totality but the insistence of language, inaugurating the split-subject of enunciation: "I am a small burning, freezing creature, naked and alone in a vast world, in a wilderness where is neither food nor water and not a single friendly soul. But I'll not be bullied." (*Animal's People*, 350).

Animal's People ends with Animal's seriocomic intoning of the following manifesto: "All things pass, but the poor remain. We are the people of the Apokalis. Tomorrow there will be more of us" (366). The novels by Sinha and Sahgal do not end with a restitution of individual to society, but they offer an alternative and contingent "conceptual vocabulary" and a "narrative grammar," to quote Slaughter again, "of free and full human personality development" ("Enabling Fictions," 1407).

"We are always *after* the empire of reason, our claims to it always short of adequate" says Gayatri Chakravorty Spivak of postcoloniality ("Poststructuralism," 228). The novels in English discussed in this chapter, however, do not seem to be worked over by the Enlightenment project associated with colonialism in a similar way. As Peter Childs says of the Indian novel in English post-1947, "The idea of Indian identity has . . . figured more prominently in narratives of Englishness as the troubled margins of the nation have increasingly been located not just at its geo-cultural edges but internally" (*Postcolonial Theory*, 23). Englishness—or Americanness, for that matter—is discussed in contemporary subcontinental writing in English in relation to the empire and the aftermaths of empire, but more often to relate to migrant, diasporic, and global ethnicities and the emergence of a collective language of uncertain ownership. These English language novels speak to the transformation of "English literature" to "literatures in English," a continental drift which, to quote Gauri

Viswanathan, "deterritorializes the national implications of English literature, and . . . refocuses attention on language rather than the nation as the creative principle of literature" ("Pedagogical Alternatives," 57–58). A final, trenchant example of this epistemic change is Mohammed Hanif's profoundly funny short story, "Butt and Bhatti," about a Muslim policeman, Teddy Butt, and his love interest, the Christian nurse Sister Alice Bhatti. The story is entrenched in the local realities of Pakistan, yet it laughs in the face of Fredric Jameson's depiction of third world literature as "the story of the private individual destiny [that] is always an allegory of the embattled situation of the public third-world culture and society" ("Third World Literature," 69). Butt is, in many ways, a sum of his parts. His hollow hypermasculinity, his brutality, covetousness, and callous abuse of women are not out of character for a police tout in a morally bankrupt law-and-order system. But he is also a man deranged by love, whose ardor he ill-advisedly expresses by ambushing Alice Bhatti at gunpoint:

"The love that I feel for you is not the love I feel for any other human being. The world might think it's the love of your flesh. I can understand this world and their thinking. I have wondered about this and thought long and hard and realized that this is a world full of sinners so I do understand what they think but I don't think like that. When I think about you, do I think about these milk pots?" He waves his Mauser across her chest. Alice looks at his gun and feels nauseous and wonders if the peace and quiet of this corridor is worth preserving. "I think of your eyes. I think of your eyes only." ("Butt and Bhatti," 128)

Nurse Bhatti collects herself and sends him packing with a calm admonishment, as one would a high-strung child. The heartbroken Butt flees in a daze and, outside the hospital, shoots the Mauser aimlessly. This unpremeditated and random gesture sets in motion waves of chaos and carnage, enough to discombobulate for three whole days a city always jittery from being in a permanent stage of siege. The failed civilian romance is not synecdochal of a failed state, though it choreographs one of its everyday breakdowns, where people are killed "while fixing their satellite dishes on their roofs" (130). "Butt and Bhatti" is not a Pakistani take on *Romeo and Juliet*. The political and the personal are thrust together by accident, like the ampersand of a moment's madness bringing together the odd couple Butt and Bhatti. Hanif delineates a Pakistan where KFC joints and billions of rupees worth of Suzukis and Toyotas juxtapose with poverty, atavistic mores, a crumbling infrastructure, and the ubiquitous threat of terror, but, far from being a national allegory, the story is one of lumpen love, the comic incompatibility of its hero and heroine amplifying one of many unrealizable narratives in life.

Irrespective of their geopolitical location, Adiga, Sinha, Hanif, and Hamid view Europe/America from outside Europe/America, and affect a provincialization of the West, retaining all the while a deep suspicion about the centripetal pull of literary and cultural nationalism. Notwithstanding universal condemnations of Fredric Jameson's delineation of third world literature as "national allegory," the efficacy of literature from the subcontinent is often related to its powerful representation of "the ambiguous and shifting relations that exist between individuals and groups in a plural community" (Mukherjee, "Anxiety," 2608). The new generation of novels discussed here, however, is about individuation in unpropitious circumstances. While the conclusion of *Midnight's Children* sees Saleem Sinai exploding under the awful pressure of the crowd, Ali Shigri in *A Case of Exploding Mangoes* takes small comfort in being "the one that got away." This moment of movement I call "emergence," which I have delineated as a literary trope associated with the vernacular canon of English, and which is not to be confused with the generalization of postcolonial English literature as "emergent" or fledgling.[21] All four novels seem to emphasize what Aamir Mufti calls the ethical possibilities of "minority existence" in modernity, even as the specter of millions of Chinese users of English changes, for the better, the literal connotations of "minority" ("Auerbach," 107).

6

hamarashakespeare.com
Shakespeare in India

Contemplating the implicit universalism of globalization, which seems to go hand in hand with its adaptability to local interest, Simon Gikandi wonders if globalization is appealing to social scientists "because of what is perceived as its conjunctive and disjunctive form and function" ("Globalization," 627). Shakespeare as a global commodity does seem to perform a "conjunctive and disjunctive" function. For example, in an essay titled "Shakuntala, Miranda, and Desdemona," the celebrated nineteenth-century Bengali novelist Bankim Chandra Chattopadhyay compares Shakespeare heroines to those of the Sanskrit poet Kalidasa, and finds them to be better *sati*s than their Indian counterparts. Bankim is using the term *sati* in the general cultural sense of "loyal in wifely duty" and "faithful": in his estimation, even the meekest of heroines like Shakuntala seems belligerent in comparison with the silently suffering Desdemona. The historical association of *sati* with the practice of bride immolation, however, makes for what Roberto Fernández Retamar calls an "alien elaboration" ("Caliban," 27) of Shakespeare in Hindu myth and belief: it momentarily reconciles recondite vernacular elements and the universal (the Hindu notion of the ultimate sacrifice of the widow on her husband's pyre and the universal ideal of self-sacrificing femininity) before doubling as a site of tension between the two. This chapter traces curious adaptations of the Shakespearean text in Indian cinema and on the Indian stage. As Christy Desmet observes, "The history of Shakespeare appropriation contests bardolatry by demystifying the concept of authorship" (*Shakespeare and Appropriation*, ed. Desmet and Sawyer, 4). In a country where Shakespeare is a mandatory part of the university curriculum in English, where Shakespeare could indeed be said to help the university reproduce itself,[1] these translations offer audacious, sometimes irreverent, instances of Shakespeare love, authorship, and revisionism.

The title of the chapter jokily refers to the Web site (www.hamarashakespeare.com) of an obscure translation project on the information highway that stages Shakespeare plays in Indian languages in Chennai every February. Shakespeare was, from the inception of British literary education in nineteenth-century India, a vital part of educational policy, placed alongside the Bible to introduce Indians to sound Protestant principles, and "widely deployed in classrooms from Calcutta to Lahore," as Ania Loomba observes ("*Hamlet* in Mizoram," 231).[2] The title Hamara Shakespeare—"Our Shakespeare"—serves well a chapter that is primarily devoted to popular, nonacademic, and improvisational Shakespeare adaptations in India, and enjoys the insouciance of players unschooled in Shakespeare making the Shakespearean corpus their own, an effrontery which marks my own critical stance as a non-Shakespearean scholar "doing" Shakespeare. Hamara Shakespeare showcased three experimental adaptations of *Macbeth* in February 2011: a Malayalam *Macbeth*, which eschews gradual plot development for a narrative that is articulated from monologues; a second play that draws on the ancient Indian performing tradition of Koodiyattam; and Vikram Iyengar's *Crossings*, a play focalizing on Lady Macbeth, which works over the verbal text constructed from the dialogue of the original with Indian classical dance, iconography, mythology, and demonology. The choice of an art form like Koodiyattam that is more dependent on facial expressions and nonverbal integers rather than speech—actors undergo lengthy and vigorous training for perfecting eye movements alone—bespeaks the assumption that Shakespeare's tale is well known enough not to require full verbal explication. "It is a story that anyone can relate to," says the celebrated Koodiyattam actor Margi Madhu, justifying the Indianized reprisal that remakes *Macbeth* in its own image.[3] Madhu's *Macbeth* yokes Koodiyattam's full affective apparatus of *Angika* (body movements), *Vachika* (verbal expression), *Satvika* (manifestation of internal feelings), and *Aharya* (extraneous) to express the psychodrama of Macbeth's life, albeit at the cost of plot detail, supporting characters, and plot endings (the play stops with Macbeth fainting at the sight of the approaching Birnam woods). The raison d'être of the local adaptation seems to be the insertion of culture-specific detail—Macbeth's victory is celebrated with the traditional orchestra of *chenda, maddhalam, edekka,* and *thimila,* while Duncan is served a traditional Kerala feast by Macbeth—and the deployment of the semiotics of an esoteric Indian dance form to reshape a classic story.[4]

The Hamara Shakespeare project is one of many cultural instances of Shakespeare adaptations in India that seem relatively untroubled by the historical and institutional context of the plays—or the play text, for that matter—and amplify the ludic possibilities of an overfamiliar yet uncanny Shakespearean story, sometimes in the service of searing political commentary relevant in the local geopolitical context. Take, for example, the popularity of *Hamlet* in Mizoram, a tribal state in the borders of Burma and India, which Ania Loomba interprets as a "negotiation between the failure of the MNF-related resistance and its possible resurgences" ("*Hamlet* in Mizoram," 243).[5] Translated into Mizo some fifty years ago, *Hamlet* is performed in Mizoram in informal venues and the open air: tape recordings of the plays can later be heard blaring from market kiosks. *Hamlet-drama,* as the Mizos call it, is rarely performed in its entirety, the provisional nature of its montage-like narrative enhanced by local exigencies, as when "Horatio is called away to his job as senior technician at Aizawl's only hospital" ("*Hamlet* in Mizoram," 243). "Is *Hamlet-drama* Shakespeare at all?" asks Loomba (245). It is evident that the Mizos are not using Shakespearean drama as a means to cultural capital: the players and the audience have a sketchy knowledge of originals and seem oblivious of Shakespeare's prestige. Or is it possible that "when Hamlet came to Mizoram, he became a Mizo," as the opening line in Pankaj Butalia's 1989 film, *When Hamlet Came to Mizoram,* goes? Loomba's essay is a response to the Butalia documentary, and she takes issue with its focus on a "wandering, lamenting Ophelia," because "the film's scopophilic gaze on Ophelia throws into sharp focus its coyness in looking at other aspects of Mizoram, notably its recent political history" (242). For Loomba, this play, "enacted in the crucible of political unease" (243), should be read instead as a symptom of radical, if temporarily baffled, (political) performativity. The Mizo *Hamlet* is unique also in the way it cannot be interpellated in the category of "postcolonial": the subaltern status of the Mizo is largely due to disenfranchising Indian (Central) government policy and the widespread cultural invisibility of the tribal in modern India.[6] It is also not possible to categorize the *Hamlet* obsession as a phase in an evolving local art form with open structures of inclusion: Mizos have no indigenous theater traditions and performances of the play are in European costume. According to Loomba, *Hamlet*-drama functions as a private theatrical, focusing on questions of beleaguered identity, playacting and dissembling, and "glamourizes individual, as opposed to collective identity" (244). The overwhelming allegorical force of the *Hamlet*-story, however, means that for this Mizo narrative of individuation "the movement of its inscription is the very possibility of its effacement" (Derrida, "No Apocalypse," 27).

This chapter has three broad sections. The first details two unusual adaptations of Shakespeare in nineteenth-century Calcutta: Girish Ghosh's Bengali translation of *Macbeth* and Mr. Barry's staging of *Othello* using an Indian "Moor." The second traces the history of "Shakespearana," the traveling theater company founded by actor-manager Geoffrey Kendal, who toured India and the Far East extensively between the 1940s and the 1970s. I read Kendal's autobiography alongside the 1965 Merchant Ivory production, *Shakespeare Wallah*, a fictional portrayal of a wandering Shakespearean troupe that captures the vicissitudes of the relationship between Shakespeare and his non-English players and playgoers. The final section, which ends with an interview with Vishal Bhardwaj, reads the acclaimed Indian filmmaker's retellings of *Macbeth* and *Othello* in the Hindi movies *Maqbool* and *Omkara*, respectively, to examine the displacements of the translated, yet unmistakeably Shakespearean, story in fraught national and regional contexts. I will hazard parsing the questions this chapter raises: Is there a consensual Shakespeare across languages and cultures? What is the relation of this world text to the mythopoeic heritage, the many languages and lived realities of the heterotopic subcontinent? How does the counterculture of Shakespeare performance in India contribute to the counterdiscourse of postcolonial modernity, one that reflects neither a vindictive remembering nor a forcible erasure of the historical conditions of its emergence, and is sustained instead by what Ian Baucom, in a different but relatable context (that of the legacy of the trans-Atlantic slave trade), calls the responsibility and promise of a "transverse [and] relational" mode of being (*Specters of the Atlantic*, 317)?

Shakespeare "on the Calcutta Boards"

"If the spirit of Garrick and Shakespeare ever recombined in a new and blessed embodiment, only then could the void left by Girish's death begin to be addressed," writes Abinash Chandra Gangopadhyay, biographer of the Bengali theater luminary Girish Chandra Ghosh (*bangla san*, 1250–1318, A.D. 1844–1912).[7] Girish Ghosh was not just the doyen of the Bengali stage but also a musician, playwright, novelist, and poet. He is also credited to have translated *Macbeth*, which opened at the Minerva Theatre on January 28, 1893. The play drew encomiums from English and Indian commentators alike. "A Bengali Thane of Cawdor is a lively suggestion of incongruity, but the reality is an admirable reproduction of all the conventions of an English stage," observed the editor of the *Englishman* (Gangopadhyay, *Girishchandra*, 266). The editor of *Indian Nation*, N. Ghosh, preferred Ghosh's Bengali translation to an erstwhile French one, while Maharaja Jatindramohan Tagore praised Ghosh for the way the seemingly untranslatable sections of the play had been borne across in Girish's Bengali script. The High Court judges Chandra Madhab Ghosh and Gurudas Bandopadhyay, along with the Barrister P. L. Ray, issued a joint review of the Classic Theatre staging of *Macbeth*, highlighting again the superior ease of the translated text: "To translate the inimitable language of Shakespeare was a task of no ordinary difficulty; but Babu Girish Chandra Ghose has performed that difficult task very creditably on the whole, and his translation is in many places worthy of the original" (Gangopadhyay, *Girishchandra*, 267).

According to his biographer, Girish's resolve to translate Shakespeare is traceable to his childhood habit of questioning limits and attempting the impossible. Gangopadhyay relates an episode from Girish's boyhood in which the child coveted the first crop of the cucumber tree in the backyard, especially since it was dedicated to the deity of the house. "I am thirsty," cried Girish inconsolably an entire evening, while still turning away offers of water. "Giri, if indeed you are thirsty, why won't you have a drink?" asked his father. "It is not a thirst for water," the boy solemnly said. "What sort is it, then?" the father insisted. "I am thirsty for the cucumber in our garden." The bemused father circumvented family rules to placate boy over God, and Girish often cited this scenario of wish-fulfillment to illustrate how he was spurred, not deterred, by prohibition or perceived difficulty. The translation of Shakespeare, Gangopadhay claims, was influenced by a comment by Gurudas Bandopadhyay, a renowned High Court judge, which acted as a dare that set Ghosh up for attempting the translation. The two men, old classmates from the Hare School, had met after a performance at the Great National Theatre of Haralal Ray's *Rudrapal*, a Bengali adaptation of *Macbeth*, and Gurudas had said that while the translation of Shakespeare into Bengali could only enrich the latter, the Shakespearean text was often lost in translation, as with the witches' speeches in *Macbeth* (Gangopadhyay, *Girishchandra*, 118).

Girish Chandra made good progress with the translation, but the manuscript was misplaced when the Atkinson Company, where he was bookkeeper, shut down. He revived the project again in 1893, at the height of his stage career, recalling his previous work from memory. The result was sensational. Instead of a literal translation, Ghosh captures the sense of the witches' discourse through a commensurability of the jargon and argot and the ambient queerness of the Weïrd Sisters. Let's take, for example, the first witch's dialogue from act 1, scene 1.[8]

First Witch: When shall we three meet again?
In thunder, lightning, or in rain?

Gangopadhyay suggests a faithful, if tame, translation:

Ābār milibo bal kothā teen jané—
Bajrodhwoni, damini, bā bāri borishané?

The Bengali thespian Utpal Dutt, translating *Macbeth* in 1975, comes with a similar, if less formal, version with his use of spoken urban Bengali:

Ābār kabé dekhā habé teenjané
Bajropāt, bidyut, ghorborshār kon diné?

Girish Chandra's translation runs as follows:

Didi lo, bal nā ābār milbo kabé teen boné—
Jakhan jhorbé meghā jhupur jhupur,
Chak chakāchak hanbé chikur,
Kad kadākad kadāt kadāt dākbé jakhan jhanjhané?

Ghosh opens with "Didi lo"—"O my sisters"—and the "teen boné" or "we three sisters," at the end of the line, instead of "teen jané" ("we three"), further emphasizes the natural, filial connection between the unnatural women. Thunder, lightning, and rain are translated into words supplemented by onomatopoeic sound. Megha, or the rain cloud, rains "jhupur

jhupur," streaks of lightning flash "Chak chakāchak," and the thunder rumbles "Kad kadākad kadāt kadāt": the language is demotic, excessive, childlike. Again, the first witch says in the original text (scene 3):

A sailor's wife had chestnuts in her lap,
And mounch'd, and mounch'd, and mounch'd.

Dutt translates this as:

Ek mājhimāllār bou chhilo boshé,
Konchodé bādām. Chibiyé, chibeyé, chibiyé
Khāchchilo āyesh koré. (13)

Dutt's Bengali verb for "mounch'd" can be translated as "chewed," the raw enjoyment of the Shakespearean depiction gestured at by the qualifier "āyesh koré," or "with indolent enjoyment." Ghosh, however, translated the words as:

Elo chulé mālar meye, boshé udom gāy
Bhor konchodé chhenchā bādām, chākum chākum khāy.

Girish Chandra captures the overt sexuality of the verbal description in the original by making the sailor's daughter bare-backed ("udom gāy") and wild-haired. Chestnuts have been replaced with scaled groundnuts ("chhenchā bādām"), a popular street-side snack in Calcutta, the munching made lascivious by lapping, lip-smacking sounds ("chākum chākum").

I will include two more examples from this translation. The first is from act 4, scene 1, 22–34:

Scale of dragon, tooth of wolf;
Witches' mummy; maw, and gulf,[9]
Of the ravin'd salt-sea shark;
Root of hemlock, digg'd i'th' dark;
Liver of blaspheming Jew;
Gall of goat, and slips of yew,
Sliver'd in the moon's eclipse;
Nose of Turk, and Tartar's lips;
Finger of birth-strangled babe
Ditch-delivered by a drab,
Make the gruel thick and slab:
Add thereto a tiger's chaudron,
For th' ingredience of our cauldron.

The Girish Ghosh translation runs as follows:

Chhédé dé nekdé baghér dānt,
Sāper ensho mishié né tār sāth;
Suntki karā daini marā,
Nonā hangor khidhéy jarā,
Tuntitā né nā chhindé,
Bār koré né bhundi phéndé;
Bishér chārar sekad khānā
Āndhār rété khundé ānā;
Débatāké gāl déchhé sénté,
Né é ihudir mété;
Chhāgolér pitti thobā,
Niyé lo kadāy chobā;
Kabar bhuinyer jhāuer dāntā,
Geroner rété kātā;
Turkir nākér bontā,
Tātārer thonttā motā;
Biyiye chhélé khānār dhāré
Mukh tipé tār déchhé shéré
Nyalnélé angul chélé,
Éné dé lo kadāy phélé,
Thakthaké ghana ghana
Karo jhol kathā shono;
Bāghér bhunri tār uporé
Mashlā rākh kadā bhoré.

Ghosh brings to bear on this scene of cauldron boiling the arcana of Bengali *rupkatha*, or fairy tales, taking care to translate the Shakespearean text to identifiable ghoulish referents and emotional integers. "Scale of dragon" is translated to the scales sloughed by a snake ("sāper ensho"), the Yew (originator of the poisonous "slips of yew") represented as "the fir tree of the graveyard" ("jhāuer dāntā").[10] The translation of the thirteen lines of third witch's speech is almost double the length, as Ghosh amplifies the suggestions of the epigrammatic language for impact. For instance, he draws out the implications of both "maw and gulf," both meaning stomach and appetite, playing on the alternative meaning of "maw" as gullet. "Tear out the throat [tunti tā né nā chhindé] and carve out the entrails [bār koré né bhundi phéndé]," the fuller explication goes. There are also occasional misreadings: Ghosh takes "ravined" ("ravenous") for "ravished with hunger." The anti-Christian implication of the "blaspheming Jew" is overlooked in its translation as "God-abusing" ("Débotāké gāl dechhé sénté") Jew, and Ghosh emphasizes the racial imaging of "Tartar's lips" by translating the phrase as "the Tartar has fat lips" ("Tātārer thonttā motā"). The "moon's eclipse" is translated to the more slangy "geron" instead of the Sanskritized "grahan" for "eclipse." Overall, the language is colloquial and earthy, Ghosh opting for verbs that emphasize the coarse, visceral aspect of the apparitions that makes them all too real. The cauldron has become an everyday wok for cooking ("kadā"), the sneaky domesticity of this unnatural scenario further emphasized by translating "gruel" or "mixture" as "sauce" ("jhol") and "ingredience" as "mashlā," commonly used to refer to household spice provisions.

The next passage for consideration from the Girish Ghosh translation of *Macbeth* is a section of Lady Macbeth's famous soliloquy in act 1, scene 5, 39–49.

> Come, you Spirits
> That tend on mortal thoughts, unsex me here,
> And fill me, from crown to the toe, top-full
> Of direst cruelty! Make thick my blood
> Stop up th'access and passage to remorse;
> That no compunctious visitings of Nature
> Shake my fell purpose, nor keep peace between
> Th'effect and it! Come to my woman's breasts,
> And take my milk for gall, you murth'ring ministers,
> Wherever in your sightless substances
> You wait on Nature's mischief![11]

The Girish Ghosh translation runs as follows:

Āy, Āy, Āy ré narakbāshi pisāchnichay!
Dākichché jighāṇshā toré āy ttarā kori;
Hara nāri komalatā hridi hoté mama,
Āpadmastok kara kothinmoy.
Kara ghana shonit-probāho
Ruddha rākho hridayer dwār,
Mānab-swabhāb-jāto anutāp jeno nāhi pashé
Na talāy uddeshyo bhishan, danda nahi uthé moné,
Jadbodhi kārjo nahi hoy samādhān!
Esho hatyā-uttejonākāri

Bhrama jārā adrishyo shoriré,
Mānāb-swabhabé paap-uttejonā hetu,
Esho esho nārir hridoyé,
Payah paribarté bish dého payadharé.

The Ghosh translation turns the evocative to descriptive: "spirits" become "evil spirits" ("pisāchnichay")," "sex" is translated into "womanly tenderness" ("nāri komalatā") the vocative itself is seen to issue from not merely the enunciating subject but her core of "jighāṇshā," or propensity for violence. As in the original, Ghosh telescopes from universal to particular in the references to nature. The translation of "compunctious visitings of nature" is made in the universalizing spirit of the Shakespearean use of "sex," with nature generalized as "human nature" ("manab swabhāb"), and not necessarily feminine nature, but he reverts to gendered language for "Come to my woman's breasts." Breasts stand interchangeably for "the milk of human kindness" in the heart ("hriday") and breast milk.

According to Hemendranath Dasgupta, author of *The Indian Stage* (1944), the tunes of the songs of the Weïrd Sisters were borrowed from *Renowned Songs of the World*, a book Ghosh had procured from Harold's firm on Dalhousie Square. Ghosh uses constellations of sounds and words in the songs that lend themselves readily to musical elaboration, as is evident in this last example from the Ghosh translation, drawn on the fourth witch's song in act 4, scene 1, lines 44–45: "Black spirits and white, red spirits and gray, / Mingle, mingle, mingle, you that mingle may." Bypassing altogether the accreted meanings of what may have been a traditional "Charm" song in the Shakespearean version, Ghosh brings to his adaptation incantatory sounds that, despite their slangy irreverence, mimic the rousing cadences of traditional Kali mantras.

Dhalā kāli, katā lāli,
Milé julé cholé aay,
Jhun jhun jhun jhun
Jhun jhun jhun.

The doggerel "Dhalā kāli, katā lāli" is Girish's literal rendering of the colors white (dhalā), black (kālo), tawny (katā), and red (lāl). The use of the word Kāli, however, ties the black, white, and red of the famous cauldron scene to the shades of red, black, and white that feature prominently in the iconography of the Hindu goddess Kāli. Seen this way, the seemingly innocuous words develop sinister undertones, evoking the protruding shield-like tongue of Kāli ("dhāl"), or the garland of severed human heads ("kātā lali") the goddess of the night wears around her neck. Ghosh could also be calling on "Dākini Jogini," the witch duo that follows the trail of Kāli. The invocation of these fierce incarnations is, however, framed in the tender and colloquial "come hither," "cholé aay." The charge of the opening line is further diffused in the onomatopoeic "jhun jhun jhun jhun," imagining perhaps the tinkling of anklets of the approaching goddess, and undergirding a different, almost daughterly, aspect of her conglomerate femininity, comparable to that of the witches. The rampaging Kāli, the devourer of time (*kāl*), bestows dark (*kālo*) formlessness to the "Weïrd" (*Macbeth* 1.3.32) and wayward sisters in the Bengali *Macbeth*. Yet again, the translation captures the repetitive auditory patterns crucial to the "enchanting" (4.1.43) effect of the witches.

After seven months of rehearsals, Ghosh's *Macbeth* opened at the Minerva in 1893. He had wanted to name the theater "The Classic," but relented to the proprietor's request to have it named Minerva. Ghosh is said to have drawn inspiration and material from the handful of British theaters in Kolkata, especially Lewis's Theatre Royal (popularly known as Lewis Theatre), and his conversations on world theater and dramaturgy with the American Mrs. Lewis, renowned actress and founder of Lewis Theatre. Ghosh had employed the famous painter Mr. Willard to design the backdrop: the "drop scene" was earmarked for special praise in reviews, especially for the way in which a watercolor painting emulated the depth and intensity of oil. The makeup artist, Mr. J. Pym, was also recruited for this production, which went on to set a new standard of excellence in Bengali theater in costume design and makeup. Both Girish Ghosh's performance as Macbeth and Tinkodi Dāsi's as Lady Macbeth, and Ardhendu Shekhar Mustafi's multiple roles (as the porter, the first witch, the old man, the first murderer of Banquo, and the Scottish doctor) were applauded in sophisticated theater circles. The production, however, failed to become popular, perhaps because of an unfair comparison with the Ghosh-authored musical *Abu Hosen*, which had opened to packed houses that same year. This put paid to Girish Ghosh's ambitions of subsequent Shakespeare translations. Girish is reported to have said, airing his misgivings about professional theater in Bengal and the specious tastes of the theater-going public, that the general audience in Bengal was not yet ready to understand drama.[12]

If Girish Ghosh's translation of *Macbeth*, with its staging of a text hitherto seen as untranslatable, marks a milestone in Bengali theater history and evolving Indic theories and practices of dramaturgy, the English theater of colonial Calcutta also witnessed a daring experimentation with Shakespeare. In 1848, James Barry, the owner of the Sans Souci, a garrison theater in Calcutta originally designed to entertain expatriate Brits, cast a native gentleman, Baisnab Caran Adhya (anglicized in reviews as "Baboo Bustomchurn Addy"), in the title role of Othello. As Sudipto Chatterjee and Jyotsna Singh wittily remark, "The Moor and the Bengali had collapsed into one for Shakespeare's sake, for novelty's sake, for the colony's sake, and—in Barry's case—for profit's sake" ("Moor or Less?" 75). While Indian students had staged performances of Shakespeare earlier—as did Henry Derozio at the Dhurrumtollah Academy in Kolkata in December 1822—rarely did an Indian perform a key role in a Shakespeare play. Addy's recruitment by Barry is symptomatic of the growing trends of realist representation and verisimilitude in casting Shakespearean characters; it also reflects a novel turn in the Indian involvement in Shakespearean theater, namely aristocratic Indian patronage of hitherto racially segregated theater. In 1835, when the Chowringhee Theatre in Calcutta faced bankruptcy, Prince Dwarakanath Tagore, grandfather of Rabindranath, had bailed it out. The *Calcutta Star* of 1848 mentions that Mr. Barry had ventured to use the "kind and gratuitous services of a Native Gentleman" with the express sanction and patronage of an elite group of princes and bābus: "Maharajah Radkaunt Bahadur; Maharaja Buddinauth Roy; Maharajah Prawnkissen Mullick and Brothers; Baboos Greeschunder Dutt and Brothers."[13]

A letter appeared on August 12, 1848, in the *Calcutta Star*, excitedly anticipating the "debut of a real unpainted nigger" which had set "the whole world of Calcutta agog": "How full it must be—by Jove, Barry and the Nigger will make a fortune" (Lal and Chaudhuri, eds., *Shakespeare*, 22).[14] The play, however, opened to mixed reviews, best exemplified by the August 19 review in the *Bengal Harkaru*:

Othello, of Shakespeare's plays, the latest and the best, was the great attraction of Thursday night—the player, however, but not the play. Performed by Baboo Bustomchurn Addy ... all expectations were, of course, centred in the young aspirant for dramatic fame, who has gallantly flung down the gauntlet to the rest of the members of the Native community. For in England, it is well known, the poetry of the mind has long given way to the poetry of motion, and Shakespeare, exiled from the country he honours so much, seeks an asylum on the Calcutta boards.... Othello's entry was greeted with a hearty welcome.... Slim, but symmetrical in person, his delivery was somewhat cramped, but, under all circumstances, his pronunciation of English was for a Native remarkably good. (cited in Chatterjee and Singh, "Moor or Less?" 76–77).

The review, which begins positively and humorously on the phenomena of the worldwide circulation and Indian appropriation of Shakespeare, however, faults Addy eventually for being the not-white, not-quite-Shakespearean actor, though the role obviously sanctions a racial and cultural variation from European models of characterization. It goes on to criticize Addy's lack of proficiency in the "art of bye-play" and poor knowledge of stage business; his incompetence in the third act; his inability to "depict the ravages of the whirlwind of jealousy which overpowers the soul of the Moor"; the inaudibility and unintelligibility of his diction. Misgivings about the spectacle of miscegenation between the brown Addy and the white Mrs. Anderson are conspicuously absent, and grudging praise is handed out in the *Harkaru* review for Addy's theatricality in passionate scenes with Iago (3.3.451) and Desdemona (4.2.37). Soon after the second performance of the play, on September 12, 1848, it was clear from the increasingly hostile responses in the English-language dailies that despite the exiled Shakespeare's propensity to travel and tread the "Calcutta boards," the Native had failed to bring him home. The Indian Othello was a thing "to fear, not to delight" (1.2.71).

The Traveling Shakespeare Company

"We would ask to see the principal—who might be a Hindu in a dhoti, a Goanese mother superior, a Christian brother, a Parsee, or a Muslim. Shakespeare was the password, and the reception was nearly always warm" (107). This is Geoffrey Kendal, writing in his autobiography *The Shakespeare Wallah* of his tours with a repertory company through Indian schools and colleges: "At one newly built Hindu college... the principal cried: 'You act Shakespeare? Ah, Shakespeare is my *guru*.' Then he quoted: 'What is man If his chief good and market of his time / Be but to sleep and feed?'" (107–8). *The Shakespeare Wallah*, a moniker coined by the Merchant Ivory film *Shakespeare Wallah* and roughly translated as "the Shakespeare vendor," is a moving record of the manager-actor Geoffrey Kendal's two long and eventful stints in India, one beginning in 1946 and the other in 1953. "Armed with Shakespeare, whose plays were so much appreciated in India, we felt that we could ignore the warnings about the nationalist movement and possible troubles," writes Kendal of his first visit to India in 1946, the dawn of the Indian Independence in 1947 (85). The band of actors, including Geoffrey Kendal and his wife, Laura Liddell, travels through Partition turbulence and Hindu-Muslim riots in the dying days of the raj, the last "durbars" or royal courts of Hyderabad, Patiala, Gwalior, Travancore, and Cochin, the hill station schools with open-air amphitheaters against the backdrop of the Himalayas, tribal outposts and tea plantations. The first chapter of "Shakespearana," Kendal's traveling company, begins in Piccadilly Circus on a hot summer's day in February 1946 and ends with Mahatma Gandhi's assassination in February 1948. At the same time as India was bringing to a violent close the history of the colonial encounter, Kendal was acting out an alternative story of cultural exchange, transaction, and friendship. In the foreword to *The Shakespeare Wallah*, Felicity Kendal writes: "My father's passion was more to do with giving than gaining, and what he wanted to give was Shakespeare—Shakespeare presented with a minimum amount of fuss to the maximum number of people—to hundreds and thousands of people, in fact, who would meet the plays often for the first time, and remember them for ever" (viii). Kendal grew to love his Indian audiences: the rows of intelligent school girls "drinking in every word and gesture" (107); the last English headmasters of Mayo College, St. Paul's, Doon School, and Sherwood College; the odd implacable Maharaja; or wannabe thespians eager to learn the stage business of Shakespearean theater. A local amateur group in Travancore thanked Kendal for providing "in such profusion answers to questions which confronted us when trying to visualize an action while reading a play." "Let Shakespeare keep India and Britain united," the letter ended cheerily (89). He loved also the hard graft of building a rostrum out of lashed benches, sorting out light and borrowing a gramophone, conscripting a washer man to iron costumes, and putting up curtains. The greenroom was often a tiny desk in a kindergarten classroom, from where thanes and witches magically appeared at the appointed time. "We became adept in the art of improvisation" (122), Kendal writes. The company powered through performances with simple props such as a blue length of cloth that could be made to ripple across the stage, like a river, or French and English flags, which, flourished from the wings, created the impression of battle scenes in *Henry V*. In more desperate times, they willed the scene into darkness (as in a large gymnasium in Hong Kong flooded with the afternoon sun) through the evocative word power of *Macbeth*. Lighting—crucial for creating different effects out of the most unpromising props (the blue backdrop, for example, would have to at times appear as a clear blue sky and as a sky at sunset at others)—was primitive. During one performance the guests at Macbeth's feast went falling with the banquet table through the makeshift stage as soon as the words "You know your own degrees / Sit down" were uttered.

Shakespearana performed Shakespeare in India as though its life depended on it. The company used local musicians, as it had to: "the songs of Elizabethan England seemed to harmonize perfectly with an Indian flute or sitar," Kendal muses (123). Some of the productions were costumed in local dress and "from this a wonderful understanding between actor and audience developed" (123). India interrupted the dramatic illusion in unforeseeable and usually hilarious ways, such as when the *dhobi* (washer man), a pile of freshly laundered clothing on his head and an iron in his hand, came up to Othello on stage to say, "*Dhobi* finished now, *sahib*" (124). Kendal and company strained to make Shakespeare legible and effective and went to great lengths to elicit audience response, sometimes pantomiming a play in "good old Elizabethan tradition" (123). They laughed at the constant mishaps, spent their days perpetually traveling thousands of miles between scholastic centers, and their annual visits were increasingly seen as a seasonal return of the Bard himself. Once, the reservation card on their rail compartment actually read, "Mr Shakespeare and His Ladies."

Despite drawing on the international cachet of the 1965 Merchant Ivory film *Shakespeare Wallah* for the title of his autobiography, Kendal felt short-changed by this picturization of his life and the travails of the wandering Shakespeare Company: "Our touring company had been a great success and had brought Shakespeare to the furthest places of India. We had hoped the film would be an affirmation of this and an illustration of what was, to us, still a wonderful way of life. But *Shakespeare Wallah* showed the Buckingham Players down on their luck, trying to cadge bookings from unsympathetic school bursars, and overwhelmed by the slick, rich, song-and-dance Bombay movies" (145). *Shakespeare Wallah*, scripted by Ruth Prawar Jhabvalla and produced by James Ivory and Ismail Merchant, tells the story of the Buckingham Players, a traveling company specializing in adaptations of Shakespeare, and their dwindling fortunes in post-Independence India. While Kendal's autobiographical account of his 1946 arrival in India and the 1953 return (to India) references a rapidly changing, modernizing, India, this upheaval does not seem to affect the transactional nature of a peripatetic theater patronized by royalty, intelligentsia, the school system, as well as middle-class and lower-middle-class audiences. The Merchant Ivory production, however, presents the company as out of place and absurd from the start, as when they perform the Spanish Armada scene from Sheridan's *The Critic* against the backdrop of an ornamental pond till an errant cow stops play. In the film, Indians are depicted as treating the spectacle as a relic of a discredited cultural regime that gave the country its beflanneled schoolboys, half-timbered mock Tudor Simla houses, and hilltop schools. For Manjula, the popular film star who feels threatened and belittled by her lover's (the Casanova Sanju's) fascination with Shakespearean actors, the Buckingham Players is no classical rep but a ragtag group of men and loose women who wear filthy costumes and work disreputable venues. She is ignorant of Shakespeare and unfazed by it, and this makes her, in the eyes of Sanju, a mere "songstress," not an actor. Manjula, dressed as if for a premiere, and press photographer in tow, disrupts the performance of *Othello* grandly as she enters the playhouse late, a fuss she repeats by leaving the play early. Faced with Sanju's anger, she says, provocatively, "But it must have been very near the end Sanju*ji*, he killed the heroine." Manjula, brought to brittle, bitter, life by Madhur Jaffrey, presumably stands for the growing impatience in the newly minted nation with European narratives of aspiration and emancipation. The "mute testimonial" of the empty wine racks at the Simla Gleneagles Hotel testifies to the steady withdrawal of the British as a real, cultural presence. India, for the Buckingham Players, is increasingly what Pym calls "a place of impermanence" (*Wandering*, 37). There is talk among the expats of leaving and Buckingham, grown "old and sour," ponders the fate of Shakespeare in India: "Nowadays, why should they care?"

Actually, they did. The Shakespeare-mad Maharaja, played delectably by the Bengali thespian Utpal Dutt, has an unlikely affinity with the Buckingham Players, for, like they, he is in troubled times, forced to consider modernizing and making sustainable his sprawling estate: "We are all forced to make cuts in the text written for us by destiny," he quips. The banquet at the Maharaja's palace is almost entirely conducted in the international, Shakespearean language. The Maharaja breaks into an impromptu performance—the "quality of mercy" speech—telling the present company that the value of Shakespeare as a cultural import lies not only in his poetry, but also his wisdom: "Who could have expressed so well the turbulences of the heart? Who could have written so profoundly on the cares of kingship?" he asks wistfully. Thoughts turn soon to the transience of worldly power and the senior Buckinghams lugubriously recite lines from the deposition scene in *Richard II* ("Let us sit upon the ground / And tell sad stories of the death of kings"), to the mild unease of the Maharaja, who had clearly underestimated the tragic dimension of turning palaces into hotels for foreign tourists. Shakespearean textuality—and the players are a vital link in the chain, which helps transmit Shakespeare from the written word to word of mouth—provides commentary, critique, and, sometimes, clownage for an Anglo-Indian tale of star-crossed lovers. It speaks with many mouths of Lizzie and Sanju's predicament in the performances that dot the narrative: through Ophelia's distraction at the clash of imperatives, Sir Toby's bawdy revelry, Othello's poisoned sense of self, the "radiant poetry" of Romeo and Juliet's love,[15] and the treachery of Antony and Cleopatra's.

Everyone's Shakespeare

The Bengali actress, writer, and director Aparna Sen's film *36 Chowringhee Lane* (1981) casually references the imperial histories and legacies of Shakespeare in India, the plays which the English brought with them to Calcutta and staged in local playhouses like the Chowringhee Theatre and Sans Souci, the entry of Shakespeare in school and college curricula, and the creation of Macaulay Minute Bengali Babus, "Indian in blood and colour but English in tastes, in opinion, in morals and intellect."[16] The film shows a year—Christmas Day to Christmas Day—in the life of the Anglo-Indian school teacher Violet Stoneham. Miss Stoneham, as she is called by her charges, lives in a derelict building in what used to be the heart of colonial administration and European shopping in Kolkata, between Chowringhee Road, Park Street, and Theatre Road, her benumbed existence a round of school, the care home where her brother Eddie lies dying, and the grave of Davie, her childhood sweetheart killed in the war. Increasingly friendless since her niece Rosemary immigrated to

Australia, she has a cat of Shakespearean pretensions, Sir Toby, to keep her company. To make matters worse, Stoneham is sidelined in the new principal's ruthless reorganization of staff, demoted from the teaching of Shakespeare to the senior girls to teaching grammar in the junior section of the prestigious all-girls school. She feels superannuated and absurd, like other reliquaries of the British raj, and yet India is all she has ever known.[17] A cultured young Bengali couple befriends her with an eye to using her flat, empty during the workday, for their daily assignations. Worn down by her brother's sickbed dementia and the indignities of the workplace, Stoneham gives the charming Nandita, an old pupil, and Samaresh, her wisecracking and self-regarding boyfriend, free use of her home to ostensibly further the out-of-job Samaresh's writing career. She feels flattered to do so, she says: "Great works of literature being written in my place and all!" They make her tea in the evenings, rifle excitedly through her family curios and memorabilia, and make her laugh. The insouciance of young love proves tonic for Miss Stoneham, so she lives a little before Samaresh lands a job and the couple move on, callously leaving behind their life on 36 Chowringhee Lane. The crushing realization of this cruel, if rather pedestrian, betrayal of the old by the young comes to Miss Stoneham on Christmas Day, as she stands locked out of a party in Nandita and Samaresh's new bungalow, where young India momentarily gives in to the nostalgia of English LP records on her old gramophone, a wedding gift to the ingrates.

36 Chowringhee Lane is not an adaptation of Shakespeare, but "what matters is the role Shakespeare plays in it," as Greenblatt says of an anecdote on H. M. Stanley in the last essay of *Shakespearean Negotiations* (162). Richly literary in sensibility, the film relies on a consensual cultural sense of Shakespeare as the classic of classics and a staple of literary cultivation. The urban, literate, and possibly anglophile audience of the movie would feel acutely the relation of the Anglo-Indian teacher's self-worth to her now usurped role as Shakespeare specialist in a posh school. They would have little difficulty imagining her disenfranchisement as she stands outside her old classroom, looking in, as the new Shakespeare teacher, armed with a special degree in English and a model of the Globe, gets Stoneham's apathetic pupils to perform *Twelfth Night* with gusto. "Shakespeare is quite heavy stuff," as Stoneham says, and it bestows form and weight on citing subjects. It is to *King Lear* that Violet Stoneham turns in the end to articulate what Harold Bloom calls "the vision and wisdom of misery"

(*Shakespeare*, 239). Alone with a mongrel in the nighttime desolation of the Victoria Memorial, carrying the Christmas cake she had baked for those she had once considered her friends, she is sure of nothing but the lessons of Shakespeare.[18] Like Lear, her "terror of being loved, of needing love" (Cavell, "Avoidance," 62), has brought calamity on her head; like Lear the blindness and dotage of old age have led to unsparing intimations of the human condition.

> Pray, do not mock me:
> I am a foolish fond old man,
> Fourscore and upward, not an hour more nor less;
> And to deal plainly,
> I fear I am not in my perfect mind. (4.7.59–63)

The movie ends with Miss Stoneham reciting Lear's words to Cordelia after they have lost the battle, a final scene of misrecognition in which Lear acquiesces to his fate in the hope that at least Cordelia will be there to share it.

> Come, let's away to prison:
> We two alone will sing like birds i' the cage:
> When thou dost ask me blessing, I'll kneel down,
> And ask thee forgiveness: so we'll live,
> And pray, and sing, and tell old tales, and laugh
> At gilded butterflies, and hear poor rogues
> Talk of court news; and we'll talk with them too,
> Who loses and who wins; who's in, who's out . . . (5.3.7–14)

The lines quoted begin "No, no, no, no!" an exclamation which reinforces again Lear's catastrophic disavowal of consequences, the obdurate imperiousness of "Come, let's away" torquing up the pitiful projection of prison cells as bolt holes of escape and his fear of further humiliation. Stoneham finishes the sorry business of the day and year in an ennobling trance that is reminiscent of Shakespeare's Lear's, moving, like the King, from the authority of provisional consolations to the freedom of the inconsolable.

As the Bengali thespian Utpal Dutt once said, "The classics were not the prerogative of an elite. They would cease to exist unless they were brought to the people" (cited in Singh, "Postcolonial/Postmodern," 38). Dutt's ideas of radical theater are possibly traceable to his disavowal of his Jesuit education in the Western classics—according to Rustom Bharucha, "the fact that he could recite Virgil and Shakespeare dismayed him" (*Rehearsals*, 55–56). He trained with Geoffrey Kendal and the traveling Shakespeare Company before joining the Little Theatre Group in Calcutta. Dutt left the Little Theatre, which staged a new play of Shakespeare every month, for a brief stint with the anti-imperialistic Indian People's Theatre Association, returning to it in 1951 to signal a shift to Bengali and a covert politicization of its message.[19] Three months after the declaration of Emergency in India in June 1975, the Little Theatre produced *Macbeth*, translated into Bengali and directed by Dutt. "There is no better play against tyranny than Shakespeare's *Macbeth*," Dutt said to Shamik Bandopadhyay in an interview.[20] He continued: "We knew that though this was a play protesting Mrs. Indira Gandhi's Emergency, it would escape detection by the obtuse Congress Party people. They would assume that this was a troupe immersed in the cultivation of Shakespeare and suspend censorship. And that's precisely what happened. There was never a protest against our *Macbeth*" (1–2). The group expanded its audience from the "minority audience" of "the Westernized intellectuals of Calcutta" (Bharucha, *Rehearsals*, 56) to the masses, touring remote villages in rural Bengal. In the foreword to Dutt's translation of *Macbeth*, Dutt outlines the interventionist stratagem of the troupe as targeted political attack that, however, went hand in hand with the study of literary masterpieces: "We will not merely shout shrilly [shob shomoy kromosho golā choriye choriye jabo nā]," he explains to Bandopadhyay (2).

"The film is not meant for Shakespearean scholars," Vishal Bhardwaj says without hostility of *Maqbool*, his 2004 adaptation of *Macbeth* (Pais, "Maqbool"). Bhardwaj's Shakespeare adaptations subscribe to Dutt's demythologizing stance toward Shakespearean classics, which led him to translate and stage them in everyday and local contexts in India. "The jealousy, the plotting and the tragedy are all still there in *Omkara*. What has changed is that we have tried to make [*Othello*] understandable to an Indian audience," says Abhishek Chaubey, who co-wrote (with Bhardwaj) the script of the film (Ramesh, "Matter of Caste"). Bhardwaj's cinematic output belongs to Indian intellectual cinema, but he also brings to that reified, ratiocinative tradition oomph, speed, coruscating humor, and the poetics of a deeply musical sensibility (Bhardwaj, a highly acclaimed composer, started his work life as accompanist for ghazal singers in Delhi's Pragati Maidan). For Bhardwaj, Shakespeare plays clearly contribute to what Alan Sinfield calls "the perpetual contest of stories that constitutes culture," reinforcing or challenging "prevailing notions of what the world is like, of how it might be" ("Cultural Materialism," 50). However, if most contemporary rewritings of Shakespeare follow the logic of modernization that brings Shakespeare in dialogic interaction with changed historical contexts, corporate and cultural ideologies, modes of aesthetic reception and performance, Bhardwaj's films seem to say that nothing much has changed about the human condition as invented by Shakespeare.[21] Referring to *Maqbool*, Bhardwaj says, "You can place this story anywhere, in the army, in a bank, in journalism. It is a vicious, furious, bleak story. It's human" (quoted in Perry, "Lights!").

Maqbool is set in the Mumbai underworld, though the imbrications of politicians, movie stars, and policemen in its nefarious goings-on make untenable the distinction between those on the right side and the wrong side of the law. The actor Irrfan Khan plays Maqbool, a trusted capo of Jahangir Khan, a mafia don affectionately called *Abbaji* by his associates.[22] The action begins with two rotten cops, Panditji and Purohit, in the process of blowing out the brains of a member from the gang of Mughal, Abbaji's arch-rival. The *janampatrikā* or horoscope of Mumbai that Panditji has finger traced on the windshield of the police van gets splattered with blood: "Sārī Mumbai khoon se bhardi! [You have covered Bombay in blood!]," Panditji rebukes Purohit. The comic duo, one of whom is incongruously named "scholar" (*pandit*) and the other "priest" (*purohit*), stands in for the Weïrd Sisters, choreographing the fate of the key characters and precipitating violent corrections that supposedly restore the balance of power (*shakti kā santoolan*). Panditji is adept in astrology, but, if Purohit is to be believed, his terrible prescience could also have something to do with his black tongue, which, according to superstitious belief in India, means that the individual's utterances are effectively speech acts that make things happen. Maqbool is rumbled by this clairvoyance when Panditji correctly predicts that Abbaji will soon delegate mafia control of Bollywood, or the Hindi film industry, to him. Confounding his confusion over Panditji's long-term prediction that he will inherit Abbaji's seat of power in a mere six months is Nimmi, Jahangir's nubile mistress, who has the hots for Maqbool, and delights in playing seductress when she is not tormenting him about his inability to act on his obvious desire for the boss's moll. The cast of characters is completed by Maqbool's comrade-in-arms, the soft-hearted gangster Kaka (Banquo), Sameera, the only child of Abbaji from his first marriage, Guddu (Fleance), Kaka's son and Sameera's lover, and Boti (McDuff), the slain gang lord Mughal's son, who has been forced at gunpoint to defect to Abbaji's outfit.

Things come to a head when Sameera's romance with Guddu is made public. Jahangir Khan, who has just spurned an international smuggling deal worth three billion rupees, seems to be losing the plot, and Nimmi plays on Maqbool's insecurities around the inevitable succession war, convincing him that when it came to questions of inheriting the underworld business, Abbaji would no doubt favor his son-in-law Guddu over a retainer like Maqbool. Their volatile love is finally consummated in Maqbool's house the night before Sameera's engagement. In a mess of lust, greed, jealousy, and half-baked suspicions over the motives of his beloved benefactor, and unable to forget Panditji's forecast about Guddu's ascent to power, Maqbool kills Abbaji while the latter is resting in his home. The lovers try to incriminate the staunchly loyal bodyguard, who had been tricked into drinking by Nimmi, and whose gun has served as the murder weapon. Maqbool takes charge of the business and makes public his affair with Nimmi, which confirms suspicions and alienates him from the crime family as well as the politicos who had backed Abbaji. Kaka is next to be murdered, and Maqbool's position is further weakened by strife and sedition within and attacks from without (orchestrated by Boti and Guddu). Meanwhile, Nimmi is with child, but the timing makes it impossible to know if the paternity is Jahangir's. The whole world seems to mock Maqbool for being the dupe of a woman, and he alternates between violent rage, hypnoid half-awake states, and befuddlement at Nimmi's rapid descent into madness. Nimmi, deranged by the pregnancy, wracked with guilt and hallucinations, is like one of the revenants in Maqbool's plague of dreams. The bumbling cops assure Maqbool that all will be well till the sea comes to his house and the unthinkable eventuality comes to be on the night of the lunar eclipse when customs officers interrupt Maqbool's boat at sea, seizing the loot that would buy the gang political protection, and the game is finally up for Maqbool. "The sea has encroached into my house," he says, anticipating a raid by the sea-patrolling police officers. Nimmi dies. Maqbool's death in the hands of Boti feels less like retribution than much-awaited release from the private carceral that is the tragic hero's lot.

Perhaps the most remarkable change in this adaptation is that "Lady Macbeth" is not the wife of Macbeth but the *biba* (mistress) of Duncan.

The intensity of the affair is choreographed with stark beauty, eros and guns coming together to dramatic effect. Nimmi extracts a declaration of love from Maqbool with a loaded gun pointed at him. When Maqbool, torn between his love for Nimmi and fealty to his master, hits back, calling her a whore and saying she should go back to the brothel, Nimmi retorts that she would willingly go back to Allah if her lover came along for the ride. Lovers' tiff over, Maqbool wipes her tears with the muzzle of a revolver. "You can die for me; you can also kill for me," Nimmi tells Maqbool. "Or kill me," she taunts, putting a marigold garland used on sacrificial goats around her neck. It is, therefore, not simply usurpation of power that the pair covets, but the gratification of their excessive and unedifying passion. In fact, Panditji's first prediction for Maqbool Miyan on the fateful night of predictions was that of love. Nimmi does not "unsex" herself (1.5.40)—there is little discernible change in her humanity or femininity in the course of the play—nor is there in her what Adelman calls an "unnatural abrogation of her maternal function" (*Suffocating Mothers*, 135).

"That whore will be the death of us all," says a gang member of Nimmi in the wake of Abbaji's murder. As Jacqueline Rose observes, "Failing in a woman, whether aesthetic or moral, is always easier to point to than a failure of integration within language and subjectivity itself." To quote Rose further on the sexual politics of *Hamlet* and *Measure for Measure*, "It is a woman who is seen as the cause of the excess and deficiency in the play," threatening identities and systems that structure "normal adult psychic and sexual life" ("Sexuality," 100). Bhardwaj adds to the bold portrayal of Nimmi's desire the unspoken class dimension of a girl prostituting herself to a criminal old enough to be her father, and with nothing but social ostracism to return to should Jahangir reject her for a new recruit. If the pervasive misogyny of the characterization of the power-mongering Lady Macbeth is inevitably reproduced in this adaptation, *Maqbool* boldly asserts that while Nimmi threatens Maqbool's subjectivity, she is also the agent that congeals it in all its messy contradictions. Nimmi, played by the statuesque Tabu, is seen in monochrome colors (black, red, and white) that seem to match the elemental colors of the protagonist's moods, a portrayal reminiscent of the way in which Kurosawa, in the *Throne of Blood*, makes Lady Washizu seem like a Noh stylization of Washizu's most extreme states of being. And yet she is no more Maqbool's shadow than she was Jahangir's. Metonymically connecting the Law of the Father with the body of the mother, she shows up sexual difference for the instability of identifications and the impropriety of object choices that it is.

In the role of the Weïrd Sisters, Bhardwaj casts Panditji and Purohit, all-too-human cops, and the vaunted "balance of power" deferred to by both is achieved less through invisible psychic machinations than through active scheming on the part of the pair, like the time they let Boti (McDuff) escape death in order to rally forces to vanquish Maqbool. They act as maladroit guardians of the crime nexus and archivists of its secrets and lies. For instance, Panditji tells Maqbool that there is little doubt that Abbaji had murdered his mentor, Lalji, a heinous act which seems to justify his protégé's eventual betrayal. "Shakti kā santoolan," as Panditji says, the correction of fire (*aag*) by water (*pāni*). Panditji and Purohit stand for the insistence of the quotidian, "of human things, human purposes, human desires" that Thomas De Quincey discerns in the knocking, and the shock of the knocks, on the gate soon after Duncan's murder ("On the Knocking," 84). Ruthless though they can be, the cops represent the banality of the law's routine violence in India, and are full of brotherly feelings in their dealings with each other. As with the knocking on the gate, their comic delinquencies and lust for life—they are seen having a peeing competition as Maqbool and Nimmi plot the murder—point to the fact that while Nimmi and Maqbool are, to quote De Quincey, increasingly "cut off from the ordinary tide and succession of human affairs," a reaction has simultaneously commenced and "the human has made its reflux upon the fiendish. . . . The pulses of life are beginning to beat again" (84–85).

Bhardwaj's *Omkara* (2006) sets *Othello* in the badlands of Uttar Pradesh in India. Omi Shukla is a half-caste thug, the right-hand man of a corrupt politician, Tiwari Bhaisaab, whose troubles with the law and frequent stints at jail have given Omkara pole position in the party. The plot thickens with Omi's abduction of his paramour Dolly on the day of her arranged marriage with Rajju. The Iago figure, Langda Tyagi, had indeed alerted his mate, Rajju, to the eventuality even as he was hijacking the wedding party, urging him to rush to the scene to save his bride, but poor Rajju's scooter had given way and all was lost. Dolly is the luminously beautiful and pampered daughter of Raghunath Mishra—aka Vakil Saab, lawyer to Bhaisaab—and the father finds it inconceivable that his delicate bloom (*phool*) of a child would willingly abscond with the casteless, uncouth Omkara. Faced with incontrovertible proof of their secret affair and mutual ardor, Vakil Saab disowns his daughter with a parting shot to Omkara that will forever haunt the union: "Can a girl who dupes her father be loyal to anyone?" ("She has deceived her father, and may thee"; *Othello* 1.3.291).

In a significant deviation from the text, Dolly is not married to Omkara right away as there is no auspicious wedding date in sight, and lives "in sin" in his house, surrounded by members of the gang and their families. Meanwhile, Bhaisaab manages to sideline his political rival Indore Singh and shakes up the organization of his party in preparation for the upcoming state elections, nominating Omkara for a party seat. Omkara's old post of *bāhubali*, translated as "henchman" or "one who lives by the force of his arms," is up for grabs, and, to Langda Tyagi's rude shock, his candidacy is spurned in favor of a new recruit, Kesu (Cassio), a college graduate, who, according to Omkara, will refresh the image of the party and attract student votes. The inexorable plot movement of *Othello* takes over, with Tyagi getting Kesu drunk and involved in a violent brawl, Omkara's anger at and rejection of Kesu, Kesu's appeal to Dolly to help restore him in Omkara's good offices, Tyagi's slow but sure cultivation of murderous jealousy in Omkara's mind around Dolly's alleged affair with Kesu. Indu, Tyagi's wife, impulsively steals an antique waistband (*kamarbandh*) gifted by Omkara to Dolly, perhaps only to wear it a few times before returning it, to Tyagi's unmitigated delight. He gives it to Kesu, asking him to gift it to his paramour, the dancing girl Billo Chamanbahar, to appease the latter. The heirloom waistband in Billo's possession finally serves as "ocular proof" (*Othello* 3.3.362) of Dolly's unfaithfulness, and Omkara smothers her to death on their wedding night. Tyagi's conspiracy goes to plan, and he leaves Kesu for dead, only Indu, discovering Omkara with his slain wife and the waistband, pieces together the story and turns on her husband. Tyagi denounces her as a liar and whore, and is killed shortly afterward by a sickle-wielding Indu. Kesu limps back into the scene, injured but alive, and inherits the fiefdom when Omkara shoots himself in the heart.

In these adaptations of Shakespearean tragedies, Bhardwaj shows little interest in writing back to the Shakespearean text, questioning its historical assumptions on race, class, and gender, addressing its occlusions or exclusions, or acting out its hitherto unexamined implications. There is also no indication whatsoever that the adapters-interpreters of the tale see Elizabethan England or Shakespeare's play as a mirror of their own cultural moment. In fact, Bhardwaj seems to trust the plot and characters to be transhistorical and transcultural enough to speak to the specifics of a local Indian context. Omkara is an outsider to the Brahmin-dominated scene of Bhaisaab's party. He is born to a Brahmin father and a mother from a lower class, hence the ostracizing tag of *ādhā baman*, or "half-Brahmin." It is not merely heroic prowess but signs of vulnerability in this macho man, and his dignified endurance of psychic wounds, that endear him to Dolly—the love affair starts with a wounded Omkara collapsing in Dolly's arms. "The moon is called the moon whether it is half or full," she says to him comfortingly. While Bhardwaj does not directly engage with the caste-ridden politics of North India, or the severe problem of caste discrimination in India as a whole, he subtly references upward-mobility narratives pertaining to caste as well as the inevitable return of caste stratification and dehumanization. Omkara stands for hundreds of "minority" undercastes exploited by upper-class political leaders for personal and party gain. He is given the sacred thread of Brahminhood upon his appointment as *bahubali*, but just as Othello, the Christian convert, "turns Turk," it is inevitable that Omkara too will forfeit the hard-earned distinction. Omkara, played by the actor Ajay Devgan, is the most dark-skinned man in the group, his insecurities about his looks stirred by the harmless banter of the playful Indu and later shamelessly exploited by Tyagi. "Like milk in a pot of coal," says Indu of the stunning color contrast between Dolly and Omkara. "Like a sweetmeat in the mouth of a crow"; "like sandalwood glowing in a pitch-dark night." Dolly, as her anglicized pet name suggests, is from a class the mercenary Omkara works for, Kesu Firangi's class (*firangi* means "English" or "foreign," a tribute to Kesu's superior charms, college degree, and guitar skills). "You are either an innocent or a witch," Omkara says of Dolly's limpid brown eyes, unusually light for an Indian. She is increasingly objectified as what Slavoj Žižek identifies as the "inhuman partner" of courtly love, the automaton who makes the hero hate her (and himself) for loving her, "an apathetic void imposing senseless, arbitrary ordeals" (*Metastases*, 102).[23] Dolly falls silent in her death scene, meeting Omkara's obscene accusations with a wilful and reproachful withholding: it is as if she knows that in a representational economy that treats her as inscrutable as well as intimately knowable words would be futile anyway. But if she does not defend herself, as Desdemona does, she does not exculpate her murderer either—her nails draw blood from Omkara's cheek as she is smothered to death.

Like Emilia, Indu, the sharp-tongued wife of Langda Tyagi, speaks up for Desdemona-Dolly and the lot of bullied women. She repeats almost verbatim (in Hindi dialect) Emilia's

They are all but stomachs, and we all but food:
They eat us hungerly, and when they are full
They belch us. (3.4.105–7)

Indu is coarse and earthy, equally at ease with all of the three warring men, and fearlessly urges Omkara to ditch the patriarchal line: "With our own scriptures demonising femininity, what chance does an ordinary woman have?" In the end she correctly suspects that the "scurvy fellow" (4.2.142) is none other than her husband, and kills him when he responds to her allegations with a violent tirade that can be summed up as "go home, whore." In a drama whose uncanny plot twists have imperceptibly changed the marital bed—the rustic wooden swing where Dolly and Omkara once made love—to a scene of murder, the homely Indu's criminal turn does not entirely surprise. As if to further explain the deviation from the Shakespearean text, Bhardwaj frames her face and body language in a manner evocative of the iconography of avenging female goddesses of the Hindu pantheon, Devi Durgā, and her dark double, Kāli.

If storm-tossed and politically troubled Cyprus is the dark id of the metropolitan center that is Venice, the setting of *Omkara* too gives the lie to Indian modernity. The morally rudderless condition of the characters is related to this dustbowl, where the law of the jungle is carried out with state-of-the-art mobile phones and guns, where a prominent politician on board a national railway train can nonchalantly ask the ticket master to reverse the direction of the train—"You heard right," Bhaisaab tells the terrified man—and where thugs carry out strip-searches of policemen. If race in early modern usage connotes a complex of clan, class, lineage, and gender, *Omkara* offers a nuanced representation of its worst depredations in its portrayal of not just the half-caste Omkara, but also Langda Tyagi. In a torrid scene, Indu likens Langda to a hungry beast. "A cheetah?" "A wolf?" "A snake?" "A chameleon?" Langda asks, his manly confidence dwindling with each diminution of feral charge. "No, you are my little bunny," Indu says as Langda's face crumples. Langda (*langda* is Hindi slang for "lame") Tyagi walks with a limp and projects from the start the sadistic fury of a clever but unrewarded man who expects to be tripped up, rendered impotent and silly, and eventually irrelevant. He is the insecure middle child between the tragic hero and the gallant, if lesser, knight who will restore social order when the tragic business is wrapped up. If Shakespeare's Iago is, as Harold Bloom states, "a free artist of himself, uniquely equipped, by experience and genius, to entrap spirits greater than his own in a bondage founded upon their inner flaws" (*Shakespeare*, 464), Bhardwaj's Langda Tyagi, undoubtedly an artist extraordinaire of psychological manipulation and torture, is also a little man whose sense of subjection and humiliation is ultimately related to economic inequities, social injustices, and uneven developments. He is the symptom of a failed state, not its cause.

The three different modes of Shakespeare transmission that I have discussed in this chapter—Ghosh's and Addy's uniquely Bengali translation of Shakespearean text and performance, Kendal's all-India travels with Shakespeare, and cinematic adaptations of Shakespeare's tragedies—testify to David Kastan's insight that Shakespeare has survived (in India, in this case) "precisely by being accessible and pliant in the hands of his lovers" (*Shakespeare and the Book*, 5). Kastan makes a distinction between (a fixed) text and (changeable) performance that seems particularly relevant to the concerns of this chapter. In chapter 3 of *Shakespeare and the Book*, "From Contemporary to Classic; or, Textual Healing," Kastan seems to suggest that while Shakespeare is an eternal contemporary on stage, amenable to changing conventions in dramaturgy or the contingent demands of staging and performance, he ought to also stand as a classic text, "worthy of having the corruptions worked by theatrical necessity, printing practice, and time recognized and repaired" (96–97).[24] The distinction between the hermetic textuality of a classic and modifying, modernizing performances is unstable, of course, each needing the threat of other to constitute itself. A cartoon of William Shakespeare appears after the roll of credits in the 1981 film *Angoor*, the most popular of Hindi film adaptations of *The Comedy of Errors*. The publicity machine of the movie was careful to avoid naming Shakespeare, possibly to keep the appeal of this family flick broad-based.[25] Filmgoers did not need telling about Shakespeare anyway, familiar as they were with the classic comedy through the mediations of two popular adaptations, the Bengali *Bhrāntibilāsh* (The Comedy of Errors; 1963), and the Hindi *Do Dooni Chār* ("Two Twos Are Four"; 1968). In the final frame of the film, the cartoon Shakespeare winks, as if returning the look, and completing the transferential circuit of surreptitious knowledge.

. . .

I met Vishal Bhardwaj, the maker of *Maqbool* and *Omkara* at his Oshiwara (Mumbai) studio on August 23, 2010. Here is a transcript of that interview.

Ankhi Mukherjee: My first question is related to my interest in the transmission and translation of metabooks. Have you read Shakespeare and did you read him in Hindi? [I read Shakespeare first in Bengali, a translation of Lamb's *Tales of Shakespeare*.] You describe *Macbeth* as a "timeless tale" in an interview. Would you agree that for many Indians, Shakespeare is not just part of the Western canon but the canon itself, in that his works embody the continuity, consensus, authority, and authenticity that we associate with timeless tales?

Vishal Bhardwaj: I was a very bad student, with no interest in studies. Shakespearean language is forced on you in school. I remember the first thing I read, *Merchant of Venice*, in ninth or tenth class, the "pound of flesh." Literature is boring. So-called classics can seem boring. I was like a common man in this respect. I remember watching *Angoor*, Gulzar's adaptation of the *Comedy of Errors*, and the Shakespeare painting that winks in the end. While I was making *Makdi*, I looked up the witches' reference. I was moved by Kurosawa's *Throne of Blood*, the basic storyline, really, where Macbeth kills King Duncan. This remained with me. [The subject of the film I was planning then was to be made in the underworld genre. Guns are more attractive to me than roses, you see. But movies should be about human relations, not just underworld. I am after the "deeper tale."]

I was traveling from Dehradun to Delhi on the *Shatabdi Express* with my stepson. I had with me Shakespeare's tales, and read *Macbeth*. I thought it would make a great story for the underworld, what with its witches, guilt, and denial. A great human tale around a crime. Cowriter Abbas suggested that cops make the best witches. I alternated between Shakespearean language and modern English as I read—my journey to Shakespeare happened on a train journey. I found the structuring of this story peculiar. . . . It is structurally solid, like *Julius Caesar* and *Hamlet*. I read everything of Shakespeare that was available, watched *Throne of Blood* and the movie about

Macbeth in a fast-food joint (Billy Morrissette, *Scotland, PA* [2001]). We have changed in the last four hundred years, but basic emotions are the same. Shakespeare's stories can be placed anytime. Beyond borders. That's what makes it a classic.

A.M.: Shakespeare is a core and compulsory part of English lit curricula all over the world, and is an icon of Englishness itself. His works constitute a supremely powerful expression of what is shared across all the potentially damaging divisions of class, caste, and interest in the nation. What do you make of his universal appeal, wherein the Shakespearean tale lends itself with equal ease for expressing the collective memory of non-Western nations and cultures?

V.B.: We may have progressed, but questions of racism persist. We fight for racism but it is still very much there. You find questions of segregation everywhere—society remains the same in its deep core.

A.M.: The thing about Shakespearean tragedy is that you feel there are murky currents of invisible agency beneath the manifest intentions of all of the characters. You tap into this beautifully through your use of the policemen in *Maqbool*, one tracing the vagaries of the stars and the other noting the violent corrections through which balance [santoolan] is restored to the world. Could you say more on this?

V.B.: To raise this question, are we writing our lives or is it all written, you have to look at the supernatural. It comes in real shapes and influences action—we sometimes call this *karma*. Tragedy has irony. It is that which cannot be undone and it makes you empathise with the sinner. Tragedy is when you can understand the guilt of the sinner. *Macbeth* is probably the most powerful play of Shakespeare. It revolves around a heinous crime, and the denial of guilt. Lady Macbeth goes insane in that denial and he starts hallucinating.

A.M.: The key preoccupations of your Shakespeare adaptations seem to be sexual love and political (and power) struggle and the devastating intersection between the two. In the process you examine the figure of the scapegoat, and the derangements of one character, be it Maqbool or Omkara or Langda Tyagi, reveal the maladies and dysfunctions of the dominant culture: attitudes toward ambition and political ascent in the case of *Maqbool* (the critic Northrop Frye said, "We go to *Macbeth* to learn what a man feels like after he has gained a kingdom and lost a soul") and collective fears about the racial or cultural other in *Omkara*. I'd like to ask you about Omkara as the figure through which you translate the fraught question of race to caste questions or to a racism without race. In *Othello*, medieval ideas of blackness as evil merge with the dehumanization of sub-Saharan Africans consequent upon the emerging slave trade. Shakespeare reflects his society's anxieties lest the truly foreign, with whom it must trade, sheds its apparent differences from the English and thus challenges an English identity defined by means of those very differences. Othello's qualities don't match with stereotypes about Muslims (or the black race). The contrast, in early-modern eyes, between Othello's inside and outside instils a collective fear that professions of Christian faith may disguise a hostile imposter-interloper. His ethnicity and color create the need for a sure test of faith.

V.B.: Hitting a woman does not make Othello-Omkara a poor Christian or a bad *dalit*. Man is judged by one trait—the way he respects a woman. Othello-Omkara for me has complexes about the beauty of his wife. And he has no respect for his own self. Not handsome and a half-caste, he wonders if he is worthy of Desdemona-Dolly.

A.M.: Yes, complicating Othello's position are the prevailing beliefs about women's infidelity, particularly to older husbands, which Iago uses to return Othello to what he considers his true Moorish nature, a violent and jealous one. My next question is related to your acute understanding of the misogyny that structures the two tragedies, where the figure of the woman, whether it is the virago Nimmi or the passive Dolly, becomes the locus of the explicit sexual concerns of the play: female chastity, cuckoldry, adultery, misogyny.

V.B.: The one big change I made in my adaptation was to make Macbeth's wife Duncan's mistress. If they were a couple instead, and killed Duncan as a husband-and-wife team, it would appear to be a straightforward bid for power. By making her the mistress of Duncan, I wanted to show how she incites and poisons him not for the throne but for herself. She herself is the trophy. To gain his beloved, he then has to kill his father. I find female characters much more fascinating than male ones. Women have more resistance than men. You can replace muscular power with machines, but there is no alternative to female resistance. Female characters take initiatives—eventually a character like Emilia is instrumental in defeating Iago.

A.M.: My book, which is primarily concerned with the relationship of so-called master texts to the mode of circulation that is world literature, treats Shakespeare adaptations such as yours as disruptive forces that shape the history and diffusion of English language. It is not just a symptom of globalization, which is often related to American triumphalism or the emergence of English as a global vernacular, but about mobility and circulation, *metissage*, as they call it in French, mutual influence and crossbreeding. Can universal truths crossbreed with singular local histories and languages without reducing them to version of themselves?

V.B.: "Localism" captures the reality of that region. It makes a fantasy believable. India is an amazing country. The dialect changes every fifty kilometers. We use local detail though great drama and cinema are beyond language. Say you are in France, and a street fight is going on. You get the meaning even if you don't have the language. *Omkara* uses a Western UP (Uttar Pradesh) dialect. The parallel to the Moor is in Omkara's darkness and fallen caste. What brings about tragedy is his deep inferiority complex. And he is "kān ka kachchā" (vulnerable to what he hears), as we say in Hindi (*laughs*).

Postscript
The Why of the What

I finally got up my courage sufficiently to ask the chill J. M. Coetzee about *The House on Eccles Street*. Did he have some particular reason for using Joyce, I lamely queried. "No particular reason," he replied.[1]

Jacques Derrida's "Che cos'è la poesia?" written ostensibly in response to the rubric "What is poetry?" for the Italian journal *Poesia*, cannot, of course, be relied upon to suggest a definition of poetry or a definitive method for reading it. Derrida describes the poem as a hedgehog or *hérisson*, quills raised at the ready and rolled in a ball in response to approaching danger on the freeway. "Vulnerable and dangerous," it is a "converted animal," Derrida says, "turned toward the other and toward itself" (*Derrida Reader*, 233, 235). Similarly, it is the intense self-absorption of a poem which makes it vulnerable, eliciting our desire to own it, and learn it by heart: "No poem without accident, no poem that does not open itself like a wound, but no poem that is not also just as wounding" (233). Derrida's hedgehog metaphor can be extended to the classic, a thing of splendid and defensive isolation as well as a textuality mutilated over time by iteration and critical intervention. To answer the question of what makes a classic we would have to renounce knowledge and "set fire to the library of poetics," as Derrida says of the critical practice enjoined by impossible questions such as "What is poetry?" (233).Borrowing Derek Attridge's distinction between "arguments" and "arguings" (he uses the latter to characterize the epistemic structure of

J. M. Coetzee's *Elizabeth Costello*), I would like to claim that the debates around "What is a classic?" are *arguings*, "utterances made by individuals in concrete situations," and not of the order of the philosophical argument, "which implicitly lays claim to a timeless, spaceless, subjectless condition as it pursues its logic" (Attridge, *J. M. Coetzee*, 198). Difficulties of defining the classic notwithstanding, we can, and I have, tried to explain and sometimes answer *why* authors and critics (and author-critics) revisit and reinvent the idea of the classic. I have also detailed the singular ways in which the temporal event of the classic is repeated: the self-situating of the latecomer to the canon (Eliot and Coetzee); the rewriting of literary influence (Said and Naipaul, after Conrad); the decoding and recoding of classics (Walcott); the creation of a vernacular canon; postcolonial mimesis and countersignature.

Literature is a linguistic act whose nature is to repeat. In his essay on a production of *Romeo and Juliet* in Paris, Derrida applies the idea of "countertime" to both the mishaps within the play and the structure of "innumerable repetitions, each staked in its particular way, under the same name," through which the classic survives: "It belongs to the series, to the still-living palimpsest, to the open theater of narratives which bear this name. It survives them, but they also survive thanks to it" (*Acts*, 433). And this is why Coetzee, when asked about the motive behind a reconfigured Marion Bloom in the novel-within-a-novel in *Elizabeth Costello*, can legitimately say there is often "no particular reason" as to why literature repeats itself. In the context of postcolonial literature, however, the idea of repetition and *contretemps* interrupting the homogenous time of the original text, has a different—and unavoidably political—charge. Margot Norris reminds us that Costello's creator has a habit of rewriting canonical authors: Daniel Defoe in *Foe*, Fyodor Dostoevsky in *The Master of Petersburg*, Franz Kafka in *The Life and Times of Michael K*. "With this fictional corpus he has succeeded better than James Joyce, or Kafka for that matter, in winning awards, including the 2003 Nobel Prize for Literature. If Coetzee writes award-winning fiction by engaging creatively with the works of other authors, why not Elizabeth Costello herself?" ("Not a Bit," 1). Norris suggests that Costello the Australian and Coetzee the South African suffer alternately from the anxiety of influence and the desire for immortality, as did Stephen Dedalus and his Irish creator. Is Costello "parasitizing" Molly Bloom, Norris speculates (adapting the rhetoric of her fictional counterpart, Elizabeth Costello), in order to reinforce associations of literary greatness with her work? Costello's mocking self-awareness of her youthful aspirations would justify this reading. "This was my great ambition: to have my place in the shelves of the British Museum, rubbing shoulders with the other Cs, the great ones: Carlyle and Chaucer and Coleridge and Conrad" (*Elizabeth Costello*, 16).

Elizabeth Costello's musings above are her opening statements in the acceptance speech for a prestigious North American literary prize: the lecture is titled "What Is Realism?" Behind her neophyte eagerness to have deposit copies of her first book promptly despatched to the leading libraries of the world, Costello explains, was the fantasy of outliving and posthumous survival as text. "What lay behind my concern about deposit copies was the wish that, even if I myself should be knocked over by a bus that next day, this first-born of mine would have a home where it could snooze, if fate so decreed, for the next hundred years, and no one would come poking with a stick to see if it was still alive" (*Elizabeth Costello*, 17). Neither the lecture nor the novel, however, dwells for long on such meretricious aims. Costello corrects the younger Costello's desire for lasting fame by emphasizing the transience of the very institutions that instigate and occasionally authenticate literary ambition. The British Museum, which is now the British Library, will "crumble and decay, and the books on its shelves turn to powder" (17). What follows in the remainder of Costello's talk is a Kafkaesque decentering of the self and its ontological props: "The word-mirror is broken, irreparably. . . . The lecture hall itself may be nothing but a zoo" (19). I mention this textual example to emphasize that while considerations of the criteria that determine transcendental value are not easily separated from the desire to write or create art, the question of the classic represents a transient, albeit valuable, moment in the life of the writer, and marks a quest that is best left unrealized. Costello, who had fondly recalled her youthful disappointment at having Marie Corelli, not Carlyle or Chaucer, as her library-shelf neighbor, ends the lecture wishing for gradual oblivion. "There must be some limit to the burden of remembering that we impose on our children and grandchildren" (20).

The canon is an achieved anxiety, an imagined unity, an inclusive stance on the diverse literary genres produced within the tradition of literature in English. It is, as Bloom says, the memory system, which receives, retains, and selectively orders works. Each literary age, movement, or reading formation, marks the place and claims of the canonical as contingent, outlines a program that serves to authorize its own attitudes and poetics, and invents a vatic tradition of its own. Canon formation in the twentieth- and twenty-first centuries—if "formation" is indeed the word for it—is increasingly carried out in deconstructive modes of critical scrutiny that not only challenge orthodoxies of the mind and dogma, as Said says of secular criticism, but the place and claims of the arbiters who have traditionally determined the nature and possibilities of literature. "Out of place" is a good working definition for many of the speaking positions showcased in the book, including that of Edward Said, who forged it as a Palestinian in the United States and an American in the Arab world. According to T. S. Eliot, the persistence of literary creativeness in any people "consists in the maintenance of an unconscious balance between tradition in the larger sense—the collective personality, so to speak, realized in the literature of the past—and the originality of the living generation" (*On Poetry and Poets*, 58). This model of transaction between an organically unified and "collective" tradition and the atomic individualism of the belated writer too has changed in two key ways. We no longer view literary periods like high modernism as a common inheritance, the "collective personality . . . realized in the literature of the past." Joseph Conrad's constitutive presence in the works of Achebe, Said, Naipaul, Harris, and Salih, for example, is incomparable with the influence of other metropolitan writers of empire fiction. In the "retrospective rearrangement" affected by postcolonial appraisals of Conrad,[2] he is not the canon but one of the anxious aftercomers to the canon, like Said and Naipaul. Second, the originality of Salih's or Naipaul's work in the heart-of-darkness tradition is best understood not in isolation but against the originality of Conrad and the diversified history of "original" Conrad rewritings. As Geoffrey Galt Harpham suggests, the canon après Conrad is perhaps neither "transcendental" nor "narrowly political" but "a massively collective production that yet reflects the deepest urgencies and anxieties of individual identity and desire" (*One of Us*, 196).

The Pakistani novelist Uzma Aslam Khan writes amusingly of the momentous day Woolf fell into her hands. The year was 1984, the fifth year of the Soviet invasion of Afghanistan next door, with the CIA pouring billions of dollars into Pakistan to fund the Holy War. It was a sweltering afternoon in the month of Ramzan in Karachi, the city disfigured with violence and civic unrest under the dictatorial rule of General Zia. Khan remembers the moment Virginia Woolf describes Shakespeare's "incandescent, unimpeded" mind in *A Room of One's Own*, for that was the very instance that she put the book down to call the Karachi Electricity Supply Corporation to demand that the electricity return to her house. "Otherwise, I promised the operator, God would punish him for denying my fasting parents even the respite of a ceiling fan. Then I went back to imagining Ms. Woolf in a long lilac dress, a thick belt around her slim waist and a lacy floppy hat to protect her delicate complexion. England was really happening; Pakistan wasn't" ("Pakistan"). Without overanalyzing the blog post, I will present it in these concluding remarks as symptomatic of the postcolonial writer's relationship with the Western canon: the idea of chance or accident shaping the encounter ("My older sister handed me a copy"); the ideational character of the great book, which leads to a comic incommensurability of fictional and real worlds, leading in turn to political awakening ("A woman is entitled to her own uninterrupted space, protected and nourished by her own money? No one had ever told me that"); the power of the classic to speak to us as if "all ages are contemporaneous" (Woolf's dynamic 1920s England and Khan's static 1980s Pakistan, coalescing in the slight figure of the disaffected woman fighting for change).[3]

At a time when those of us in the arts and humanities in the United Kingdom are trying to understand the implications of teaching subjects that are *not*, to quote the language of the recent higher education White Paper, "strategically important" but will be increasingly expensive, with high recommended fee levels, at a time when we are anxious about the future of the university as a multiversity, it can seem self-indulgent to worry about calibrations and contestations of nonmonetary value.[4] British universities, as Stefan Collini rightly points out, "have been national cultural institutions that more closely resembled, say, the British Museum or the BBC rather than, say, Bhs or BP" ("Browne's Gamble"). What the Browne Report and the ensuing White Paper have brought about is the withdrawal of the present annual block grant of approximately 3.9 billion that the government makes to students to underwrite their teaching, signaling a shocking abdication of the state's financial responsibility toward higher education, and ushering its new regulatory, policing function vis-à-vis the university. The rise in fees, combined with the withdrawal of direct public funding for the teaching of the humanities in the United Kingdom, has introduced a competitive logic of the marketplace whereby students are no longer "our partners in a joint enterprise of learning and understanding," but "consumers seeking the cheapest deals that will enable them to emerge with the highest earning prospects," as the historian Keith Thomas writes in the *London Review of Books* ("Universities"). Common sense dictates, then, that we promptly replace the question of the classic with burning questions such as "Why higher education?" or "What is a university?" or, as Stefan Collini's new book title goes, "What are universities for?" We could, alternatively, argue that times of great social and cultural change are propitious for assessing and inventing the relationship between the world, the text, and the critic, to use Edward Said's enduring formulation. T. S. Eliot's 1944 Virgil Society address, with which I began this book, was given during the Blitz. Coetzee's "What Is a Classic?" lecture obliquely references South African cultural negotiations between domestic and international discourses at a time of political upheaval. As Said says, "criticism is worldly and in the world so long as it opposes monocentrism" (*World*, 53), whether it is the monocentrism of war, the suzerainty of autocratic states, or the philistinism of regimes of government regulation and audit, as embodied in the Browne Report and the White Paper.

If a large section of this book is devoted to the questioning, staging, and transmission of the classic, an equally pressing question has been that of postcolonial revisionism. In my examining of different kinds of postcolonial rewritings, I have tried to avoid suggesting the "first in the West" formula of cultural production, where the postcolonial writer's evaluation of the canon and displacement of its loci of signification are interpreted as modes of colonial mimicry, a compulsory rite of passage for arrivistes and wannabes. The historical "belatedness" of the postcolonial anglophone writer's inclusion in the metropolitan canon of English literature is always in danger of being identified with a certain civilizational lag that Dipesh Chakrabarty talks about in his essay "Belatedness as Possibility" (*Indian Postcolonial*). Evoking the Deleuzian definition of repetition as "singularity without concept," or a singularity that is "non-exchangeable and non-substitutable," Chakrabarty proposes postcolonial repetition as a form of newness, neither second-best nor deficient.[5] I have also strongly resisted "the empire writes back" formula, which has been routinely debunked over the years, but attaches still to the phenomenon of postcolonial rewriting of canonical texts. The localized insurrection involved in "seizing the language of the centre and re-placing it in a discourse fully adapted to the colonized place" (*Empire Writes Back*, 37), neither pays attention to the differentiations and disparities of power in the "colonized place," nor does it automatically make standard international English multidialectical, whereas this project highlights the exciting variety of postcolonial cultural production and unmistakable complementarities between English and anglophone cultures. The term *postcolonial* has been thoroughly interrogated and qualified, its temporalities and spatial span, its range of locations and positions between indigeneity and planetary forms of belonging addressed in the context of each topic and the thesis as a whole: it does *not*, in the final analysis, amount to rooted and antagonistic reprisals of colonial power/knowledge and representational politics. I have made no effort to explain away cultural and historical difference or the very political unconscious of literature through the finite interpretive resources of this mode of literary criticism: there is, as ever, "too much truth for art to hold" (Coetzee, *Doubling*, 99).

This project has particularly focused on texts that share many features of world literature, if by that category we mean "a literature that seeks to be disseminated, read, and received around the world so as to change the world and the life of a given people within it," as Pheng Cheah's uncomplicated but powerful definition goes ("What Is a World?" 36). I have, in my critical interrogation of the primal moment of canon formation—the staging of the question "What is a classic?"—speculated on whether the corpus of world literature is organized by relatable principles of selection, organization, and exclusion. In his how-to book on world literature, David Damrosch rises to the challenge of the all-important question, "And so, what to read?" with "an organized approach" (*How to Read*, 125): take hints from a favorite author; root around great literary figures, for there is usually more in the literary culture where the masterpiece came from; enroll in a college or university course; read scholarly monographs on the subject and dip into the ready-made archives of world literature offered by Bedford, Longman, and Norton; lead a less xenophobic life, study and travel abroad. The case of postcolonial world literature that I have examined in this book is well served by these gentle critical exhortations, a far cry from the ambivalent musings of an exhausted, middle-aged Eliot on the exhaustibility of language and literature in a classic. Although world literature does away with the minutiae of linguistic and national identity and neutralizes differences (between and within literatures) in the equality of rights in a way its postcolonial counterpart cannot afford to, some of the same critical criteria seem to hold true for these linked phenomena: world literature or no, literary value remains under the careful custodianship of writers, mandarins, and universities, while international publishing houses keep churning out the world's greatest classics. As Damrosch cautions, "purely random reading . . . will rapidly become bewildering" (125).

So, where are we on the question of the classic? "Authors and titles move in and out of critical fashion, so while there is a core list of classics that will never go out of print, the canon isn't set in stone," says Judith Luna, commissioning editor of the Oxford World's Classics series. Each generation of critics and scholars chooses its own classics to respond most nearly to its own immediate preoccupations, Luna says: "Fashionable areas such as Gothic literature, or colonial and postcolonial literature, mean we can publish titles that might not otherwise be thought of as 'classics' alongside Homer or Jane Austen."[6]

I would like to close with two recent cultural events that show the familiar pattern of reviving a classic through noncompliance with established modes of reception. In 2011, Faber and Faber, in partnership with Touch Press, a reputed digital publisher with a science-dominated list, produced *The Waste Land* app. For £7.99, readers could have access to six audio versions of the poem, including readings by Alec Guinness and Eliot himself, historical photographs, a filmed version by Fiona Shaw, and commentary from poets and critics, including Heaney, Winterson, Oxford don Craig Raine, and the rock singer Frank Turner. As well as a plain version of the text, the app includes notes and a facsimile of the first draft, complete with Ezra Pound's editorial comments and markings. According to Henry Volans, the head of digital at Faber, where Eliot had worked for over forty years, *The Waste Land* was the only possible poem they could start with. That year also saw the release of Roland Emmerich's film *Anonymous*, which claims that "Shakespeare" was actually Edward de Vere, Seventeenth Earl of Oxford, while William Shakespeare was a homicidal, semiliterate buffoon who impersonated the anonymous playwright, hoodwinking London audiences and contemporary society alike. Historians and literary critics have been apoplectic at the historical errata, the lack of substantiating evidence, and the offensive class assumptions driving Emmerich's (and

Sony's) conspiracy theory. The Shakespeare Birthplace Trust has started a pamphlet war of sorts by releasing an e-book and an online video, titled *Was Shakespeare a Fraud?* Coetzee would probably say of the pointless exercise of authorizing Shakespeare that "as long as the classic needs to be protected from attack, it can never prove itself classic."[7]

Notes

INTRODUCTION

1. These words, spoken by Walcott on the *South Bank Show*, a television arts magazine show on the ITV network in the UK, are cited in Burnett, *Derek Walcott*, 179.

2. According to Benjamin, "the most distinguished trait of a collection will always be its transmissibility" (*Illuminations*, 66). He likens the collector's attitude to the collection to "the attitude of an heir," only here the issue of inheriting or bequeathing—"transmissibility"—is neither contained within filiative structures nor spatially determined. The "mountains of cases" that occasion the writing of this essay are just as valuable for their material contents as for the memories of movement they constellate.

3. Vendler's review appeared in the November 24, 2011, issue of the *New York Review of Books*, and is available at www.nybooks.com/articles/archives/2011/nov/24/are-these-poems-remember/?pagination=false. Rita Dove's response in the December 22 issue of the *NYRB* can be found here: www.nybooks.com/articles/archives/2011/dec/22/defending-anthology/?pagination=false.

4. See Said's discussion of the difference between "filiation" and "affiliation," in "Secular Criticism," *The World, the Text, and the Critic*, 1–13. Affiliation goes beyond instinctual filiation "to become a form of representing the filiative processes to be found in nature, although affiliation takes validated nonbiological social and cultural forms" (23). I discuss this further in the Chapter 1.

5. For an elaboration on the idea of "secular" in Said's formulation of "secular criticism," see Robbins, "Secularism"; see also Mufti, "Auerbach."

6. I quote here from Foucault's introduction to the journals of the hermaphrodite Herculine Barbin, where he describes sexual practices that cannot be contained within the discursive formation of heterosexuality as "a world of pleasures in which the grin hangs about without the cat." See Michel Foucault, ed., *Herculin Barbin, Being the Recently Discovered Memoirs of a Nineteenth-century Hermaphrodite*, trans. Richard McDougall (New York: Colophon, 1980), x; cited in Butler, *Gender Trouble*, 32.

CHAPTER 1

1. When the Booker Prize was established in 1968, it was touted as an English-language Prix Goncourt, an award that would encourage the wider reading of the "very best in fiction" across the United Kingdom and the Commonwealth. Celebrated winners include Naipaul, Gordimer, Rushdie, Golding, Byatt, Coetzee, Ondaatje, Okri, McEwan, and Atwood.

2. Mantel went on to win the Man Booker Prize in 2009 for her *Wolf Hall*. *Bring Up the Bodies*, the sequel to *Wolf Hall*, won the Booker Prize in 2012.

3. James English details an instance of alleged prize fixing where a group of forty-eight influential African-American writers, including Maya Angelou, Toni Cade Bambara, Amiri Baraka, and Alice Walker, demanded and secured the 1988 Pulitzer Prize for Toni Morrison's *Beloved*. The intervention, according to James English, was in the form of a petition to the *New York Times Book Review* that stated pointedly that James Baldwin (who was recently deceased) "never received the honor of these keystones to the canon of American literature: the National Book Award and the Pulitzer Prize: never" (*Economy*, 238). The statement goes on to link Baldwin to Morrison, who, despite her formidable international reputation, "has yet to receive the keystone honors of the National Book Award or the Pulitzer Prize" (238). The Morrison-Pulitzer "scandal" raises uncomfortable questions about racist occlusion as well as egregious forms of affirmative action. *Beloved* is undoubtedly a literary classic, and English himself points out that "Morrison and *Beloved* make singularly bad targets for the decline-of-standards polemic" deployed by Reagan conservatives in the wake of the controversy (240). I refer to this "case" to point out the relevance of this putative bid for canonicity to the cultural contestations key to my topic. Does a worthy winner bring her value and "future, if not present" canonicity to the prize, as English argues, or do value and canonicity issue from prizes and cultural arbiters (and critics)?

4. I am referring here to the terms used by Jonathan Kramnick to describe the formation of the English literary canon in eighteenth-century England. The historical circumstances Kramnick describes as crucial to canon formation—the transformation of the reading public and print capitalism—are also particularly relevant to the contingent staging of the classic question. *Making the English Canon*, 15.

5. The essay appears in Sainte-Beuve's *Causeries*. I have used Prendergast's translation of the relevant passages.

6. As Peter Ackroyd observes, the wartime lectures—"What Is a Classic?" "The Social Function of Poetry," "The Music of Poetry," and "The Classics and the Man of Letters"—reiterate the themes of "common language," or the "changing language of common intercourse," and "common style." The dereliction of war had fostered a sense of national identity, which manifested in Eliot's work as a unity of the "letters of the past" and a formal, if exceedingly fragile, order called European literature (*T. S. Eliot*, 270–71).

7. London's blue plaques mark buildings in which historical luminaries lived and worked. Founded in 1866, the program of the blue plaques is believed to be the oldest of its kind in the world and has been run successively by the Royal Society of Arts, the London County Council, the Greater London Council, and, since 1986, English Heritage. The plaque scheme has steadily raised awareness about London's historical buildings and, in some cases, has saved them from demolition. It has been instrumental in inspiring conservation movements such as the Society for the Protection of Ancient Buildings (founded in 1877) and the National Trust (founded in 1895).

8. There exists a long critical tradition of comparing T. S. Eliot to Virgil. In 1944, W. F. Jackson Knight identified Eliot's poetry as Virgilian. Kermode, while reviewing *On Poetry and Poets* in 1958, detected in Eliot the Virgilian qualities of gravity, labor, pietas, and a sense of destiny. He elaborated on the topic again in *The Classic* (1975). Donald Davie and Elizabeth Porges Watson have both written influential essays on Eliot's treatment of Virgil, and Gareth Reeves's *T. S. Eliot: A Virgilian Poet* (1989) demonstrates how Virgil informs Eliot's ideas about politics, society and religion, not just literature, and yokes Eliot's poetic and cultural thought.

9. See Christopher Prendergast, *The Classic*, 46. Prendergast points out that the term *function* in Sainte-Beuve's essay, borrowed from Matthew Arnold, is possibly the first use of the term in relation to the task of criticism.

10. According to Damrosch, world literature is conceptualized in three ways (that are not mutually exclusive): "As an established body of classics, as an evolving canon of masterpieces, or as multiple windows on the world." In Damrosch's formulation, the classic, identified with Greek and Roman literature, is a work of foundational value, above reproach and reappraisal. The masterpiece, on the other hand, displays the genius of the classic but not its transcendental and inscrutable nature, and activates dialogue and transference between the antique and the modern. The third category is valued for the inroads into foreign worlds it offers, irrespective of the intrinsic value of the works themselves. (*What Is World Literature?* 15).

11. The question "What is a classic?" can be said to have a deconstructive logic because the form and coherence of the classic is posited by this very questioning. The classic in turn provokes and sustains the critical and cultural anxiety around questions of classical value, without being reducible to critical or cultural anxieties. Critics don't make classics any more than writers do: the classic is a form of textuality that joins strength to strength for a sustained confrontation.

12. Both Prendergast and Compagnon note the contraction of the global vision of "Qu'est-ce qu'un classique?" in the 1858 lecture "De la tradition en littérature et dans quel sens il la faut entendre" (On Tradition in Literature and the Way in Which It Should Be Understood). Echoing Compagnon, Prendergast suggests that the difference could be attributed to the respective functions of the critic and the professor: "Maintaining the tradition and preserving the canon of taste is the

special task of the professoriate, to be handed down through the self-producing mechanism of the educational institution to its students" (62).

13. Derrida's "Geopsychoanalysis: '... and the rest of the world," is a cautionary essay on the failure of international psychoanalysis, but here the totalizing frame of reference is American, not European. Derrida seizes on a formulation in the IPA's proposed constitution of 1977, which lists the association's main geographical areas as "America north of the United States—Mexican border; all America south of that border; and the rest of the world." The "rest," Derrida observes with amusement, includes "Europe, the native land and old mother country of psychoanalysis, a body tattooed all over with psychoanalytic institutions and apparatuses; but the self-same 'rest of the world' also connotes all that virgin territory . . . where psychoanalysis, to put it bluntly, has never set foot" ("Geopsychoanalysis," 65).

14. *Midnight's Children*, by Salman Rushdie, was judged the best-ever winner of the Booker Prize for the second time in 2008. The Best of Booker marked the prize's fortieth anniversary. A similar contest—the Booker of Bookers—was held in 1993 to coincide with its twenty-fifth birthday, and came to the same conclusion. The shortlist for the 2008 award, chosen by biographer Victoria Glendinning, broadcaster Mariella Frostrup, and John Mullan, professor of English at the University of London, was put to public voting. The shortlist included the Australian Carey, the South Africans Coetzee and Gordimer, and the Indian-born Rushdie. Of the six shortlisted novels, five deal with colonial-postcolonial experience.

CHAPTER 2

1. While Conrad's critical pronouncements are often traced to his metatextual pieces, the letters and essays, especially the celebrated preface in *The Nigger of the "Narcissus,"* his role as critic is indissociable from his painstaking development of the formal structures of narrative: delayed decoding, impressionist techniques (especially in the way that they represent time), the plurality of versions and meanings of the same event, "frame-tales and flashbacks" (Gorra, *After Empire*, 560).

2. Said describes the intellectual in the postcolonial and global world as a "wanderer, going from place to place for his material, but remaining a man essentially *between* homes" (*Beginnings*, 368).

3. See Patrick Brantlinger's "Epilogue" in *Rule of Darkness*, and "Romance and Reification: Plot Construction and Ideological Closure in Joseph Conrad," in Fredric Jameson, *The Political Unconscious*. Brantlinger draws on Fredric Jameson's analysis of the schism between Conrad's modernist will-to-style and mass-culture tendencies of romance conventions to argue that this split "corresponds to the contradiction of an anti-imperialist novel that is also racist": "In the direction of high style the story acquires several serious purposes, apparently including its critique of empire. In the direction of reified mass culture it falls into the stereo-

typic patterns of race thinking common to the entire tradition of the imperialist adventure story or quest romance" (*Rule*, 265).

4. As Ian Watt points out, the use of the word *invincible* here is poignant, and clearly shows Conrad's awareness that solidarity is under the threat of defeat. The preface's view of solidarity, Watt insists, "must be interpreted mainly as conative, as Conrad's explanation of what he was trying to achieve" (*Conrad*, 107).

5. Conrad makes a similar point in a letter to Hugh Walpole: "If I had not known English I wouldn't have written a line for print in my life." *Collected Letters of Joseph Conrad*, vol. 6 (1917–19), 227.

6. See Foucault, "Of Other Spaces": "We are in the epoch of simultaneity: we are in the epoch of juxtaposition, the epoch of near and far, of the side-by-side, of the dispersed. We are at a moment, I believe, when our experience of the world is less that of a long life developing through time than that of a network that connects points and intersects with its own skein" (22).

7. It is telling that Walter Benjamin cites from *The Shadow-line* in *The Arcades Project* to substantiate his "theory of the trace," the idea that interiority—such as the privacy of a hotel room—is crisscrossed with reminders and remainders of the life preceding and surrounding it. In the context of *The Shadow-line*, the "trace" could be said to refer to the anxiety of miscegenation that structures narratives of Englishness, or the relation of the individual to his own spatial reference (*Arcades Project*, 227).

8. Bhabha is commenting on a Derek Walcott poem ("Names") here (*Collected Poems*, 305), more specifically the lines

A sea-eagle screams from the rock,
and my race began like the osprey
with that cry,
that terrible vowel,
that I!

According to Bhabha, the "I" is pronominal in the way it marks the "avowal of the enslaved colonial subject in the symbolic agency of history." It is postnominalist in that it shores up social identity as "articulations of difference—race, history, gender—[that] are never singular or binary" (*Location*, 234).

9. As Harpham astutely comments, "Conrad's work constitutes a continual calculation of distance from this—what to call it?—source, origin, navel, prime meridian, mine, mint, destructive element, explosive device, Inner Station." *One of Us*, 100.

10. Friedrich Nietzsche, *The Gay Science, with a Prelude in Rhymes and an Appendix of Songs*, trans. Walter Kaufmann (New York: Vintage Books, 1974), 178; cited in Said, *Reflections*, 82.

11. This is uncannily similar to Conrad's letter of June 19, 1896, to Garnett:

Other writers have some starting point. Something to catch hold of. The start from an anecdote—from a newspaper paragraph. . . . They lean on dialect—or on tradition—or on history—or on the prejudice or the fad of the hour; they trade upon some tie or some conviction of their time—or upon the absence of these things—which they can abuse or praise. But at any rate they know something to begin with—while I don't.

See Edward Garnett, *Letters from Joseph Conrad, 1895–1924* (Indianapolis: Bobbs-Merrill Company, 1988); cited in Said, *Joseph Conrad*, 54.

12. This was originally serialized in two parts in the *Sunday Times Magazine* in 1974, later published in the nonfiction book *The Return of Eva Peron*.

13. Malik posed as a black power messiah in the 1960s. He stayed in London between 1957 and 1971, notoriously as pimp, drug dealer, and property racketeer in the first decade. He was arrested in 1967 under race-relations legislation for an antiwhite speech, and a "conversion" to Islam followed, after which he was hailed as an underground black leader by the press. He presented himself as a guerrilla, setting up communes, first in Islington, and then his native Trinidad, when he had to flee England to avoid a trial for robbery and extortion. In Trinidad, Malik reinvented himself yet again, advocating a peaceful revolution based on a return to the land. In 1972, Gale Benson, a twenty-seven-year-old English woman, was found stabbed to death and buried in the commune (where she had been living with her boyfriend Hakim Jamal). The motives of the murder remain unsolved, but Malik is reported to have ordered it as a blood ritual to bring the gang closer in guilty camaraderie. According to Naipaul, Benson, being white, English, middle class, and female, presented a composite figure against which Malik could galvanize black anger and resentment. There were other murders in the commune—"for no reason except that of blood, and because he was now used to the idea of killing with a cutlass" (*Return of Eva Peron*, 89)—and Malik was eventually found guilty and hanged in 1975.

CHAPTER 3

1. Walcott describes his poetic skill as "that of a magpie," in "What the Twilight Says" (*What the Twilight*, 93). Terada is possibly referring to T. S. Eliot's comments on mature poets in "Philip Massinger" (1920); the passage is worth quoting in full for its classification of the mature and the good among poets:

One of the surest of tests is the way in which a poet borrows. Immature poets imitate; mature poets steal; bad poets deface what they take, and good poets make it into something better, or at least something different. The good poet welds his theft into a whole of feeling which is unique, utterly different from that from which it was torn; the bad poet throws it into something which has no cohesion. A good poet will usually borrow from authors remote in time, or alien in language, or diverse in interest.

See *Selected Essays*, 206. See also Christopher Ricks's development of this idea of "previous consciousness" and its legacy for the belated poet in *Allusion to the Poets* (Oxford: Oxford University Press, 2002).

2. "The realm this poet comes from is a real genetic babel," observes Brodsky in *Derek Walcott* (ed. Bloom), 35.

3. See Walcott, *What the Twilight* (9). Walcott calls the chiasmic figure of the Caribbean poet negotiating indigent local reality with the English (language) medium of his poetry "the mulatto of style."

4. Prendergast is citing from *Nouveaux lundis*, xiii, 284, and 305.

5. Walcott in interview with D. J. Bruckner, "A Poem in Homage to an Unwanted Man" (1990), in *Critical Perspectives*, ed. Hamner (397). Walcott also cites Timon of Athens as a source for the characterization of Philoctete. Rei Terada points out that the Homeric model of Walcott's Philoctete is "an anti-Greek Greek hero," abandoned by Odysseus and his crew on the island of Chryse because of a festering wound brought on by a snakebite, and increasingly disenchanted with the cause of the war (*Derek Walcott's Poetry*, 197).

6. Terada points out that these aesthetic questions are contextualized against a world that no longer lets the poet believe in correspondence: "When one suffers from the 'exile of divorce' (a 'divorce,' as in Williams's *Paterson*, from community as well as from a single partner), reflecting surfaces return 'disfiguring' images" (139).

7. This accusation is often echoed by critics. Commenting on Walcott's *Epitaph for the Young*, which experiments with blatant imitation of other writers' lines, Stewart Brown says "even in these poems the 'masters' were not chosen arbitrarily; they all spoke to Walcott's ambition and situation in various ways (*Derek Walcott*, ed. Harold Bloom, 85).

8. This theme is also addressed in "Latin Primer" in *The Arkansas Testament*, where the schoolmaster in tweed jacket and tie contemplates the incongruity of teaching Latin to "lithe black bodies" that would "die in dialect": "where were those brows heading / when neither world was theirs? (23).

9. See Greenwood, *Afro-Greeks*. For related scholarship on the classical influences of Caribbean literature, see *Crossroads in the Black Aegean*, ed. Goff and Simpson; *Classics and Colonisation*, ed. Goff; and *Classics in Postcolonial Worlds*, ed. Hardwick and Gillespie.

10. *The World's Great Classics*, 50 vols. (New York: Colonial Press, 1899–1901; Grolier 1969)

11. The original title of the *Waste Land*, borrowed from Sloppy in Charles Dickens's *Our Mutual Friend*.

12. Walcott claims that he wrote "The Castaway" in solitary confinement in a beach house in Trinidad, surrounded by "the sea and the vegetation." This experience led him to think of the image of the West Indian artist "as someone who was in a shipwrecked position." See Hirsch, "Art of Poetry" (213).

13. *Creole continuum* is a term used in translation studies that refers to the fact that there is not one standard variety of the Creole to which all speakers conform, a wide spectrum of varieties. The continuum ranges from the highly presti-

gious variety, known as acrolect, to the least prestigious type of lexifier, known as basilect. The intermediary ranges are known as mesolects. Guyanese Creole English and Jamaican Creole English are often cited as examples of Creoles with a perceptible Creole continuum, while Barbadian Creole English is virtually indistinguishable from standard British English.

14. See Gilroy, *Black Atlantic*, for a discussion of the "rhizomorphic, fractal structure" of the black artist's transcending of the structures of nation-state and "the constraints of ethnicity and national particularity" (19), which in turn leads to an "intercultural and anti-ethnocentric account of modern black history and political culture" (4).

CHAPTER 4

1. *Oriental Herald* (1829); cited in *Derozio*, ed. Chaudhuri, 421.
2. *Oriental Magazine* 1.10 (October 1843); cited in *Derozio*, ed. Chaudhuri, 39.
3. Ibid.
4. A significant form of postcolonial rewriting takes the form of a "postcolonializing" of European writers. In "Postcolonializing Shakespeare," for instance, Ato Quayson offers a postcolonial interpretation of *The Merchant of Venice* by showing how Jewishness functions as an indigent detail in the text that obstructs the resolution of the plot in the formula of Shakespearean romantic comedy. Quayson argues that were we to conflate race with class momentarily, we would find ideological continuities between the occlusion of Shylock in Venetian society and that of any "cipher of otherness" within a dominant Western culture. The postcolonial method illuminates not just "the formation of sensibilities in the period in which the plays were originally produced" but also the "genealogy of ideas that arguably persist in varying forms to the present day" (*Postcolonialism*, 161).

Edward Said's *Culture and Imperialism* is an inaugural influence in the history of such materialist interpretations. *The Postcolonial Jane Austen* (ed. Park and Rajan), which follows Said's lead in going through the links between British literature and imperial activity in the nineteenth century, does not, however, simply shore readings of Austen's imperial thematics and determinations, her nationalism or the question of Englishness. It brings to bear instead, under the auspices of the "postcolonial," questions of class, race, and gender, which mobilize new constellations of meaning and new readerships. "*Why* we read Jane Austen is also a function of *how* we read Jane Austen," as Rajeswari Sunder Rajan puts it (21). See also Terry Collits's *Postcolonial Conrad*, which examines the efficacy of Conrad's works in the discursive field of postcolonial studies, and *Semicolonial Joyce*, a collection of essays edited by Derek Attridge and Marjorie Howes, which attempts to situate Ireland's colonial history in Joyce's work.

5. Cooppan cites Derek Attridge's valuable insight that "[in] *the event of the allegorising reading* . . . one may be doing justice to the singularity and inventive-

ness of a literary work by responding to its invitation to allegorize, to its quality of what we might call 'allegoricity,' because in so doing we are working through the operations of its meaning—irrespective of whether we arrive at some stable allegorical scheme" (Attridge, *J. M. Coetzee*, 61).

6. Alcoff, "Problem," 115.

7. McDonald, *Literature Police*, 304.

8. "Not all people exist in the same Now," wrote Ernst Bloch in 1932. "They do so externally, by virtue of the fact that they may be seen today. But that does not mean that they are living at the same time with others" (Bloch, "Nonsynchronism," 22). See also Joshi's discussion of nonsynchronism in *Another Country* (250).

9. Sartre states in the preface to *The Wretched of the Earth* that "the status of the 'native' is a nervous condition introduced and maintained by the settler among colonized people *with their consent*." (*The Wretched of the Earth*, 7–31).

10. As Joseph Slaughter and others have pointed out, *Nervous Conditions* is set in the political turmoil of the period between 1965 and 1980, its fictional events bookended by the last resurgence of white supremacist rule in Rhodesia (in the form of the Unilateral Declaration of Independence in 1965), and the independence of Zimbabwe in 1980.

CHAPTER 5

1. In stark contrast to the Globe-trotter, Kipling aligns himself to a traveler, whose outward restlessness does not affect his mental makeup, especially the strength of his previously acquired convictions. "One of the advantages of foreign travel is that one takes such a keen interest in, and hears so much about, Home. Truly, they change their trains, but not their train of thought, who run across the sea" (*From Sea to Sea*, 405).

2. Pollock is describing an overhaul in political structures and administrative agendas in late middle-period India, when matters of regional governance take precedence over the dream of imperial expansion. As kings became less the figureheads of "cosmic imperia" and more the "overlords of existing regional polities," the universal applicability of Sanskrit loses ground to vernaculars that better articulate and authorize regional political space while also aiming for transregional diffusion. The key characteristic of the emergent cosmopolitan vernaculars, Pollock suggests, is that they "usurp the position of the superposed literary formation" and "recreate the condition of the imperial culture at the level of the region" ("Cosmopolitan," 31–32).

3. See Appiah, "Loyalty to Humanity."

4. Bhabha quotes Kristeva, *Strangers to Ourselves*, 13.

5. See Viswanathan, "Currying Favor." See also Roy, "'Englishing' India," which treats the nineteenth-century introduction of English education in India as a formalization of processes that had been in motion for several decades. Debjani

Ganguly provides an excellent overview of the vicissitudes of the English language in India in her "The Language Question in India."

6. *Parliamentary Debates* (1813), vol. 26; cited in Viswanathan, "Currying Favor," 92.

7. The quote is from Viswanathan, "Beginnings." Viswanathan is here commenting on the long-standing effects of the Macaulay Minute of 1835, which advocated the teaching of English to Indians. According to Viswanathan, "the strategy of locating authority in the texts of English literature all but effaced the sordid history of colonial expropriation, material exploitation and class and race oppression behind British world dominance" (22).

8. "Late Style: Adorno, Lampedusa, Cavafy," lecture, University of Minnesota, Minneapolis, February 22, 1999; cited in Timothy Brennan, "Resolution," in *Edward Said*, ed. Bhabha and Mitchell (43–55).

9. *Hazaar* is Urdu-Hindi for "a thousand." The line from Chatterjee's *English, August* runs as follows: "Amazing mix, the English we speak. *Hazaar fucked*. Urdu and American,' Agastya laughed, 'a thousand fucked, really fucked. I'm sure nowhere else could languages be mixed and spoken with such ease" (Chatterjee, *English, August*, 1).

10. Mukherjee, *Perishable*, 167.

11. Ibid., 171.

12. For critiques of vernacularizations of English speech and writing see Mukherjee, "Anxiety of Englishness"; Khair, *Babu Fictions*; Aravamudan, *Guru English*; Joshi, *Another Country*; Srivastava, "Pidgin English."

13. According to Harold Bloom, *poetic misprision* is inextricable from the question of poetic influence, especially when it involves two strong poets, and "proceeds by a misreading of the prior poet, an act of creative correction that is actually and necessarily a misinterpretation" (*Anxiety of Influence*, 30).

14. As Stephen Morton points out, the pages of the Guppee army refer to the chapters of the Koran, which are not arranged in a linear order, and beseech a readerly intervention whereby each new interpretation rearranges the narratives in novel, coherent wholes (85).

15. In an influential essay, Marianne Hirsch describes the relationship of the second generation to traumatic historical events, and the phantom constitution of memories of events that preceded their births, as "postmemory." This concept is particularly relevant for Anam's work in the way it draws on the family as a space of transmission, and emphasizes the role of gender in conveying remembrance. Hirsch, "Generation of Postmemory."

16. Ahmad draws an analogy from powerful capitalist firms, which "originating in particular imperialist countries but commanding global investments and networks of transport and communication, proclaim themselves nevertheless as being *multi*nationals and *trans*nationals, as if their *origins* in the United States or the Federal German Rupublic was a mere myth and as if their ability to accumu-

late surplus value from a dozen countries or more was none other than an *excess* of belonging" (Ahmad, "Rushdie's *Shame*," 1463). ."

17. See www.themanbookerprize.com/news/stories/1146.

18. The gas leak at the Union Carbide factory at Bhopal is one of the worst industrial disasters in history. The Bhopal factory was built in the 1970s by the Dow Chemical Company to manufacture pesticide, but the venture proved unprofitable following years of bad monsoons and crop failures and the plant fell into disrepair. The Union Carbide factory, instead of dismantling the unit, cut costs through reducing the number of skilled maintenance staff. Despite several warnings of a major toxic release, safety issues were grossly neglected and Union Carbide made no efforts to secure the factory or safeguard the densely packed neighborhoods nearby. On December 2, 1984, the plant leaked over forty tonnes of lethal methyl-isocyanate (MIC) gas: twenty thousand people were killed and more than a hundred thousand people remain chronically ill in the aftermath. About half a million people have injuries relatable to the gas leak. The victims were awarded a one-off payment of three hundred Sterling per head by Union Carbide.

19. See Giancarlo Maiorino, "Picaresque Econopoetics: At the Watershed of Living Standards," in *The Picaresque: Tradition and Displacement*, ed. Giancarlo Maiorino (Minneapolis: University of Minnesota Press, 1996): 1–39.

20. Ranajit Guha uses the Hegelian concept of *die Weltgeschichte* to outline the processes of abstraction through which historical phenomena are drained of particularities and history itself becomes a philosophical concept. History becomes the philosophy of history and the "concreteness of the human past [is] made to yield to the concept of World-history" (*History*, 3).

21. As Gayatri Spivak has demonstrated in several literary critical exercises, vernacular colonial literature challenges the contrast often made, "in 'western' colonial discourse studies, between western literature as 'central' and third world literature . . . as 'marginal' or 'emergent'" ("Burden," 282).

CHAPTER 6

1. In *Cultural Capital*, Guillory, contemplating the relative autonomy of educational institutions, wonders if "the duration of educational institutions can be shown to be (in part) an effect of formal objectifications of reproduction, such as canons of texts." "Institutions of reproduction," Guillory continues, "succeed by taking as their first object not the reproduction of social relations but the reproduction of the institution itself" (57).

2. For the most comprehensive and astute analysis of the instrumentality of English literary education in the civilizing mission of the empire, see Viswanathan, *Masks of Conquests*. See also Spivak, *Lie of the Land*; and Joshi, *Another Country*. Harish Trivedi's *Colonial Transactions* supplements Viswanathan's work in its in-

sistence that despite the power imbalance between the two sides, the colonial encounter was characterized by cultural traffic and exchange. Focusing, as she does, on strategies of epistemic domination perfected by colonial rulers, Viswanathan self-consciously omits the responses of the native population to the exertions of the East India Company on their behalf: the history of the Indian response, Viswanathan argues, "can, and perhaps must, be told separately for its immensely rich and complex quality to be fully revealed" (12). This chapter follows the lead of Joshi and Trivedi to gesture toward the "immensely rich and complex quality" of that story across colonial and postcolonial history.

3. Cited in Nileena M. S., "Revisiting *Macbeth*," *The Hindu*, March 13, 2011; available at hamarashakespeare.com.

4. See Ania Loomba, "Local-Manufacture Made-in-India Othello Fellows," in *Post-Colonial Shakespeares*, ed. Loomba and Orkin (143–63), for a detailed discussion of the use of the four-hundred-year-old form of Kathakali, derived from Koodiyattam, for a spectacular adaptation of *Othello*. "I realised that at first I only asked what it was doing to Shakespeare," says Loomba. "Slowly, I was compelled to invert that question, and try and understand what the production was doing to Kathakali" (151). Two insights in this essay are particularly useful to this discussion. The first is that with Kathakali, the context of the Shakespeare adaptation is within "indigenous performative and intellectual histories rather than in simply the colonial heritage of English literary texts in India" (159). The second is what Loomba perceives as the disturbing erasure of race, which is not even inflected in class or communal differences to reflect the schisms relevant to Indian society, in such adaptations. Kathakali's hypertrophic conventions, Loomba concludes, "subvert or simply bypass those of Shakespeare's play" (162).

5. The Mizoram National Front, or MNF, is a regional political party originally formed to protest against the negligence and inaction of the Indian central government in the face of famine in the Mizo areas of the Assam state in 1959. The MNF had a major uprising in 1966, and evolved into an underground separatist movement. The front lay down arms after signing the Mizo Accord in 1986 with the government of India.

6. Comparing Hamlet-drama to a Delhi-based adaptation of *Hamlet*, Loomba observes that "Delhi Shakespeare remains Western in a way that Hamlet-drama does not. . . . Mizoram is further removed from Delhi than Delhi is from London ("*Hamlet* in Mizoram," 244).

7. See Gangopadhyay, *Girishchandra*, 5; my trans. Incidentally, the editor of *Sadharani*, Akshoy Chandra Sarkar, referred to him as the "Garrick of Bengal" in an 1879 review of Ghosh's double act as Ram and Meghnad in Michael Madhusudan Dutt's *Meghnādbodhkabya*.

8. I have used Arden editions throughout for my quotations of Shakespeare, but have relied on the Shakespeare text (publication details unknown) provided by Girish Ghosh's biographer, for the sections on Ghosh's translation.

9. "Witch's" in the original. The punctuation in Gangopadhyay's version is also discrepant from the original. On line 28, "Slivered in the moon's eclipse" has become "Sliver'd." "Chawdron" in line 33 is spelled "chaudron."

10. The fir tree, a signifier of northern climes, is ubiquitous in representations of England and Europe in Bengali literature; audiences would have been familiar with the type from the iconography of English and translated texts, and also from the variant of the fir that grows in hill stations in India.

11. Other than the capitalization of "spirits" in line 39 and that of "nature in" in 49, and the substitution of "murth'ring" for "murd'ring," the text has no variations, in marked contrast with the one cited before.

12. This is mentioned in the introduction to Girish Chandra Ghosh's complete works and runs as follows: "Nātok dekhar jogytālabhé ihāder ekhano bahu batsar lāgibé—nātok bujhibār sādhāron darshak ekhano Bānglāy tairi hoyni [It will take them (the masses) years to become astute theatergoers. The average Bengali in the audience is not ready yet to comprehend (serious) theater]" (*Girish Rachanabali*, 23).

13. Amal Mitra's *Kalkatay Bidesi Rangalay* (Foreign Theaters in Calcutta) (Calcutta: Prakash Bhaban, 1967), cited in Chatterjee and Singh, "Moor or Less?" 69–70.

14. Despite the buzz around the appearance of an authentic Moor, the opening performance of James Barry's *Othello* was interrupted by a local military commanding officer of the British East India Company, who refused to let his men act as extras in the production, and the police were also involved, though there is no evidence to suggest that this disruption was racially motivated (Chatterjee and Singh, "Moor or Less?" 75–76).

15. According the G. K. Hunter, Romeo and Juliet counter the rhetoric of society with "radiant poetry," expressive of their mutually felt desires and outlook. See "Shakespeare and the Traditions of Tragedy."

16. The Macaulay Minute on English Education (1835), argued forcefully by Thomas Macaulay, recommended an education which would invent a new social identity for Indians, who would then serve as interpreters between the British rulers and the "millions whom [they] governed." Samaresh and his milieu evoke stereotypes of colonial mimic men.

17. She, however, has no friends outside the Anglo-Indian community and speaks no Bengali. On their first meeting with Miss Stoneham, Samaresh pretends to sing to Nandita as he asks her in Bengali to press their case for the flat. True to her lifelong misgivings, Stoneham's cross-cultural romance—"If we mix closely with Indians they also mix nicely with us," she says optimistically at the height of her relationship with Samaresh and Nandita—comes to a precipitate end, the callous rejection of the Bengali couple cynically echoing Rosemary's betrayal in the hands of her Indian beau.

18. Sen is clearly evoking the pervasive animal imagery of a play that de-

scribes the "unaccomodated man" to a "poor, bare, forked animal" (2.4.262). As Marjorie Garber observes, in *King Lear* dogs figure negatively as the byname of human wretchedness and lowliness—"mongrel," "cur," "whoreson dog"—but also as faithful household creatures, whose barking at Lear on the Heath was perhaps the ultimate sign of his banishment from the socius. The unconditional loyalty of dogs is also contrasted with dramatic effect to filial disloyalty. As Cordelia says despairingly,

> Mine enemy's dog,
> Though he had bit me, should have stood that night
> Against my fire. (4.7.36–38)

See Garber, "Shakespeare's Dogs," *Profiling*, 182–94.

19. See Bharucha, *Rehearsals of Revolution*; and Utpal Dutt's own *Towards a Revolutionary Theatre*. See also Jyotsna G. Singh, "Different Shakespeares," which elaborates, with specific examples drawn from theater and education, the changing roles of Shakespeare in Indian cultural self-definition.

20. See foreword by Shamik Bandopadhyay, in Utpal Dutt's Bengali translation of *Macbeth*. All quotations from this foreword are translated by me.

21. I am referring to Harold Bloom's argument in *Shakespeare: The Invention of the Human*. While Bloom attributes Shakespeare's adaptability to the "global and multicultural" universalism of his works (3), Bhardwaj seems to value Shakespeare for the way in which the classic tales negotiate historical difference. Bhardwaj's tragic heroes are embedded in sociopolitical contexts, and, unlike their European counterparts, individuation does not entail a break from the communal life of the tribe. The tragic heroes of Bhardwaj's Shakespeare adaptations do not have soliloquies or asides: the psychic malady of the hero is not contained in character alone, but functions metonymically as social contagion. The protagonist is eventually scapegoated for the regeneration of the civic state.

22. *Abbaji* can be translated as "godfather." The activities of the crime gang, as Panditji tells A. C. P. Devsare, involve rent collection, land acquisition, contract killing, and protection of minorities, which in this case refers to the Muslim population of Mumbai and in India.

23. Twice in the movie, Omkara utters the old scriptural phrase in Sanskrit, *triya charitram*, which runs as follows: "Triya charitram, purushasya bhagyam, devo na janati, kuto manushya." To translate: "A woman's character and a man's destiny—even the Gods don't have a clue, let alone humans."

24. Kastan is citing Lewis Theobold's statement that on the page Shakespeare "stands, or ought to stand, in the nature of a classic writer" (*Shakespeare and the Book*, v). See *Shakespeare Restored* (London, 1726).

25. See Rajiva Verma, "Shakespeare in Hindi Cinema," in *India's Shakespeare*, ed. Trivedi and Bartholomeusz, 269–90.

POSTSCRIPT

1. Margot Norris quotes Austin Briggs, in conversation with J. M. Coetzee at Hamilton College (November 2001). Briggs, who reviewed three of the published segments of *Elizabeth Costello* in the spring 2002 issue of the *James Joyce Quarterly*, is referring here to the fourth novel written by the eponymous protagonist of *Elizabeth Costello*, which is titled *The House on Eccles Street* and has as its main character none other than Joyce's Molly Bloom. See Margot Norris, "Not a Bit Like Molly Bloom."

2. The phrase is used by Fritz Senn to describe Joyce's rewriting of Homer's *Odyssey*. See "Book of Many Turns."

3. Pound, "Praefatio," 6.

4. The *Browne Review*, or "Independent Review of Higher Education Funding and Student Finance," was undertaken to consider the future direction of higher-education funding in England. It was launched on November 9, 2009, and published its findings on October 12, 2010. It was chaired by Lord Browne of Madingly, the former chief executive of BP, and recommended wide-ranging changes to the system of university funding, including removing the cap on the level of fees that universities can charge. The *Higher Education White Paper*, published in June 2011, is a publication of ministers' views for the future of the education sector, and is premised on the findings of the *Browne Review*. The White Paper states that though graduates will pay more toward the cost of their degrees, the government's proposals will improve their experience as students; expand their choices; make universities more accountable to students than ever before.

5. Gilles Deleuze, *Difference and Repetition*, trans. Paul Patton (New York: Columbia University Press, 1994), 1; cited in Chakrabarty, "Belatedness as Possibility."

6. Conversation with Judith Luna, June 1, 2012.

7. Coetzee, "What Is a Classic?" 19.

Bibliography

Abraham, Taisha. "An Interview with Arundhati Roy." *Ariel* 29.1 (1998): 91.

Abrams, M. H. *A Glossary of Literary Terms*. Chicago: Holt, Rineherd and Winston, 1985.

Achebe, Chinua. "An Image of Africa." *Research in African Literature* 9.1 (Spring 1978): 1–15.

Ackroyd, Peter. *T. S. Eliot: A Life*. New York: Simon and Schuster, 1984.

Adelman, Janet. *Suffocating Mothers: Fantasies of Maternal Origin in Shakespeare's Plays, "Hamlet" to "The Tempest."* New York: Routledge, 1992.

Adiga, Aravind. *The White Tiger*. London: Atlantic Books, 2008.

Agamben, Giorgio. *The Open: Man and Animal*. Stanford, CA: Stanford University Press, 2004.

Ahmad, Aijaz. *In Theory: Nations, Classes, Literatures*. London: Verso, 1992.

———. "Reading Arundhati Roy Politically." In *Arundhati Roy's The God of Small Things*, ed. Alex Tickell, 110–20. London: Routledge, 2007.

———. "Rushdie's *Shame*: Postmodernism, Migrancy, and Representation of Women." *Economic and Political Weekly* 26.24 (June 15, 1991): 1461–71.

Alcoff, Linda Martin. "The Problem of Speaking for Others." In *Who Can Speak? Authority and Critical Identity*, ed. Judith Roof and Robin Wiegman, 97–119. Urbana: University of Illinois Press, 1995.

Ali, Monica. *Brick Lane*. Chatham, England: Quality Paperbacks Direct, 2003.

Altieri, Charles. *Canons and Consequences Reflections on the Ethical Force of Imaginative Ideals*. Evanston, IL: Northwestern University Press, 1990.

———. "The Hermeneutics of Literary Indeterminacy: A Dissent from the New Orthodoxy." *New Literary History* 10.1 (1978): 71–99.

———. "An Idea and Ideal of a Literary Canon." *Critical Inquiry* 10.1 (1983): 37–60.

———. "Organic and Humanist Models in Some English Bildungsroman." *Journal of General Education* 23 (1971): 220–339.

Anam, Tahmima. "First Look: Tahmima Anam." *The Guardian*, November 24, 2007.

———. *A Golden Age*. London: John Murray, 2007.
———. "PW Talks with Tahmima Anam." *Publishers Weekly*, October 15, 2007.
Anand, Mulk Raj. "Pigeon Indian: Some Notes on Indian English Writing." *World Literature Written in English* 21.2 (1982): 325–36.
Anderson, Benedict. "El Mulhadado País." In *The Spectre of Comparisons: Nationalism, Southeast Asia, and the World*, 333–59. London: Verso, 1998.
———. *Imagined Communities: Reflections on the Origin and Spread of Nationalism*. London: Verso, 1991.
———. *The Spectre of Comparisons: Nationalism, Southeast Asia, and the World*. London: Verso, 1998.
Appadurai, Arjun. *Modernity at Large: Cultural Dimensions of Globalization*. Minnesota: University of Minneapolis Press, 1996.
Appiah, Anthony. "Loyalty to Humanity." *Boston Review* 19.5 (October–November 1994).
Apter, Emily. *Continental Drift: From National Characters to Virtual Subjects*. Chicago: University of Chicago Press, 1999.
———. "Global *Translatio*: The 'Invention' of Comparative Literature, Istanbul, 1933." *Critical Inquiry* 29.2 (2003): 253–81.
———. *The Translation Zone: A New Comparative Literature*. Princeton, NJ: Princeton University Press, 2006.
Appadurai, Arjun. "Grassroots Globalization and the Research Imagination." In *Globalization*, ed. Arjun Appadurai, 1–20. Durham, England: Durham University Press, 2000.
———. "The Hermeneutics of Literary Indeterminacy: A Dissent from the New Orthodoxy." *Literary Hermeneutics*. Special issue of *New Literary History* 10.1 (1978): 71–99.
———. *Modernity at Large: Cultural Dimensions of Globalization*. Minneapolis: University of Minnesota Press, 2003.
Arac, Jonathan. "Anglo-Globalism?" *New Left Review* 16 (2002): 35–45.
Aravamudan, Srinivas. *Guru English: South Asian Religion in a Cosmopolitan Language*. Princeton, NJ: Princeton University Press, 2005.
Armstrong, Isobel. Review of *The Poetry of Browning: A Critical Introduction*, by Philip Drew. *Review of English Studies*, n.s., 23.89 (1972): 90–93.
Ashcroft, Bill, Gareth Griffiths, and Helen Tiffin, eds. *The Empire Writes Back*. New York and London: Routledge, 1989.
Attwell, David. "Coetzee's Estrangements." *Novel* 41.2–3 (2008): 229–43.
Attridge, Derek. *J. M. Coetzee and the Ethics of Reading: Literature in the Event*. Chicago: University of Chicago Press, 2004.
Attridge, Derek, and Marjorie Howes, eds. *Semicolonial Joyce*. Cambridge: Cambridge University Press, 2000.

Bandopadhyay, Shamik. "Mukhabandha." Foreword to *Shakespeare: Macbeth*, trans. Utpal Dutt. Kolkata: Thema, 2006.

Barker, Francis, and Peter Hulme. "'Nymphs and Rapers Heavily Vanish': The Discursive Con-Texts of *The Tempest*." In *Alternative Shakespeares*, ed. John Drakakis, 191–205. London: Methuen, 1985.

Baucom, Ian. "Gloablit, Inc.; or, The Cultural Logic of Global Literary Studies." *PMLA* 116.1 (2001): 158–72.

———. *Out of Place: Englishness, Empire, and the Locations of Identity*. Princeton, NJ: Princeton University Press, 1999.

———. *Specters of the Atlantic: Finance Capital, Slavery, and the Philosophy of History*. Durham, NC: Duke University Press, 2005.

Baugh, Edward. *Derek Walcott*. Cambridge: Cambridge University Press, 2006.

Beckett, Samuel. *Samuel Beckett*. Vol. 4, *Poems, Short Fiction, Criticism*. Ed. Paul Auster. New York: Grove Press, 2006.

Benítez-Rojo, Antonio. *The Repeating Island: The Caribbean and the Postmodern Perspective*. Trans. James E. Maraniss. Durham: Duke University Press, 1992.

Benjamin, Walter. *Illuminations: Essays and Reflections*. Ed. Hannah Arendt. New York: Schocken, 1969.

———. *The Arcades Project*. Cambridge, MA: Harvard University Press, 2002.

Bhabha, Homi K. *The Location of Culture*. London: Routledge, 1994.

———. *Nation and Narration*. London: Routledge, 1990.

———. "Of Mimicry and Man: The Ambivalence of Colonial Discourse." *October* 28 (1984): 125–33.

———. "Unpacking My Library Again." *Journal of the Midwest Modern Language Association* 28.1 (1995): 5–18.

———. "Unsatisfied: Notes on Vernacular Cosmopolitanism." *Postcolonial Discourses: An Anthology*. Ed. Gregory Castle. Oxford: Blackwell Publishing, 2000. 38–52.

———. "The World and the Home." *Social Text* 31–32 (1992): 141–53.

Bhabha, Homi, and W. J. T. Mitchell, eds. *Edward Said: Continuing the Conversation*. Chicago: University of Chicago Press, 2005.

Bharucha, Rustom. *Rehearsals of Revolution: The Political Theater of Bengal*. Honolulu: University of Hawaii Press, 1983.

Bingham, Harry. "You Say Potato, I Say *Ghoughbteighpteau*." *The Guardian*, September 29, 2007.

Bloch, Ernst. "Nonsynchronism and the Obligation to Its Dialectics." *New German Critique* 11.4 (1977): 22–38.

Bloom, Harold. *Anxiety of Influence: A Theory of Poetry*. New York: Oxford University Press, 1973.

———, ed. *Derek Walcott*. Philadelphia: Chelsea House, 2003.

———. *Shakespeare: The Invention of the Human.* London: Fourth Estate, 1999.

———. *The Western Canon: The Books and School of the Ages.* New York: Riverhead, 1994.

Bourdieu, Pierre. *Distinction: A Social Critique of the Judgement of Taste.* Trans. Richard Nice. 1st French ed., 1979. New York: Routledge, 1986.

Brantlinger, Patrick. *Rule of Darkness: British Literature and Imperialism, 1830–1914.* Ithaca, NY: Cornell University Press, 1988.

Brathwaite, Edward Kamau. *The Development of Creole Society in Jamaica 1770–1820.* Oxford: Oxford University Press, 1971.

———. "English in the Caribbean: Notes on Nation Language and Poetry." In *English Literature: Opening Up the Canon,* ed. Leslie A. Fiedler and Houston A. Baker, Jr., 15–53. Baltimore: Johns Hopkins University Press, 1979.

Brennan, Timothy. *At Home in the World: Cosmpolitanism Now.* Cambridge, MA: Harvard University Press, 1997.

———. "The Cultural Politics of Rushdie Criticism: All or Nothing." In *Critical Essays on Salman Rushdie,* ed. M. Keith Booker, 107–28. Boston: G. K. Hall, 1999.

———. "Edward Said and Comparative Literature." *Journal of Palestine Studies* 33.3 (Spring 2004): 23-38.

———. *Salman Rushdie and the Third World: Myths of the Nation.* London: Macmillan, 1989.

Breslin, Paul. "The Cultural Address of Derek Walcott." *Modernism/Modernity* 9.2 (2002): 319–25.

———. "Derek Walcott's 'Reversible World': Centres, Peripheries, and the Scale of Nature." *Callaloo* 28.1 (Winter 2005): 8–24.

———. *Nobody's Nation: Reading Derek Walcott.* Chicago: University of Chicago Press, 2001.

Brodsky, Joseph. "The Sound of the Tide." In *Less Than One: Selected Essays,* 164–65. New York: Farrar, Straus and Giroux, 1986.

Bunzl, Matti, et al., eds. *Postcolonial Studies and Beyond.* Durham, NC: Duke University Press, 2005.

Burnett, Paula. *Derek Walcott: Politics and Poetry.* Gainsville: University Press of Florida, 2000.

Calvino, Italo. *The Literature Machine: Essays.* Trans. Patrick Creagh. 1980. Repr., London: Vintage Books, 1997.

Cartelli, Thomas. "After *The Tempest*: Shakespeare, Postcoloniality, and Michelle Cliff's New, New World Miranda." *Contemporary Literature* 36.1 (1995): 82–102.

Casanova, Pascale. "Literature as a World." *New Left Review* 31 (2005): 1–11.

———. *The World Republic of Letters.* Trans. M. B. Debevoise. Cambridge, MA: Harvard University Press, 2004.

Cavell, Stanley. "The Avoidance of Love: A Reading of *King Lear.*" In *Disowning Knowledge in Seven Plays of Shakespeare*, 39–123. Cambridge: Cambridge University Press, 2003.
Chakrabarty, Dipesh. "Belatedness as Possibility: Subaltern Histories, Once Again." In *The Indian Postcolonial: A Critical Reader*, ed. Elleke Boehmer and Rosinka Chaudhuri, 163–76. London: Routledge, 2011.
———. *Habitations of Modernity*. Chicago: University of Chicago Press, 2002.
———. "Postcoloniality and the Artifice of History: Who Speaks for 'Indian' Pasts?" *Imperial Fantasies and Postcolonial Histories.* Special issue of *Representations* 37 (1992): 1–26.
———. *Provincializing Europe: Postcolonial Thought and Historical Difference.* Princeton, NJ: Princeton University Press, 2000.
———. "Radical Histories and the Question of Enlightenment Rationalism: Some Recent Critiques of Subaltern Studies." *Econonomic and Political Weekly* (April 8, 1995): 751–59.
———. "Universalism and Belonging in the Logic of Capitalism." *Public Culture* 12.3 (2000): 653–78.
Chatterjee, Sudipto, and Jyotsna G. Singh. "Moor or Less? The Surveillance of Othello." In *Shakespeare and Appropriation*, ed. Christy Desmet and Robert Sawyer, 65–82. New York: Routledge, 1999.
Chatterjee, Upamanyu. *English, August: An Indian Story*. London: Faber and Faber, 1989.
Chattopadhyay, Bankim Chandra, Brajendranath Bandopadhyay, and Sajanikanta Das, eds. *Bijnan-rahasya, Samya, Vividh Prabandha*. Kolkata: Bangiya Sahitya Parishad, 1938.
Chaudhuri, Rosinka, ed. *Derozio, Poet of India: The Definitive Edition*. New Delhi: Oxford University Press, 2008.
Cheah, Pheng. *Spectral Nationality: Passages of Freedom from Kant to Postcolonial Literatures of Liberation*. New York: Columbia University Press, 2003.
———. "What Is a World?: On World Literature as World-Making Activity." *Daedalus: Journal of the American Academy of Arts and Sciences* 137.3 (Summer 2008): 26–38.
Cheng, Vincent J. *Joyce, Race, and Empire*. Cambridge: Cambridge University Press, 1995.
Childs, Peter, ed. *Postcolonial Theory and English Literature: A Reader*. Edinburgh: Edinburgh University Press, 1999.
Cleary, Joe. "The World Literary System: Atlas and Epitaph." Review of *The World Republic of Letters*, by Pascale Casanova. *Field Day Review* 2 (2006): 196–219.
Coetzee, J. M. *Age of Iron*. New York: Random House, 1990.
———. *Boyhood: Scenes from Provincial Life*. New York: Penguin Books, 1998.

———. *Diary of a Bad Year*. 2007. Repr., London: Vintage Books, 2008.
———. *Doubling the Point: Essays and Interviews*. Ed. David Attwell. Cambridge, MA: Harvard University Press, 1992.
———. *Elizabeth Costello*. London: Vintage Books, 2004.
———. *Foe*. London: Penguin Books, 1987.
———. *The Master of Petersburg*. New York: Viking Press, 1994.
———. "The Novel Today." *Upstream: A Magazine of the Arts* 6.1 (1988): 2–5.
———. "The Sympathetic Imagination: A Conversation with J. M. Coetzee." *Brick* 67 (2000): 37–47.
———. "What Is a Classic?" *Stranger Shores: Essays, 1986–1999*. London: Vintage Books, 1992: 1–19.
———. *Youth*. London: Secker and Warburg, 2002.
Collini, Stefan. "Browne's Gamble." *London Review of Books*, April 11, 2010.
———. *What Are Universities For?* London: Penguin Books, 2012.
Collits, Terry. *Postcolonial Conrad: Paradoxes of Empire*. New York: Routledge, 2005.
Compagnon, Antoine. "Sainte-Beuve and the Canon." *Modern Language Notes* 110.5 (1995): 1188–99.
Conrad, Joseph. *The Collected Letters of Joseph Conrad*. Ed. Frederick R. Karl. 4 vols. New York: Cambridge University Press, 1983– .
———. *Congo Diary and Other Uncollected Pieces*. Ed. Zdzislaw Najder. London: Doubleday, 1978.
———. *Heart of Darkness: An Authoritative Text, Backgrounds and Sources, Criticism*. 3rd ed. Ed. Robert Kimbrough. 1902. Repr., New York: W. W. Norton, 1988.
———. "Henry James: An Appreciation." *North American Review* 180.578 (January 1905): 102–8.
———. *The Mirror of the Sea and A Personal Record*. Oxford: Oxford University Press, 1988.
———. *The Nigger of the "Narcissus" and Other Stories*. Ed. Allan H. Simmons. London: Penguin Classics, 2007.
———. *Notes on Life and Letters*. Ed. J. H. Stape, with Andrew Busza. Cambridge: Cambridge University Press, 2004.
———. *The Secret Agent: A Simple Tale*. Ed. Peter Lancelot Mallios. 1907. Repr., New York: Modern Library, 2004.
———. *The Shadow-line: A Confession*. London: Dent and Sons, 1917.
———. *Tales of Unrest*. London: Penguin Books, 1977.
———. *Typhoon and Other Tales*. Ed. Cedric Watts. Oxford: Oxford University Press, 1998.
Cooppan, Vilashini. "Interconnections." *PMLA* 112.2 (1997): 278–79.

———. *Worlds Within: National Narratives and Global Connections in Postcolonial Writing*. Stanford, CA: Stanford University Press, 2009.
Cornell, Drucilla. *The Philosophy of the Limit*. New York: Routledge, 1992.
Culler, Jonathan. "Anderson and the Novel." *Diacritics* 29.4 (Winter 1999): 19–39.
———. *The Literary in Theory*. Stanford, CA: Stanford University Press, 2007.
Damrosch, David. *How to Read World Literature*. Oxford: Wiley Blackwell, 2009.
———. *What Is World Literature?* Princeton, NJ: Princeton University Press, 2003.
Dangarembga, Tsitsi. *Nervous Conditions*. 1988. Repr., Banbury: Ayebia Clarke Publishing, 2004.
Das, Kamala. "An Introduction." *Feminist Studies* 26.3 (Autumn 2000): 727–28.
Dasgupta, Hemendranath. *The Indian Stage*. Vol. 3 (1944). Available at Internet Archives, www.archive.org/details/indianstagevoliio29646mbp (accessed May 22, 2013).
Defoe, Daniel. *The Life and Adventures of Robinson Crusoe*. Ed. Angus Ross. London: Penguin Books, 1985.
Deloughrey, Elizabeth. "Island Writing, Creole Cultures." In *The Cambridge History of Postcolonial Literature*, 2 vols., ed. Ato Quayson, 2: 802–32. Cambridge: Cambridge University Press, 2011.
De Quincey, Thomas. "On the Knocking at the Gate in *Macbeth*." In *Confessions of an English Opium-Eater*, ed. Grevel Lindop, 81–85. Oxford: Oxford University Press, 1996.
Derrida, Jacques. *Acts of Literature*. Ed. Derek Attridge. New York: Routledge, 1992.
———. *A Derrida Reader: Between the Blinds*. Ed. Peggy Kamuf. New York: Columbia University Press, 1991.
———. "Geopsychoanalysis: '. . . and the rest of the world.'" In *Psychoanalysis and Race*, ed. Christopher Lane, 65–91. New York: Columbia University Press, 1998.
———. "No Apocalypse, Not Now (Full Speed Ahead, Seven Missiles, Seven Missives)." Trans. C. Porter and P. Lewis. *Diacritics* 14.2 (1984): 20–31.
———. "Of an Apocalyptic Tone Recently Adopted in Philosophy." *Oxford Literary Review* 6.2 (1984): 3–37.
———. "Onto-Theology of National-Humanism (Proglomena to a Hypothesis)." *Oxford Literary Review* 14.1–2 (1992): 3–23.
Desani, G. V. *All About H. Hatterr*. 1970. Repr., New York: The New York Review of Books, 1986.
Desmet, Christy and Robert Sawyer, eds. *Shakespeare and Appropriation*. London: Routledge, 1999.Dickens, Charles. *Great Expectations*. Ed. Angus Calder. London: Penguin Books, 1985.

Dickens, Charles. *Great Expectations*. Ed. Angus Calder. London: Penguin Books, 1985.
Dimock, Wai Chee. "Literature for the Planet." *PMLA* 116.1 (2001): 173–88.
———, ed. *Shades of the Planet: American Literature as World Literature*. Princeton, NJ: Princeton University Press, 2007.
———. *Through Other Continents: American Literature Across Deep Time*. Princeton, NJ: Princeton University Press, 2006.
Disraeli, Benjamin. *Sybil; or, The Two Nations*. Oxford: Oxford University Press, 1981.
Drakakis, John, ed. *Alternative Shakespeares*. London: Methuen Publishing, 1985.
Duffy, Enda. *The Subaltern Ulysses*. Minneapolis: University of Minnesota Press, 1994.
During, Simon. "Postmodernism: Or, Post-Colonialism Today." *Textual Practice* 1.1 (1987 Spring): 32-47.
Dutt, Utpal, trans. *Shakespeare: Macbeth*. Foreword by Shamik Bandopadhyay. Kolkata: Thema, 2006.
———. *Towards a Revolutionary Theatre*. Kolkata: M. C. Sarkar and Sons, 1982.
———. "A Weapon of Change." *Sunday*, November 3, 1985, 2–3.
Eagleton, Terry. *Exiles and Émigrés: Studies in Modern Literature*. London: Chatto and Windus, 1970.
———. *Heathcliff and the Great Hunger: Studies in Irish Culture*. London: Verso, 1995.
Eliot, T. S. *On Poetry and Poets*. New York: Farrar, Straus and Giroux, 1957.
———. *Selected Essays*. London: Faber and Faber, 1999.
———. "Virgil and the Christian World." *On Poetry and Poets*. New York: Farrar, Straus and Giroux, 1957: 121-131.
———. *What Is a Classic? An Address Delivered Before the Virgil Society on the 16th of October 1944*. London: Faber and Faber, 1945.
English, James F. *The Economy of Prestige: Prizes, Awards, and the Circulation of Cultural Value*. Cambridge, MA: Harvard University Press, 2005.
Etherton, Michael. *The Development of African Drama*. London: Hutchinson University Library for Africa, 1982.
Fanon, Frantz. *Black Skin, White Masks*. Trans. Charles Lam Markmann. London: Pluto Press, 1986.
———. *The Wretched of the Earth*. Trans. Constance Farrington. New York: Grove Press, 1963.
Fee, Margery. "Who Can Write as Other?" In *The Post-Colonial Studies Reader*, ed. Bill Ashcroft, Gareth Griffiths, and Helen Tiffin, 242–48. New York: Routledge, 1995.

Forster, John. *The Life of Charles Dickens*. Vol. 2. New York: Charles Scribner's Sons, 1900.
Foucault, Michel. "Of Other Spaces." *Diacritics* 16 (Spring 1986). 22–29.
Freud, Sigmund. "Beyond the Pleasure Principle." In *The Standard Edition of the Complete Psychological Works of Sigmund Freud*, 24 vols., ed. and trans. James Strachey, 18: 7–64. London: Hogarth Press, 1953–74; 1955.
Gandhi, Leela. *Postcolonial Theory: A Critical Introduction*. New York: Columbia University Press, 1998.
Gangopadhyay, Abinashchandra. *Girishchandra*. Ed. Swapan Majumdar. 1927. Repr., Kolkata: Dey's Publishing, 1977.
Ganguly, Debjani. "The Language Question in India." In *The Cambridge History of Postcolonial Literature*, 2 vols., ed. Ato Quayson, 2: 649–80. Cambridge: Cambridge University Press, 2011.
Garber, Marjorie. *Profiling Shakespeare*. New York: Routledge, 2008.
Garnett, Edward. *Letters from Joseph Conrad: A Personal Remembrance*. Boston: Little, Brown, 1924.
Gates, Henry Louis. *The Signifying Monkey: A Theory of African Literary Criticism*. New York: Oxford University Press, 1989.
Ghosh, Amitav. *The Hungry Tide*. London: HarperCollins Publishers, 2004.
———. "The March of the Novel Through History: The Testimony of My Grandfather's Bookcase." *Kenyon Review* 20.2 (1998): 13–24.
———. *The Shadow Lines*. London: Bloomsbury Publishing, 1988.
Ghosh, Bishnupriya. "An Invitation to Indian Postmodernity: Salman Rushdie's Contextual Cultural Hybridity." In *Critical Essays on Salman Rushdie*, ed. M. Keith Booker, 129–53. New York: G. K. Hall, 1999.
Gikandi, Simon. "Globalization and the Claims of Postcoloniality." *South Atlantic Quarterly* 100.3 (2002): 627–58.
Gilkes, Michael. *Wilson Harris and the Caribbean Novel*. London: Longman Caribbean, 1975.
Gilroy, Paul. *The Black Atlantic: Modernity and Double Consciousness*. Cambridge: Harvard University Press, 1993.
Girish rachonaboli: Pratham khanda. Kolikata: Sahitya Sansad, 1969.
Goff, Barbara, ed. *Classics and Colonisation*. London: Duckworth, 2005.
Goff, Barbara, and Michael Simpson, eds. *Crossroads in the Black Aegean*. Oxford: Oxford University Press, 2007.
Gordon, Lyndall. *T. S. Eliot: An Imperfect Life*. New York: W. W. Norton, 1999.
Gorra, Michael. *After Empire: Scott, Naipaul, Rushdie*. Chicago: University of Chicago Press, 1997.
———. "Joseph Conrad." *Hudson Review* 59.4 (Winter 2007): 541–71.

Greenblatt, Stephen. *Shakespearean Negotiations.* Berkeley: University of California Press, 1988.
Greenwood, Emily. *Afro-Greeks: Dialogues Between Anglophone Caribbean Literature and Classics.* Oxford: Oxford University Press, 2009.
Guha, Ranajit. *History at the Limit of World-History.* New York: Columbia University Press, 2002.
Guillory, John. *Cultural Capital: The Problem of Literary Canon Formation.* Chicago: University of Chicago Press, 1994.
———. "The Ideology of Canon Formation: T. S. Eliot and Cleanth Brooks." *Canons* issue of *Critical Inquiry* 10.1 (September 1983): 173–94.
———. "The Ordeal of Middlebrow Culture." *Transition* 67 (1995): 82–92.
Habermas, Jürgen. "Further Reflections on the Public Sphere." Trans. Thomas Burger. In *Habermas and the Public Sphere*, ed. Craig Calhoun, 421–61. Cambridge: MIT Press, 1992.
Hamid, Mohsin. *The Reluctant Fundamentalist.* New York: Penguin Books, 2007.
Hamner, Robert D., ed. *Critical Perspectives on Derek Walcott.* Washington, DC: Three Continents, 1993.
———. *Derek Walcott.* New York: Twayne Publishers, 1993.
———. *Epic of the Dispossessed: Derek Walcott's "Omeros."* Columbia: University of Missouri Press, 1997.
Hanif, Mohammed. "Butt and Bhatti." *Granta* 112: 119–31.
———. *A Case of Exploding Mangoes.* London: Random House, 2008.
Hanscombe, Gillian, and Suniti Namjoshi. "Writing the Rag-Bag of Empire." In *Engendering Realism and Postmodernism: Contemporary Women Writers in Britain*, ed. Beate Neumeier, 391–406. Amsterdam: Rodopi, 2001.
Hardwick, Lorna, and Carol Gillespie, eds. *Classics in Postcolonial Worlds.* Oxford: Oxford University Press, 2007.
Harlow, Barbara. "Sentimental Orientalism: *Season of Migration to the North* and *Othello.*" In *Season of Migration to the North by Tayeb Salih: A Casebook*, ed. Mona Takieddine-Amyuni, 75–79. Beirut: American University of Beirut, 1985.
Harpham, Geoffrey Galt. *One of Us: The Mastery of Joseph Conrad.* Chicago: University of Chicago Press, 1996.
Harris, Wilson. *Palace of the Peacock.* London: Faber and Faber, 1960.
———. "Tradition and the West Indian Writer." In *Tradition, the Writer and Society: Critical Essays*, 28–33. London: New Beacon Books, 1967.
Hartman, Geoffrey H. "War in Heaven." Review of *The Anxiety of Influence: A Theory of Poetry*, by Harold Bloom. *Diacritics* 3.1 (1973): 26–32.
Hirsch, Edward. "The Art of Poetry XXXVII." *Paris Review* 101 (1986): 196–230.
Hirsch, Marianne. "The Generation of Postmemory." *Poetics Today* 29.1 (Spring 2008): 103–28.

Huggan, Graham. *The Postcolonial Exotic: Marketing the Margins*. London: Routledge, 2001.
Hughes, Ted. *A Dancer to God: Tributes to T. S. Eliot*. London: Faber and Faber, 1992.
Hulmes, Keri. *The Bone People*. London: Picador, 1984.
Hunter, G. K. "Shakespeare and the Traditions of Tragedy." In *The Cambridge Companion to Shakespeare*, ed. Stanley Wells, 123–41. Cambridge: Cambridge University Press, 1986.
Jameson, Fredric. *The Political Unconscious: Narrative as a Socially Symbolic Act*. Ithaca, NY: Cornell University Press, 1981.
———. "Third World Literature in the Era of Multinational Capitalism." *Social Text* 15 (1986): 65–88.
Johnson, David. *Shakespeare and South Africa*. Oxford: Clarendon Press, 1996.
Jones, Lloyd. *Mister Pip*. London: John Murray, 2007.
Joshi, Priya. *In Another Country: Colonialism, Culture, and the English Novel in India*. New York: Columbia University Press, 2002.
Joyce, James. *Daniel Defoe*. Ed. and trans. Joseph Prescott. Buffalo Studies 1. Buffalo: State University of New York, 1964.
Kakutani, Michiko. "No Headline." *New York Times Book Review*, November 13, 1985.
Kaplan, Carola M., Peter Lancelot Mallios, and Andrea White, eds. *Conrad in the Twenty-first Century: Contemporary Approaches and Perspectives*. New York: Routledge, 2005.
Kastan, David Scott. *Shakespeare and the Book*. Cambridge: Cambridge University Press, 2001.
Kendal, Geoffrey. *The Shakespeare Wallah*. Foreword by Felicity Kendal. Middlesex, England: Penguin Books, 1986.
Kenner, Hugh. "In the Footsteps of the Master." *New York Times*, November 9, 1975.
Kermode, Frank. *The Classic*. London: Faber and Faber, 1975.
Khair, Tabish. *Babu Fiction: Alienation in Contemporary Indian Novels*. New Delhi: Oxford University Press, 2001.
Khan, Uzma Aslam. "Pakistan: Women and Fiction Today." Available at http://worldpulse.com/magazine/articles/pakistan-women-and-fiction-today (accessed May 22, 2013).
Kincaid, James R. "Rhetorical Irony, the Dramatic Monologue, and Tennyson's 'Poems' (1842)." *Philological Quarterly* 53.2 (1974): 220–36.
Kipling, Rudyard. *From Sea to Sea and Other Sketches: Letters of Travel*. Vol. 1. London: Macmillan, 1904.

Kirsch, Adam. "The *Five-foot Shelf* Reconsidered." *Harvard Magazine* (November–December 2011). Available at www.harvardmagazine.com/2001/11/the-five-foot-shelf-reco.html (accessed May 22, 2013).

Kortenaar, Neil ten. "Writers and Readers, the Written and the Read: V. S. Naipaul and *Guerillas*." *Contemporary Literature* 31.3 (1990): 324–34.

Kramnick, Jonathan. *Making the English Canon: Print-Capitalism and the Cultural Past, 1700–1770*. Cambridge: Cambridge University Press, 1998.

Kristeva, Julia. *Strangers to Ourselves*. Trans. Leon S. Roudiez. New York: Columbia University Press, 1991.

Lamming, George. *The Pleasures of Exile*. Ann Arbor: University of Michigan Press, 1960.

Lamos, Colleen. *Deviant Modernism: Sexual and Textual Errance in T. S. Eliot, James Joyce, and Marcel Proust*. Cambridge: Cambridge University Press, 1998.

Lal, Ananda, and Sukanta Chaudhuri, eds. *Shakespeare on the Calcutta Stage: A Checklist*. Kolkata: Papyrus, 2001.

Lasdun, James. "The Empire Strikes Back." *The Guardian*, March 3, 2007.

Lawrence, D. H. *The Collected Letters of D. H. Lawrence*. Ed. Harry T. Moore. 2 vols. London: Heinemann, 1962.

Lehman, Robert S. "Eliot's Last Laugh: The Dissolution of Satire in *The Waste Land*." *Journal of Modern Literature* 32.2 (2009): 65–79.

Letters from Conrad: 1895–1924. Ed. Edward Garnett. London: Nonesuch Press, 1928.

Levine, George. *The Realistic Imagination: English Fiction from Frankenstein to Lady Chatterley*. Chicago: University of Chicago Press, 1981.

Lloyd, David. *Anomalous States: Irish Writing and the Postcolonial Moment*. Durham, NC: Duke University Press, 1993.

Loomba, Ania. *Gender, Race, Renaissance Drama*. Manchester, England: Manchester University Press, 1989.

———. "*Hamlet* in Mizoram." In *Cross-Cultural Performances: Differences in Women's Re-Visions of Shakespeare*, ed. Marianne Novy, 227–50. Urbana: University of Illinois Press, 1993.

Loomba, Ania, and Martin Orkin, eds. *Post-Colonial Shakespeares*. New York: Routledge, 1998.

Lukács, Georg. *The Theory of the Novel: A Historico-Philosophical Essay on the Forms of Great Epic Literature*. Trans. Anna Bostock. Cambridge, MA: MIT Press, 1971.

Lyotard, Jean François. "Going Back to the Return." In *The Languages of Joyce: Selected Papers from the 11th International James Joyce Symposium, Venice 12–18 June 1988*, ed. R. M. Bollettieri Bosinelli, Christine van Boheemen, and C. Vaglio Marengo, 193–210. Philadelphia: John Benjamins, 1992.

Madge, Elliot Walter. *Henry Derozio: The Eurasian Poet and Reformer.* Ed. Subir Ray Choudhuri. Kolkata: Naya Prokash, 1982.

Makdisi, Saree S. "The Empire Renarrated: *Season of Migration to the North* and the Reinvention of the Present." *Critical Inquiry* 18.4 (1992): 804–20.

Martin, Murray. "Who Is the Colonist? Writing in New Zealand and the South Pacific." *World Literature Today* 68.3 (Summer 1994): 488–92.

McDonald, Peter D. *The Literature Police: Apartheid Censorship and Its Cultural Consequences.* Oxford: Oxford University Press, 2009.

McKeon, Michael. *The Origins of the English Novel, 1600–1740.* Baltimore: Johns Hopkins University Press, 1987.

———, ed. *Theory of the Novel: A Historical Approach.* Baltimore: Johns Hopkins University Press, 2000.

Mellors, John. "Mimics into Puppets: The Fiction of V. S. Naipaul." *London Magazine* 15.6 (1976): 117–21.

Memmi, Albert. *The Colonizer and the Colonized.* London: Earthscan Publications, 2003.

Millett, Kate. *Sexual Politics.* Champaign: University of Illinois Press, 1970.

Moretti, Franco. "Conjectures on World Literature." *New Left Review*, n.s. 1 (2000): 54–68.

———. *Modern Epic: The World System from Goethe to García Márquez.* Trans. Quentin Hoare. New York: Verso, 1996.

———. "The Slaughterhouse of Literature." *Modern Language Quarterly* 61.1 (2000): 207–27.

Morris, Rosalind C. ed. *Can the Subaltern Speak? Reflections on the History of an Idea.* New York: Columbia University Press, 2010.

Morton, Stephen. *Salman Rushdie: Fictions of Postcolonial Modernity.* London: Palgrave Macmillan, 2008.

Mufti, Aamir R. "Auerbach in Istanbul: Edward Said, Secular Criticism, and the Question of Minority Culture." *Critical Inquiry* 25.1 (1998): 95–125.

———. "Global Comparativism." *Critical Inquiry* 31.2 (2005): 472–89.

Mukherjee, Ankhi. "The Death of the Novel and Two Postcolonial Writers." *Modern Language Quarterly* 69.4 (December 2008): 533–55.

———. "'What Is a Classic?': International Criticism and the Classic Question." *PMLA* 124.5 (2010): 1026–42.

Mukherjee, Meenakshi. "The Anxiety of Englishness: Our Novels in English." *Economic and Political Weekly.* 28.48 (November 27, 1993): 2607–11.

———. *The Perishable Empire: Essays on Indian Writing in English.* Oxford: Oxford University Press, 2000.

Naipaul, V. S. *An Area of Darkness: An Experience of India.* 1964. New York: Vintage Books, 1981.

———. *A Bend in the River.* 1979. Repr., London: Picador, 2002.
———. *A Congo Diary.* Los Angeles: Sylvester and Orphanos, 1980.
———. *A House for Mr Biswas.* 1969. Repr., London: Picador, 2002.
———. *The Enigma of Arrival: A Novel in Five Sections.* 1987. Repr., New York: Random House, 1988; London: Picador, 2002.
———. *Finding the Centre: Two Narratives.* London: André Deutsch, 1984.
———. *Guerrillas.* London: André Deutsch, 1975.
———. "In the Middle of the Journey." In *The Overcrowded Barracoon and Other Articles*, 41–46. London: André Deutsch, 1972.
———. "The Irascible Prophet: Interview with Rachel Donadio." *New York Times*, August 7, 2005.
———. *Literary Occasions: Essays.* Ed. Pankaj Mishra. London: Picador, 2004.
———. *The Mimic Men.* London: Vintage Books, 2001.
———. "The Novelist V. S. Naipaul Talks About his Work to Ronald Bryden." *Listener*, March 22, 1973, 367–68.
———. *The Return of Eva Peron.* London: André Deutsch, 1980.
———. "Two Worlds: Nobel Lecture, 2001." *PMLA* 117.3 (2002): 479–86.
———. *A Writer's People: Ways of Looking and Feeling.* London: Picador, 2007.
———. "Writing Is Magic." Interview by Francis Wyndham. *Sunday Times*, November 10, 1968, 57.
Nandy, Ashis. *The Intimate Enemy: Loss and Recovery of Self under Colonialism.* New Delhi: Oxford University Press, 1983.
Newman, Judie. *The Ballistic Bard: Postcolonial Fictions.* London: Arnold, 1995.
Ngũgĩ wa Thiong'o. *Moving the Centre: The Struggle for Cultural Freedoms.* London: James Currey, 1993.
Ngũgĩ wa Thiong'o, and Micere Githae Mugo. *The Trial of Dedan Kimathi.* London: Heinemann, 1976.
Nietzsche, Friedrich. *Beyond Good and Evil: Prelude to a Philosophy of the Future.* Ed. Rolf-Peter Horstmann and Judith Norman. Trans. Judith Norman. Cambridge: Cambridge University Press, 2002.
Nixon, Rob. "Caribbean and African Appropriations of *The Tempest*." *Critical Inquiry* 13.3 (1987): 557–78.
———. *London Calling: V. S. Naipaul, Postcolonial Mandarin.* Oxford: Oxford University Press, 1992.
———. "Neoliberalism, Slow Violence, and the Environmental Picaresque." *MFS: Modern Fiction Studies* 55.3 (2009): 443–67.
———. "Preparations for Travel: The Naipaul Brothers' Conradian Atavism." *Research in African Literatures* 22.2 (1991): 177–90.
Nolan, Emer. *James Joyce and Nationalism.* London: Routledge, 1995.
Norris, Margot. "Not a Bit Like Molly Bloom." *James Joyce Broadsheet* 74 (2006): 1.

Nussbaum, Martha. "Patriotism and Cosmopolitanism." *Boston Review* 19.5 (October–November 1994): 3–6.

Okunoye, Oyeniyi. "Dramatizing Postcoloniality: Nationalism and the Rewriting of History in Ngugi and Mugo's *The Trial of Dedan Kimathi*." *History in Africa* 28 (2001): 225–37.

Ondaatje, Michael. *Anil's Ghost*. London: Bloomsbury Publishing, 2000.

Orgel, Steven. "The Authentic Shakespeare." *Representation* 21 (1988): 5–25.

Pais, Arthur J. "Maqbool Is Not Meant for Shakespearean Scholars." *Rediff India Abroad* (November 6, 2003). Available at www.rediff.com/movies/2003/nov/06vishal.htm (accessed May 22, 2013).

Pamuk, Orhan. "Nobel Lecture: My Father's Suitcase." Nobel lecture, December 7, 2006. English translation available at www.nobelprize.org/nobel_prizes/literature/laureates/2006/pamuk-lecture_en.html (accessed May 22, 2013).

Park, You-me, and Rajeswari Sunder Rajan, eds. *The Postcolonial Jane Austen*. New York: Routledge, 2000.

Parrinder, Patrick. *Nation and Novel: The English Novel from Its Origins to the Present Day*. Oxford: Oxford University Press, 2006.

Parry, Benita. *Conrad and Imperialism*. London: Macmillan, 1983.

Perloff, Marjorie. *21st-Century Modernism: The "New" Poetics*. Malden, MA: Blackwell, 2002.

Perry, Alex. "Lights! Sound! Fury!" *Time*, February 16, 2004. Available at www.time.com/time/magazine/article/0,9171,591352,00.html (accessed May 22, 2013).

Pollock, Sheldon. "The Cosmopolitan Vernacular." *Journal of Asian Studies* 57.1 (1998): 6–37.

Pound, Ezra. "Praefatio" to *The Spirit of Romance*. New York: New Directions, 1968.

Prakash, Gyan. "Postcolonial Criticism and Indian Historiography." *Social Text* 31–32 (1992): 8–19.

Pratt, Mary Louise. "In the Neocolony: Destiny, Destination, and the Traffic in Meaning." In *Coloniality at Large: Latin America and the Postcolonial Debate*, ed. Mabel Moraña, Enrique D. Dussel, and Carlos A. Jáuregui, 459–75. Durham, NC: Duke University Press, 2008.

Prendergast, Christopher. *The Classic: Sainte-Beuve and the Nineteenth-Century Culture Wars*. Oxford: Oxford University Press, 2007.

Pym, John. *The Wandering Company: 21 Years of Merchant Ivory Films*. London: British Film Institute, 1983.

Quayson, Ato. *Postcolonialism: Theory, Practice, or Process?* Cambridge: Polity Press, 2000.

Ramazani, Jahan. *The Hybrid Muse: Postcolonial Poetry in English*. Chicago: University of Chicago Press, 2001.

———. "Modernist Bricolage, Postcolonial Hybridity." *Modernism/Modernity* 13.3 (September 2006): 445–63.
Ramesh, Randeep. "A Matter of Caste as Bollywood Embraces the Bard." *The Guardian*, July 29, 2006.
Reeves, Gareth. *T. S. Eliot: A Virgilian Poet*. London: Macmillan, 1989.
Retamar, Roberto Fernández. "Caliban: Notes Towards a Discussion of Culture in Our America." *Massachusetts Review* 15.1–2 (1974): 7–72.
Richards, Thomas. *The Imperial Archive: Knowledge and the Fantasy of Empire*. London: Verso, 1993.
Ricks, Christopher. *Allusion to the Poets*. Oxford: Oxford University Press, 2003.
Robbins, Bruce. "Introduction Part I: Actually Existing Cosmopolitanism." In *Cosmopolitics: Thinking and Feeling Beyond the Nation*, ed. Pheng Cheah and Bruce Robbins, 1–19. Minneapolis: University of Minnesota Press, 1998.
———. "A Portrait of the Artist as a Social Climber." In *The Novel*, vol. 2, *Forms and Themes*, ed. Franco Moretti, 409–35. Princeton, NJ: Princeton University Press, 2006.
———. "Secularism, Elitism, Progress, and Other Transgressions on Edward Said's *Voyage In*." *Social Text* 40 (Fall 1994): 25–37.
Rose, Jacqueline. "Sexuality in the Reading of Shakespeare: *Hamlet* and *Measure for Measure*." In *Alternative Shakespeares*, John Drakakis, 95–118. London: Methuen, 1985.
Roy, Modhumita. "'Englishing' India: Reinstituting Class and Social Privilege." *Social Text* 39 (Summer 1994): 83–109.
Rushdie, Salman. *Ground Beneath Her Feet*. London: Vintage Books, 2000.
———. *Haroun and the Sea of Stories*. London: Viking Books, 1990.
———. *Imaginary Homelands: Essays and Criticism, 1981–91*. London: Granta, 1992.
———. *Joseph Anton: A Memoir*. London: Jonathan Cape, 2012.
———. *Midnight's Children*. 1981. Repr., London: Vintage Books, 1995.
———. *The Moor's Last Sigh*. London: Jonathan Cape, 1995.
———. *The Satanic Verses*. Dover, England: Consortium, 1992.
———. *Shame*. London: Vintage Books, 1995.
———. *Step Across This Line: Collected Non-Fiction, 1992–2002*. London: Vintage Books, 2002.
Sahgal, Nayantara. *Rich Like Us*. 1985. Repr., New Delhi: HarperCollins Publishers, 2003.
Said, Edward. "Beginnings." In *Power, Politics, and Culture: Interviews with Edward Said*, ed. Gauri Viswanathan, 3–38. New York: Pantheon, 2001.
———. *Beginnings: Intention and Method*. New York: Columbia University Press, 1985.

———. *Culture and Imperialism*. New York: Alfred A. Knopf, 1993.
———. *Freud and the Non-European*. London: Verso, 2003.
———. "An Interview with Edward W. Said." In *Conrad in the Twenty-first Century: Contemporary Approaches and Perspectives*, ed. Carola M. Kaplan, Peter Lancelot Mallios, and Andrea White, 283–303. New York: Routledge, 2005.
———. *Joseph Conrad and the Fiction of Autobiography*. Cambridge, MA: Harvard University Press, 1966.
———. *Orientalism*. New York: Vintage Books, 1978.
———. *Out of Place: A Memoir*. London: Granta, 1999.
———. *Reflections on Exile and Other Literary and Cultural Essays*. London: Granta, 2001.
———. *The World, the Text, and the Critic*. Cambridge, MA: Harvard University Press, 1983.
Sahgal, Nayantara. *Rich Like Us*. 1985. Repr., New York: HarperCollins Publishers, 2003.
Sainte-Beuve, Augustin. "Qu'est-ce qu'un classique?" *Causeries du lundi*. 3rd ed. Vol. 3. Paris: Michel Levy, 1875–78.
Salih, Tayeb. *Season of Migration to the North*. Trans. Denys Johnson-Davies. London: Heinemann, 1969.
Sedgwick, Eve Kosofsky. *The Coherence of Gothic Conventions*. London: Routledge, 1986.
Senn, Fritz. "Book of Many Turns." In *Joyce's Dislocutions: Essays on Reading as Translation*, 127–36. Baltimore: Johns Hopkins University Press, 1984.
Seth, Vikram. *A Suitable Boy*. New York: HarperCollins Publishers, 1993.
Shah, Bina. "Pakistan's Literary Boys' Club." *The Guardian*, October 15, 2010. Available at www.guardian.co.uk/commentisfree/2010/oct/15/pakistan-literary-boys-club (accessed May 26, 2013).
Shah, Saeed. "As Their Country Descends into Chaos, Pakistani Writers Are Winning Acclaim." *Guardian*, February 17, 2009.
Shakespeare, William. *Macbeth*. Ed. Kenneth Muir. London: Arden Shakespeare, 1984.
———. *Othello*. Ed. E. A. J. Honigmann. London: Arden Shakespeare, 2006.
Shamsie, Kamila. *Burnt Shadows*. London: Bloomsbury Publishing, 2009.
Sinfield, Alan. "Cultural Materialism and the Politics of Plausibility." In *New Casebooks: Othello*, ed. Lena Cowen Orlin, 49–77. New York: Palgrave Macmillan, 2004.
———. *Faultlines: Cultural Materialism and the Politics of Dissident Reading*. Berkeley: University of California Press, 1992.
Singh, Jyotsna M. "Different Shakespeares: The Bard in Colonial/Postcolonial India." *Theatre Journal* 41.4: 445–57.

———. "The Postcolonial/Postmodern Shakespeare." In *Shakespeare: World Views*, ed. Heather Kerr et al., 29–43. Newark: University of Delaware Press, 1996.
Sinha, Indra. *Animal's People*. London: Simon and Schuster, 2007.
Slaughter, Joseph R. "Enabling Fictions and Novel Subjects: The *Bildungsroman* and International Human Rights Law." *PMLA* 121.5 (2006): 1405–23.
———. *Human Rights, Inc.: The World Novel, Narrative Form, and International Law*. New York: Fordham University Press, 2007.
Spivak, Gayatri Chakravorty. "The Burden of English." In *The Lie of the Land: English Literary Studies in India*, ed. Rajeswari Sunder Rajan, 275–99. Delhi: Oxford University Press, 1992.
———. "Coetzee's *Foe* Reading Defoe's *Crusoe/Roxana*." In *Consequences of Theory: Selected Papers from the English Institue, 1987–88*, ed. Jonathan Arac and Barbara Johnson, 154–80. Baltimore: Johns Hopkins University Press, 1991.
———. *Death of a Discipline*. Kolkata: Seagull, 2004.
———. *Outside in the Teaching Machine*. New York: Routledge, 1993.
———. "Poststructuralism, Marginality, Postcoloniality, and Value." In *Literary Theory Today*, ed. Peter Collier and Helga Geyer-Ryan, 219–44. London: Polity Press, 1990.
———. *The Spivak Reader*. Ed. Donna Landry and Gerald Maclean. New York: Routledge, 1996.
———. "Translation as Culture." *Parallax* 6.1 (2000): 13–24.
Srivastava, Neelam. "Pidgin English or Pigeon Indian?" *Journal of Postcolonial Writing* 43.1 (2007): 55–64.
Stead, C. K. "Keri Hulme's *The Bone People* and the Pegasus Award for Maori Literature." *Ariel* 16.4 (1985): 102–7.
Subrahmanyam, Sanjay. "Diary." *London Review of Books*, November 6, 2008, 42–43.
Suleri, Sara. *The Rhetoric of English India*. Chicago: University of Chicago Press, 1992.
"Tears, Tiffs, and Triumphs." *Guardian*, September 6, 2008.
Terada, Rei. *Derek Walcott's Poetry: American Mimicry*. Boston: Northeastern University Press, 1992.
Thieme, John. *Derek Walcott*. Manchester: University of Manchester Press, 1999.
Thomas, Keith. "Universities Under Attack." *London Review of Books*, December 15, 2011.
Tickell, Alex, ed. *Arundhati Roy's The God of Small Things*. London: Routledge, 2007.
Trivedi, Harish. *Colonial Transactions: English Literature and India*. Kolkata: Papyrus, 1993.
Trivedi, Poonam, and Dennis Bartholomeusz, eds. *India's Shakespeare: Translation, Interpretation, and Performance*. Newark: University of Delaware Press, 2005.

Vendler, Helen. *Coming of Age as a Poet: Milton, Keats, Eliot, Plath*. Cambridge, MA: Harvard University Press, 2003.

Viswanathan, Gauri. "The Beginnings of English Literary Study in British India." *Oxford Literary Review* 9.1–2 (1987): 2–26.

———. "Currying Favor: The Beginnings of English Literary Study in British India." *Social Text* 19–20 (Autumn 1988): 85–104.

———. *Masks of Conquests: Literary Study and British Rule in India*. New York: Columbia University Press, 1989.

———. "Pedagogical Alternatives: Issues in Postcolonial Studies." In *Between the Lines*, ed. Deepika Bahri and Mary Vasudeva, 54–63. Philadelphia: Temple University Press, 1996.

Vogt-William, Christine. "'Language is the skin of my thought': Language Relations in *Ancient Promises* and *The God of Small Things*." In *The Politics of English as a World Language*, 393–404. Amsterdam: Rodopi, 2003.

Walcott, Derek. *Another Life*. New York: Farrar, Straus and Girous: 1973.

———. *The Arkansas Testament*. New York: Farrar, Straus and Giroux, 1987.

———. "Caligula's Horse." *Kunapipi* 11.1 (1989): 138–42.

———. "The Caribbean: Culture or Mimicry?" *Journal of Interamerican Studies and World Affairs* 16.1 (1974): 3–13.

———. *Collected Poems, 1948–1984*. London: Faber and Faber, 1982.

———. *Conversations with Derek Walcott*. Ed. William Baer. Jackson: University of Mississippi Press, 1996.

———. *Dream on Monkey Mountain and Other Plays*. New York: Farrar, Straus and Giroux, 1970.

———. "The Figure of Crusoe: On the Theme of Isolation in West Indian Writing." In *Critical Perspectives on Derek Walcott*, ed. Robert D. Hamner, 33–40. Washington, DC: Three Continents, 1993.

———. *The Fortunate Traveler*. New York: Farrar, Straus and Giroux, 1981.

———. *The Gulf and Other Poems*. London: Jonathan Cape, 1969.

———. Interview with Nancy Schoenberger. *Threepenny Review* 15 (1983): 16–17.

———. "Leaving School." *Critical Perspectives on Derek Walcott*, ed. Robert D. Hamner, 51–57. Washington, DC: Three Continents, 1993.

———. "Meanings." *Savacou* 2 (September 1970): 51.

———. "The Muse of History." In *What the Twilight Says: Essays*, 36–64. New York: Farrar, Straus and Giroux, 1998.

———. *Omeros*. London: Faber and Faber, 1990.

———. "On *Omeros*: An Interview." *Caribana* 3 (1992–93): 38–39.

———. *Pantomime*. In *Remembrance and Pantomime*, 90–170. New York: Farrar, Straus and Giroux, 1990.

———. "Reflections on *Omeros*." *South Atlantic Quarterly* 96.2 (1997): 229–46.

———. *Selected Poems*. London: Faber and Faber, 2007.
———. *Tiepolo's Hound*. London: Faber and Faber, 2000.
———. *What the Twilight Says: Essays*. New York: Farrar, Straus and Giroux, 1998.
———. *White Egrets*. London: Faber and Faber, 2010.
———. "Young Trinidadian Poets." *Sunday Guardian*, June 19, 1966, 5.
Watt, Ian. *Conrad in the Nineteenth Century*. Berkeley: University of California Press, 1979.
Waugh, Patricia, ed. *Literary Theory and Criticism: An Oxford Guide*. Oxford: Oxford University Press, 2006.
Weiss, Timothy. *On the Margins: The Art of Exile in V. S. Naipaul*. Amherst: University of Massachusetts Press, 1992.
White, Hayden. *The Content of the Form: Narrative Discourse and Historical Representation*. Baltimore: Johns Hopkins University Press, 1987.
Wood, James. "An Indelicate Balance: The Noisy Pluralism of Indian Fiction." *New Republic*, December 1997, 32–37.
———. "Noisy Pluralism." *New Republic*, December 29, 1997.
Woolf, Virginia. "How Should One Read a Book?" *The Common Reader, Volume II*. 1932. Repr., ed. Andrew McNeillie, 258–70. London: Vintage Books, 2003.
Young, Robert J. C. "English and the Language of Others." *European Review* 17.1 (2009): 203–12.
———. "Postcolonial Remains." *New Literary History* 43.1 (Winter 2012): 19–42.
Žižek, Slavoj. *The Metastases of Enjoyment: Six Essays on Woman and Causality*. London: Verso, 1994.

Index

Abrams, M. H.: on dramatic monologues, 171
Achebe, Chinua, 116, 119; and Conrad, 52–53, 63, 95–96, 217; *An Image of Africa*, 95–96; *Things Fall Apart*, 96
Ackroyd, Peter, 224n6; *T. S. Eliot*, 32, 36
Adelman, Janet, 204
Adhya (Addy), Baisnab Caran, 193–94, 209
Adiga, Aravind, 175, 181; *The White Tiger*, 161, 164–69, 172, 173, 177, 178
affiliation vs. filiation, 30, 55, 117–18, 223n4
Agamben, Giorgio: on human freedom, 176; *The Open: Man and Animal*, 175–76
Ahmad, Aijaz: on capitalism, 160, 232n16; on English language, 147; on excess of belonging, 160, 232n16; on Roy's *God of Small Things*, 157
Ajayi, Ade: on Omotoso, 132
Alcott, Louisa May: *Little Women*, 140
Ali, Ahmed: *Twilight in Delhi*, 155; use of English by, 154–55
Ali, Monica: *Brick Lane*, 160; use of English by, 160
alternative canons, 9–13, 18–19, 21–22, 45, 113, 115–16, 153
Altieri, Charles: on canon formation, 6–7, 42; "Idea and Ideal," 6–7; on ideological overdeterminations, 42; on Kermode, 44; on literature about literature, 127
Anam, Tahmima, 232n15; *A Golden Age*, 159–60
Anand, Mulk Raj, 154, 155
Anderson, Benedict, 116, 126
Andri?, Ivo, 3
Angelou, Maya, 224n3
Angoor, 209, 210
anticolonialism, 115, 126, 127, 132, 150–51
anxiety of influence, 19, 20, 96, 137, 215
Apocalypse Now, 95

Appadurai, Arjun, 42; on delocalised transnations, 161
Appiah, Anthony, 148
Apter, Emily, 106, 172; *Continental Drift*, 19; on marketing of Third World difference, 161–62; *The Translation Zone*, 19
Arabic literature: *hakawati* style, 123
Arac, Jonathan: on English language, 144
Aravamudan, Srinivas, 155
arguings vs. arguments, 214–15
Armstrong, Isobel, 170
Arnold, Matthew, 29, 40, 41, 225n9
Ashbery, John, 81
Ashcroft, Bill: *The Empire Writes Back*, 115–16, 220
Attridge, Derek: on allegory, 230n5; on arguments vs. arguings, 214–15; on canonization, 39; *Semicolonial Joyce*, 126, 230n4
Attwell, David: on Coetzee, 128
Atwood, Margaret, 116, 119; *The Blind Assassin*, 28; and Booker Prize, 28
Auden, W. H., 1, 56, 80
Austen, Jane, 119, 230n4

Bach, Richard: *Jonathan Livingstone Seagull*, 175
Bakhtin, Mikhail, 106
Baldwin, James, 224n3
Ballantyne, R. M., 128
Bambara, Toni Cade, 224n3
Bandopadhyay, Gurudas, 186–87
Bandopadhyay, Shamik, 201
Bangladesh: Bengali in, 151; contemporary novels in, 22; English language in, 151; Muktijuddho/Liberation War, 159
Bankim Chandra. *See* Chattopadhyay, Bankim Chandra

Banville, John: *The Sea*, 28
Baraka, Amiri, 11, 12, 224n3
Barbin, Herculine, 223n6
Barker, Francis, 115
Barry, James, 185, 193, 235n14
Barth, John: *Lost in the Funhouse*, 165
Baucom, Ian, 185; on globalizing imaginary, 42
Baudelaire, Charles: "Les sept vieillards," 94–95
Baugh, Edward, 98, 101, 103, 105
Bearden, Romare, 79–80
Beckett, Samuel, 6, 56; "Dante . . . Bruno. Vico . . . Joyce," 38
Belatedness, 3, 7, 20, 22, 70, 80, 111, 117–118, 120, 123, 132, 142, 217, 219, 228n1
Bellow, Saul, 6
Bengali, 151, 159, 186, 187–94, 201, 209, 210
Bengali Babus, 198, 235n16
Benítez-Rojo, Antonio, 113–14
Benjamin, Walter: *The Arcades Project*, 227n7; on renewal of existence, 5; on theory of the trace, 227n7; on transmissibility of collections, 4, 223n2; "Unpacking My Library," 5, 23; on writing books, 23
Benson, Gale, 228n13
Bhabha, Homi, 5, 44, 171; on the alienated self, 119–20; on Benjamin, 5; on cosmopolitanism, 148–49, 151–52; and "DissemiNation," 125; on enunciation, 119–20, 126; *The Location of Culture*, 57–58, 73, 78; on Naipaul and Conrad, 57, 78; on pronomial vs. postnominalist "I," 57–58, 227n8; on the unhomely, 73; "Unsatisfied: Notes on Vernacular Cosmopolitanism," 148–49
Bhardwaj, Vishal: on localism, 213; *Makdi*, 210; *Maqbool*, 185, 201, 202–5, 210, 211, 212, 236n22; *Omkara*, 185, 201, 205–9, 210, 213, 236n23; on Shakespeare, 210–13, 236n21; and Western literary canon, 210
Bharucha, Rustom, 200–201; *Rehearsals of Revolution*, 236n19
Bhrāntibilāsh, 209
Bibhuti Bhushan, 2
Bingham, Harry: on English language, 144–45; *This Little Britain*, 144
Bin Laden, Osama, 174
Black Power movement, 76
Bloch, Ernst: "Nonsynchronism," 231n8
Bloom, Harold: on aesthetic value, 9–10, 45–46; *Anxiety of Influence*, 67, 81, 142, 232n13; on canonicity, 112, 142; on class, 9–10, 45; on influence, 117; on *King Lear*, 199–200; on literary Art of Memory, 13, 31; on poetic misprision, 232n13; on School of Resentment, 10; *Shakespeare: The Invention of the Human*, 236n21; on Shakespeare's adaptability, 236n21; on Shakespeare's Iago, 209; on strangeness of canonical works, 31; *The Western Canon*, 9–10, 18, 31, 45–46; on Vendler, 11; on Walcott, 80–81
Blyton, Enid, 139, 140, 145
Boileau-Despréaux, Nicolas, 104
Booker Prize, 27–28, 29, 128, 161, 164, 169, 224nn1,2, 226n14
Bourdieu, Pierre: on cultural capital, 29; on cultural consumption, 28–29; *Distinction*, 28–29
Bradbury, Malcolm, 28
Brantlinger, Patrick, 122; on Conrad, 226n3; *Rule of Darkness*, 52
Brathwaite, Edward Kamau: on Caribbean nation language, 134–35; on Creole societies, 103; on Dante, 135; on T. S. Eliot, 135; on unconventional English, 134–35
Brecht, Bertolt, 80
Brennan, Timothy: *At Home in the World*, 18; on Said, 56; *Salman Rushdie and the Third World*, 18
Breslin, Paul, 83, 137
Briggs, Austin, 237n1
British East India Company, 149, 234n2, 235n14
British Universities and Browne Report, 218–19, 237n4
Brodsky, Joseph, 86, 229n2
Brontë, Charlotte: *Jane Eyre*, 77, 121, 122, 140; *Vilette*, 140
Brontë, Emily: *Wuthering Heights*, 77, 106
Brooks, Gwendolyn, 11, 12
Browne Report, 218–19, 237n4
Brown, Stewart, 229n7
Buckingham, J. S., 111
Bunzl, Matti: *Postcolonial Studies and Beyond*, 17
Burgess, Anthony, 153

Burnett, Paula, 95
Butalia, Pankaj: *When Hamlet Came to Mizoram*, 184
Byron, Lord, 112

Caiso, 103
Calvino, Italo, 3
Calypso, 99, 100, 103, 104–5, 106
canonicity: canon formation, 6–7, 13, 31, 42; as dynamic, 113–14, 118, 216–17, 221; as exclusive, 9; and Joyce, 126–27; as normalizing agent, 8–9; in postcolonial literature, 18–19, 113–14, 115–16, 118–19; relationship to classics, 30–31; transmission of the canon, 13
Can the Subaltern Speak?, 15
capitalism, 48, 61, 94, 133, 168, 177, 178; Ahmad on, 160, 232n16; movement of capital, 16, 42, 165; as transnational, 161, 232n16. *See also* globalization
Carey, Peter, 226n14
Carson, Anne, 81
Cartland, Barbara, 145
Casanova, Pascale, 44; Cleary on, 48; "Literature as a World," 47–48; on Naipaul, 47; *The World Republic of Letters*, 19, 47
Cather, Willa, 159
Cavell, Stanley, 200
center-periphery relationship, 140, 219–20; the Empire writing back, 115–16, 144, 219; the European metropolis, 34, 38, 72, 118, 122, 135–36, 149, 208; in literary criticism, 18, 20, 22, 35, 44, 47–48, 86, 233n21
Cervantes, Miguel de, 7
Césaire, Aimé, 121, 137
Chakrabarty, Dipesh, 47, 123; "Belatedness as Possibility," 219; on fragmented histories, 22, 161; on Indian autobiographies, 132; on Marx, 168
Chamoiseau, Patrick, 137
Chatterjee, Sudipto, 193
Chatterjee, Upamanyu, 168; *English, August*, 232n9; on "hazaar fucked" English, 153, 232n9
Chattopadhyay, Bankim Chandra, 2; on *satis*, 182; "Shakuntala, Miranda, and Desdemona," 182
Chaubey, Abhishek, 201

Cheah, Pheng, 126; on world literature, 220
Chekhov, Anton: *The Seagull*, 101; *Three Sisters*, 6
Cheng, Vincent, 126
Childs, Peter: *Post-Colonial Theory and English Literature*, 121, 179–80
Chowringhee Theatre, 193
Christie, Agatha, 145
Clark, Alex, 28
class, 22, 100, 145, 164–66, 204, 206, 208, 221–22; Bloom on, 9–10, 45; and literary criticism, 121, 230n4; middle class, 43, 164, 174; the poor, 175–79; relationship to consumption, 28–29; upper classes, 33, 132, 147, 207; working class, 164
Cleary, Joe: on Casanova, 48
Coetzee, J. M.: and Booker Prize, 28, 224n1, 226n14; on center and periphery, 135–36; and Defoe, 127, 215; and Dostoevsky, 128, 215; on T. S. Eliot, 37–39, 41, 46–47; on Herbert, 39–40; on *The House on Eccles Street*, 214, 237n1; and Joyce, 214, 215, 237n1; and Kafka, 215; on literary criticism, 29, 39–41; as outsider writer, 44, 48–49; on the perduring, 44; on Pound, 38; on provincial, national, and metropolitan literature, 135–36; and South African apartheid, 41; on truth and art, 220; and Western literary canon, 116, 119, 215–17
Coetzee, J. M., works of: *Boyhood*, 38; *Diary of a Bad Year*, 44, 128; *Elizabeth Costello*, 215–16, 237n1; *Foe*, 127–28, 215; *The Life and Times of Michael K*, 215; *The Mastering of Petersburg*, 128, 215; *Stranger Shores*, 20; "What Is a Classic?," 7, 14, 20, 29, 30, 31–32, 37–41, 44, 45, 46–47, 55, 149, 215, 219, 222, *Youth*, 38, 45
Coleride, Samuel Taylor, 14–15, 29; "Rime of the Ancient Mariner," 101
Collini, Stefan, 218, 219
Collits, Terry, 60, 61; *Postcolonial Conrad*, 230n4
colonial fiction, 50, 51, 62, 69
Compagnon, Antoine, 46, 225n12
comparativism, 123
Condé, Maryse, 106
Conrad, Joseph: and Achebe, 52–53, 63, 95–96, 217; on art, 53, 54, 60, 61–62, 71, 227n4; attitudes regarding

imperialism, 51–52, 226n3; attitudes regarding race, 52–53, 62–63, 121, 226n3; correspondence, 61–62; and English language, 55–56, 64–65, 227n5; Harpham on, 55, 59, 217, 227n9; and Wilson Harris, 52–53, 217; on imagination, 71–72; and literary criticism, 50, 52–53, 59–60, 62–63, 121, 226nn1,3; and Naipaul, 1, 20–21, 50, 54, 55, 56–57, 59, 63, 66–78, 122, 127, 215, 217, 227n11; and narrative, 57–66, 72–73, 226n1; vs. Nietzsche, 63–64; on the novel, 50, 54, 60; as outsider writer, 36, 55–56, 64; Parry on, 51; and postcolonial literature, 20–21, 50–51, 54–57, 59, 62, 63, 64–65, 66–78, 122, 124, 125, 127; and Rushdie, 6; and Said, 20, 50, 51, 56–57, 58, 59–66, 215, 217; and Salih, 122, 123, 124, 125, 217; and Walcott, 21, 80, 91–98, 137

Conrad, Joseph, works of: "Author's Note" to *A Personal Record*, 55; autobiographical works, 20, 50, 55, 56, 58–60, 61–62, 64–65, 66; *Congo Diary*, 68, 70; *Heart of Darkness*, 52–53, 60, 62–63, 64, 68, 69, 70–71, 73–74, 88, 91, 95, 96, 121, 122, 123, 125, 127, 217; "Henry James," 54, 67; "The Lagoon," 73; *Lord Jim*, 67, 68; *The Mirror of the Sea*, 61, 75; *The Nigger of the "Narcissus,"* 53, 57–58, 60; *Nostromo*, 56, 66, 75; *A Personal Record*, 55, 58–60, 61, 64–65, 67, 70, 71; *The Secret Agent*, 74–76, 77–78; *The Shadow-line*, 57, 58–59, 227n7; *Victory*, 96

contrapuntality, 51, 113, 123
Cooppan, Vilashini, 113, 127
Coppola, Francis Ford: *Apocalypse Now*, 95
cosmopolitanism, 38, 154, 161–62, 164; Bhabha on, 148–49, 151–52; Pollock on, 148, 151–52, 231n2
counterreading, 18, 19, 21, 119, 122, 125
Crane, Hart, 80
Crane, Stephen, 137
Creole English: Creole continuum, 104, 229n13; creolization, 104, 105, 113; and Walcott, 21, 80, 103–8
Culler, Jonathan: "Anderson and the Novel," 116; *The Literary in Theory*, 19
cultural capital, 29, 184
cultural translations, 113
curriculum formation, 113

Dalrymple, William, 153
Damrosch, David: on the classic, 42–43, 225n10; definition of masterpiece, 42–43, 44, 225n10; on glocalism, 22, 172; *How to Read*, 220, 221; *What Is World Literature?*, 19, 42–43, 91, 225n10
Dangarembga, Tsitsi: on Englishness, 139–40; *Nervous Conditions*, 133, 137–40, 231n10
Dante Alighieri, 36, 38, 44, 80, 106; *De vulgari eloquentia*, 135
Dasgupta, Hemendranath: *The Indian Stage*, 191
Dāsi, Tinkodi, 192
Das, Kamala: "An Introduction," 151
Davie, Donald, 225n8
Davy, Humphry, 151
death, 88–89
De Chirico, Giorgio: *The Enigma of Arrival*, 134
Defoe, Daniel: and Coetzee, 127, 215; *Robinson Crusoe*, 121, 127, 131; Walcott and Crusoe, 21, 82, 98–103
De Freitas, Michael, 76
Deledda, Grazia, 3
Deleuze, Gilles, 219
DeLillo, Don, 174
DeLoughrey, Elizabeth, 131
democracy, 16
De Quincey, Thomas, 205
Derozio, Henry, 193; *The Fakir of Jungheera*, 112; "Harp of India," 111, 113; and nationalism, 111–13; and Western literary canon, 112
Derrida, Jacques: "Che cos'è la poesia?," 214; on countertime, 215; on Fichte, 46; "Geopsychoanalysis '...and the rest of the world'," 226n13; "No Apocalypse," 185; "Onto-Theology of National-Humanism," 46; on the poem as hedgehog, 214; on psychoanalysis, 226n13
Desani, G. V.: *All About H. Hatterr*, 153–54
Desmet, Christy, 182–83
Devgan, Ajay, 207
Devi Durga, 208
diaspora, 113, 160–61
Dickens, Charles: *David Copperfield*, 1, 142; *Great Expectations*, 117, 140–43; *Oliver Twist*, 1

Dimock, Wai Chee: on canon revision, 118; on creolization, 104, 105; on nonstandard space and time, 46; on the planet, 18; *Through Other Continents*, 19, 46, 104; on world literature, 8
disenfranchisement, 67
Disraeli, Benjamin: *Sybil*, 164, 166
Do Dooni Chār, 209
Donadio, Rachel, 69
Donne, John, 105, 108
Dostoevsky, Fyodor, 3, 128, 215
Dove, Rita: on Baraka, 11, 12; on Merrill, 11; and *Penguin Anthology of Twentieth-Century American Poetry*, 10–12; on Vendler, 11–12
Drabble, Margaret, 27
dramatic monologues, 171–72
Dryden, John, 14–15; *MacFlecknow*, 105; *The Medall*, 105
Du Bellay, Joaquim, 84
Duffy, Enda, 126
During, Simon, 130
Dutt, Michael Madhusudan: *Meghādbodhkabya*, 234n7
Dutt, Smarajit, 114
Dutt, Utpal, 187, 188, 197; on the classics, 200–201; Towards a Revolutionary Theatre, 236n19

Eagleton, Terry: *Exiles and Émigrés*, 48, 56; on Joyce, 127
Edel, Leon, 61
Eliot, Charles William: on Harvard Classics, 3
Eliot, George: *Middlemarch*, 1
Eliot, T. S., 1, 27, 56, 79, 80, 137; alienation of, 37; on cultural homogeneity, 32–33; on dead languages, 8, 32, 35; on English language, 35; Hughes on, 36–37; on Kipling, 36; on literary creativeness, 217; on literary criticism, 29, 40; on mature poets, 228n1; as outsider writer, 36, 48–49; on talent, 63, 142; on tradition, 34, 63, 142, 217; on Vigil's *Aeneid*, 34–35, 37–38, 225n8; voice of, 135; and Walcott, 1, 21, 80, 94–95, 97, 137; and World War II, 32, 36, 37, 41, 224n6
Eliot, T. S., works of: *On Poetry and Poets*, 217, 225n8; "Philip Massinger," 228n1; "Virgil and the Christian World," 34–35;

The Waste Land, 36, 37, 94–95, 97, 221; "What Is a Classic?," 14, 16, 20, 29, 30, 31–39, 41, 44, 45, 46–47, 55, 149, 215, 219, 220, 224n6
Emecheta, Buchi, 122
emergence, 181, 233n21
Emmerich, Roland: *Anonymous*, 221–22
English, James: on cultural and political capital, 29; *The Economy of Prestige*, 29; on Pulitzer Prize and Morrison's *Beloved*, 224n3
English language: Chinese speakers, 144, 181; and Conrad, 55–56, 64–65, 227n5; T. S. Eliot on, 35; English studies, 8, 10, 15, 19, 114–15; English vernacular canon, 19, 22, 145, 146–47, 151–53, 181; as global vernacular, 22, 34, 42, 55–56, 144–45, 175, 213; most-translated authors in, 145; word count of, 144–45
Englishman, 186
Etherton, Michael, 133
European *Bildungsroman*, 117, 119, 133, 137–43, 153, 173, 175, 177–78
European *Künstlerroman*, 133–34
European metropolis, 19, 34, 38, 72, 118, 122, 135–36, 149, 208
European travelogue, 92, 93, 119
exclusiveness, 9, 11–12, 13–14, 30

Faber and Faber, 1, 32, 221
Fanon, Franz, 121, 171; *Black Skin, White Masks*, 119–20; *The Wretched of the Earth*, 231n9
Faulkner, William, 159
Fee, Margery, 128
Fernández Retamar, Roberto, 182; on Caliban, 113
Fichte, Johann Gottlieb: *Discourse to the German Nation*, 46
Firdousi, 34
Flaubert, Gustave, 3; *Salammbô*, 34
Ford, Ford Maddox, 74
Foucault, Michel, 223n6; on epoch of space, 8, 56; "Of Other Spaces," 8, 227n6; on simultaneity, 227n6
France, Anatole: on literary criticism, 59–60
Fraser, Antonia, 27
French language: word count, 145
Freud, Sigmund, 62; *Beyond the Pleasure Principle*, 35; case studies, 124

Frostrup, Mariella, 226n14
Frye, Northrop: on *Macbeth*, 212
Fukuyama, Francis, 120

Gandhi, Indira, 201
Gandhi, Leela: on postcolonial literature, 131
Gandhi, Mahatma, 177, 195
Gangopadhyay, Abinash Chandra, 187, 235n9; on Girish Ghosh, 186–87
Ganguly, Debjani, 151, 231n5
Garber, Marjorie, 236n18
García Márquez, Gabriel: *Chronicle of a Death Foretold*, 174
Gates, Henry Louis, 103
gender, 10, 13, 15, 22, 45, 160, 163, 191, 206, 208, 227n8, 232n15; feminism, 9; and literary criticism, 114, 121, 230n4; misogyny, 204, 212
genres, 22, 119; intergenre novels, 20, 50; rewriting of, 131–43. *See also* European Bildungsroman; European travelogue
German language: word count, 144–45
Ghosh, Amitav, 119; on the fictional bookcase, 3; *Hungry Tide*, 162–63; "The March of the Novel Through History," 2–3; *Sea of Poppies*, 155; *The Shadow Lines*, 133, 162; on universal literature, 3; and Western literary canon, 2–3
Ghosh, Chandra Madhab, 186
Ghosh, Girish Chandra, 185, 234n7; *Abu Hosen*, 192; on Bengali audiences, 192, 235n12; translations of Shakespeare, 186–93, 209, 234n8, 235nn9–11
Ghosh, N., 186
Gikandi, Simon: on globalization, 182
Gilkes, Michael, 53
Gilroy, Paul: *Black Atlantic*, 230n14
Gissing, George: *The Private Papers of Henry Ryecroft*, 134
Glendinning, Victoria, 226n14
Glissant, Édouard, 137
globalization, 17, 41–42, 52, 148, 172, 213; as cultural, 8, 31, 47; as economic, 152, 170; Gikandi on, 182; as literary, 118; as neocolonialism, 120, 161; as uneven, 178
global-local binary, 22, 47, 172
global migration, 17
Goethe, Johann Wolfgang von, 6
Gogol, Nikolai, 7
Gordimer, Nadine, 226n14

Gordon, Lyndall: *T. S. Eliot*, 36
Gorky, Maksim, 3
Gorra, Michael: *After Empire*, 52, 70, 226n1; on Conrad, 60–61, 70, 226n1; on Rushdie, 155
Gramsci, Antonio, 65
Greenblatt, Stephen: *Shakespearean Negotiations*, 199
Greenwood, Emily: *Afro-Greeks*, 88
Griffiths, Gareth: *The Empire Writes Back*, 115–16, 220
Guardian, 10, 174; and Booker Prize, 27–28; "Tears, Tiffs, and Triumphs," 27–28
Guha, Ranajit, 233n20
Guillory, John: on Bloom's *Western Canon*, 9; on canonicity, 31; *Cultural Capital*, 12–13, 18, 146–47, 233n1; on dominant and dominated cultures, 12–13; on educational institutions, 233n1; on English vernacular canon, 145, 146–47; "The Ideology of Canon Formation," 13, 31; on institutions of reproduction, 233n1; on prehistory of canon-formation, 13, 31; on singularity of classics, 13; on Standard English, 147; on transmission, 13
Guinness, Alec, 221

Haiti, 95
Hamara Shakespeare, 183–84
Hamid, Mohsin, 181; *The Reluctant Fundamentalist*, 161, 169–72, 173; on Zia dictatorship, 174
Hamner, Robert, 85
Hamsun, Knut, 3
Hanif, Mohammed: "Butt and Bhatti," 180–81; *A Case of Exploding Mangoes*, 161, 172–75, 181
Hardy, Thomas: *The Woodlanders*, 77
Harlow, Barbara, 123
Harpham, Geoffrey Galt: on Conrad, 55, 59, 217, 227n9; *One of Us*, 55, 59, 217
Harris, Wilson, 116, 122, 137; and Conrad, 52–53, 217; on Conrad's *Heart of Darkness*, 52–53; *Palace of the Peacock*, 53–54; *The Secret Ladder*, 53; "Tradition and the West Indian Writer," 52–53, 83
Hartman, Geoffrey, 67
Harvard Classics, 3
"Hazaar fucked" English, 153, 232n9

Heaney, Seamus, 81, 84, 221
Hegel, G. W. F., 42; on *Weltgeschichte*, 233n20
Heidegger, Martin, 175–76
Heller, Joseph, 174
Hemingway, Ernest, 6, 56
Herbert, Zbigniew, 39–40
Higher Education White Paper, 218–19, 237n4
Hill, Geoffrey, 81
Hindi, 159, 209, 210, 213, 232n9
Hinduism, 178, 182, 208
Hirsch, Edward, 99
Hirsch, Marianne: on postmemory, 232n15
hoarding of classics, 4, 5
Hobbes, Thomas, 104
Homer, 34, 79, 80, 89, 237n2
Horace, 40, 104
Howes, Marjorie: *Semicolonial Joyce*, 126, 230n4
Huffington Post, 10
Huggan, Graham: on global culture industry, 18; *The Postcolonial Exotic*, 18
Hughes, Ted: on Eliot's poetry, 36–37
Hugo, Victor, 3
Hulme, Keri: *The Bone People*, 128–31
Hulme, Peter, 115
Hunter, G. K., 235n15
hybridity, 72, 113, 118, 129, 152, 176–77

identity, 2, 4, 6, 7–8; national identity, 116, 146–47, 170, 224n6
imagination, 9, 71–72, 82, 83
imitation, 67, 84, 97, 102, 112, 113, 119, 121, 215; postcolonial politics of mimesis, 21, 79, 101, 102, 229
imperialism, 15, 70, 83, 96, 98, 117, 120, 122, 232n16; of Britain, 16, 70, 90, 125, 198, 230n4, 232n7, 233n2; and the classic, 35–36, 43, 46; Conrad's attitudes regarding, 51–52, 56, 226n3; as cultural, 170; and European novels, 70; and Joyce, 126
India: Calcutta, 16, 185–94, 198, 201; caste discrimination in, 207; Charter Act of 1813, 149–50; Chennai, 183; contemporary novels in, 22; corruption in, 165, 166; cosmopolitan vernaculars in, 148; Emergency era, 176–77, 201; English Education Act of 1835, 150; English education in, 149–51, 152, 183, 198, 231n5, 232n7, 233n2; Kendal's Shakespeare troupe in, 16, 23, 185, 194–98, 201, 209; Mizoram, 184–85, 234nn5,6; nationalism in, 111–12, 114, 195; "nationsroman" in, 133; reception of Shakespeare in, 16, 114, 183, 186–94; relations with Pakistan, 170; Shakespeare adaptations in, 16, 19, 22–23, 114, 182–213, 234nn4,6; Union Carbide's factory at Bhopal, 177, 233n18; Uttar Pradesh, 205, 213
India Gazette, 112–13
Indian Nation, 186
Indian People's Theatre Association, 201
individualism, 164, 217
individuation, 67, 175, 181, 185, 236n21
influence, 21, 112, 117, 215, 217; anxiety of, 19, 20, 96, 137, 215
intergenre novels, 20, 50
intertextuality, 80–81, 94, 95, 104
Irving, Washington: *The Legend of Sleepy Hollow*, 171
Ivory, James, 196
Iyengar, Vikaram: *Crossings*, 183

Jackson Knight, W. F., 225n8
Jaffrey, Madhur, 197
James, Henry, 61
Jameson, Frederic: on Conrad, 226n3; *Political Unconscious*, 56; on third world literature, 180, 181
Jhabvalla, Ruth Prawar, 196
Johnson, David: on South African English studies, 115
Johnson, Samuel., 14–15, 29
Jones, Lloyd: *Mister Pip*, 140–43
Joshi, Priya: on Ali, 154–55; *Another Country*, 231n8, 233n2; on the "nationsroman," 133, 173
Joyce, James, 56, 131, 156; Beckett on, 38; and Coetzee, 214, 215, 237n1; *Finnegans Wake*, 97; and Ireland, 126, 230n4; and postcolonial studies, 126–27; *Ulysses*, 97, 126, 237n2; and Walcott, 21, 79, 80, 96–97, 137

Kafka, Franz, 7, 215
Kālī, 191–92, 208
Kalidasa, 182
Kapoor, Raj, 157
karma, 178, 211

266 Index

Kastan, David: on Shakespeare's survival, 209, 236n24
Kathakali, 234n4
Keats, John, 81
Kendal, Felicity, 195
Kendal, Geoffrey: Shakespeare troupe in India, 16, 23, 185, 194–98, 201, 209; *The Shakespeare Wallah*, 194–95, 196, 197
Kenner, Hugh: on Kermode, 32
Kenya: independence struggle, 132–33; Mau Mau war, 133
Kermode, Frank: *The Classic*, 18, 31, 32, 33–34, 35–36, 37, 43–44, 225n8; on Eliot and Virgil, 225n8; on the empire and the classic, 35–36; on Sainte-Beuve, 33–34; on secular canon-formation, 31; on surplus of signifier, 31, 43; on survival of the classic, 31
Khair, Tabish, 160
Khan, Irrfan, 202
Khan, Usma Aslam: on Woolf, 217–18
Khayyam, Omar, 156
Kincaid, Jamaica: *Lucy*, 133
Kincaid, James, 172
Kipling, Rudyard: T. S. Eliot on, 36; *From Sea to Sea*, 145–46, 231n1; on the globetrotter, 145–46, 231n1; on India, 145–46; *Kim*, 121; "Letters of Travel," 145–46; "Mandalay," 162; on travelers, 231n1
Kirsch, Adam: on Harvard Classics, 3
Koodiyattam, 183–84, 234n4
Koran, 4, 156–57, 232n14
Kortenaar, Neil ten, 76
Kramnick, Jonathan: on English literary canon, 224n4; on literature, 9; "Making of the English Canon," 9, 224n4
Kristeva, Julia: *Strangers to Ourselves*, 149
Kureishi, Hanif: *The Buddha of Suburbia*, 133
Kurosawa's *Throne of Blood*, 204, 210

Labov, William, 103
La Malinche, 120
Lamb's *Tales from Shakespeare*, 1, 210
Lamming, George, 116; on Caliban, 121–22; *Pleasures of Exile*, 121–22
Lamos, Colleen: *Deviant Modernism*, 35; on Virgil and Eliot, 35
Landon, L. E., 112
Lasdun, James, 172

Lawrence, D. H., 56, 67; *Lady Chatterley's Lover*, 139
Leavis, F. R.: on Conrad, 50; *The Great Tradition*, 50
Lee, Hermione, 27–28
Lehman, Robert, 95
Lessing, Doris: *In Pursuit of English*, 133
Levine, George, 66
Lewis, C. S., 130
Lewis Theatre, 192
Liddell, Laura, 195
literary ambition, 19, 58, 216
literary apprenticeship, 1, 21, 47, 80
literary criticism, 13–15, 19, 46, 118, 126, 152–53, 220; and Booker Prize, 27–28; center-periphery model in, 18, 20, 22, 35, 44, 47–48, 86, 233n21; and class, 121, 230n4; J. M. Coetzee on, 29; and Conrad, 50, 52–53, 59–60, 62–63, 121, 226nn1,3; T. S. Eliot on, 29, 40; function of, 40, 41, 225n9; and gender, 114, 121, 230n4; impersonality vs. personality in, 20, 28, 45; international, 19, 34, 44, 46; and literary standards, 8, 10–12, 14, 29, 31–32; nation/narration theme in, 126–29; and postcolonial rewriting, 119–20, 121; and race, 52–53, 62–63, 114, 121, 226n3, 230n4; relationship to the classic, 29, 30, 31–32, 39–41, 217, 225n11; Said on, 13–14, 30, 50, 55, 61, 119, 152–53, 217; worlding of, 44–45
literary standards, 8–12, 28, 35, 39, 40–41, 43, 45–46, 216, 221; and literary criticism, 8, 10–12, 14, 29, 31–32
Little Theatre Group, 201
Llosa, Vargos: *El hablador*, 116
Lloyd, David: on Joyce, 126–27
localism, 213
London's blue plaques, 36–37, 225n7
Loomba, Ania: "*Hamlet* in Mizoram," 183, 184–85, 234n6; "Local-Manufacture Made-in-India Othello Fellows," 234n4
Lukács, Georg, 56
Luna, Judith: on classics, 221

Macaulay, Thomas: and Charter Act, 150; "Minute on English Education," 198, 232n7, 235n16
MacCabe, Colin, 126
Machado de Assis, Joachim Maria, 7
Madge, E. W., 112

Madhu, Margi, 183
Maiorino, Giancarlo, 177
Makdisi, Saree, 123, 125
Malayalam, 159, 183
Malik, Abdul, 76, 78, 228n13
Malkani, Gautam, 155
Mannoni, Octave, 121
Mantel, Hilary, 28; *Wolf Hall*, 224n2
Maqbool, 185, 201, 202–5, 210, 211, 212, 236n22
marginalization, 13, 14, 56, 67
Marlowe, Christopher, 108
Martin, Murray, 129
Marx, Karl, 168
Maugham, William Somerset, 128
Maupassant, Guy de, 3
McDonald, Peter: on Coetzee, 136
Mellors, John, 77
Melville, Herman, 7, 97, 128, 130–31
Memmi, Albert, 175
Merchant, Ismail, 196
Merchant Ivory Productions: *Shakespeare Wallah*, 185, 194, 196–98
Merrill, James, 11, 81
Michael X, 76, 228n13
Millett, Kate: on *Lady Chatterley's Lover*, 139
Milton, John, 35, 108, 112, 151
Minerva Theatre, 186, 192
Mishra, Pankaj: on Roy's *God of Small Things*, 157
misogyny, 204, 212
misprisions, 81, 156, 232n13
Mizoram National Front (MNF), 184, 234n5
Montaigne, Michel de, 104
Moore, Thomas: "The Harp of Erin," 113; "Lallah Rookh," 112
Moretti, Franco: on asymmetry in international power, 144; on literature as planetary system, 17–18; *Modern Epic*, 19; "The Slaughterhouse of Literature," 42
Morrison, Toni: *Beloved*, 224n3
Morris, Rosalind C., 15
Morrissette, Billy: *Scotland, PA*, 211
Morton, Stephen, 232n14
Mufti, Aamir, 181; on global comparativism, 123; on Said, 14, 123
Mugo, Micere: *The Trial of Dedan Kimathi*, 132–33
Mukherjee, Meenakshi, 162; on Rao, 154; "The Anxiety of Indianness," 154, 181

Mullan, John, 226n14
multinational corporations, 232n16

Nabokov, Vladimir, 44
Naipaul, V. S., 116, 119; Casanova on, 47; and Conrad, 1, 20–21, 50, 54, 55, 56–57, 59, 63, 66–78, 122, 127, 215, 217; on global travel, 70; on heart-of-darkness tradition, 50; on intergenre novels, 20, 50; Jimmy Ahmed in *Guerrillas*, 4; and the *Künstlerroman*, 133–34; on literary form, 5; on Narayan, 154; narrative style, 72–73; on the novel, 66, 67, 68, 69–70, 73, 77, 78; on organized societies, 68, 73, 78, 227n11; private English literary anthology of, 1–2; on self-transcendence, 16; use of English by, 155; and Western literary canon, 1–2, 153
Naipaul, V. S., works of: *Among the Believers*, 69; *An Area of Darkness*, 67; *A Bend in the River*, 63, 69, 70–72, 122, 127; *Bend in the River*, 68; *Beyond Belief*, 69; *A Congo Diary*, 68, 122; "Conrad's Darkness"/"Conrad's Darkness and Mine," 68–69, 73; *The Enigma of Arrival*, 70, 78, 133–34; *Guerrillas*, 74, 76–78, 127; *A House for Mr Biswas*, 133; *Literary Occasions*, 1–2, 5, 15, 21, 54, 66, 68–69, 70, 73, 153; "Michael X and the Black Power Killings in Trinidad," 76, 228n13; *The Mimic Men*, 54, 67, 78, 133; *The Mystic Masseur*, 133; "A New King for the Congo," 69; "Two Worlds," 153; "Writing is Magic," 78
Namjoshi, Suniti, 155
Nancy, Jean-Luc: on communauté désoeuvrée, 116
Nandy, Ashis: on colonialism, 16–17, 114; *Intimate Enemy*, 16–17
Narayan, R. K., 154
Nashe, Thomas: *The Unfortunate Traveller*, 94
national identity, 116, 146–47, 170, 224n6
nationalism, 14, 37, 46, 51, 52, 111–13, 125–27, 147, 149, 150–51, 152, 181, 230; in India, 111–12, 114, 195
national literature, 21–22, 118, 135–36
Nazism, 95, 100
neoliberalism, 175, 178
Newman, Judie, 4, 76; *The Ballistic Bard*, 18
Newton, Isaac, 151

Index

New York Review of Book: "Are These the Poems to Remember?," 10–12
New Zealand: Pakeha and Maori in, 128–29; South Island, 131
Ngũgĩ wa Thiong'o: *The Trial of Dedan Kimathi*, 132–33
Nietzsche, Friedrich: *Beyond Good and Evil*, 14; vs. Conrad, 63–64; on history, 63–64; on the question mark, 14
Nixon, Rob, 115; on Conrad, 69, 70; on Naipaul, 69, 70, 127; on Shakespeare, 121–22; on Sinha's *Animal's People*, 177
Nobel Prize in Literature, 145, 215
Nolan, Emer, 126
nonreading, 22, 137–43
nonsynchronism, 137, 231n8
Norris, Margot: on Coetzee and Joyce, 215–16
nostalgia, 19, 29, 120, 136, 169, 199
Nussbaum, Martha: on cosmopolitanism, 148

O'Connor, Flannery, 159
Okunoye, Oyenlyi, 132
Omkara, 185, 201, 205–9, 210, 212, 213, 236n23
Omotoso, Kole: *Just Before Dawn*, 132
Ondaatje, Michael: *Anil's Ghost*, 162–63
Oriental Herald Review, 111
Orientalism, 149, 150, 153
Oriental Magazine, 112
originality, 21, 31, 34, 63, 64, 112, 174, 217
overdetermination, 42, 45
Ovid, 86–88
Oxford, Edward de Vere, Earl of, 221–22

Paine, Thomas, 151
Pakistan: contemporary novels in, 22; English language in, 151; relations with India, 170; relations with United States, 217; Urdu in, 151; Zia dictatorship, 172–73, 174, 218
Pampa, 148
Pamuk, Orhan, 3; "My Father's Suitcase," 2; and Western literary canon, 2, 4; on writing, 23
Park, You-me: *The Postcolonial Jane Austen*, 119, 230n4
Parringer, Patrick, 134
Parry, Benita: on Conrad, 51–52; *Conrad and Imperialism*, 51–52
Pater, Walter, 60

Paz, Octavio, 44
Penguin Anthology of Twentieth-Century American Poetry, 10–11
Perloff, Marjorie, 37
Phillip, Caryl: *The Final Passage*, 133
Phillip, Theophilus: "The Bedbug," 104–5
Piers Plowman, 84
politics, 4, 8, 10, 12, 14, 17, 30, 31, 50, 61, 79, 86, 218, 220
Pollock, Sheldon: on cosmopolitanism, 148, 151–52, 231n2; on Sanskrit, 148, 231n2; "The Cosmopolitan Vernacular," 148
Pope, Alexander: *Dunciad*, 105
postcoloniality: meaning of, 15–17, 111, 120–21; postcolonial representation, 3, 16–17, 18, 85–86; postcolonial studies, 10, 17, 18, 113, 126–27, 230n4. *See also* postcolonial literature
Postcolonial Jane Austen, The, 119, 230n4
postcolonial literature: and anxiety of influence, 67, 81, 96, 137, 215; autobiography in, 132; canonicity in, 18–19, 113–14, 118–19; and Conrad, 20–21, 50–51, 54–57, 59, 62, 63, 64–65, 66–78, 122, 123, 125, 127; as counterreadings, 18, 19, 21, 119, 122, 125; and cultural globalization, 47; and nationalism, 111–12, 125–27; postcolonial rewriting, 19, 20–22, 80, 91–98, 100, 113, 115–25, 126, 127–28, 131–43, 144, 215, 217, 219–20, 230n4; relationship to world literature, 17–18, 19, 220–21; as rewriting genre, 131–43; and Shakespeare, 114–15, 121–22, 131; Suleri on, 15–16
Pound, Ezra, 38, 44, 56, 80, 137, 221
poverty, 138, 175–79
Prakash, Gyan: on the postcolonial, 117
Pratt, Mary Louise: "In the Neocolony," 120–21, 142; on postcoloniality, 120–21
Premchand, Munshi: Hindi chronicles, 165
Prendergast, Christopher, 33, 40, 84, 224n5, 225nn9,12
Pulitzer Prize, 224n3
Pym, John, 197

Quayson, Ato: on Merchant of Venice, 230n4; "Postcolonializing Shakespeare," 230n4

Rabelais, François, 106

race, 13, 22, 45, 82, 86, 96, 129, 140, 145, 190, 192, 194, 206, 208, 212, 228n13, 234n4; Conrad's attitudes regarding, 52–53, 62–63, 121, 226n3; and literary criticism, 52–53, 62–63, 114, 121, 226n3, 230n4; racism, 11, 12, 34, 52–53, 62–63, 71, 96, 100–101, 121, 122, 175, 211, 224n3, 226n3, 228n13, 232n7. *See also* slavery
Raine, Craig, 221
Rajan, Rajeswari Sunder, 119; on Austen, 230n4; *The Postcolonial Jane Austen*, 119, 230n4
Ramazani, Jahan: on transnational poetics, 155; on Walcott, 84, 86
Rao, Raja: *Kanthapura*, 154
Ray, Haralal: *Rudrapal*, 187
Ray, P. L., 186
Reeves, Gareth, 36; *T. S. Eliot*, 225n8
repetition, 117–18, 215, 219–20
rereading, 31, 96, 113; nonreading as, 137–43
Rhodesia, 231n10
Rhys, Jean, 80, 107–8, 116, 118, 119, 137; *Wide Sargasso Sea*, 3, 77, 122
Richardson, Samuel: *Clarissa*, 77
Richards, Thomas, 121
Ricks, Christopher, 137; *Allusion to the Poets*, 228n1
Rimbaud, Arthur, 95
Robbins, Bruce, 133, 163
Rochester, John Wilmot, Earl of: *Satyr Against Reason and Mankind*, 104–5
Rose, Jacqueline, 204
Roy, Arundhati: "'Englishing' India," 231n5; *God of Small Things*, 157–59; use of English by, 157–59
Roy, Modhumita, 150–51
Rushdie, Salman: on Bhabha, 125; and Booker Prize, 27–28, 226n14; and Conrad, 6; critical reception of, 155; on elective affinities, 6; on the novel and the nation-state, 125; on temporary human beings, 173–74; use of English by, 155–57; and Western literary canon, 7–8, 119
Rushdie, Salman, works of: "The Empire Writes Back to the Centre," 115–16; *Ground Beneath Her Feet*, 36; *Haroun and the Sea of Stories*, 156–57, 232n14; *Imaginary Homelands*, 7, 152; *Joseph Anton*, 5–8; *Midnight's Children*, 27–28, 47, 133, 156, 157, 181, 226n14; *Moor's Last Sigh*, 125; *Satanic Verses*, 156–57, 173–74; *Shame*, 156

Sahay, Raghuvir, 114
Sahgal, Nayantara, 175; *Rich Like Us*, 161, 176–77, 179
Said, Edward, 44, 172; on affiliation vs. filiation, 30, 55, 117–18, 223n4; on autonomy of art, 50; on colonial novels, 62; and Conrad, 20, 50, 51, 56–57, 58, 59–66, 215, 217; on contrapuntality, 123–24; on Dicken's *Great Expectations*, 117; on elaboration, 65; on exilic marginality, 62, 152; on fiction of autobiography, 65–66; on *Heart of Darkness*, 62–63; on history, 117; on imperialism, 117; on intellectuals, 226n2; on literary criticism, 13–14, 30, 50, 55, 61, 119, 152–53, 217; on lost causes, 20, 65; on monocentrism and criticism, 219; on Nietzsche, 63–64; on noncoercive human community, 146; on *Nostromo*, 56, 66; on orientalism, 65; on repetition, 117–18; on secular criticism, 14, 30, 223n5; on textuality of texts, 20, 45; on Western critical consciousness, 13–14, 30
Said, Edward, works of: *Beginnings*, 56, 63, 152–53; "Conrad: The Presentation of Narrative," 64, 65; *Culture and Imperialism*, 31, 58, 62, 63, 70, 117, 123, 230n4; *Joseph Conrad and the Fiction of Autobiography*, 61–62; *Orientalism*, 124; *Out of Place*, 65, 175; *Reflections on Exile*, 57, 62, 64, 65, 66, 123; *The World, the Text and the Critic*, 13–14, 30, 45, 50, 63, 64–65, 117, 119
Sainte-Beuve, Augustin: *Causeries*, 224n5; definition of the classic, 33–34, 84; "De la tradition en littérature et dans quel sens il la faut entendre," 225n12; on Flaubert's *Salammbô*, 34; "Qu'est-ce qu'un classique?," 14, 33–34, 40, 46, 225nn9,12
Salih, Tayeb: and Conrad, 122, 123, 124, 125, 217; *Season of Migration to the North*, 3–4, 63, 122–25, 133; and Western literary canon, 3–4, 123
Sanskrit, 148, 182, 231n2, 236n23
Sans Souci theater, 193, 198
Sarat Chandra, 2

Index

Sarkar, Akshoy Chandra, 234n7
Sartre, Jean-Paul, 138, 231n9
satire, 21, 104, 105–6, 173
Saunders's "Troubadour," 112
Schoenberger, Nancy, 84
Schopenhauer, Arthur, 60
Schweitzer, Albert, 95
Scotland, PA, 211
Scott, Sir Walter, 112
Sealy, Allan: *The Trotter-Nama*, 133
selectiveness, 11–13, 18, 113, 220
self-archiving, 1–2, 4, 5
Semi-colonial Joyce, 230n4
Sen, Aparna: *36 Chowringhee Lane*, 198–200, 235nn16–18
Senn, Fritz, 237n2
September 11th attacks, 161, 169, 170
Seth, Vikram, 119; *A Suitable Boy*, 152, 167–68; *Beastly Tales*, 155
sexuality, 10, 13
Shakespeare Birthplace Trust: *Was Shakespeare a Fraud?*, 222
Shakespeare Wallah, 185, 194, 196–98
Shakespeare, William, 35, 112, 151; adaptations in India, 16, 19, 22–23, 114, 182–213, 234nn4,6; authorship controversy, 221–22; Caliban, 102, 113, 121–22, 131; in colonial India, 16, 114, 183, 186–94; in contemporary Indian cinema, 16, 23, 182, 198–213; Desdemona, 182; and Hollywood, 120; Kendal's troupe in India, 16, 23, 185, 194–98, 201, 209; Lamb's *Tales from Shakespeare*, 1, 210; and postcolonial literature, 114–16, 121–22, 131; Shakespeare studies, 114–15; textuality vs. performance, 209; translations of, 114, 145, 186–93, 201, 234n8
Shakespeare, William, works of: *Antony and Cleopatra*, 198; *Comedy of Errors*, 209, 210; *Hamlet*, 89–90, 97, 184–85, 198, 204, 210, 234n6; *Henry V*, 196; *Julius Caesar*, 1, 210; *King Lear*, 123, 199–200, 236n18; *Macbeth*, 114, 183–84, 185, 186, 187–93, 196, 201, 202–5, 210–12; *Measure for Measure*, 204; *Merchant of Venice*, 210, 230n4; *Midsummer Night's Dream*, 131; *Othello*, 16, 123, 124, 182, 185, 193–94, 197, 198, 201, 205–9, 212, 234n4, 235n14; *Richard II*, 198; *Romeo and Juliet*, 120,
198, 215, 235n15; *The Tempest*, 102, 113, 115, 121–22, 131; *Timon of Athens*, 229n5; *Twelfth Night*, 198, 199
Shakuntala, 182
Shamsie, Kamila: *Burnt Shadows*, 161
Shekhar, Ardhendu, 192
Shelley, Percy Bysshe, 29, 112
Sheridan's *The Critic*, 197
Sholokhov, Mikhail, 3
Shri 420, 157
Sienkiewicz, Henryk, 3
Sinclair, Upton, 3
Sinfield, Alan, 201–2
Singh, Jyotsna, 193; "Different Shakespeare," 236n19
singularity of classics, 13, 140
Sinha, Indra, 175, 181; *Animal's People*, 161, 177–79
Sjöberg, Leif, 80
Slaughter, Joseph, 179; on Dangarembga's *Nervous Conditions*, 137, 138, 139–40, 231n10; on human rights and the *Bildungsroman*, 177–78; on surrogate microrepublics, 163
slavery, 114, 121, 133, 185, 212; Walcott on, 86, 94, 99, 103, 136
Smith, Zadie: *White Teeth*, 133
social mobility, 133–34
South Africa: apartheid in, 41; CNA award in, 135, 136; English studies in, 115
Spivak, Gayatri Chakravorty: on alternative canons, 45; on anti-imperialist revolution, 132; on canon-apocrypha opposition, 45; on colonial discourse studies, 233n21; *Death of a Discipline*, 18, 48; on demographical frontiers, 48; on empire of reason, 117, 179; on English education in India, 152; on English studies, 10; on gendered subalternity, 15; *Lie of the Land*, 233n2; *Outside in the Teaching Machine*, 10, 44, 157; on the planet, 18; on R. K. Narayan, 152; on Rushdie, 157; on translation, 147–48; on upward race-mobility, 41
Sri Lankan contemporary novels, 22
Stanley, H. M., 199
Stead, C. K.: on Hulme's *The Bone People*, 128, 131
Steinbeck, John, 3
Stendhal, 3

Stephenson, Robert Louis, 128
Stevens, Wallace, 81
Strindberg, August, 80; *Miss Julie*, 101
subalternity, 15, 113, 160, 164, 184–85
subcultures, 13
subject-in-process, 22
Subrahmanyam, Sanjay: on Adiga's *White Tiger*, 165, 168
Suleri, Sara, 2, 119; on canonicity, 118; on Naipaul, 74; on postcolonial literature, 15–16; *The Rhetoric of English India*, 15–16, 74; on Western literary canon, 117
Sutherland, John, 28
Swift, Jonathan: *A Tale of a Tub*, 105
Synge, J. M., 80

Tabu, 204
Tagore, Maharaja Jatindramohan, 186
Tagore, Prince Dwarakanath, 193
Tagore, Rabindranath, 2, 9, 193
Terada, Rei, 87; on Walcott, 79, 89, 98, 104, 228n1, 229nn5,6
Tharoor, Shashi: *The Great Indian Novel*, 133
Theobold, Lewis, 236n24
Thieme, John, 98, 105
36 Chowringhee Lane, 198–200, 235nn16,17
Thomas, Dylan, 80, 137
Thomas, Keith, 219
Throne of Blood, 204, 210
Tiffin, Helen: *The Empire Writes Back*, 115–16
Tolkien, J. R. R., 130
Tolstoy, Leo, 3
tradition: American tradition, 56, 159–60; Arabic oral tradition, 123; Caribbean mock-heroic tradition, 21, 105–6; T. S. Eliot on, 63, 142, 217; fabulist traditions, 155; great tradition of English literature, 70, 101, 148; heart-of-darkness tradition, 50, 69, 92, 93, 96, 122, 125, 217; relationship to the classic, 21, 31–32, 33–34, 36; Walcott on, 21, 136–37
translation studies, 19, 229n13
transmission, 113, 119; of the canon, 13; of knowledge, 39; of tradition, 33
Tremain, Rose, 28
Trivedi, Harish: *Colonial Transactions*, 233n2; on Shakespeare studies, 114
Turgenev, Ivan, 3
Turner, Frank, 221

Two Nations theory, 164

universality, 9, 34, 35–36, 46–47, 48
Urdu, 151, 155, 159, 232n9

Valmiki, 34
Vendler, Helen: *Coming of Age*, 37; on dilemma of idiom, 37; *The Harvard Book of Contemporary American Poetry*, 12; on *Penguin Anthology of Twentieth-Century American Poetry*, 10–12; on Walcott, 81–82, 94
Verne, Jules: *Twenty Thousand Leagues Under the Sea*, 1
Virgil, 34–36, 37, 44, 80, 225n8
Viswanathan, Gauri, 149–50, 179–80, 232n7; *Masks of Conquest*, 233n2
Vogt-William, Christine: on Roy's *God of Small Things*, 159
Volans, Henry, 221
Voltaire, 151
Vyasa, 34

Walcott, Derek, 16, 119, 215; and Achebe, 95–96; on assimilation, 80; on Auden, 1; on Bearden, 79–80; and "Best of the World's Classics," 80, 90–91; and Calypso, 99, 100, 103, 104–5, 106; and Christ, 79, 99; on the classic, 21, 84–85; on collective amnesia, 82, 83; and Conrad, 21, 80, 91–98, 137; Creole modernism of, 21, 80, 103–8; on decomposition as composition, 21; and Defoe's Crusoe, 21, 82, 98–103; and disfigurement as figuration, 21, 79; education of, 88, 97; and T. S. Eliot, 1, 21, 80, 94–95, 97, 137; and Homer, 79, 80, 85, 89; on imagination, 82, 83; and intertextuality, 80–81; and Joyce, 21, 79, 80, 96–97, 137; and mimicry, 79, 80, 101, 104, 105; as "mulatto of style," 81, 229n3; multinational self-representation of, 80; on poetry, 80, 82, 83; and postcolonial latecomers, 21, 79; and postcolonial politics of mimesis, 21, 79, 101, 102; Ramazani on, 84, 86; and Rhys, 80; and Shakespeare, 79, 80, 89–90, 91, 102; and simultaneity, 79–80; on slavery, 86, 94, 99, 103, 136; Terada on, 79, 87, 89, 98, 104, 228n1, 229nn5,6; on Timon of

Athens, 229n5; on tradition, 21, 136–37; on unstable sets of resemblances, 21, 79; Vendler on, 81–82, 94; and Western literary canon, 1, 4, 93, 108; and Yeats, 80–81, 137
Walcott, Derek, works of: *Another Life*, 82, 83, 85, 97; *The Arkansas Testament*, 88, 229n8; "Caligula's Horse," 82; "The Caribbean," 82; *The Castaway*, 229n12; "Crusoe's Journal," 83, 98, 99; *Epitaph for the Young*, 229n7; "The Figure of Crusoe," 82, 98–99; "The Fortunate Traveler," 93–96; "Greece," 89; "Gros Islet," 88; "Hic Jacet," 83; "Homecoming: Anse La Raye," 88; "Hotel Normandie Pool," 86–88; "Jean Rhys," 107–8; "Koenig of the River," 95; "Latin Primer," 229n8; "Leaving School," 97; "Meanings," 21, 88; "The Muse of History," 83, 136–37; "Names," 227n8; *Omeros*, 79, 80, 82–83, 84, 85–86, 87, 89–93, 97, 137, 229n5; "On *Omeros*," 84; *Pantomime*, 21, 99–103; "Reflections," 79–80; "Ruins of a Great House," 81, 108; "The Schooner *Flight*," 83, 84, 86, 89; "The Spoiler's Return," 21, 103–7; "The Star-Apple Kingdom," 83; *Tiepolo's Hound*, 81, 82; "Volcano"/*Sea Grapes*, 96–98; *What the Twilight*, 21, 80, 82, 83, 88, 98, 103, 136; "What the Twilight Says," 81, 103, 108, 228n1; "Young Trinidadian Poets," 80
Walcott, Warwick, 89–90, 91

Walker, Alice, 224n3
war on terror, 161, 171
Watson, Elizabeth Porges, 225n8
Watt, Ian, 60, 227n4
Waugh, Patricia: on imaginary unities, 9; *Literary Theory and Criticism*, 9
Weldon, Fay, 28
West, Rebecca, 27
White, Patrick, 116
Williams, William Carlos: *Paterson*, 229n6
Winterson, Jeanette, 221
Wood, James: on Rushdie, 155
Woolf, Virginia, 131; "How Should One Read a Book?," 14–15; Uzma Aslam Khan on, 217–18; *A Room of One's Own*, 218
world literature, 8–9, 42–43, 213, 225n10; relationship to postcolonial literature, 17–18, 19, 220–21
World's Great Classics, The, 90, 91
Wright, Jay, 81

Yeats, William Butler, 131; "Meditations in Time of Civil War," 81; "On a House Shaken by the Land Agitation," 81; *Supernatural Songs*, 81; and Walcott, 80–81, 137
Young, Robert: on English language, 152; on postcolonial studies, 17

Zia ul-Haq, Muhammad, 172–73, 174, 218
Zimbabwe, 231n10
Žižek, Slavoj, 207

Cultural Memory in the Present

Jean-Pierre Dupuy, *The Mark of the Sacred*

Henri Atlan, *Fraud: The World of* Ona'ah

Niklas Luhmann, *Theory of Society, Volume 2*

Ilit Ferber, *Philosophy and Melancholy: Benjamin's Early Reflections on Theater and Language*

Alexandre Lefebvre, *Human Rights as a Way of Life: On Bergson's Political Philosophy*

Theodore W. Jennings, Jr., *Outlaw Justice: The Messianic Politics of Paul*

Alexander Etkind, *Warped Mourning: Stories of the Undead in the Land of the Unburied*

Denis Guénoun, *About Europe: Philosophical Hypotheses*

Maria Boletsi, *Barbarism and Its Discontents*

Sigrid Weigel, *Walter Benjamin: Images, the Creaturely, and the Holy*

Roberto Esposito, *Living Thought: The Origins and Actuality of Italian Philosophy*

Henri Atlan, *The Sparks of Randomness, Volume 2: The Atheism of Scripture*

Rüdiger Campe, *The Game of Probability: Literature and Calculation from Pascal to Kleist*

Niklas Luhmann, *A Systems Theory of Religion*

Jean-Luc Marion, *In the Self's Place: The Approach of Saint Augustine*

Rodolphe Gasché, *Georges Bataille: Phenomenology and Phantasmatology*

Niklas Luhmann, *Theory of Society, Volume 1*

Alessia Ricciardi, *After* La Dolce Vita: *A Cultural Prehistory of Berlusconi's Italy*

Daniel Innerarity, *The Future and Its Enemies: In Defense of Political Hope*

Patricia Pisters, *The Neuro-Image: A Deleuzian Film-Philosophy of Digital Screen Culture*

François-David Sebbah, *Testing the Limit: Derrida, Henry, Levinas, and the Phenomenological Tradition*

Erik Peterson, *Theological Tractates*, edited by Michael J. Hollerich

Feisal G. Mohamed, *Milton and the Post-Secular Present: Ethics, Politics, Terrorism*

Pierre Hadot, *The Present Alone Is Our Happiness, Second Edition: Conversations with Jeannie Carlier and Arnold I. Davidson*

Yasco Horsman, *Theaters of Justice: Judging, Staging, and Working Through in Arendt, Brecht, and Delbo*

Jacques Derrida, *Parages*, edited by John P. Leavey

Henri Atlan, *The Sparks of Randomness, Volume 1: Spermatic Knowledge*

Rebecca Comay, *Mourning Sickness: Hegel and the French Revolution*

Djelal Kadir, *Memos from the Besieged City: Lifelines for Cultural Sustainability*

Stanley Cavell, *Little Did I Know: Excerpts from Memory*

Jeffrey Mehlman, *Adventures in the French Trade: Fragments Toward a Life*

Jacob Rogozinski, *The Ego and the Flesh: An Introduction to Egoanalysis*

Marcel Hénaff, *The Price of Truth: Gift, Money, and Philosophy*

Paul Patton, *Deleuzian Concepts: Philosophy, Colonialization, Politics*

Michael Fagenblat, *A Covenant of Creatures: Levinas's Philosophy of Judaism*

Stefanos Geroulanos, *An Atheism That Is Not Humanist Emerges in French Thought*

Andrew Herscher, *Violence Taking Place: The Architecture of the Kosovo Conflict*

Hans-Jörg Rheinberger, *On Historicizing Epistemology: An Essay*

Jacob Taubes, *From Cult to Culture*, edited by Charlotte Fonrobert and Amir Engel

Peter Hitchcock, *The Long Space: Transnationalism and Postcolonial Form*

Lambert Wiesing, *Artificial Presence: Philosophical Studies in Image Theory*

Jacob Taubes, *Occidental Eschatology*

Freddie Rokem, *Philosophers and Thespians: Thinking Performance*

Roberto Esposito, *Communitas: The Origin and Destiny of Community*

Vilashini Cooppan, *Worlds Within: National Narratives and Global Connections in Postcolonial Writing*

Josef Früchtl, *The Impertinent Self: A Heroic History of Modernity*

Frank Ankersmit, Ewa Domanska, and Hans Kellner, eds., *Re-Figuring Hayden White*

Michael Rothberg, *Multidirectional Memory: Remembering the Holocaust in the Age of Decolonization*

Jean-François Lyotard, *Enthusiasm: The Kantian Critique of History*

Ernst van Alphen, Mieke Bal, and Carel Smith, eds., *The Rhetoric of Sincerity*

Stéphane Mosès, *The Angel of History: Rosenzweig, Benjamin, Scholem*

Pierre Hadot, *The Present Alone Is Our Happiness: Conversations with Jeannie Carlier and Arnold I. Davidson*

Alexandre Lefebvre, *The Image of the Law: Deleuze, Bergson, Spinoza*

Samira Haj, *Reconfiguring Islamic Tradition: Reform, Rationality, and Modernity*

Diane Perpich, *The Ethics of Emmanuel Levinas*

Marcel Detienne, *Comparing the Incomparable*

François Delaporte, *Anatomy of the Passions*

René Girard, *Mimesis and Theory: Essays on Literature and Criticism, 1959–2005*

Richard Baxstrom, *Houses in Motion: The Experience of Place and the Problem of Belief in Urban Malaysia*

Jennifer L. Culbert, *Dead Certainty: The Death Penalty and the Problem of Judgment*

Samantha Frost, *Lessons from a Materialist Thinker: Hobbesian Reflections on Ethics and Politics*

Regina Mara Schwartz, *Sacramental Poetics at the Dawn of Secularism: When God Left the World*

Gil Anidjar, *Semites: Race, Religion, Literature*

Ranjana Khanna, *Algeria Cuts: Women and Representation, 1830 to the Present*

Esther Peeren, *Intersubjectivities and Popular Culture: Bakhtin and Beyond*

Eyal Peretz, *Becoming Visionary: Brian De Palma's Cinematic Education of the Senses*

Diana Sorensen, *A Turbulent Decade Remembered: Scenes from the Latin American Sixties*

Hubert Damisch, *A Childhood Memory by Piero della Francesca*

José van Dijck, *Mediated Memories in the Digital Age*

Dana Hollander, *Exemplarity and Chosenness: Rosenzweig and Derrida on the Nation of Philosophy*

Asja Szafraniec, *Beckett, Derrida, and the Event of Literature*

Sara Guyer, *Romanticism After Auschwitz*

Alison Ross, *The Aesthetic Paths of Philosophy: Presentation in Kant, Heidegger, Lacoue-Labarthe, and Nancy*

Gerhard Richter, *Thought-Images: Frankfurt School Writers' Reflections from Damaged Life*

Bella Brodzki, *Can These Bones Live? Translation, Survival, and Cultural Memory*

Rodolphe Gasché, *The Honor of Thinking: Critique, Theory, Philosophy*

Brigitte Peucker, *The Material Image: Art and the Real in Film*

Natalie Melas, *All the Difference in the World: Postcoloniality and the Ends of Comparison*

Jonathan Culler, *The Literary in Theory*

Michael G. Levine, *The Belated Witness: Literature, Testimony, and the Question of Holocaust Survival*

Jennifer A. Jordan, *Structures of Memory: Understanding German Change in Berlin and Beyond*

Christoph Menke, *Reflections of Equality*

Marlène Zarader, *The Unthought Debt: Heidegger and the Hebraic Heritage*

Jan Assmann, *Religion and Cultural Memory: Ten Studies*

David Scott and Charles Hirschkind, *Powers of the Secular Modern: Talal Asad and His Interlocutors*

Gyanendra Pandey, *Routine Violence: Nations, Fragments, Histories*

James Siegel, *Naming the Witch*

J. M. Bernstein, *Against Voluptuous Bodies: Late Modernism and the Meaning of Painting*

Theodore W. Jennings, Jr., *Reading Derrida / Thinking Paul: On Justice*

Richard Rorty and Eduardo Mendieta, *Take Care of Freedom and Truth Will Take Care of Itself: Interviews with Richard Rorty*

Jacques Derrida, *Paper Machine*

Renaud Barbaras, *Desire and Distance: Introduction to a Phenomenology of Perception*

Jill Bennett, *Empathic Vision: Affect, Trauma, and Contemporary Art*

Ban Wang, *Illuminations from the Past: Trauma, Memory, and History in Modern China*

James Phillips, *Heidegger's Volk: Between National Socialism and Poetry*

Frank Ankersmit, *Sublime Historical Experience*

István Rév, *Retroactive Justice: Prehistory of Post-Communism*

Paola Marrati, *Genesis and Trace: Derrida Reading Husserl and Heidegger*

Krzysztof Ziarek, *The Force of Art*

Marie-José Mondzain, *Image, Icon, Economy: The Byzantine Origins of the Contemporary Imaginary*

Cecilia Sjöholm, *The Antigone Complex: Ethics and the Invention of Feminine Desire*

Jacques Derrida and Elisabeth Roudinesco, *For What Tomorrow . . . A Dialogue*

Elisabeth Weber, *Questioning Judaism: Interviews by Elisabeth Weber*

Jacques Derrida and Catherine Malabou, *Counterpath: Traveling with Jacques Derrida*

Martin Seel, *Aesthetics of Appearing*

Nanette Salomon, *Shifting Priorities: Gender and Genre in Seventeenth-Century Dutch Painting*

Jacob Taubes, *The Political Theology of Paul*

Jean-Luc Marion, *The Crossing of the Visible*

Eric Michaud, *The Cult of Art in Nazi Germany*

Anne Freadman, *The Machinery of Talk: Charles Peirce and the Sign Hypothesis*

Stanley Cavell, *Emerson's Transcendental Etudes*

Stuart McLean, *The Event and Its Terrors: Ireland, Famine, Modernity*

Beate Rössler, ed., *Privacies: Philosophical Evaluations*

Bernard Faure, *Double Exposure: Cutting Across Buddhist and Western Discourses*

Alessia Ricciardi, *The Ends of Mourning: Psychoanalysis, Literature, Film*

Alain Badiou, *Saint Paul: The Foundation of Universalism*

Gil Anidjar, *The Jew, the Arab: A History of the Enemy*

Jonathan Culler and Kevin Lamb, eds., *Just Being Difficult? Academic Writing in the Public Arena*

Jean-Luc Nancy, *A Finite Thinking*, edited by Simon Sparks

Theodor W. Adorno, *Can One Live After Auschwitz? A Philosophical Reader*, edited by Rolf Tiedemann

Patricia Pisters, *The Matrix of Visual Culture: Working with Deleuze in Film Theory*

Andreas Huyssen, *Present Pasts: Urban Palimpsests and the Politics of Memory*

Talal Asad, *Formations of the Secular: Christianity, Islam, Modernity*

Dorothea von Mücke, *The Rise of the Fantastic Tale*

Marc Redfield, *The Politics of Aesthetics: Nationalism, Gender, Romanticism*

Emmanuel Levinas, *On Escape*

Dan Zahavi, *Husserl's Phenomenology*

Rodolphe Gasché, *The Idea of Form: Rethinking Kant's Aesthetics*

Michael Naas, *Taking on the Tradition: Jacques Derrida and the Legacies of Deconstruction*

Herlinde Pauer-Studer, ed., *Constructions of Practical Reason: Interviews on Moral and Political Philosophy*

Jean-Luc Marion, *Being Given That: Toward a Phenomenology of Givenness*

Theodor W. Adorno and Max Horkheimer, *Dialectic of Enlightenment*

Ian Balfour, *The Rhetoric of Romantic Prophecy*

Martin Stokhof, *World and Life as One: Ethics and Ontology in Wittgenstein's Early Thought*

Gianni Vattimo, *Nietzsche: An Introduction*

Jacques Derrida, *Negotiations: Interventions and Interviews, 1971–1998*, edited by Elizabeth Rottenberg

Brett Levinson, *The Ends of Literature: The Latin American "Boom" in the Neoliberal Marketplace*

Timothy J. Reiss, *Against Autonomy: Cultural Instruments, Mutualities, and the Fictive Imagination*

Hent de Vries and Samuel Weber, eds., *Religion and Media*

Niklas Luhmann, *Theories of Distinction: Re-Describing the Descriptions of Modernity*, edited and introduced by William Rasch

Johannes Fabian, *Anthropology with an Attitude: Critical Essays*

Michel Henry, *I Am the Truth: Toward a Philosophy of Christianity*

Gil Anidjar, *"Our Place in Al-Andalus": Kabbalah, Philosophy, Literature in Arab-Jewish Letters*

Hélène Cixous and Jacques Derrida, *Veils*

F. R. Ankersmit, *Historical Representation*

F. R. Ankersmit, *Political Representation*

Elissa Marder, *Dead Time: Temporal Disorders in the Wake of Modernity (Baudelaire and Flaubert)*

Reinhart Koselleck, *The Practice of Conceptual History: Timing History, Spacing Concepts*

Niklas Luhmann, *The Reality of the Mass Media*

Hubert Damisch, *A Theory of /Cloud/: Toward a History of Painting*

Jean-Luc Nancy, *The Speculative Remark: (One of Hegel's bon mots)*

Jean-François Lyotard, *Soundproof Room: Malraux's Anti-Aesthetics*

Jan Patočka, *Plato and Europe*

Hubert Damisch, *Skyline: The Narcissistic City*

Isabel Hoving, *In Praise of New Travelers: Reading Caribbean Migrant Women Writers*

Richard Rand, ed., *Futures: Of Jacques Derrida*

William Rasch, *Niklas Luhmann's Modernity: The Paradoxes of Differentiation*

Jacques Derrida and Anne Dufourmantelle, *Of Hospitality*

Jean-François Lyotard, *The Confession of Augustine*

Kaja Silverman, *World Spectators*

Samuel Weber, *Institution and Interpretation: Expanded Edition*

Jeffrey S. Librett, *The Rhetoric of Cultural Dialogue: Jews and Germans in the Epoch of Emancipation*

Ulrich Baer, *Remnants of Song: Trauma and the Experience of Modernity in Charles Baudelaire and Paul Celan*

Samuel C. Wheeler III, *Deconstruction as Analytic Philosophy*

David S. Ferris, *Silent Urns: Romanticism, Hellenism, Modernity*

Rodolphe Gasché, *Of Minimal Things: Studies on the Notion of Relation*

Sarah Winter, *Freud and the Institution of Psychoanalytic Knowledge*

Samuel Weber, *The Legend of Freud: Expanded Edition*

Aris Fioretos, ed., *The Solid Letter: Readings of Friedrich Hölderlin*

J. Hillis Miller / Manuel Asensi, *Black Holes / J. Hillis Miller; or, Boustrophedonic Reading*

Miryam Sas, *Fault Lines: Cultural Memory and Japanese Surrealism*

Peter Schwenger, *Fantasm and Fiction: On Textual Envisioning*

Didier Maleuvre, *Museum Memories: History, Technology, Art*

Jacques Derrida, *Monolingualism of the Other; or, The Prosthesis of Origin*

Andrew Baruch Wachtel, *Making a Nation, Breaking a Nation: Literature and Cultural Politics in Yugoslavia*

Niklas Luhmann, *Love as Passion: The Codification of Intimacy*

Mieke Bal, ed., *The Practice of Cultural Analysis: Exposing Interdisciplinary Interpretation*

Jacques Derrida and Gianni Vattimo, eds., *Religion*

The authorized representative in the EU for product safety and compliance is:
Mare Nostrum Group
B.V Doelen 72
4831 GR Breda
The Netherlands

www.ingramcontent.com/pod-product-compliance
Lightning Source LLC
Chambersburg PA
CBHW032134250426
43661CB00077B/1929